SCANDAL, WILD LIVING, AND MUSIC SO HOT IT SMOKED— HE LIVED THE GOLDEN AGE OF ROCK 'N' ROLL

The multitude came to its feet as the thin blond decked out in red pants, wine sharkskin jacket and white shoes strode onstage. He was a sight to behold, this gaudy Ball of Fire, this veloured Vulcan whose dispositions were unstoppable and whose talent was matchless.

Having hardly twenty minutes to work his magic, Jerry wasted no time on warming up. He hammered the keys until his fingertips were bruised by the barrage. He jumped to his feet, kicking the piano stool into the wings, grabbed the mike positioned between his legs and pounded the keys with his fist. He played the piano with his elbows, his bootheels, and ended the song by sitting on the keys. A single curl unraveled over his forehead, and as the heat wave rose, his long blond hair streamed into his face and over his eyes. Withdrawing a silver comb and whipping his tresses back in place provoked screams and cheers; tearing his jacket off was the sign for the faithful to come forward to the altar.

"Whole Lot of Shakin'" started a riot. Girls fainted. The crowd mobbed the stage, hands held high, grasping for the pianist whenever he moved too close to the edge. For his final selection, Jerry waited for the pandemonium to subside, then hit the keys four times briskly:

You shake my nerves and you rattle my brain.
Too much love drives a man insane.
You broke my will, but what a thrill.
Goodness gracious, great balls of fire!

GREAT BALLS OF FIRE

The Uncensored Story of Jerry Lee Lewis

Myra Lewis with Murray Silver

ST. MARTIN'S PRESS/NEW YORK

St. Martin's Press titles are available at quantity discounts for sales promotions, premiums or fund raising. Special books or book excerpts can also be created to fit specific needs. For information write to special sales manager, St. Martin's Press, 175 Fifth Avenue, New York, N.Y. 10010.

Grateful acknowledgment is made for permission to quote from the following songs:

"End of the Road" by Jerry Lee Lewis, copyright © 1956, Knox Music, Inc.

"Great Balls of Fire" by Jack Hammer and Otis Blackwell, copyright © 1957, Hill and Range Songs, Inc. All rights controlled by Unichappell Music, Inc. (Rightsong Music, Publisher) International Copyright Secured. ALL RIGHTS RESERVED.

"Lewis Boogie" by Jerry Lee Lewis, copyright © 1958, Knox Music, Inc.

"Hang Up My Rock and Roll Shoes" by Chuck Willis, copyright © 1959, Tideland Music/Picadilly Music

"It Won't Happen with Me" by Raymond L. Evans, copyright © 1961, Knox Music, Inc.

"Whenever You're Ready" by Cecil Harrelson, copyright © 1966, Shelby Singleton Music, Inc.

"Who's Gonna Play This Old Piano" by Ray Griff, copyright © 1972, Blue Echo Music

Published by arrangement with William Morrow and Company, Inc.

GREAT BALLS OF FIRE

Library of Congress Catalog Card Number: 82-9085

ISBN: 0-312-91641-8   Can. ISBN: 0-312-91642-6

Printed in the United States of America

Quill edition published 1982
First St. Martin's Press mass market edition/July 1989

10 9 8 7 6 5 4 3 2 1

Acknowledgments

PORTIONS OF THIS BOOK NOT ORIGINAL WITH MYRA and Jerry Lee Lewis are the generous gifts of Cecil Harrclson, Lois and J. W. Brown, Jud Phillips and Elmo Lewis. Also providing information indispensable to the work are Phoebe Lewis, Rusty Brown, Jane Lewis Brown, Otis Lee Brown, Lillie Lewis, John Lewis, Stella Herron Calhoun, Dorothy Barton Lewis Russell, Jane Mitcham Lewis Wilkinson, Rev. Jimmy Lee Swaggart, Henry Brown and Grace Merrill.

Thanks to the following for details: Slim Whitman, Jack Clement, Jimmy Van Eaton, Carl Perkins, Johnny Cash, Horace Logan and Bob Sullivan at KWKH, and Joe Moise of the Atlas Sewing Center, Baton Rouge, Louisiana. For court records: Clyde Webber, clerk, Vidalia, Louisiana, Clint Crabtree, clerk, and Sally Foppiano, deputy clerk, Shelby County Circuit Court, Memphis, Tennessee. Thanks also to Brother Robert Hogan, director of admissions, Sister Catherine McCafferty, and Pearl Ellis, librarian, all of the Southwestern Assembly of God College, Waxahachie, Texas.

Thanks to Kay Martin and Gary Skala, presidents emeriti of the Jerry Lee Lewis International Fan Club, for letters, newsletters, photos, itineraries, and twenty-five years of sacrifice, dedication and friendship. And thanks to Wim de Boer and Barry Gamblin for taking up where Kay and Gary left off.

For invaluable critical assistance, thanks to our agent, Denise Marcil.

Thanks to our friends the Malones, Marie and Jim Yorg, Judy

Orr, Dean Phillips, Jim Kingsley, Don Sylvester, John Pearce, Mark Sabel and Carolyn and Bob Russell.

Above all, thanks to our families for their love and support without which this book would not have been possible.

Photo credits: Eric Beaumont, Phillip Parr, Terry Adams, Stephen Terry, Phoebe Lewis, Louis Cahill, The Buddy Holly Memorial Society, and Murray Silver.

For the glory of God, who delivered us all to the other side.

Contents

Prologue

IT WAS THE MEDIA EVENT OF THE SPRING silly season, when all of Fleet Street had nothing better to do than go callithumping across London on the morning of May 22, 1958, to meet and greet America's latest rock regent, Jerry Lee Lewis. Photographers jockeyed for position, cubs and aces elbowed one another, calling for a moment's notice from the singer who had set the world to shakin'. His second record for a jackleg label out of Memphis had become the biggest-selling single in the history of popular music, equaled only by his next two efforts, and he expected to capture England without opposition.

To one side a girl stood unnoticed till she caught the eye of a rogue reporter blocked from access to the star. As he approached, she turned away, hoping he would leave if ignored.

"And who are you, miss?" the reporter asked.

"Jerry's wife," she muttered.

"His wife? I didn't know he was married," the newsman said, sensing a lead. "Mind if I ask you a few questions?" And before she could answer, she was pushed toward a waiting limousine.

At the Lewises' hotel in the fashionable Mayfair district of London, reporters awaited an audience with rock's royal family, among them the man whose discovery of a secret marriage pressed him into further investigation of Jerry Lee Lewis's background. Jerry was cautious, having sensed something in the reporter's manner which made him wonder whether the curiosity about his wife was friendly.

"How old is Myra?" asked the reporter.

"Fifteen," Jerry said, adding two years to Myra's age to ward off scandal.

The next morning, Myra and Jerry were handed copies of the early editions of the London newspapers. Ominous headlines— "Meet Myra From Memphis—Wife at 15!" and "Jerry Brings Wife No. 3, Fair and 15, Like a Well-Scrubbed Fourth-Former!" —gave way to the following day's revelations that Myra was in fact thirteen years old, Jerry's cousin, and his second bigamous linkup to boot. Photos of Myra dwarfed accounts of war in Tunisia and de Gaulle's takeover of the French government.

It was fun at first, all this attention, especially for Myra, who had been kept a secret for six months to prevent such a scene from happening. It was when the press turned self-righteous, first by making fun and then by making an example of the Lewises, that the game came to an end. Jerry, who had become accustomed to celebrity, was baffled by the bother over such trivial matters as his marriages. Further, the sudden switch from immortality to immorality did nothing to alter his arrogance. "Who's this guy de Gaulle? He seems to have gone over bigger than us. What's so great about him?" said Jerry when one paper failed to print his picture on page one. But Fleet Street was to turn the tide of public support against him. "Clear Out This Gang!" cried one editorial, and others called for a boycott of Jerry's concert dates and his immediate deportation. His fans turned on him, disrupting his performances with taunts of "Baby snatcher!" and "Go home, kiddy thief!" Members of the House of Commons debated Jerry's fate in open sessions of Parliament, and as the Home Office instigated extradition procedures, the six-week tour was canceled. Jerry's producers abandoned him, his music was blacklisted from the airwaves and promoters kept hands off. After the initial shock came anger, then Jerry's resolute determination to start over again, changing neither his stage persona nor his private lifestyle. And all the while, the press bombarded Jerry with questions.

"Who are you?"

"What are you?"

"Where did you come from?"

"How did you get this far?"

They did not like his answers.

Here are the answers.

1 *Another Place, Another Time*

NINETEEN THIRTY-FIVE WAS A FINE YEAR FOR babies in the Deep South. People would later look back and marvel at the young'uns born in that year, in particular two who became movers and shakers of the shakin' movement. To Gladys and Vernon Presley of Tupelo, Mississippi, a son was born on the eighth day of the first month—Elvis, coolest of the cool, the man who would be king of rock 'n' roll. Three hundred miles down the road to the southwest, a son was born to Mamie and Elmo Lewis who became both friend and foe of the king, taking the crown for himself and losing it in a series of bloodless but noisy coups. And in March of the same year, Mamie's sister and Sun Swaggart celebrated the birth of their son, Jimmy Lee, a man of God whose toughest task would be saving the souls of those who rocked and rolled.

Jerry Lee Lewis claimed to have been "born feet first and rocked ever since." Elmo and Mamie were expecting his birth in October, but he signaled his arrival on September 29. Doc Campbell insisted on attending the delivery despite having drunk away the afternoon, but passed out at the same time the Lewises' son was entering the world. Mamie cried out for help, and Elmo fished for a tiny hand to grab and found instead a tiny foot. Failing to recognize the inherent danger of strangulation during a feet-first delivery, Elmo took hold of the little piggies and tugged his son to freedom. The little man came out wailing at a pitch and volume which roused the doctor.

"Looks like you did a pretty fair job without me, Elmo," Doc Campbell said when he had revived. "The boy is in fine shape. Sorry I wasn't much help, but it's Sunday, an' I wasn't expectin' any business. What are you gonna name the li'l fella, anyhow?"

"Jerry Lee. The Lee is for my daddy, Leroy," said Elmo.

"The Lee is for his uncle Lee Calhoun," Mamie disputed.

Thus it began, the tug of war wherein young Jerry was the emotional rope, pulled this way and that between parents. They created a perfect contradiction: a man who loved to hate and hated to love, who denied himself salvation, who tortured his mind with guilt and his body with poison, moving away from those he needed and alienating himself from the things he wanted most—life, love and faith.

Jerry Lee Lewis came to life in the midst of poverty and bearing the mark of maleficent spirits. Incest and murder, bigamy and rebellion, child marriages and hard drinkin' were all inherent characteristics of Leroy's clan, a people terrible from their beginning onward. Jerry Lee Lewis was a product of this environment and a culmination of all that had gone before him, his misfortunes having begun fifty years before he entered the world. No other aspect of Jerry's heritage is as important to the development of his tastes and attitudes as his pioneer ancestry, reflected in everything from the innovative music he created to the scandals he started. And like his forefathers, he looked at life with a primitive fear of God and an altered perception of the law, explaining many of the seemingly inexplicable events that happened to him. Jerry represents the whole spectrum of his ancestry—preachers and pagans, doctors and derelicts—and the odd polarity of his nature is the direct result of strong, contrary influences bred in the bone. Where his extraordinary talent came from, nobody knows.

Jerry's grandfather, Leroy, died fifteen months after Jerry's birth. Her husband's death came as no surprise to Arilla, who had been expecting it daily for the past twenty years. Lee had neglected a cancerous growth on his back, wasting money she gave him for treatment on whiskey. The family was summoned to Snake Ridge for the funeral, where Robert Jay had removed his father's corpse from the casket during the nightlong wake and fitted his stiffened form into his favorite rocking chair on the front porch. He retrieved the old man's corncob pipe and molded it into his right hand, then tied a string to the rocker's leg and trailed it off into the bushes just as a gathering of grieving kin arrived. No one noticed that the man rocking on the porch was the deceased until one of the children pointed and said, "Mama, looky, Grampa." There damn near was a double funeral when Elmo caught up with his little brother.

Leroy was interred in the family cemetery on Snake Ridge as the presiding preacher was hard pressed to recall acts of Christian kindness to mention in the last rites. As he spoke of Lee's undying devotion to his family, many offered silent protests to the contrary while others wondered at what had become of the once-prosperous family estate. Lee Lewis was gone, but he left others bearing his name who would carry on in his style as if the dead hand guided them through the next fifty years, visiting the iniquity of the fathers upon the children unto the third and fourth generation.

Elmo ran a bootleg whiskey concession which had increased to the point where he was forced to run off three hundred gallons twice a week to meet the demand. He was just beginning to produce a potable liquor when the revenuers came to buy out his franchise. Elmo was sentenced to serve five years in the penitentiary at Angola, in the same blockhouse he helped build as a carpenter. Lee Calhoun, Elmo's benefactor and Mamie's favorite in-law, was also nabbed in the raid. Being a man of great wealth, he had the quiet opportunity to buy his freedom, but also being a man of great greed, he elected to take a year-long vacation at the government's expense and kept his fortune intact. Fortunately, Lee had socked away a substantial sum for rainy days such as these, and his wife and Elmo's family would not initially face hardship. The rest of the clan rallied round to lend support of every kind. Whatever consolation they could provide would not begin to offset the abuses rained down on Elmo by his ever-loving wife. He spent many months in Angola wondering whether Mamie would make good her threat not to wait for his return.

On an August evening before Jerry's third birthday, his eight-year-old brother met with fatal misfortune. Mamie and her sister Stella were waiting supper on Elmo, Jr., when a loud commotion caused them to run to the window. A crowd gathered at the scene of an accident one block away in front of Nelson's superette. A neighbor was dispatched to the Lewis house with the news; Mamie answered the knock with Jerry on her hip.

"Miz Lewis, there's been a accident . . ."

"Elmo?" she quaked with alarm.

"He jumped out of a wagon just as some drunk in a flatbed truck swerved to miss a bus that had come to a stop . . ."

"Elmo?"

"The tailgate caught your boy in the back of the head."

"Elmo!" Mamie wailed, piercing Jerry through the heart and echoing in Angola.

The sombrous ceremony, the steady flow of kindred mourners and the strident cries of his mother were confusing to Jerry. He approached the casket and called out, hoping to stir his sleeping brother. He patted the pinewood planks till his mother pulled him away, then held on to her tightly as her tears of grief washed over him. Grief over the tragic death of a loved one was the first powerful emotion Jerry felt; suffering was the first feeling he could remember. In the beginning, there was pain.

On the dreary afternoon of August 6, 1938, a saddened throng lingered at a simple grave on Snake Ridge awaiting the sheriff's delivery of Elmo. He was allowed to attend the burial in the company of armed officers. His hands were uncuffed so that he might embrace his wife and the guards allowed him to procede to the gravesite unattended, but they posed with loaded shotguns to discourage any attempt at escape from custody. At the conclusion of the brief ceremony, Elmo was returned to the auto, shackled and placed in the backseat between guards for the long drive back to prison.

The absence of Elmo from Jerry's life during the formative years left an indelible mark on the child. His mother became his sole influence. She was his counselor, coach, teacher, preacher and best friend. Her preferences became his; her fears were deeply ingrained into his conscience. Mamie drew Jerry closer to her during the absence of her husband. The loss of her firstborn made her remaining son dearer still. If Elmo would not do right by her, she would make sure that her son would never disappoint her. As much as Jerry might do for her, it was never quite enough.

After serving almost twelve months of his sentence, Elmo was moved from Angola to a minimum-security prison farm in New Orleans. Conditions were so poor that there were no quarters for prisoners, no food and no clothes. There was also no fence, and Elmo decided during the middle of a work detail to quietly walk away. The clothes he wore were nondescript and gave no hint of being the uniform of an incarcerated criminal. He hitchhiked home and walked in unannounced, much to Mamie's surprise. He had not been missed at the prison farm, and after a few anxious days he quit looking for men with guns sent to retrieve him.

Elmo had not been missed at home, either. He was a stranger. The respect of his son had died of neglect in the same way his wife's feelings had withered. Mother and child were closer than close, and Dad was on the outside looking in. Mamie asserted herself as head of the household. Elmo, freed from prison, served a life sentence performing odd jobs and running his wife's errands.

World War II cut into America like a new and different Depression. There was work and more money, but nothing to buy. Niceties were sacrificed in support of the war effort. Gasoline was rationed. Even clothing styles were altered to cut away excess cloth so that there was more to go around. Elmo and Mamie traveled the Southwest following defense-plant jobs and left seven-year-old Jerry with Aunt Stella and Uncle Lee. They treated him to a finer standard of living than he had ever known, showering him with all of the things their son would have had. He had new clothes. He had his own bed in his own bedroom. He was given an allowance and was not made to save one cent of it.

For Jerry and his friends, many of the sacrifices made on behalf of the war effort were made for them by their parents. Going without shoes made little difference to country boys, and if the army needed all of America's broccoli, it was fine with Jerry. The only sacrifice he was unprepared to make was giving up Saturdays at the movies. Each and every week, Jerry met his cousins Mickey Gilley and Jimmy Lee Swaggart at the box office of the Arcade to see a western starring Gene Autry, Hopalong Cassidy or Johnny Mack Brown. And every Sunday, in the company of their families, the boys went to church. Church was a better show than the one they had seen the day before.

The evangelists that passed through Ferriday had settled in permanently. The persistence of Mamie and Stella convinced Lee Calhoun that theirs was a worthy cause. Actually, it was the morning prayer meetings in Lee's living room which convinced him that a permanent site was needed. Mamie preached. Her sisters were among her first converts, and once the Holy Spirit moved a sister, she began testifying and the congregation began to grow. On the Monday following the initiation of the newest members, Papa Herron was surprised to find his daughters still dancing in the Spirit.

Mamie grabbed her father and whirled him around. He was shocked, at first. Shaking and hollering is no way to treat a seventy-three-year-old man first thing in the morning. Then the old man began jumping about, raising a muffled roar about Jesus. Papa got the Spirit and he hadn't been to church yet.

Like most eight-year-olds, Jerry wasn't able to find the Holy Spirit as readily as his parents, but enjoyed the psalm singing and dancing in the Spirit. He asked his daddy to show him how to play the guitar and make music of his own. He had a difficult time negotiating the fretwork with his short, stubby fingers, but nevertheless took the guitar to school every day and played at recess. His teacher said that if Jerry would devote a fraction of the time spent with the guitar on schoolwork, he would do much better. He might even pass.

During the Christmas following his ninth birthday, Jerry became instantly attracted to the piano owned by his aunt Stella. He sat at the spinet and, untutored, pecked out "Silent Night" on mostly black keys. Jerry looked at his hands as if he had just discovered them and figured out what they were for: a recovery of secrets known to the soul in previous existences.

The first pianist Jerry sought to emulate was a preacher who pounded a heavy bass line with his left hand, hammered out simple melodies with the right and flipped through the Testament at the same time. Brother Janway was the best preachin' piano player in those parts, and Jerry Lee and Jimmy Lee were in the first pew whenever he came to town. Jimmy wanted to play the piano, too. He prayed that the Holy Spirit would fill him with the special gift that would enable him to play like Brother Janway and move congregations to new heights of religious ecstasy. He bargained that in exchange for that ability his talent would never be used for material gain except in service to the Lord. "And if I ever go back on my promise, Lord, you can paralyze my fingers," he pledged. Jimmy felt the hand of God, and lo, he was moved and inspired. At the conclusion of prayer meetin', he sat at the piano and began playing basic progressions. He was thrilled with his ability, confident that God had answered his prayers.

To Jerry, piano playing seemed like a very simple, very natural thing to do. His confidence in his own ability to master the instrument did not require the aide of divine intervention. It wasn't something to pray over. Besides, Jerry didn't think Brother Janway was half as good as Old Sam, who was featured nightly at Haney's Big House in the Chocolate Quarters of Ferriday where he played and sang with a passion unequaled by Brother Janway's religious fervor. Sam played the blues, rollicking tunes like "Shanty Town" and "Harbor Lights" and pumpin', stompin' versions of "Drinkin' Wine Spo-Dee-O-Dee." Jerry wanted to play like Old Sam. He wanted to move people to new heights on dance floors.

On Friday and Saturday nights, Jerry fetched Jimmy across the tracks into Chocolate Quarters to watch the blues musicians from open windows and doorways to the colored nightclubs. The Big House attracted such great musicians as B. B. King, Muddy Waters and Piano Red, and the boys studied the masters attentively until Haney chased them away. The following day, as Jimmy rehearsed his hymnal, Jerry attempted to recreate what he had heard the night before. Something important was happening.

Elmo had a fair working knowledge of the piano. He sat Jerry down at Stella's spinet and began his son's first lessons by showing him how to play minor chords. Elmo passed along what little expertise he had, and nature seemed to do the rest. Within ninety days of practicing three and four hours a day, Jerry had reached what his father thought was perfection on the piano. His mother declared her son was a natural.

Now Jerry wanted a piano of his own.

Night and day, Jerry could talk of nothing else besides music, and Elmo saw the perfect chance to win the worship of his son by giving him the piano he wanted so desperately. The problem was that Elmo had been making just enough money to keep his family going on a week-to-week, hand-to-mouth basis. Only recently had he been able to purchase his first house, and there was not enough money left over for such an expensive luxury. Hardship mattered little to his young son, who was totally affixed to the one burning desire of demanding music from ivory keys. If only the boy hadn't the talent, it would be easier to say no.

As a last resort, Elmo went to the bank. He did not qualify for a loan, so his only alternative was to take out a mortgage on his house for nine hundred dollars. With this money he bought a nearly new upright made by the Starck Company. How strange the handsome and imposing fixture seemed among the few sticks of frail furniture in the Lewises' humble home. How happy was Jerry, who did not touch ground from the front door to the piano bench where he positioned himself permanently and pounded the keys with short, stubby punches. He practiced long and played hard, so hard that he wore through the ivory covers and dug out pits in the wooden keys. Music was more than alleviation from boredom and poverty, it was the only way Jerry could express himself honestly and without fear of contradiction or mistake.

The only misfortune befalling the well-meaning Elmo was that his son was not old enough to work as a pianist in nightclubs and at dances. Hence, no money was made from Elmo's investment; happiness was the only dividend, the future was the only chance for profit. It was not an explanation bank officers could understand. The mortgage on the Lewis house was foreclosed when Elmo could not meet the payments, but at least his boy had his piano.

Jimmy Lee Swaggart became Jerry's classmate in weekly piano lessons. Jimmy was very polite and always attentive. Jerry was his opposite. He had an uncontrollable urge to pump life into every passage, whether it was a waltz, scale or Christmas carol. Their instructor, Mr. Griffin, demanded strict adherence to the lesson book, but after a few bars of perfect form, instinct asserted itself, Jerry dropped his eyes from the printed page and let animal magic resound from the keys. After three lessons, Mr. Griffin was still unable to displace the influence that Old Sam had over his young pupil.

"Wrong!" Mr. Griffin screamed for the sixth time. "Wrong, wrong, wrong! You're not paying attention to your instructions. Everything you play is too loud and too fast. Now, here's how to play it."

"If you wanna know how to play it," Jerry retorted, "*here's* how it goes."

Mr. Griffin was outraged. The lessons were over; student and teacher had reached a mutual termination of tutorship.

The rift with Mr. Griffin was minor in comparison to the running battle Jerry had with all of his schoolteachers. He learned only that which interested him: history according to the Bible and the piano according to Old Sam; he would learn to count with large stacks of money, and geography by traveling four continents. Jerry preferred to wear out the seat of his britches on a piano bench to a school bench.

Fortunately, Jerry was the first person teachers thought of whenever the school met at assembly and the need arose for a pianist. He could barely read and hardly write, but he played the piano like a master. Though he'd failed the fourth grade, Mrs. West waived him on to the fifth after Jimmy, one of Mrs. West's former pets, testified to the beating Jerry would receive from his parents if he stayed back.

Jerry worked a paper route to earn spending money for Saturdays at the movies. Westerns were his favorite films and horror movies ran a close second, but the film that made the biggest impact on young Jerry was *Down Among the Sheltering Pines*, starring Al Jolson. Here was the greatest showman Jerry had ever seen. Supercharged by the performance, Jerry ran home to his piano and developed an even greater respect for Jolson upon discovering the difficulty of achieving a passable impersonation of his style. Next to Jimmie Rodgers, there was no one in Jerry's world like Al Jolson.

Occasionally, the members of the Texas Street Assembly of God asked Jerry to play piano at their meetings. Some of the parishioners were partial to his lively treatment of gospel hymns, while others objected that songs about Jesus should not sound too much like boogie-woogie. No complaints were raised, however, when Jimmy Lee Swaggart played the hymns in his cut-and-dried, simple way, and between the two, Jimmy played a more acceptable psalm than his versatile cousin. No matter: Jerry preferred playing for tent revivals, where he was encouraged to let loose. Excitement was the evangelistic drawing card, and no one was a better draw in Ferriday than the twelve-year-old Lewis boy. Members of the Texas Street church saw that their decision to ban Jerry from playing at their meetings had been too hastily made when the transient revivals threatened to take the play away from the established church. Other churches asked Jerry to put in appearances, and WNAT radio in Natchez offered to broadcast him live every afternoon.

"Won't you come back and play for your old friends at Texas Street?" the penitent came to beseech him.

"I'll pray about it, brother," Jerry replied in his offhand way, "I'll pray about it."

As he became a minor celebrity at local revivals and talent shows, Jerry soon discovered that with fame comes the attention of pretty girls. He wasn't much to look at—the tall, lanky figure with hair cut short on the sides and a high nest of curls on top, teeth overlapped and shuffled like a spread deck of playing cards and ears that stuck out—but classmates marveled at his skill on the keyboard, and friendships could be made without opening his mouth except to sing. A young lady named Faye Bryant was Jerry's first love, a stimulant for a blossoming ego, an excitable girl whom he found fun in impressing with his manual dexterity. Jerry did not make much time for Faye because, at thirteen, he preferred raising hell with the boys.

Jerry's partner in crime was Cousin Jimmy, who was still fighting an unresolved battle between heaven and hell and raised Cain on Saturday and asked forgiveness on Sunday. Saturday nights, after being chased away from Haney's, the boys went shoplifting. Getting caught hardly concerned either of the vandals, since Pa Swaggart was chief of police. Under cover of night, Jerry and Jimmy crept along Louisiana Street into the alley behind Vogt's drugstore and the Ellis five-and-ten. If the last show was over at the Arcade, the only people out and about were two blocks away at the King Hotel. Breaking into any of the shops in the business district would then be no more difficult than lifting a rusty latch or picking a simple lock, and the boys could shop leisurely throughout the stores for odds and ends which the owners would not readily miss. Later in the week, the desperadoes would happen by the police station to inquire if there were any leads on the thieves breaking into stores lately.

Unlike Jerry, Jimmy was given to fits of conscience about their escapades. The boys were drifting apart. Jimmy became a serious student and attended church twice weekly without fail. His nightly capers with his cousin were excused away by homework assignments, and the Arcade was off-limits, too. There was something in what the preacher said about movies taking people further away from God.

Jerry was Jimmy's foil. Never an industrious student, and a churchgoer only on special occasions or when services were meted out as punishment, Jerry preferred hunting and fishing, moviegoing and thrill-seeking. He antagonized Jimmy with devilments, tempting him to forsake his goal of becoming a preacher. When words failed him, Jerry even balanced on the beams of the Mississippi River Bridge to tear Jimmy's attention away from Bible study.

Jimmy made several efforts to reform his wayward cousin. Jerry went along with it for a while, attending church every other week, then turned away when Jimmy pressed too hard for redemption. The cousins reached a fundamental division over the concept of talent and its uses and applications: Jimmy claimed that God-given talents are for the glory of God; Jerry was of the opinion that God-given talents are for the glory of the talented. Jimmy played piano only in church; Jerry, for anyone standing still long enough to listen.

Elmo was determined that his talented son be heard by the general public. He was not defeated by the setback which had taken his house away. He found work with Standard Oil to pay for a new home, and at all other times searched for stages for his son to play on. Elmo and Jerry happened to be in town one Saturday when they noticed a big commotion over at the grand opening of the new Ferriday Ford agency. The dealership was giving away free Cokes, and a fiddler and guitarist were playing through a rickety public-address system to raise a crowd. A piano sat unplayed. Elmo asked permission for his son to play the idle keyboard.

Jerry had never been amplified by a public-address system. Not knowing how sensitive a microphone could be, he placed the stand between his legs with the top of the device inches from his lips and nervously began "Hadacol Boogie." His confidence began to build as the audience smiled and clapped and tapped their feet in time to the music. They applauded. They asked for more. Jerry continued to play while Elmo passed the hat. The collection of loose change netted thirteen dollars. Thirteen whole dollars for a few minutes' fun with a piano. It was more money than vending newspapers yielded in an entire week.

Unhappily, there were not many occasions where a fourteen-year-old boy could play before a paying crowd. It was a technicality that could be cured only by time. Until then, Elmo hoisted Jerry's upright into the bed of his truck and drove him around the countryside in search of an audience. As Jerry played, Elmo passed the hat.

Jerry was certain that success waited somewhere for a person of his talent, but if there was a fortune to be found, it wasn't in Ferriday. The natural starting point seemed to be New Orleans, the home of so many of the great musicians Jerry had seen at Haney's. He set out on Highway 61 without giving much thought as to what he would do if he made it the more than two hundred miles to Bourbon Street. When he failed to come home that night, Mamie began to worry. By midnight, she had paced through a pair of shoes, and made Elmo drag the highway between Jonesville and Natchez, stopping at the police station and hospital before ending the search. Mamie remained awake through the night, answering every creak of a floorboard hoping her son had come home. The telephone rang at sunup, and fearing bad news, Mamie made Elmo answer.

"Mr. Lewis, this is the desk sergeant at the police station in New Orleans. Do you have a fifteen-year-old boy named Jerry, Mr. Lewis? About five-foot-eight, a hunnert an' thutty pound, blon' hair and blue eyes?"

"That sounds like him. Can I speak to him?" Elmo asked.

"In a minnit, Mr. Lewis. He's here with us. We picked him up last night walkin' the streets. Said he was lookin' for a job. We thought he looked a mite young . . . Hello? . . . Mr. Lewis?"

Elmo slammed the receiver home and dragged Mamie out of her chair and into their new '49 Ford as the operator tried to make another connection. Mamie, still unsure as to the safety of her son, asked her husband whether he was dead.

"Not yet," said Elmo.

At the police station in New Orleans, Jerry tried to avoid strangulation by explaining he had been kidnapped and driven to New Orleans against his will. That excuse bought him four seconds before he was forced to come up with another.

"Mr. Lewis," the sergeant interrupted, "do you mistreat this boy?"

"Not till today," Elmo hollered, "but when we get home . . ."

"Reason I ask, sir, is young Jerry here tol' us a lot about bein' beaten and worked to the bone—"

"I'll beat what bones ain't been worked, an' that's just about all of 'em," Elmo threatened. "Gimme five minutes with him is all I ask."

When the dust had settled and Elmo was silenced by hoarseness, Jerry's explanation came pure and simple. "I come here for one reason, to get a job playin' the piano. I know I'm good. I couldn't get a job at home where folks know I'm too young, so I come here where they don't know me. I seen guys here ain't half as good as me. I know I can make a million dollars playin' the piano, if I jus' had the chance."

"We know that, boy," Elmo said with compassion, "but you don't look any older down here than you do at home. Nobody'll hire you. What are you gonna do? Starve? I know they's folks on the radio an' teevee what ain't half as good as you, an' I'll take you to the station person'ly. But you can't run off an' leave your mother this way. So, for now, you come home with us."

Jerry returned home without a fight, but it wasn't too long before one of the TV people he had referred to sponsored a benefit for the Heart Association in Monroe, and Jerry asked his father to keep his promise. The show sponsor was Ted Mack, the talent scout who had premiered a program on Sunday nights the year before and allowed people from every walk of life to exhibit whatever talent they thought they possessed before a national audience. Very few of Ted's guests on *Amateur Hour* became successful in show business, but the show itself was popular. Elmo took Jerry to meet Mack lest he run away again and audition on his own.

"My boy can play anythin' you can name on the piano," Elmo bragged in response to a supervisor's question about Jerry's talent.

"Not on this stage, he can't. Mr. Mack doesn't want any boogie-woogie, none of that jazz. He wants the light classics, the classic classics and the popular songs. Now, can your boy do any of that?"

"Heard what I said?" Elmo replied, then instructed his son to play something slow for the audition.

Jerry nodded, and played a rendition of "Goodnight Irene" by the book.

"I guess he'll do," the supervisor said. "Next, please."

Jerry was scheduled to close the show. When at last his turn came, he was past being ready, but the audience had grown listless and inattentive, having been subjected to off-key warblers and misfiring magicians. Jerry could not tolerate indifference. He didn't mind if the crowd disliked him as much as if they ignored him completely. He knew what to do, the same thing Old Sam would do—play boogie-woogie. His flamboyance hushed the crowd, who then began to clap for the first time with more than just polite applause. Jerry was splendid, his spidery arms stretching end-to-end over the keyboard, his look mischievous and determined. Before he could be ushered offstage, he completed a low-down and dirty version of "When the Saints Go Marching In," and left no doubt as to who was the gathering's favorite performer. Ted Mack, stern and unmoved, fanned himself with his hat, then reluctantly doled out ten dollars to Jerry as winner of the contest.

Encouraged by the reception in Monroe, Elmo took his son to the WNAT radio station in Natchez, where he won a spot on a live broadcast from their studio every Saturday. Jerry was alloted thirty minutes, along with The Singing Green Sisters, to play anything he wanted. His repertoire, consisting mainly of Jimmie Rodgers, traditional folksongs and gospel hymns, was liked enough by a local market to provide advertiser sponsorship.

"You can keep your part in the show for as long as you can keep a sponsor," the station manager told Jerry. "There ain't a whole lotta money in it for you, but, who knows, you might make a record someday."

Natchez rises from the banks of the Mississippi River and climbs steep cliffs overlooking the valley that Ferriday rests in. The town remains suspended in time by the marvelous white columned mansions that survived the ravages of civil war but fell into disrepair and abuse until civic pride recently restored them to their former majesty. In 1950, the town was beseiged by the teen terrors Jerry Lee Lewis and Cecil J. Harrelson. Cecil's daddy, by virtue of being a local cop, promoted the pair to a privileged class above the law. Cecil was sometimes cautious in testing his father's patience, but Jerry cut a wide path from Natchez to his home in the farming community of Black River and was the first local hellion bestowed with a title. Mr. Harrelson nicknamed Jerry the "Black River Stallion."

Jerry and Cecil met, or rather collided, in the school library. Cecil was browsing through stacks and reached for a particular title when another hand snatched it away. Cecil recognized the slab-sided sneak thief as the guy rumored to have stolen his motorbike. Cecil pushed Jerry, and Jerry shoved him back. They were to have settled it after school, but Cecil's foe was long gone. Cecil caught up with Jerry at the pool hall, and Jerry, claiming to have forgotten all about the fight, invited Cecil to shoot a game of eight ball instead.

Thus began a long-lasting and often-tested friendship. Jerry and Cecil recognized in each other vast similarities, not the least of which was a quiet veneration for religious principles. Though they shared great talents for mischiefmaking, they knew a time would come when they would have to make amends to God, if not to aggravated policemen, burgled shopowners and embittered parents of young girls. Most important to their relationship, Cecil inspired in Jerry a respect which he rarely held for any man.

Together, the two friends rushed headlong into adolescence. At fourteen, they learned to drive, drink beer and smoke cigars. And when the time came, they double-dated. The girls didn't stand a chance against the two-man tag team of Jer and Cece.

On Friday nights, that part of Highway 65 running through the center of Ferriday looked like a stock-car racetrack. Jerry and Cecil drove as if using brakes was against the law. They began their run at the top of a hill on the other side of the Mississippi River Bridge, and by the time the old shandrydan made Ferriday six miles away, the speedometer was flitting around one hundred miles per hour. They were fixed with a built-in alibi for eyewitnesses, claiming they were always being mistaken for the Marks boy, who owned a car like Cecil's.

The drive-in had just let out on a particular Friday night when Jer and Cece topped the hill leading into town doing ninety with a Louisiana state trooper in hot pursuit. A half-mile of cars were lined up in both lanes and Cecil had no choice but to go around them, whipping his car onto the soft shoulder. He raised a dust storm which stopped everyone, including the trooper, dead in their tracks.

"Hell, at this rate I can beat the eleven-minute record to Lake St. John," Cecil said to Jerry, who turned around in his seat to watch for flashing lights.

"Betcha cuppa coffee you can't," Jerry said, and Cecil stomped the accelerator, pushing the wheezing crate toward Dead Man's Curve. Jerry jumped into the backseat and cowered on the floor as Cecil took the curve on two wheels and blew past Lake St. John in record-breaking time.

"Now, how 'bout that cuppa coffee," Cecil called to the backseat.

The boys were not expecting the eluded trooper to be waiting at the Harrelsons' house when they arrived. With cool aplomb, they prepared to recite their litany of excuses.

"Where you boys been tonight?" Cecil's daddy asked, having been briefed on a high-speed chase by the trooper.

"Oh, nowhere in particular," Cecil evaded. "We were up on the levee and over in Jonesville earlier. Why? Trouble?"

"You know anything about the ruckus over at the drive-in?"

"What ruckus?"

"Car come through flyin' low 'long about midnight, and the officer here says it looked a lot like your'n."

"Must've been the Marks boy," Cecil said, falling back on the stand-by excuse. "You know, you been havin' a lotta trouble with him lately."

"No, wudn't him. He's been too many places at the same time lately. Officer says two boys, one blond, maybe."

"Must've been Truman King," Cecil shifted. "He's got a car exactly like this'n, too."

"Wasn't Truman. He's the first one I thought of, an' then I remembered he's in jail already."

"Must've been nigras, then," Cecil concluded, and headed for bed.

Truman King was a good excuse for anything that went wrong in Ferriday. He had a history of being wherever there was trouble. He and Jerry had been caught stealing a pistol from a gun shop once. Serious consequences were at stake until Uncle Lee Calhoun came forward and greased many palms and the whole thing was forgotten. Uncle Lee told his nephew it was going to be his last miracle, and the next time he was caught pulling a stunt like that, Jerry could forget Lee's number. Truman, with eight lives left, chanced one on breaking into a power plant and filching a battery worth six thousand dollars, thinking if it was able to illuminate Ferriday it was perfect for transforming his hot rod into a rocket ship. Instead of setting the land speed record, Truman went to prison.

With Truman out of the way and when the Marks boy could be accounted for, Jerry and Cecil were down to blaming the town's troubles on blacks, the age-old ultimate scapegoat. "Whatever happens in the next few days, I mean, if anyone should ask you about me, tell 'em you saw me the night before talkin' to some ol' nigra in a pickup truck," Jerry told Cecil. "I gotta plan, an' I may need an excuse."

Two days later a policeman brought Jerry to the Harrelson's house with his hands cuffed behind his back. When Cecil came to the door, Jerry winked at him and continued to stand silent.

"Cecil, did you happen to see young Jerry here last night anywheres?" the officer asked.

"Yessir, I did. He was pulled up to a stop light over on Carolina Street talkin' to some ol' nigra in a pickup truck. Blue, I think."

"Okay, then, I guess I'll have to let you go, Jerry," the officer said.

"What's this about, anyhow?" Mr. Harrelson wanted to know.

"I caught young Jerry here tryin' to sell a car battery that belonged to Don Henry Wickham. Natchally, I thought he stole it."

"I tol' you I bought it off some ol' nigra that had a bunch of 'em in the back of his pickup truck." Jerry glared.

"All right," said Mr. Harrelson, "but the next time you wanna sell a battery, Jerry, sell the whole damn car with it."

With this latest incident added to his lengthening record, and his best excuses used up, there could be no more stealing or tearing up and down the highway for a while. Girls were about the only game left to play. In spite of outward appearances, nicknames and legends, both Cecil and Jerry were raised as every southern gentleman to respect women, and under a penalty worse than death imposed by their religion, there was to be absolutely no sexual contact until marriage. Not liquor, not instinct, nor hot summer nights in the arms of two-dollar whores could tempt the boys into the sin of fornication. They could only speculate as to what pleasures awaited the uninitiated.

On a night free of obligations, Jerry and Cecil crossed the river into Natchez for an evening of girl-watching at the skating rink and stopped at the Hilltop Club for a beer. It was early and no one else was in the place. In a corner sat an old piano which was played by one of several men the Hilltop employed at a couple of dollars a night.

"Barkeep, mind if m' friend here plays your piano some?" Cecil called.

"Yes, I do. Nobody touches that piano tonight 'cept Floyd."

"Hey, he ain't gonna eat it, he just wants to limber up."

"No."

"Keep askin' him," Jerry nudged Cecil. "Make him let me."

"Mister, m'friend here thinks that's a real nice—"

"I said no and I meant it," the bartender interrupted.

"Look," Cecil's voice rose, "if you don't let this man play your damn piano, he's gonna get to be very hard to keep quiet, so you might as well let him play the damn thing five minutes, so's he'll leave us both alone."

"Okay, okay, play the sonofabitch."

"Thanks, Cece," Jerry said, flexing his fingers. He walked jauntily toward the piano and took his place at the keyboard sticky with spilled drinks, poked middle C a few times and discovered the piano had never been introduced to a tuning fork. Looking for certain keys to avoid, he drifted in and out of his favorite tunes, and the bartender approached Cecil with a fresh beer he hadn't ordered.

"Say, buddy, your friend play around here?"

"Sure. He's on the radio every Saturday, sometimes with his cousin Jimmy, sometimes with his cousin Mickey on Guitar. They ain't got a band, just fool around at fairs an' such. He's played in church, but never in no bars," Cecil said, hiding the fact that Jerry was underage for employment in night clubs.

"Think he'd like a job here?"

"Think he likes to eat?" Cecil answered.

"I can't pay him much, but he might make a few bucks in tips," the bartender said.

"That don't matter, he's just lookin' for a place to play. When does he start?"

"Tomorrow's all right with me."

"Good," said Cecil, walking over to Jerry with the proposition. Jerry smiled when he heard the offer. "Hell, I knew it. All he needed was to hear a little."

The next night, Jerry played his first engagement for hire at the Hilltop Club and took home ten dollars. It was not as much as he imagined his first salary would be, but he figured it was an ideal way to spend the summer.

Cecil worked as a clerk in a department store. He was waiting on a middle-aged black woman one afternoon when he spotted Jerry passing by.

"There goes the Killer," Cecil said aloud to himself.

The black lady reeled and cried out an alarm. "Killer! Where's the killer?" she yelled, not knowing whether to run or hide or call the police.

Cecil told Jerry the story when he saw him later that evening, and the boys had a good laugh at the lady's expense. "Killer, where's the killer?" Cecil cried in his best impersonation, sending his friend into fits of laughter. The joke got a lot of mileage, and the boys greeted each other on the street with loud shouts of "Here comes the Killer!" "Killer" was a nickname that stuck. Both boys used it when referring to the other, or for people whose names they did not know or couldn't remember. And as popular catch phrases will sometimes do, "killer" came to be used as a superlative in describing styles of clothing, haircuts, cars and songs.

* * *

In the afternoons, before reporting to work at the Hilltop, the Killer busied himself with repairing an old '41 Ford. He did not have a talent for fixing things mechanical, and while working under the hood, he gouged his right hand with a screwdriver. The wound was not serious but required wearing a burdensome bandage, and with the use of his right hand encumbered, the Killer's attack on the keyboard was altered. The left hand pounded out a more prominent bass line while the favored hand pawed a lighter melody, an alteration to which he became accustomed. Playing unaccompanied in the corner of a crowded bar taught him to play with force, flourish and volume in order to be heard above the noise and loud conversations. Necessity, the mother of attention-getting inventions, and mischance, the practical inconvenience of overcoming handicap, helped forge the Killer's innovative style.

Other pianists also contributed to the development of Jerry's range. Fats Domino recorded his first song in 1949 and made it all the way to Number 6 on the national rhythm-and-blues charts, thereby becoming the vanguard of a small group of pianists who would make boogie-styled blues popular. Another pianist, Moon Mullican, had a country-western hit in 1950 with "I'll Sail My Ship Alone." Moon was a white man dressed in a cowboy getup who played swing, blues, Cajun, country, pop, honky-tonk and Dixieland randomly and equally well, sometimes blending the characteristics of one with another in the same way Jerry drew evenly from his background in gospel, folk and country styles.

Albert Luandrew, better known as Sunnyland Slim, visited Haney's Big House with Muddy Waters many times in 1950 and taught Jerry the blues with "Orphan Boy Blues" and "Back to Korea Blues." Hudson Whittaker, whose stage name was Tampa Red, came through Ferriday to play his brand of boogie, "Midnight Boogie," "It's a Brand New Boogie" and "Boogie Woogie Woman."

Twelve years Jerry's senior, Hank Williams came out of Alabama in the late forties to sign on with the "Louisiana Hayride," a troupe of musicians that toured the South. Like Jerry, Hank revered Jimmie Rodgers, and as a young boy was inspired by a black street musician who taught him everything he knew about the blues. Hank patterned himself after Ernest Tubb and Roy Acuff, and in 1949 introduced his "Lovesick Blues" to a Grand Ole Opry crowd that forced him to encore the song six times. In the next year, Hank continued his meteoric rise with "Long Gone

Lonesome Blues" and "Why Don't You Love Me," and until his untimely death at age twenty-nine, three years later, he created more than two dozen classics to become one of America's finest singer/songwriters. Along with Al Jolson and Jimmie Rodgers, only Hank Williams was ever spoken of with reverence by Jerry —all the rest he would lump together as imitators and pretenders, except, of course, himself.

In the summer of 1951, shortly before his sixteenth birthday, Jerry spent most afternoons shooting ducks or billiards and every night playing piano at either the Hilltop or Blue Cat clubs in Natchez. Briefly, he held a job pouring cement on the construction site of a new school, quitting because hard labor raised calluses on his precious palms. He was often seen in the company of Gloria Nell Childs, his latest romantic interest.

If three days in a row passed without excitement, Jerry became restless. Sitting in Cecil's auto one afternoon with no particular place to go, Jerry had been momentarily silent, a sure sign that a wild new scheme was in the works.

"Only one thing to do, Cecil," Jerry mused. "Go to New Orleans. I been there and I liked it."

"Sounds good to me," said Cecil, who was always agreeable. "When do we leave?"

"I see nothin' wrong with right now."

Jerry and Cecil had no intention of staying in New Orleans. They only wanted to stretch their legs, hunt up a few girls and find a thrill. While walking around downtown, they passed a novelty shop that had a handpainted sign hanging in the window which read: "Record Your Voice—$2." They went inside and found a tiny studio in the rear with an old piano and a set of mismatched drums. The man at the counter took Jerry's money and said, "Do whatever you want, only do it inside of five minutes—and no cussin'."

Jerry sat at the piano guessing at what would be the first sounds that he would record and settled on an old country tune entitled, "Don't Stay Away 'til Love Grows Cold." The proprietor went into an adjoining room and switched on a two-track tape recorder. When the first selection was completed, Jerry decided to record an original, untitled composition, a rambling instrumental that he made up as he went along, mixing his favorite boogie rhythms and pounding bass lines. The proprietor put as much of Jerry's music on one side of the 78-rpm record as room would allow and etched "Don't Stay Away" onto the other. A few minutes later, he came out with a small black disc and handed it to Jerry. When the boys had played the recording enough times to have aggravated the proprietor, Jerry delicately lifted the record from the turntable and carried it all over New Orleans, joking with strangers, "Have you heard my latest recording?"

Having done what he wanted to do most, Jerry was ready to return to Ferriday before the posse formed. Cecil drove him home, where Elmo and Mamie were waiting with an unfriendly reception. Jerry looked at them, then at the black plastic disc that had yet to leave his grip, and handed it to Cecil.

"Here, I want you to have this," Jerry said to his best friend. "There'll be others."

In the winter of '51, a tent revival came to Wisner, a hamlet thirty miles northwest of Ferriday. The evangelist who organized the prayer meet was Reverend Jewell E. Barton of Sterlington, a township branching off from Monroe. Reverend Barton was searching for a local pianist to take part in his convocation and had received many recommendations that he call for the Lewis boy over in Ferriday. The boy appeared before the assembled multitude, delighted to be of service.

Reverend Barton's daughter, Dorothy, tagged along to the revival and took a shine to young Jerry. She was seventeen, a religious girl and a proper young lady who was not allowed to date. She thought that it would be nice if Jerry could be her first. Jerry, always inspired by the admiration of pretty girls, performed especially well for Reverend Barton's revival.

At Christmas, Elmo moved his family to Monroe to follow the movable carpentry trade. In the spirit of Christian good will and fellowship, Reverend Barton and his family facilitated the migrants by finding them a small house close to theirs in Sterlington and helped the Lewis children through the first awkward days of school.

Jerry joined the subfreshman class at Linville High in Marion, nearly twenty miles from his new home. Although Jerry and Dorothy were hardly a year's difference in age, three grades separated them in school. Dorothy was in the eleventh grade and Jerry was still in the eighth, the seventh having been a particularly difficult

two years. Nevertheless, Jerry quickly made friends and during
the first semester was elected president of his class.

Jerry had a mad crush on Dorothy. The first time he called on
her, the Reverend Mr. Barton slammed the door in his face. Reverend Barton knew the devil when he saw him. It might have been
the end of an inglorious love affair had not the quick reflexes of
the nimble lad enabled him to sandwich his foot in the door edgewise, gaining entrance by feigning a broken toe. Jerry was adept
at handling the icy reception, and artfully concealed his Black
River Stallion alter ego behind a pious and well-mannered front.
Reverend Barton listened to cunning circumventions of his questions concerning Jerry's ambitions, and thought he had come to
know an aspiring preacher instead of the piano poundin' Killer.

When they had been friends for exactly forty-five days, Jerry
surprised Dorothy on a Thursday after school with a small, inexpensive engagement ring purchased with money he had gotten from
his aunt Stella. Dorothy did not know if the token meant they were
engaged, engaged to become engaged or just going steady. She was
excited just the same, whatever it meant, and ran home to show
Mother, who failed to join in her excitement. The next day at
school, Dorothy woefully returned the ring to her momentary
sweetheart.

"I figgered that might happen," said Jerry.

"And I can't see you anymore," Dorothy said.

"I figgered that might happen, too. But we can go on seein'
each other anyhow, can't we? Quiet-like?"

"I don't see how. My parents are very upset. They may never
let me out of the house again long as I live."

Jerry watched the Barton house late into the night without a
sign from Dorothy. As Romeo anticipated, Juliet was not allowed
out on Friday night. Or Saturday night. The only time she left the
house during the entire weekend was to attend church on Sunday
morning. Furthermore, the Reverend decided to keep her home
from school until he could decide what to do next. He didn't want
his daughter anywhere near Jerry Lee Lewis, and if necessary, he
was prepared to move to another town or send her away somewhere out of the reach of the Black River Stallion. Dorothy
missed three days of classes before her father realized that inat-
tendance jeopardized her grades and that she would have to return
before it was too late to salvage the semester. Dorothy returned to

Linville High on Thursday and made a beeline for her boyfriend to tell him what had happened. When Jerry had heard the awful story, he was peeved into a proposal.

"Let's get married. That'll fix 'em," he said.

"That's crazy." Dorothy frowned. "How can we get married now? We don't have no money, no jobs, nowhere to live—"

"That don't matter," Jerry interrupted. "It didn't matter to my folks when they got hitched, an' my ol' man still ain't got no money or a job or a place to live."

"What'll we do? Where'll we go?"

"I don't know. Yes, I do. We'll do what my folks always do—we'll go see my aunt Stella an' uncle Lee. They'll help us."

And with that, Jerry's marriage proposal was accepted. He and his betrothed drove to Ferriday and appeared on the Calhouns' doorstep, two vulnerable virgins in search of vindication, star-crossed lovers looking for shelter from the storm. Uncle Lee, fixer of all that was wrong with the Lewis clan, looked at their hopefully expectant faces and sensed the purpose of their mission. His suspicion was confirmed by Jerry's poorly worded explanation.

"We *have* to get married," Jerry told them.

"Oh, I see," said Stella, thinking a prenatal emergency had arisen. "Lee, better call the courthouse an' see what can be done."

Lee pulled his nephew aside and whispered, "Listen, boy, how far along has this thing gone?"

"Pretty far," said Jerry, not perfectly sure what his uncle meant by the question.

"Well, don't worry, son, we'll have you all fixed up in a jiffy."

Lee disappeared into the next room to make a few phone calls while Jerry rejoined his fiancée and aunt, who were busy with hurried preparations. "You can have the place next door rent-free," Stella was saying to Dorothy. "We own a little apartment next door and a place across the street that we're savin' for Mamie an' Elmo when they move back to town. What we don't already have furnished, we'll give you as a weddin' present."

Dorothy was overcome by the Calhouns' unrestrained generosity, and it was only the beginning. Stella led her nephew into the parlor for a quiet curtain lecture, then sent him bounding out of the room with a bankroll to purchase a wedding ring, a new suit of clothes and a trousseau for the bride. Lee was on the phone to one of his many friends at the courthouse expediting the formalities of obtaining a marriage license. He gave the clerk the vital information, falsifying facts and figures to make the teens of legal marrying age on paper. Jerry's age was advanced five years to make him twenty-one, Dorothy's by one year to boost her to eighteen, and "farmer" was given as Jerry's profession.

Jerry and Dorothy were joined in holy matrimony in a hastily conducted ceremony performed by Reverend W. W. Hall and attended by Cecil Harrelson, the Calhouns and Stella's daughter and her husband. Next of kin were notified through the safety of a long-distance telephone call. After the shock and disappointment came the quiet resignation that there was nothing to be done other than wish the newlyweds a long and happy life together. Mamie took the news hardest, and began packing for the move back to Ferriday which would not take place for several weeks yet.

Linville High School dropped Mr. and Mrs. Lewis from the roll on March 4 when the honeymooners failed to return to class, having decided against it now that they were adults and did not have to be plagued with a useless education. The charity of the Calhouns seemed boundless, so Jerry did not feel the necessity of having to support himself and his wife. Rent was free and the apartment was furnished; all that was needed was food on the table, and that, too, was usually provided by Aunt Stella. They lived in the luxury of their honeymoon cottage until Elmo and Mamie returned to Ferriday and took the house across the street from the Calhouns. Mamie, who could not bear separation from her boy, insisted Jerry move back home. The honeymoon was over. From his father came many a subtle hint that Jerry find honest work, instead of hanging around the pool hall all day and playing piano in a den of iniquity all night.

"It ain't been too hard a life, has it, Jerry?" Elmo began. "Sleep late, shoot pool all day, hunt, fish, come home to a hot meal that don't cost you. I b'lieve I could learn to like that myself, so what I think I'll do is put you to work an' let me stay home a spell. Now, what d'ya think you might like to do? Carpenterin'?"

"No, I b'lieve I'd like to preach," Jerry said tactically. "Yep, I think I heard the call. But it takes years of study, Lord knows, an' that takes schoolin' an' schoolin' takes money an' money's the one thing I ain't got."

"We'll give you the money," said Stella brightly, trying to be of help.

"Oh, but there ain't a Bible school anywheres near here," said Jerry, retreating into the nearest available excuse.

"Then we'll help you find one," said Stella.

This generous offer silenced everyone until Elmo piped up, "Perfect. Send him off somewhere so he can get right with God. Cut out all this foolishness. It'll help the boy find hisself."

After all excuses had been exhausted, Aunt Stella and Uncle Lee, benefactors of the faith and cornerstones of the Pentecostal church, heard Elmo's and Mamie's prayers and answered them. Mamie's hopes that her only son would become a preacher were closer to realization.

"I've found a school near Dallas, Texas," Aunt Stella reported a few days later when Jerry hoped the matter had been forgotten. "It's the Southwestern Bible Institute in Waxahachie, and it sounds just perfect. Lee and I insist Jerry go at our expense. We never had a son, but would've wanted him to be a man of the cloth, and Jerry's been like a son to us. If there's ever gonna be a preacher in this family, we have high hopes it'll be Jerry."

Jerry was stunned by the offer. His hand had been called by One higher, much higher. "I don't know what to say," he said, more in truth than modesty.

"Then it's settled," said Stella happily. "Oh, there's so much to be done and so little time to do it in before the semester starts in September. Let's see, you'll be needin' new clothes—the school is very strict about appearance. And you and Dorothy will not be allowed to live in the dormitory, of course, so we'll have to find rooms for you somewhere nearby."

Jerry had only to appear at the bus station on the first day of September to bid farewell to his family; Stella had taken care of all other arrangements. The Calhouns laid out sufficient cash for an apartment and essentials for the first semester. Jerry wore a new suit, also a gift from his aunt. A neat stack of crisp white linen shirts wrapped in brown paper was under one arm, a satchel containing the rest of his belongings under the other. The farewell was practically the first time Reverend Barton had spoken to his daughter since her elopement. However, Jerry's enrollment in Bible school had gained his approval.

When they arrived at the Dallas outpost of Waxahachie, Jerry and Dorothy sought out the small college in the 1200 block of Sycamore Street and from there circled the campus looking for rooms to rent. They found a small, comfortable furnished efficiency, and as Dorothy scoured the local want ads for jobs, Jerry reported for induction.

At the dean of registration's office, Jerry glanced at the rigid standards governing appearance, speech and demeanor. Although he came to like the idea of getting a higher education, going to Southwestern Bible Institute was not unlike going to prison. His primary complaint was too many rules, for which he had a poor memory. Rules were for the other suckers. Rules followed Jerry; Jerry did not follow rules.

After completing registration paper work, Jerry posed for a photograph with his wife and three classmates, including his cousin David Beatty, and asked the photographer to send a copy to his parents. "They won't b'lieve I'm here till they get this," he laughed.

The picture was not the image of the Black River Stallion. He was swallowed by a jacket four sizes too large. The sacklike cut hid all but a patch of plain white shirt and a swatch of horizontally striped tie. He wore pants overcut to begin with, the crotch hanging almost to the knee, the cuffs drooping over thick-soled shoes which were in the last squeaky stage of being broken in. His long blond hair was combed straight back in its typical furrowed fashion, a pattern of growth inherited from his mother's family. He was an unmemorable face in the crowd. His transformation had begun. And so had the revolution.

As Jerry began the first day of class, Dorothy began her new job at a nursery attending to plants and trimming shrubbery. She hadn't the least experience with horticulture, and was as unfamiliar with her work as her husband was with his. Jerry meanwhile made an honest effort to redeem himself as a serious scholar. He got no help. The classes in Pentecostal doctrine, biblical history and scriptural interpretation were as long and hot and dry as the parchment they had been written on, and were made worse for Jerry by his having to endure every moment neatly buttoned into starched shirt with jacket and tie in place. After one week of exemplary scholasticism, the priest-ridden atmosphere stirred Jerry's ancient recalcitrance. Dorothy waited supper later and later with each passing day. In time, he neglected to come home for dinner, and then not until early morning. Dorothy was afraid that one of these nights he wasn't going to come home at all.

"I have to study," Jerry explained. "Study, study, study is all I ever do all day an' all night. It's a long road to where I'm goin', an' it takes a lotta work. You can ask your pa if I'm lyin'."

Dorothy soon tired of spending all day at work and all evening at home without her newlywedded husband. She had no friends to call, and daffodils and begonias made poor conversationalists at work. When the silence of solitude began to thunder in her ears, Dorothy called home to Mother. "Wire me bus fare, Mamma," she said, "I wanna come home."

Mrs. Barton sent the money to her daughter immediately, and Dorothy was packed and gone before Jerry had taken time to notice her absence. He panicked when he discovered his wife had done what he considered unthinkable: deserted him just because he was devoting all of his time to his studies. His initial impulse was to catch the next bus after her, but it became a matter of pride, and Jerry was not about to go running after Dorothy making excuses for crimes which he wasn't sure she knew he had committed. He decided to treat Dorothy as in the wrong and act accordingly. He got approval from his parents for deciding to stay at school to finish the semester, and complete cooperation from his sympathetic female "study partner." Dorothy refused to weaken, but Jerry's study partner surrendered.

Of all the impressions Jerry made upon the staff at the school, his piano playing clearly outshined any promise he had for preaching. He was not an exciting speaker, relying on a limited stock of evangelical clichés, but impressed his audiences with an uncanny ability to quote Scripture, including verse and line number. Once seated at the piano, Jerry's music succeeded where plain speech could not follow. He was appointed honorary pianist at daily chapel services by the dean of students, rising to the occasion by coaxing grandiloquent chords out of the church's tiny spinet.

Jerry's contributions to chapel service became the favorite feature of otherwise dreary devotions. The more somber the service, the more entertaining he became, until the sermons seemed like little more than long-winded introductions to Jerry Lee Lewis and His Pumping Piano. The congregation silently pleaded for relief from preachment, erupting into unprecedented displays of fervency in vocalizing hymns. Jerry became caught up in the conflicting emotions of wanting to inspire and wanting to entertain. He was as excitable at the piano as a handclapping, handkerchief-waving preacher was on his pulpit. Emotion could not be contained, and Jerry picked an inappropriate time to release it.

While Jerry was tapping out the introductory strains to the canticle "My God Is Real," a sudden retrogression took place. He decorated the hymn with a bright glissando, and the tune took off where the composer had not intended any such change in the beat. As Jerry's mood swung from godly to devilish, "My God Is Real" began to boogie and the gathering broke into smiles and giggles, except for the deans, who collectively sat bolt upright and looked at each other for confirmation of the delusion. Dean Moore rose to his feet, bounded across the platform and scotched the recital before Jerry hit his big finish.

"This is an outrage!" the dean bellowed. "Desecration! Brother Lewis, in my office, immediately."

Jerry walked out of the sanctuary in shame. He appeared at the dean's office fearing the very worst punishment the institute was able to prescribe. A meeting of the discipline committee was hastily convened and they delivered a harsh verdict: expulsion. Boogie-woogie was the quickest ticket to perpetual perdition, the eighth deadly sin.

Jerry was penitent, his schoolmaster pitiless. Unable to summon a suitable defense, he made an attempt at apology, stopping as he watched it produce not the slightest effect on Dean Moore's demeanor. Jerry turned and walked away as a note was entered into his permanent record: "The termination of this student resulted from his choice to disregard the rules of the institute."

No official written explanation was issued by Southwestern Bible Institute to Jerry's parents. He had as long as it took to return home to conceive an explanation which would sound plausible and minimize the severity of the repercussions he was sure to experience from his family. Jerry's version of his excommunication, the annotated account, was offered along with the theatrics of glossy-eyed bewilderment.

"I don't understand it," he told his family. "I didn't do anything wrong. I played piano jus' like I always have, the way ever'body has always liked it, only this time they didn't like it. 'Shout unto the Lord, all the earth,' says the Bible. 'Serve the Lord with gladness. Come before His presence with singing.' I served Him gladly. I sang. I shouted. I didn't mean to break any rules, honest."

"I'm only s'prised you lasted as long as you did," said Elmo.

"That's enough outta you, Elmo," said Mamie, who believed her son when he said he had reformed.

"I wanna preach," Jerry claimed, "but I wanna play piano, too. Is it my fault I don't play like some ol' lady? It jus' comes out thataway natchally. I can't help it."

"Now what will you do, son?" Elmo asked, looking for telltale signs of the con in the boy.

"First thing is see about Dorothy. I'm goin' to Sterlington an' see if I can't patch things up. Then I'm comin' back here with her or without her an' make my way over to Texas Street to spread the Good Word."

The return of Jerry Lee to the Barton house was a near-repeat of his first visit, the only difference being Reverend Barton didn't want to let him in at all. Forgiveness, the Reverend's stock in trade, was what Jerry asked for, and the womenfolk sympathized with his tale of woe. However, the story they heard was not the same one Jerry's parents had listened to earlier.

"Oh, it was terrible," Jerry beseeched his wife. "When you left, I didn't know why. I didn't know where you went. I couldn't find you. I couldn't eat, I couldn't sleep, I couldn't study. My grades went bad, so I quit an' came to get you. I couldn't go on like this. If school is keepin' us apart, an' if I have to make a choice, then I'll take you over Bible school ev'ry time."

When asked to put himself in the same position, Reverend Barton became Jerry's strongest ally. Now it was Dorothy's turn to make explanations to the master of turning the tables.

"I don't wanna keep you from your mission in life," she said. "I know you have to answer to God before you answer to me, but it seemed like you never got around to me at all. Maybe you shoulda been to school before we got married."

"Maybe, but that's all over now. I ain't goin' back to school. I can serve God without a diploma. I'm gonna preach at Mamma's church. Now, are you comin' with me or not?"

"Yes," said Dorothy; her parents fairly pushed her out the door.

The couple returned to Ferriday and took up residence with Elmo and Mamie. Once again Jerry was among the small number of proselytes at the Texas Street Assembly of God on Wednesdays and Sundays. The smattering of book learning he picked up in Waxahachie in one semester had grown by word of mouth into a full-fledged education, and the congregation was anxious to hear

Brother Lewis testify. On the evening of Jerry's inaugural sermon, there was a record attendance owing to a large turnout of his family and friends. The topic of his address was the evils in everyday life, and the prime target was television.

"You can tell when the devil's in a man's house 'cause you can see his tail stickin' up through the roof. Y'know what the devil's tail looks like?" he asked as the crowd leaned forward to hear the revelation. "A television antenna, that's what the devil's tail looks like."

The crowd murmured its approval. There were many who held the invention as the work of the Devil, and preachers warned that, like motion pictures, television was another of Satan's devices to pervert the truth and lure man away from God. For weeks, Jerry's analogy was repeated around town. Citizens of Ferriday marveled at the wonderful education the boy had received in such a short time at school. As Elmo proudly explained of his son, "He's always been a quick study."

Dorothy was proud of her husband the preacher. She led the kind of life her parents lived, and Jerry earned the respect of everyone who heard him preach. He regained her trust, and Dorothy felt secure in knowing that never again would she have cause to complain about Jerry placing other aspects of his life, or other women, before her.

The second honeymoon did not last long. Dorothy and Jerry never remained in one place for long, as Elmo continued to parade his family from one residence to another, from the Calhouns' place in Ferriday to Clayton to a shack in Vidalia on the Natchez Highway. It was during one of these moves that Dorothy discovered a letter with a Waxahachie postmark addressed to Jerry in flowery script, a love note from her husband's study partner confessing how much she missed burning the midnight oil with Brother Lewis. Healed wounds reopened and the marriage entered the initial stage of dissolution.

Jerry attempted to explain away the evidence as a one-time indiscretion brought about only by his weakened emotional condition after Dorothy left him. She fussed and fumed but did not leave him as she threatened, for she knew they would never see each other again. Dorothy retreated, whiling away her days working at Lee's drugstore. Jerry spent most of his time at the pool hall. Guest appearances at church became irregular. He had come full circle; the revolution was complete.

Southwestern Bible Institute failed to modify Jerry beyond the cosmetic improvements of cleaning up his language and appearance; he never, ever used the Lord's name in vain, and learned to like wearing white dress shirts. The school could not in such a short time recast his ambitions or convert the Killer into a saint. He did not understand how anyone could be as good as the Bible instructed in order to find God's favor, and knew he was fighting a losing battle. Tormented by his shortcomings and lacking the strength to change, Jerry lost the desire to preach.

Jerry began a new job at the Swan Club. He did not consider a bar to be a proper place for a preacher's daughter and a former preacher's wife, so Dorothy was forbidden to watch him work. She did not like the new arrangement whereby she came home from the drugstore as Jerry was heading for work at the club. She was in bed when he came home and he was still asleep when she went to work the following morning.

On an August Sunday, Jerry was a guest soloist at the Holiness Church in Natchez. There he met Jane Mitcham, a high school junior who was witnessing the Pentecostal spectacle for the first time with a friend. For Jane, it was love at first sight. For Jerry, it had happened before. He could never enter a town without stealing the heart of every virgin who cast eyes upon him. Jerry paid no attention to Jane, but learned where he could find her if he wanted her.

On a Friday night later in the month, Cecil Harrelson thought he spied the unmistakable wavy-haired blond head in the company of a woman other than his wife. Several times thereafter, he saw Jerry's car parked in clandestine spots popular with young lovers on the same nights he knew Dorothy to be home alone. Jerry's movable boudoir, the same '41 Ford he had always driven, was still in pretty fair shape for parking on deserted roads late at night and playing in the backseat. Many an unborn son and daughter were stained into the fabric of its upholstery. On such a night, Dorothy discovered her husband in the midst of his vaunted virility at the drive-in movie. She had a witness, too.

Fear placed Jerry on the offensive. He followed Dorothy home and told her to pack her bags, he was taking her home to Sterlington. There was no use in pleading, the damage was done, the marriage was over. "I've gotten a girl in trouble," he lied. "Her brothers are huntin' me with hide whips. I ain't got no choice. I'm gonna have to marry her."

Dorothy was crushed. In Sterlington, she sought the advice of J. H. Dormon, attorney at law, who told her that a divorce could be filed no sooner than thirty days from the start of their separation. Her complaint, he assured her, would be on the clerk of court's desk first thing on the morning of September 18.

"Who will testify as your witness, Mrs. Lewis?" Dormon asked.

"Cecil Harrelson," she answered.

Jerry had an abbreviated explanation of the entire course of events for Cecil, who found himself in the awkward position of having to testify against his best friend in a divorce proceeding. "What d'ya want me to do about this testifyin' thing, Jerry? You want me to go to court an' tell 'em about you an' Jane?"

"No, you ain't gotta tell 'em about Jane. Dorothy don't even know Jane's name. Tell 'em whatever they wanna hear an' agree to whatever she wants an' let that be the end of it. Tell 'em you don't know who the girl was, but it happened an' that's all there is to it."

"Ain't you goin' to court?" Cecil asked.

"Hell, no. I ain't even gonna answer the damn petition. After a while the court'll give her a judgment an' the whole thing'll be over."

Jerry considered the preliminary separation had already made him a free man. The divorce decree was a mere formality. He didn't see the sense in waiting for a final judgment before marrying again, but he was careful not to mention it to Jane lest he scare her away. Jane was told nothing of the divorce, for she had been told nothing of Dorothy. Jane had not the first inkling that she had been dating a married man.

On the Friday before Dorothy was to file for divorce, complications set in. Jerry became impatient waiting for the legal process to take effect and decided there was no sense in putting off his marriage to Jane since both events were certain of happening anyway; the proper order made no difference to him. With wedding ring in pocket, Jerry picked up Jane after school and proposed they drive over to Fayette, Mississippi, and get married immediately. The subject had been mentioned several times in recent days, and Jane was ready, willing and able. Her sister, Jewell, had been prepared to serve as witness at a moment's notice, and the threesome was far into the thirty-mile drive before the first intelligent questions were posed.

"Why we goin' to Fayette?" Jane wanted to know.

"Three reasons," Jerry replied, "nobody knows us, there's no wait an' no questions asked."

"Where we goin' afterward?" asked Jewell, who had never tagged along on a honeymoon and wasn't sure she wanted to.

"To my folks' place," said Jerry.

"My folks ain't gonna like this," Jane worried. "They want me to finish school an' I ain't got much longer to go. Can't we live with my folks till I finish school? It won't be so bad, an' its just for a li'l while."

"Don't matter to me," said Jerry.

"Goody," said Jane.

"Boy, won't Mom 'n' Dad be thrilled," Jewell joked. "Comp'ny's comin'."

At the courthouse in Fayette, Jewell waited in the car for Jerry and Jane, who returned in five minutes with legal permission to marry. The license listed only their names, ages and parents' names. The address given for both parties was 1040 North Pine, Natchez, and was erroneously listed as the Elmer Lewis residence. Having learned from his uncle Lee, Jerry lied that he was twenty-one and added a year to Jane's age to make her eighteen. The clerk did not ask for proof of identification, nor did he inquire about previous marriages or present occupations. They were directed to the nearest minister, a Methodist named Matheny who was constantly on call. When the brief ceremony was concluded, Jerry and Jane and Jewell drove back to Natchez, where they breezed into the Mitcham house and shocked her parents with the happy news. Jerry moved a few of his things into Jane's bedroom and sat down at the kitchen table wondering what was for supper.

"Fix me somethin' to eat, I got to be goin'," Jerry said to Jane.

"Where?"

"Swan Club. Work. Friday's a big night."

"Sounds like fun."

"You ain't goin'," said Jerry.

"Why not?" Jane whined.

"My wife don't hang out in bars."

"But we jus' got married," she cried.

"Congratulations," he silenced her, "but it ain't proper."

He kissed his wife of a few hours good-bye and left her, as he would on many nights to follow, to spend the first night of their honeymoon at home with her parents, waiting for him to return from work. Before getting into his car, Jerry heard voices rising in angry protest over the elopement. The whole affair was off to a bad start.

Jerry was served with Dorothy's complaint for divorce one week later, on September 18. Cecil appeared in court to verify her charge that "defendant did commit an act of adultery on August 18, 1953, with a woman named Jean Jones in a 1951 Model Ford automobile near Ferriday, Louisiana." According to plan, Jerry saved attorney's fees by ignoring the suit and waited for justice to proceed without him. Meanwhile, the new Mrs. Lewis was kept a secret, and no one informed Jerry that his bigamous marriage to Jane was null and void.

Preaching and piano playing, bigamy, adultery and divorce— Jerry had far greater issues to worry about. He was six days past his eighteenth birthday and the draft was threatening to borrow two years of his life. His pal Cecil had been faced with the same dilemma earlier in the year.

"Ain't you scared of bein' drafted, Cecil?" Jerry wanted to know.

"Nossir, I am not," he said matter-of-factly.

"How come?"

"'Cause they wrapped up the big blast in Korea two months ago an' nobody's in the mood to fight, so I reckon they won't be needin' us."

"I don't wanna go in no army," Jerry complained.

"You won't have to," Cecil reassured.

"How do you know?"

"I don't. Just don't worry about it."

"I am worried. I don't trust 'em. Go with me to register."

Cecil took Jerry to the registrar's office of the Selective Service in Natchez and watched over his shoulder as the clerk recorded Jerry's vital statistics. When this was completed, the clerk handed Jerry his draft card and told him to retain it in his possession at all times and present it on demand.

"To who?" Jerry asked.

"To anybody that asks," the clerk said.

"Why would they ask?"

"Because . . . look, are you tryin' to gimme a hard time? Just take this form and fill it out, cowboy, and return it to me when you're finished," the clerk said flatly.

"I don't like the looks of this," Jerry said. "I don't like the looks of this at all."

"What's the matter now?" Cecil said under strain.

"Hell, I've only been here five minutes, an' they already gimme a membership card. I'm as good as in already. When do they gimme the damn gun?"

"That's not a membership card," Cecil said. "Ever'body gets one o' those."

"Ever'body in the army."

"Quiet. Now fill out the damn form an' let's get the hell outta here 'fore they throw us both in the stockade."

"You do it," Jerry said, pushing the paper at Cecil.

"Me? I can't answer your questions. You do it."

"No, no. Fill it out so's they won't want me. Tell 'em whatever it is they don't wanna hear. C'mon, Cecil, you know how."

"All right, so you won't go into the army. You'll go to jail."

"For how long?" Jerry asked.

Cecil shrugged.

"Good. I been to jail an' the food's fair an' the hours ain't bad."

"Not where they send draft dodgers," Cecil said. "They'll ship you off to Angola, an' it ain't nothin' like the local lockup."

"Hey, that gimme an idea. They won't take me in the army if I have a record, will they?"

"No."

"Then write down that I been to jail a buncha times."

"It has to be for real bad stuff—rape, robbery, things like that," Cecil explained. "They don't turn you down for speedin' an' runnin' red lights."

"Put it down then," said Jerry, "the real bad stuff."

"If you say so," Cecil agreed. "Let's see, Series Twelve, Court Record, that's the one. Okay, it says to check one, 'I have or have not been convicted or adjudicated of a criminal offense, other than minor traffic violations.'"

"Have."

"Okay, have. 'List the offense, date of conviction, court and sentence of each charge,'" Cecil continued. "Well, what do you want me to put?"

"Go ahead, you're doin' fine. Jus' make it good."

"Right," Cecil said, and proceeded to confess a list of contrived crimes, including murder.

With one glance at Series Twelve, the Selective Service promptly filed Jerry's registration form in the reject pile. Cecil went one step further in securing his pal's future by leaning on a friend to give Jerry a job playing piano in the lounge of the Avis Hotel in Monroe.

"That's just about the nicest thing anybody's ever done for me, Cecil," said Jerry. "But it won't give us a chance to get together much."

"I'm leavin' town, anyway," said Cecil. "I got a job workin' the oil wells in the Gulf. I'll be leavin' for Texas next week. So, best of luck, Killer. I know I'll be hearin' good things about you real soon."

The Killer had two wives until October 8, 1953, when Judge Heard granted Dorothy a divorce after Jerry defaulted by failing to file an answer to the complaint. Jerry had already deserted his new bride for the bright lights of the Avis Hotel. A two-hundred-mile round trip was too far to travel every day, so he remained in Monroe while Jane finished school in Natchez. After two months, Jerry returned, making a pledge similar to the one made to Dorothy, proclaiming his desire for Jane had made living apart too difficult and that he would never leave her again. It was a promise he made near weekly, for the lovebirds were constantly breaking up and making up. Fights typically were over finances and Jerry's tendency to squander butter-and-egg money on the movies. If the quarrel reached the intensity where milk bottles and butcher knives were thrown instead of curses, Jerry ran away for two or three days until Jane cooled off. It was during one of these separations that Jane made the mistake of going on a date with another man. Her attempt at making Jerry jealous turned him into a green-eyed monster.

Jane silenced Jerry's accusations with a few of her own, such as the secret of his first marriage. For the sake of a provisional peace, Jerry dropped the affair until he needed ammunition for the next skirmish. Mamie had an even better memory of Jane's contrived courtship, and used it to promote discord between her son and his wife. Never again could harsh words pass between them without the indiscretion being thrown in Jane's face. Jerry had felt the sting of jealousy and he didn't like it. The idea of another man despoiling his possession provoked an incurable mental aberration which Jerry carried the rest of his life. Jane had gone too far in trying to teach him a lesson.

Jane was expecting a child at the end of the year. The news troubled the expectant father. He was eighteen, married to his second wife and still living with his parents. He performed twice a week at prayer meets and never made a dime as a soldier of the Lord. He could play the devil's music six nights a week in a Natchez roadhouse and make as much as one hundred dollars. His cousin Jimmy, who had surrendered his life to Christ, tried to convince Jerry it was a far better thing to do the Lord's work for the reward that waits in heaven than gain the whole world and lose his soul. Although Jerry could never completely renounce his religion, he could not make the same commitment Jimmy honored.

Jerry listened to both sides of the argument before making a decision as to which path he should take—the wide gate that leads many down streets paved with gold to destruction, or the narrow gate few can find that leads to life everlasting. In the dark night of his soul, torn between heaven and hell, Jerry hearkened to instinct and, after a few brief bouts with a conscience that had a voice amazingly similar to Jimmy's, decided to be true to himself. His natural tendency told him to do what he did best: rock 'n' roll.

Jerry appeased his conscience by bargaining to play the devil's music only as long as it took to earn money to feed his family and fund a church of his own, to take from Satan so that he could serve the Lord. In that way, if it was possible, he hoped to have worldly wealth and heavenly peace by selling his soul to God after ransoming it from the devil. Is it not written: "God helps them that help themselves"?

"He who is not with Me is against Me," saith the Lord. In other words, "No deal."

"Aha," said Satan gleefully, "another holdout."

His decision made, it was no more difficult for Jerry to find a job playing in a nightclub than to ask the question once. The Wagon Wheel in Natchez was his only stop in his quest for employment. Paul Whitehead, the resident one-man band, was a blind pianist in need of support from a man of many talents who could play drums, guitar and an occasional four-chord bar on piano. Jerry auditioned on all three instruments and won the position. He agreed to work for ten dollars a night and tips. Tips sometimes included pep pills from truck drivers, which the energetic teen had little use for; he would have preferred a spare dime.

Blind Paul played an assortment of rhythm and blues, country and western, and whatever patrons requested. Most of the time, Jerry drummed a steady beat for Paul to keep time. He rarely got the chance to show off on piano unless Paul played one of his few numbers on the trumpet. And as the year 1954 rolled away, Blind Paul sang sad songs to people who hardly listened, and whom he could not see. His quest to record a hit song had led him down many blind alleys, and he was proficient at making excuses for what might have been. From his perch behind a mismatched drum kit, Jerry stared out at the lifeless crowd with no more vision of the fading horizon than his mentor.

On November 2, 1954, Jane gave birth to a son. Like his daddy before him, Jerry named his firstborn Junior, befitting one who would live in his father's shadow, inheriting his talents as well as his weaknesses. This new obligation scared Jerry. He resented Jane for having the child, believing she conceived intentionally to keep him from running away with another woman. After all, Jerry reasoned, Jane was once the "other woman."

Times grew increasingly tough for Elmo and Mamie and their extended family. They were scarcely able to keep their heads above water on the farm situated at the end of the road in the community of Black River. Elmo sowed his sweat into the soil and scrabbled a garden for vegetables, squeezing life's barest necessities from laying hens and milk cows. The house where the seven members of Elmo's clan lived was a shotgun model—three rooms divided by curtains hung in spaces designed for doors which were never installed. Closets consisted of two-penny nails driven into bare walls. Water was hoisted from a well by a wooden bucket. Hot in summer, cold in winter and wet when it rained, the shack's only token of happiness, pleasure or amusement was Jerry's well-worn upright. And when Black River was on the rise, Elmo and Jerry raced to roll the piano out of the house and onto the truck before the flood filled the house to the rafters. After the water subsided, some brave soul had to climb into the rafters and clear out a cheerless nest of rattlesnakes lest they crawl into bed some cold night. That was home on Black River.

The fights between his parents, the quarrels with his wife, the squalling of kid sisters, the cries of his hungry infant son and the curse of poverty combined to make Jerry sick at heart and bored with life. The solution, as in his youth, was to run away to a place where there was no one to remind him of who he was or his responsibility to those he had left behind—a place where his talent could be discovered and money could be made.

The likely place to start was Shreveport, where the program director at KWKH radio had six years before organized a touring country-music show called the "Louisiana Hayride." It was, after all, the place where Jerry's hero, Hank Williams, got his start. And, notably, in October 1954, an unknown Elvis Presley signed on in a Hayride opening spot for eighteen dollars a night. Following in his predecessors' footsteps, Jerry walked into Henry Logan's office at KWKH in search of a job with the Hayride as staff pianist.

"I'm afraid we don't have an openin' right now," Logan told Jerry. "I've had the same piano player for the past five years, a boy by the name of Floyd Cramer, an' we don't need another. Have you got a record out?"

"Nossir, I don't," said Jerry, "but I can play anything."

"Then what I suggest you do is head for Nashville and audition for the record companies," Logan said. "Everyone makin' it big in country music winds up there sooner or later. Why don't you come back to the studio tonight after hours an' record a dub to take with you. It'll make you look more perfessional. Just ask our engineer, Bob Sullivan, an' he'll get you goin'. If you get somethin' started in Nashville, come back an' see me."

At the end of the KWKH broadcast day, Jerry went into the studio to record two songs on a quarter-inch Magnacord tape recorder which were then transcribed onto a reference disc, what musicians refer to as a "dub." Jerry played "If I Ever Needed You" and Hank Snow's "I Don't Hurt Anymore," and when finished, walked aimlessly in the midnight air wondering what to do with his sample. Nashville, as Henry Logan had advised, was his only alternative to going home.

Jerry did not know anyone in Nashville, nor whom to call when he got there. He had no car and few dollars and could not afford to wait long for success to find him. Investing most of what money he had in a dollar-a-night room at the Bell Hotel, Jerry began his search for the people who could make him a star before the rest of his cash ran out. He walked into one record company after another and heard many polite refusals from producers who were too busy, too successful or too important to waste time on an unknown. He was told to come back when his name could be heard on the radio.

Funds were exhausted quickly, and Jerry walked the streets looking for work in the after-hours clubs that dotted the city. He stumbled onto an upstairs and out-of-the-way joint owned by a singer named Roy Hall and auditioned for a temporary opening in Roy's band. Late at night, Jerry played piano and entertained the same record producers and Opry stars who had refused to audition him in their offices. He played his heart out for every famous face and important personage and silently suffered when they were too drunk to notice. He would not give up.

Jane regarded Jerry's determination as desertion. He had left her penniless with their six-week-old infant. When the rent came due, Jane moved in with her sister, who had a hard enough time providing for her own family. Jane had no alternative but to file for nonsupport and ask the court to provide her with a temporary monthly payment of forty dollars. The court granted her motion; Jerry, unwilling and unable to abide the sanctions, was safe out of reach of the court's jurisdiction.

A bright moment in the otherwise disappointing venture was Jerry's visit to the Grand Ole Opry. Making his way backstage, he was befriended by Del Wood, whose one and only hit, "Down Yonder," had earned her a spot on the Opry two years before. Del's kind words of encouragement in the midst of indifference and hostility were not forgotten when Jerry brought her onstage with him at the Opry twenty years later, long after they had exchanged places.

After a month in Nashville without a glimmer of hope, Jerry was close to quitting on the country music capital when he paid a visit to Chet Atkins at RCA. Chet was a much-sought-after session guitarist and was supposed to be an authority on what the public would buy and what it took to become a success.

"Boy, go home and learn to play a guitar," was Chet's advice to Jerry. "A piano ain't never gonna make you no money."

Penniless, brokenhearted and wounded in spirit, Jerry trudged out of Nashville along Highway 65 and looked homeward. Home, where his mother would celebrate his return. Home, where his father would look up briefly from his labor to see his only son worse from wear and lower his head again to the fields. Home, where his wife would have him thrown in jail for nonsupport.

He would remain apart from his wife until the estimated costs of separation and divorce far outweighed the obligations of living with Jane and Junior. He would propose a reconciliation at a time when Christian kindness temporarily filled his heart and shortly before having to come up with another support payment. There would be peace until it was discovered Jane was pregnant again. Lacking an accurate perception of human gestation, it would be left to Jerry and his mother to suppose the child was not of Jerry's making; too little time had passed since their reunion for the miracle to take place.

Poverty and failure, hatred and jealousy, fear and doubt were what waited for Jerry five hundred miles down a lonesome highway. On the outskirts of Nashville, as traffic ceased along the road, he crawled into a ditch and went to sleep. "The way is dark, the night is long, I don't care if I never get home. I'm waitin' at the end of the road."

2 Milkshake Mademoiselle

THE MUSIC INDUSTRY BASED IN NEW YORK was completely unprepared for what was happening in the South. As long as Decca had the Crosbys and Columbia had Sinatra, it didn't matter if a handful of hayseeds had no place to peddle country tunes or blues ballads. The corporate giants in Gotham could not have cared less, in fact were hoping that an enterprising gambler would take it upon himself to seek out and improve the talent walking the streets of southern towns. What the country needed was a good five-cent recording studio, and the first man willing to take a chance on the underdeveloped talent in Memphis, Tennessee, was Sam Phillips.

Sam was working as a disc jockey when a hillbilly singer named Buck Turner loaned him the money to set up a studio in return for the educated use of that equipment in the production of Buck's demonstration records. Sam set up a twelve-foot-square studio at 706 Union Avenue in a building that contained a shipping room and an auto upholstery firm in adjoining areas. He stuck acoustic tile on the walls, slapped on a coat of light green paint, installed a one-track tape recorder and hung out a sign that read: "Memphis Recording Service." It was the only studio south of Chicago where a man with two bucks could walk in off the street and leave an hour later with his work grooved into black waxen plastic.

Sam operated at a break-even point by taping dubs for singers who then signed with established labels, cutting Sam out of the serious money to be made by pressing records and distributing them himself. It had to be proven over and over that he could make a decent return on an investment before he was convinced that he wanted a label of his own. His lack of courage in his convictions and failure to recognize the potential in his cottage industry let dozens of discoveries slip away. In time, Sam would have money to finance the start of many careers, but confidence, the thing which he lacked most in himself, would never be found in anyone else.

Sam's Sun Record Company flew under a bright yellow banner consisting of a crowing cock standing in the ellipse of a rising sun, its rays illuminating ten bars of nondescript musical notes. The first releases appeared in March 1952, all black artists singing the blues. Sam didn't get many white customers, and he knew a fortune awaited the man who could find the best of all possible worlds—a white singer with a black soul—for he knew that as good as any black singer was, he could never tap the big money from white audiences. The color bar in music had not been lifted, and a large segment of society wanted it to remain firmly in place.

There was one boy, nineteen years old, who spent off-hours in the Sun studio recording songs for his mother and demos for Sam. His name came to mind in 1954 when Sam was unable to locate the singer of another demo he had received in the mail. Sam's secretary found the boy's name on file and called him in to talk about cutting his first single.

The song was "Without You." The singer was Elvis Presley. Sam had found his magic combination: white man with black soul.

Shortly thereafter, Sam recorded Elvis's first single, a composition by Arthur Cruddup entitled "That's All Right, Mama." The "Louisiana Hayride" added Elvis to their tour at the end of the year and Sam was then able to get him an opening slot on the Grand Ole Opry. Soon the people of the Southeast were flocking to see the Hillbilly Cat, the king of western bop.

Elvis was the vanguard of the rock 'n' roll movement. He led the parade in rose-colored Cadillacs, dressed in glittery suits of pink and black, beckoning boys and girls to follow. He was a phenomenon that divided society into generations of musical tastes. He altered the normal pattern of daily life by teaching teens a new way to walk, talk and comb their hair. And below the illumined surface of the black-leather-clad figure was the primitive beat of black music, blamed for working a satanic magic on virgins and unraveling the moral fiber of America's youth.

Late in 1955, Elvis conquered the country-western market with his fifth attempt on Sun Records, "Mystery Train." Sam Phillips

had succeeded in breaking Nashville's hold on the market, and
when the song hit the top of the national charts, Colonel Tom
Parker wasted no time in contacting Elvis's parents and sweet-
talking them into letting him negotiate a contract for their boy
with a major label. His next call was to friends at RCA to set up a
conference between their top brass and Sam Phillips, keeper of
the key. Sam knew Elvis was a hot property, but he wasn't sure
why a big company in New York would want him.

When Sam heard RCA's offer to buy Elvis's contract from Sun,
he went into shock: thirty-five thousand dollars for this truck
driver, this kid with one country hit. Furthermore, RCA wanted
all of Sun's master tapes on Elvis along with Sam's publishing
subsidiary in exchange for their promise to pay Elvis all of the
royalties due him from Sun, which he had yet to collect. On top
of it all, the kid was getting five thousand dollars just for signing
his name to the contract. For Sam, the value of the transaction
was climbing to over fifty thousand dollars. He sold Elvis and
released him gladly, certain that he could find a hundred guys like
him. It was the deal of the century, only Sam wasn't on the receiving end.

Nineteen fifty-six will always be remembered as the year Elvis
conquered the hearts and minds and bodies and souls of teenaged
America. "Heartbreak Hotel" was Number 1 in the country and
rhythm-and-blues charts. RCA taught Sam Phillips a valuable lesson in promotion, and being an apt pupil, Sam poured Carl Perkins into Presley's mold and forged "Blue Suede Shoes" into a
top-ten hit in the same charts and topped Elvis by crossing over
into the pop field. It looked as though Sam had done the impossible by replacing Elvis with one better when catastrophe struck as
Carl took to the road on his first national tour. An automobile
accident seriously injured Carl and his brother, causing a six
month layoff. Carl's career, only just beginning, was temporarily
over. Before Elvis's recording year was through, "Don't Be
Cruel" and "Hound Dog" were Number 1 hits in all three charts,
and "Love Me Tender" sold another million. He was commanding
$1,250 a night to perform and had a string of television appear-
ances lined up. Ed Sullivan, fearing Elvis's gyrations might put
older viewers into culture shock, dictated that his cameraman not
expose Elvis below the waist.

Rock 'n' roll music was the issue of a critical conflict brewing in the boardrooms of the industry's major companies. With Presley's pelvic punctuation of sexually implicit lyrics, the old-line music publishers and their artists condemned rock as immoral. "It's not music, it's a disease," said Mitch Miller. Frank Sinatra said, "Rock 'n' roll is lewd—in plain fact, dirty. It's phony and false, and sung, written and played for the most part by cretinous goons." The New York *Daily News* attacked disc jockey Alan Freed as an inciter of juvenile delinquency. Parents were calling radio and television stations with complaints, threatening to boycott sponsors' products. Those who tried but could not destroy rock 'n' roll attempted, as Ed Sullivan did, to censor it when rehabilitation failed.

In the other camp, the public demand from the younger set had made Chuck Berry's "Roll Over Beethoven" the watchword of their faith. Fats Domino tallied three chartbusters, including his biggest, "Blueberry Hill." Buddy Holly turned up in Nashville to record his first single, and Gene Vincent, Eddie Cochran and more and more newcomers every day followed Elvis into the studios. The businessmen who were to become the new establishment were doing their level best to facilitate the phenomenon. Sam Phillips, still shopping for the next Elvis, opened Stars, Inc. to handle bookings for Roy Orbison, Johnny Cash and other fledgling acts trying to stake out unclaimed territory. This was excitement, this was pandemonium: Big business could smell big bucks; kids united into a culture; newspapers had something new to attack; moms and dads had something else to bitch about. And nobody had any idea what was going to happen next. How did all of this craziness effect Jerry Lee Lewis? He wanted in.

With a second child on the way and another mouth to feed, Jerry was forced into working for a living when the Wagon Wheel failed to yield more than the fifty dollars a week he had been making. Manual labor was out. His eighth-grade education was an embarrassment to him and disqualified him from positions requiring brains and basic skills. When all else fails, turn to sales.

Jerry heard about a company in Baton Rouge needing door-to-door salesmen to peddle sewing machines. The company's come-on stated that their salesmen's incomes were limited only by their own desire and determination. Brimming with boundless supplies of both, Jerry drove to Baton Rouge and found the Atlas Sewing Center and its owner, Joe Moise.

"What happens is, you pick up the machines here, take 'em back home and run 'em around door-to-door. You give the customer the machine to keep, get a ten-dollar deposit and send me their name and address which you get 'em to write down on these little cards," Moise explained. "Then what I do is send the customer a coupon book, and every month they mail me their payment until they've purchased the machine. Get the idea?"

"Yessir," said Jerry, "I give 'em the machine, get the deposit, fill out the card an' send it to you. You take it from there."

"Right. Then I get my money, you get your commission, the buyer gets the machine, ever'body's happy. Unnerstand?"

"Easy 'nough," said Jerry.

"All right, we'll have my field manager, Mr. Chapman, get you squared away with your first order and we'll see how you do."

Jerry returned to Ferriday with a trunkload of Atlas sewing machines and began calling on friends and neighbors who found it difficult to take him seriously. Jerry tried every angle—the slick talker, the penniless preacher and the poor family-man approach, none of them finding any sympathy or success. Day after day, door after door, from Baton Rouge to Monroe, from Black River to Natchez, Jerry hawked his wares, cursing that no one wanted to buy one of his sewin' sonsofbitches. Finally, he devised a cunning scheme which turned his luck around.

"Afternoon, ma'am," Jerry greeted his next customer. "I'm from the Atlas Sewin' Center in Baton Rouge, an' I'm happy to tell you that you can take advantage of a special offer whereby you can have this bran' new sewin' machine for only ten dollars. That's right, ten dollars."

"What's the catch?"

"No catch."

"I'll take it."

"I jus' knew you would," said Jerry. "All you have to do is fill out this li'l card for me an' gimme the ten bucks an' the machine is yours to keep."

Jerry accepted the deposit, retrieved the signed card and moved on to the next stop. His buyers were unconcerned with reading the fine print on the card, which legally committed them to a long series of payments commencing one month after Jerry was long gone. Business was so good with the new sales tactic that he was returning for more machines twice weekly. In very little time, he had become the company's top salesman, with a record number of kills.

For some pigeons, Jerry devised a modified artifice to gain their trust. As part of a company promotion, Jerry notified a number of lucky folks that they'd "won" a sewing machine. All he asked them to do was fill out a card for his records and pay shipping and delivery costs, totaling the coincidental amount of ten dollars. This plan worked better than the first. Untold scores of Atlas bargains and prizes were pawned off on the unsuspecting and ignorant, all of whom were surprised to find a coupon book in the mail four weeks later. Many thought it was a clerical error and threw the payment schedule away.

The first complaints were not received by Mr. Moise until Jerry was into his third record-breaking month. Moise was collecting curious notes from all over the state asking unintelligible questions about free prizes and what the hell was the big idea behind billing for what was already bought and paid for. Soon Moise's office was deluged with orders on one side of his desk and a mountain of equal size of complaints on the other. A cursory glance through both piles revealed that the salesman at the bottom of the whole mess was our man Lewis.

"Lewis, aren't you tellin' these people about the balance they owe the company?" Moise asked upon Jerry's return to Baton Rouge for more machines.

"Sure, sure. It's right there on the card. Maybe they get confused."

"You wouldn't be lendin' to that confusion, would you, Lewis? You bein' a preacher an' all, it don't seem likely. . ."

"I ain't a preacher anymore. I play piano in church sometimes, but mostly in honky-tonks on weekends."

"Well, boy," Moise said, giving our man Lewis the axe, "you'd better try to make some money playin' the piano, 'cause you sure as hell ain't gonna make it sellin' no sewin' machines."

On March 16, 1956, Jane Lewis felt familiar signs of an infant preparing to make its way into the world. Ronnie Guy Lewis, named for his maternal grandfather, was begot and born to the misfortunes of having dark hair, dark eyes and a correctible case of clubfeet, all traits in common with the stranger Mamie claimed had fathered the child—the man Jane dated once to make Jerry jealous. Jerry came to the decision that regardless of whom the child looked like, he didn't want it, couldn't afford it, and told Jane to give it away. "I don't even want you to bring it home from the hospital," he said to her.

Jane could say nothing in reply. She looked into Jerry's eyes and saw hatred and jealousy and fear and doubt, the constant questioning stare revealing his woeful inner conflict. He refused to raise another man's child, but how could he be sure? Jerry shared his mother's intuitive opinion that Ronnie was not a Lewis, and that was enough for him. No matter what the true determination of the boy's legitimacy, Jerry did not want him.

"What do you want me to do with the baby?" Jane asked, fearing the cold, blunt honesty with which her husband answered.

"Give it to your sister Jewell to raise. I don't want to see it."

Mamie stood behind her son's decision, which left Ronnie unwanted outside the paternal protective umbrella. Jerry Lee, Jr., was always in his grandmother's care, but his brother never shared the doting affections Mamie showered on Junior. Ronnie went home to Jewell's house from the hospital. Jerry was glad to have both children out of sight, while Jane, a mother of two, had no one to care for.

There was no love lost between Jerry and Jane. They spent as much time apart as they did together and their marriage was in a constant state of flux. He prohibited her from watching him work in nightclubs and preferred that she stay at home and do nothing until it was time to go to church. He did not want her with him, nor did he want her in the company of another man. Once a woman belonged to the Killer, no one else could have her, even after his desire for her had waned. Jane was imprisoned by the jealousy which she had fostered in Jerry.

In the midst of settling the problem of Ronnie, no one seemed to notice the blossoming of Frankie Jean, Jerry's twelve-year-old sister. Frankie had a steady boyfriend named Johnny Frank Edwards. Johnny Frank was sixteen, and was the first person ever to pay any attention to her. Attention was something Frankie hardly got in a home where her talented brother was the favorite child and her sister, Linda Gail, was the baby. Her mother always referred to her as "Poor Frankie," stuck in the middle.

Nevertheless, Poor Frankie captured everyone's attention when she came home late one afternoon introducing Johnny Frank as her newlywedded husband. The idea seemed perfectly suited to Jerry's way of thinking: Frankie was almost a fully grown woman who knew her own mind, tender years notwithstanding. So Jerry served as her witness along with the ever-ready Uncle Lee, who supplied the clerk at the courthouse with the falsified information that the bride was sixteen. The newlyweds followed tradition by moving in with Elmo and Mamie. By day, Frankie continued to attend the fifth grade. By night, when homework was out of the way, Frankie and Johnny were lovers.

The marriage was mercifully short and, thankfully, no children were born to the child bride. Frankie Jean's ardor had sufficiently cooled so that another marriage would not be attempted till after she had completed grade school.

The rock 'n' roll wars breaking out in the Northeast had reached a point of full scale confrontation between promoters and parents. Adults were banding together to prevent Alan Freed from staging live performances of popular acts. In reply, Freed preached that rock 'n' roll was no more dangerous than the Charleston and Black Bottom crazes of prior generations. The adults were placated and rock won out, or so it happened in the script of the movie *Don't Knock the Rock*, starring Freed, Little Richard and Bill Haley. Teens turned on by cinematic tough guys flocked to the theaters to watch kids much like themselves struggling through familiar battles with parents and teachers. Every kid in America had a celluloid counterpart whom he could relate to; in every kid was a young rebel, a mini Jimmy Dean trying to get out. From the ragtag ranks of rock 'n' roll rabble came solidarity.

Jerry clung to the hope that there was room for him in the burgeoning popular-music business. He was flat broke. Any excursions into recording country would require financial backing, and that meant Papa would have to be sold on a pitch more foolproof than the one devised for selling sewing machines.

"Papa, you've heard tell of this Elvis Presley," Jerry began. "He's my age, a country boy from Tupelo, a member of the Assembly of God, and was drivin' a truck for a livin' when he comes along an' records a coupla songs an' now he's all over the radio an' teevee. An' I tell you where he got his start—a li'l place in Memphis where I hear anybody can jus' walk in, sit down an' play. Now, what we oughta do is head straightaway for Memphis an' talk to the head man 'bout me doin' the same thing as Elvis."

"I ain't got the money to send you, son," Elmo said.

"Look, Papa, we only got to go for the day. We ain't gotta spend a whole week there. Jus' the one chance is all I need. Ten minnits with these people is all I'm askin' for. I know I can make it happen."

"I know, boy. Tell you what, gimme a few days to try an' raise a few extry dollars . . ."

"Thank you," Jerry said repeatedly. "Thank you, thank you."

For the next several weeks, Elmo squeeeeezed the eggs out of his laying hens, sold them to Nelson's supermarket and socked the extra money away. He had a new Ford already two payments behind and a stack of bills that would have to wait another month. Again he placed his fortunes in jeopardy to afford his son happiness, remembering the dreams he'd had as a boy before life played a mean trick and made him a carpenter instead of Jimmie Rodgers.

Elmo had fifteen dollars in egg money, and when combined with the few dollars Jerry was able to save from the Wagon Wheel, it gave the pair enough to make a short trip to Memphis at the end of September. The drive took all day and part of the night, and when they arrived, they drove around downtown until they found Union Avenue and Sun Records, then circled the vicinity for a cheap hotel. The found an old fleabag where Elmo rented a bed for a dollar and snuck Jerry in the back door. Jerry found it impossible to sleep. He sat at the window and watched the streets below. Along about five A.M., the city of Memphis sent trucks along the streets to wash the dreams off the sidewalks in front of the Sun studio. As the sun lipped the horizon, Jerry offered a silent prayer to heaven.

"God, You know I'm a sinner. You know I love You. You've given me this talent, and I'm askin' for Your help to put it to use. All I'm askin' for is one hit record, an' I'll take the money an' set up a li'l church an' dedicate the rest of my life to You, like Jimmy Lee. That seems fair, don't it?"

His pact with God made, Jerry dressed and was ready to make music when his father rose at dawn as was his custom. Jerry dragged Elmo downstairs and up the street to Sun Records. It was long before seven, and Sun wouldn't be open for hours. The pair stood before the small storefront and peered inside. It didn't look like much, nothing like Jerry supposed Elvis Presley's launching pad should look like.

"Let's go to the corner, get a bite to eat, wait for 'er to open up," said Elmo. Jerry was not interested, but went with his father to the corner eatery.

The boys had breakfast. They boys had lunch. Jerry kept his eye on the street, watching for the arrival of anybody famous or who looked like he might work in a recording studio. At long last, a young girl arrived to unlock the front door. A man walked in behind her, Elmo and Jerry close on his heels. The girl introduced herself to the visitors as Sally, the receptionist. Elmo did the talking.

"I wanna get my boy here an audition. We come all the way from Ferr'day, Louzanna, an' we ain't got much money. Where do we sign up an' what'll it cost?"

"There's nothing to sign and auditions are free, unless you want Jack to make a dub for you to take home," said Sally.

"Free, you say."

"That's right. What kind of music does your son play?"

"Piany . . ." said Elmo.

"Just like Chet Atkins," Jerry joked meanly.

Upon overhearing the last remark, a man walked into the outer office from the studio. His name was Jack Clement and he was the engineer whose job it was to record whoever walked in the front door, the Elvises and the imitators, the hopefuls and the has-beens. He had, in the short time he worked at Sun, recorded Carl Perkins, Johnny Cash, Roy Orbison, Billy Riley, Warren Smith, Sonny Burgess and Harold Jenkins before he changed his name to Conway Twitty. Some had talent and some were lucky, and Jack had learned to tell the difference. Sam taught him not to be too hasty in denying anyone with two dollars the chance to make music.

"So, you're as good as Chet Atkins on the piano," Jack joked with Jerry. "Tell you what, you play that one over there in the corner an' we'll see."

Jerry walked into the small green pokey-dot room—the one where Carl shined blue suede shoes, Johnny walked the line and

Elvis said, "That's all right"—and taking his place at the Wurlitzer spinet, began to play pop hits and his own special home-grown boogies, the kind which could get a guy thrown out of church.

"No, no, no," Jack interrupted. "We don't want no rock 'n' roll. Elvis has that all locked up. Play somethin' else. Do country."

The request was music to Jerry's ears. He could play Jimmie Rodgers and Hank Williams all day long. Jack nodded in approval of Jerry's treatment of the George Jones hit "Seasons of My Heart," and recorded the song for Sam to hear.

"Any good?" Elmo asked Jack after hearing Jerry's repertoire.

"Mister, if I didn't think he was good, I wouldn't've had him play so long. I got it on tape, and I'll get Mr. Phillips to listen to it when he gets back from the deejay convention. He'll give you a call in about two weeks or so. Leave a number with Sally where we can reach you."

Jerry left the studio walking three feet above ground. For the first time, he had found encouragement from someone who knew something about music. With a recommendation from the man who had recorded the best in the business, Jerry knew the last of his ten-dollar-a-night jobs supporting Blind Paul at the Wagon Wheel were over.

"Look out, now, Paul," Jerry said when next he took his place with the trio, "I may not be back here much longer, y'know. Sam Phillips will be callin' me any day now."

"Uh-huh," Paul said, as if he had heard that story many times before. "But, for now, Jerry, why don't we play somethin' for these folks an' try to meet the rent." Like a sightless oracle, Paul was a man of insight who had heard a long lifetime of show-biz accolades and promises. He had learned to take everything in his small stride, and knew there was nothing that can be said to settle a young man with stars in his eyes and a heart filled with hope.

Blind Paul was also right; Sam Phillips did not call Jerry Lee.

How, then, did Jerry Lee Lewis come to Sun Records and begin his career? Had it not been for his cousin's heart murmur, a misdelivered newspaper and an electrical accident, the world might never have heard of Jerry Lee Lewis, for it was these unlikely elements which brought about his return to Memphis and the rising of the curtain. The three errors befell Jerry's cousin, J. W. Brown, who then came to bring Jerry back to his beginning.

J. W. or Jay Brown, the last of four children born to Elmo's sister Jane and Henry Brown, grew up in Winnsboro, a stone's throw north of Ferriday. In the early forties, the Brown family entertained at dances, calling their band The Brown Bombers, then The Mississippi Hot Shots so as not to be confused with boxer Joe Lewis. In the afternoons, the band performed live over WMIS radio in Natchez and booked dates from the station's offices. Coming attractions were publicized by gluing a snapshot of the family exhibiting two guitars, a dog and a cat onto a typewritten sheet of paper listing date and place and nice comments about themselves.

Business was going great till Uncle Sam broke up the act by drafting brother Otis Lee into the army. Too young to serve at the inception of the war, J. W. joined a seismograph crew working the oil fields in the Gulf of Mexico. When Jay wasn't working, he was in the company of Miss Lois Neal. When Jay's work moved him to Natchez, he thought about Miss Lois night and day, sometimes to the exclusion of whatever he was doing. One afternoon, while lost in the memory of Miss Lois's dark-eyed stare, J. W. forgot all about an ax he was swinging and drove the blade into his foot. That's when the boy knew he was in love. He figured he'd better marry before he killed himself.

The Browns had not been married long before J. W. began ordering his wife around. One of the first things he ordered was a baby. Lois had heard that birthing babies was no picnic. She understood there was some pain involved, and when her time came, she knew firsthand the meaning of "gut-wrenching torture." The daughter born to Lois and J. W. Brown on July 11, 1944, was named Myra Gale, borrowed from a best friend's cousin. Myra was just what Jay wanted; he was in high heaven. Lois decided it would be a long time before she tried a stunt like that again.

Having turned eighteen, Jay was eligible for the draft. The army turned him down because he had flat feet. The navy gave him a closer look but passed on him when the doctor discovered a heart murmur, the result of a boyhood bout with rheumatic fever. At home, Jay found a job as a lineman for the electric company.

The electric company put Jay in the hospital and then in show business.

For five years, Jay worked the lines in Winnsboro, until he spotted an ad in a misdelivered Memphis newspaper asking for linemen. It looked bold-type promising, and Jay drove to Memphis on an impulse to apply for the job. As the only experienced man who answered the ad, Jay was put to work immediately at a first-rate salary. Six years later, as Jerry Lee Lewis impatiently whiled away October 1956 waiting for a telephone call from Sam Phillips that never came, his Tennessee cousin Jay was becoming dissatisfied with his job. After a decade of climbing poles and fidgeting with high-tension wires, Jay thought he had gone too long without accident and maybe it was time to move on to something else. He spoke of his teen years playing in a band with increasing frequency, and mentioned his seldom-seen piano-playing cousin in Ferriday as a possible partner in a new musical venture.

While in the process of coating fragile live wires with rubber insulation at the top of ninety-foot poles, Jay's luck ran out. With a slight audible snap, the end of a wire came out of its sleeve, the loose end whipping around like a Texas sidewinder until it struck Jay in the back, producing a sound like cannon shot as six thousand volts of electrical current flowed through his body and exploded from the palm of his left hand, incinerating his clothing and disintegrating his wristwatch. Because the current did not cross his heart, as in an electrocution, he survived miraculously. Jay was confined to bed for three days, during which he solemnly swore he would never climb another pole. His hopes of returning to music were destroyed as he gazed at his heavily bandaged hand which experienced no sensation.

Jay's foreman offered him an easy job inspecting lines as a troubleshooter until he got his nerve back. Jay declined lineman's work in any capacity, but the company awarded him full salary for one year as compensation for his injury. Jay had it made, a whole year with nothing to do but sit back and collect paychecks. And, by golly, that left mitt was starting to feel better already. Might even feel like playing a guitar soon.

"Think I'm gonna take a few days an' visit fam'ly," Jay told Lois. "Goin' down to Lou'siana an' see the folks, maybe find Jerry Lee. We may get somethin' started yet."

By the time Jay arrived in Ferriday on a Saturday night, Jerry had already left for work at the Wagon Wheel. Jay drove to Natchez and parked in front of the roadside tavern. The faint beat of the band wafted out into the cool night air in muted thumps and blares, reminding Jay of fifteen years before when he and his brothers played at the Wheel. He walked inside and found a table in the back and listened to the combo, paying special attention to the man he recognized from a photograph as his cousin. At the break, Jerry moved from behind the drums to the bar to speak with a friend. Jay took the stool next to him and introduced himself.

"Hey. I'm your cousin J. W. from Memphis, your aunt Jane's son."

"Oh, yeah," Jerry said, shaking his hand. "I heard about you. What brings you down here?"

"Came to see you."

"Yeah? What for?"

"I got some time off with nothin' to do. I thought about puttin' a band together. I play guitar an' I hear you play piano pretty good."

"Sure, but it seems like a mighty long way to come for a song," said Jerry.

For the last set, Jerry moved from the drums to the piano and set about the keys in his pumpin' boogie. Jay was impressed.

"Man, you gotta come to Memphis," he said excitedly. "We could get a record goin'."

"Oh, man, I done been to Memphis," said Jerry. "And Nashville. Sam Phillips over at Sun Records was s'posed to call me, but hasn't. What do I wanna go back up to Memphis for?"

"We could go see what's wrong with Sam—"

"Nah. Look, J. W., I do all right where I am. I'll get on with a record company soon enough. Jus' takes time, is all."

Jay, thirty years old and ten years Jerry's senior, was insistent. Jerry was flattered, and the flame he had felt a few weeks before at his audition was rekindled. Jay looked like there might be something to him, or maybe it was only his new Cadillac that got in Jerry's eye.

"Come on back to Memphis with me," Jay asked once more.

"Naw, forget it," said Jerry.

On Sunday, as the Lewises and Swaggarts and Gilleys made

their pilgrimage to the Assembly of God, Jay made the long drive home alone, arriving in early evening. He was telling Lois and Myra how good Jerry was as a musician and how disappointed he was to leave him in Louisiana when the telephone interrupted his report. Myra answered.

"Who's this?" asked the voice on the other end.

"Myra."

"Myra, this is your cousin, Jerry Lee Lewis. I'm in Memphis, an' I'm lookin' for your house."

"Daddy, come quick, it's Jerry," she announced.

"Jerry? Where are you? A drugstore. Which one? Okay, stay put an' I'll come get you," Jay said, and hung up the receiver. "Well, I'll be damned, he came after all. I gotta go get him."

"I wanna go, too, Daddy," Myra said.

"You finish your homework," said Lois. "I'll set another place for supper. Will he be stayin' here with us?"

"I guess so," Jay answered, heading out the door. "He prob'ly spent his last dime on that phone call."

Myra was sitting at the dining room table finishing her homework when Jerry entered the house. He was decked out in jeans, cowboy boots and red plaid shirt. His ears stuck out beneath a fresh haircut and he sported a neatly trimmed goatee. Myra thought he was cute. Lois and J. W. thought he looked like a weirdo.

"Easy, now, Myra," Jay said to his blushing daughter, "Jerry here is a married man. Ain't that right, Jerry?"

"Shucks," Myra said animatedly.

Jerry smiled and watched her for several moments. He then spied a new piano in the living room. "Who plays?" he asked, rubbing the blond wood.

"I bought it for Myra," Jay said of the toy he had bought for himself.

"Do you mind?" Jerry asked Myra, who had never touched the keys.

"No, go ahead," she said, and Jerry sat down to play until dinner was ready.

For the first meeting between Myra and Jerry, something more dramatic than homework, dinner and a brief piano recital was called for, yet the quickest sight could not penetrate the deep thoughts behind seemingly innocent glances. If it is possible for love at first sight to exist without the participants realizing it in so many words, then that was the very case with Myra and Jerry.

At the dinner table, Jerry was allowed several minutes to gaze at Myra unrestricted by shyness and modesty. His gimlet eyes gravitated toward her face, plain and unpainted but commonly handsome. He became detached from his identity as her cousin and looked at her beyond the barriers of family. He saw an attractive girl, who she was and what she was and her tender years made no difference. Myra regarded Jerry in the same unattached manner. As cousins, second cousins to be exact, she was permitted to love him by virtue of their kinship. The preliminary matter of learning to like the stranger was overcome the moment he stepped in the front door. He was a man in the pride and prime of his life. She was an innocent child. He was worldly-wise; she, a clean slate.

What could have interested a twenty-one-year-old, twice-married father of two in his twelve-year-old cousin, a girl who was just as plain as her name? Bushy-browed, buck-toothed and splotchy-faced—that was the Myra Gale Brown that Jerry Lee Lewis fell in love with at first sight. Yet in little more than a year, he would be the king of rock 'n' roll, and she the child bride who cost him his crown.

The second day of Jerry's visit to Memphis was filled with surprises, the first of which was a warm welcome from Sam Phillips when Jerry and Jay arrived at Sun Records.

"Oh, yeah, Jerry, I was gonna call you," said Sam with a big smile. "Come on in here and let's you 'n' me talk. But first, why don't you play a few songs for me. Jay, you can fill in on guitar."

As a tape recorder waited to take down every note, Jerry played the Ray Price hit "Crazy Arms," delivering an upbeat version of the honky-tonk ballad with his harder, driving rhythm. Jerry's handiwork showed off a series of progressions and catchy counterpoint patterns, crossing middle C both ways. His melody lines were pure grass roots, not likely to be taught by music instructors or printed in piano primers. He played a modified version of the traditional song "If the World Keeps On Turning" and Gene Autry's "You're the Only Star (In My Blue Heaven)," attracting other musicians hanging around the studio that day to come in and join him. Jerry sang "Little Green Valley," another old-time country tune that Sam favored, and like everything else he would ever play, he dressed the song in his pumping, bass-driven manner, a marvel of pastiche. Sam nodded his approval in time with the music and smiled at the sound he had been hoping to find.

Lastly, Jerry sang a song he had written about his home entitled "End of the Road." It was the first and one of very few songs he ever attempted to write. The autobiographical lyric was the result of spontaneous inspiration. There was no deep thought, only a naive description of home in the language of a pure and candid soul. Jane, the wife he had conveniently left behind, had told Jerry that, like himself, the little ditty would never amount to much. Contrary to her appraisal, Sam found his greatest need satisfied by the young blond singer from Louisiana. He had the blue-collar attitude, a natural unsophistication and an infectious personality. Sam walked into the control room, motioning for J. W. to follow.

"You live here in Memphis, Jay?" Sam asked.

"Yessir, I do, over on Coro Lake."

"Reason I ask, Jay, is I think the boy has a lotta talent and sounds real good, but I don't know that if I spend a thousand dollars on him today, he's liable to be in California tomorrow."

"What do you mean?"

"Well, to tell the truth, he's just about the weirdest-lookin' guy I've ever seen walk in here. Looks like a drifter to me."

"I've known him an' his mamma an' daddy all my life, sir, an' I promise you, Jerry Lee ain't like that," said Jay.

"If you'll promise me that you'll come up here with him and work hard every day, an' if he can live with you so you can keep an eye on him an' help him, I'll put a record out on him," said Sam.

"You gotta deal," Jay declared.

The boys were elated. They ran out of the studio shouting rebel yells, jumped in Jay's Cadillac and sped for home with the news. Sam was already at work. He took the one-track tape of the freshly recorded audition, and after playing it through several times culled "Crazy Arms" and transcribed it onto one side of a reference disc. He then hand-delivered his find to his old pal Dewey Phillips, a deejay at WHBQ. Two years before, Sam had personally delivered to Dewey the initial pressing of Elvis's

"That's All Right, Mama." Sam had rarely called on Dewey since then, but when he did, Dewey listened. So would all of Memphis.

Myra was at home that evening lying across her bed listening to the radio while piddling with her homework when she heard Dewey say, "I gotta brand new song recorded today in Memphis in the same studio and by the same man that discovered Elvis. Mr. Sam Phillips from Sun Records tells me he's found a new singer that he says is gonna be right up there with the Big E, Carl Perkins and Johnny Cash. I'm gonna play this song for you to judge, so listen close, then call me here at the station at JA6-5656 and give me your verdict. This cut is one you've heard before by Ray Price called 'Crazy Arms' and the singer's name is Jerry Lewis, so here it is, Memphis, what do you think?"

Myra jumped to her feet at the sound of her cousin's name and screamed for her mother and daddy to come quickly. They rushed to her room in a panic, saw Myra standing on her bed staring, and searched the room for whatever had scared her. Jerry was right behind them. Myra pointed to the radio and shouted, "listen."

"What?" they asked in unison.

"Jerry!"

As the music played, Jay turned up the volume beyond the set's capacity and filled the room with the joyful noise. All eyes were glued to the radio as if they expected to see Jerry as well as hear him. Jerry was entranced. Jay slapped him on the back as he stood with his hands on his hips, head cocked to one side, a broad smile wreathing his face. His heart soared at his success. His prayers had been answered. It was a miracle.

"The results are in," Dewey announced, "and it seems like a few Presley fans think this boy has a ways to go yet. Sixty listeners say they like it, forty say they don't. Tell you what, let's listen one more time to 'Crazy Arms' by Jerry Lewis, and I want the forty who called to say they didn't like it to call me back and let me know if you have a diff'rent second opinion. Oh, and incidentally, folks, some of you asked, no, this ain't Jerry Lewis, the comedian. This is a boy who just turned twenty-one and is from down in Lou'siana. So let's try it one more time, whaddya say?"

Jerry was only the least bit disheartened by his fair showing in the poll. Myra ran to the telephone to call in her biased verdict, and Dewey came back with news of a drastic reversal when the record finished its repeat.

"Seems like that second time around changed a lotta minds. Thirty-nine out of forty say they like 'Crazy Arms' after all. One, maybe it's Elvis himself," Dewey laughed, "says he still don't go for Jerry Lewis's new song. So, I guess we have what is just about a unanimous decision for this newcomer, and I'm sure we'll be hearing a lot more of him on Sun Records in the near future."

Sam Phillips contemplated releasing "Crazy Arms" based on the reception to its inaugural airplay, but elected to wait until Jerry put a show together in order to gain the public exposure necessary for creating a demand. If Jerry was going to live up to potential, he would have to put together the kind of wildly shocking show that had made Elvis a scandal and then a success. Jerry had never seen Elvis perform. He did not know how to create a wildly shocking show. He still played as though he were sitting in the corner of a crowded bar. He would have to start from scratch by finding a band and enough suitable material to play and someone to book dates and introduce Jerry's wildly shocking show to the public. Sam, ever cautious and close with a dollar, insisted that the machine behind the man be well tuned and running smoothly before he took another step.

Every morning throughout November, Jerry and Jay reported for work at the studio, where they sifted through stacks of current hit records to incorporate into their act. As eager as Jerry was to record, he found it impossible to work under anyone's direction. He did not like friendly advice. He did not like taking orders from producers or suggestions from engineers. He preferred to play each selection once without stopping for changes and corrections, then moving along to the next number. Rarely did he play a song more than twice unless it was for his own amusement, and never in the same way as before, causing Jack to tape rehearsals and practice sessions lest he be denied a second chance. Jack simply turned on the tape recorder, sat back and waited for Jerry to deliver.

The quickest friendships among studio musicians were made with guitarist Roland Janes and drummer Jimmy Van Eaton, who were borrowed from Billy Riley's band to record Jerry's music. From Sonny Burgess's group Jerry borrowed another drummer, Russell Smith. When J. W. Brown was not playing bass or guitar in rehearsals, he was locked away in Sam's office plotting the first steps in breaking in the new act.

The next order of business was finding a manager. The man who immediately came to mind was Bob Neal, a former deejay who had been Elvis's first manager and booking agent. Like the Phillips brothers, Neal had made the mistake of signing Elvis to a one-year contract and found himself cut out of the deal by Tom Parker. Neal and Sam regrouped to form Stars, Inc. to manage the Sun roster and hired a WHBQ deejay looking for a break as a singer and a little extra cash to act as emcee for their shows. His name was Wink Martindale, and the height of his career came twenty years later as host of a television game show.

Taking on Jerry Lee Lewis as a client should not have posed a problem for Bob Neal, who could guarantee any act a regimen of roadhouses, schoolhouses and lounges to play. Much as he might help with a few leads, Neal judged Jerry unready to take advantage of a full-time agent. J. W. Brown took up the slack by spending hours on the telephone hunting up small-paying jobs. The first engagement Jay booked was in Conway, Arkansas, for the paltry sum of thirty dollars, followed by a date in Clarksdale, Mississippi, for the same amount. Sight unseen and sound unheard, Jay was able to fast-talk his way into similar weekend bookings in towns where they would not have to travel more than a hundred miles in any direction from Memphis, enabling them to return home after the show. Jay agreed to play in any place that had a piano; all the boys had to do was pack a three-piece drum kit in the trunk of the car, load Jay's bass and amplifier in the backseat, and go boppin' to the high school hop. The drums were the property of Russell Smith, who took leave of the studio band to play the first club dates. The trio was lucky if they had a fifty-dollar night, tips included, and Jay, still on the Memphis Light and Gas payroll, gave his share to Cousin Jerry. When Sam was satisfied that Jerry was a safe bet, he decided to release "Crazy Arms" as his first single, provided the tour of weekend one-nighters continued. Because Jerry was the first white popular singer/pianist to come down the pike, Sam sought to distinguish his latest discovery with the tag "Jerry Lee Lewis and His Pumping Piano."

On any Saturday afternoon in the fall of '56, the boys piled into Jay's Cadillac and headed for one of a thousand roadhouses dot-

ting the highways that linked Memphis to the rest of Dixie. Although the trip lasted one evening, Jay required a fifth of bourbon
to keep the dust down, and Russ would necessarily have to bring
his own since Jay wasn't much for leaving any in his bottle. Jerry
was in charge of the bubble gum and en-route entertainment—a
stack of comic books, a sack of cherry bombs and a high-powered
spotlight for shining in bedroom windows as a late-night prank.

It would be sundown when the party rolled into the town they
would play that night. Marked by small, hand-painted signs with
names like Bo Peep's, Bamboo Ranch or Ice Cold Beer On
Draught, the places were easy to pass several times without spotting them. Every club was the same: The air was thick with
smoke and bourbon and cheap perfume, as thick as the plangent
sounds of the trio. The guitar blared brazen and metallic from the
amplifier, the rim shots ringing like distant gunfire. Placing a
microphone stand between his legs, Jerry called out the lyrics to
the numbers, avoiding flat and faulty keys on the antique keyboard. The patrons sat at tables inches away from the musicians,
too engrossed in their conversations to be concerned with the
music. After a few rounds of drinks set in, there was a shuffle of
feet as couples got up to dance while others played grab ass in the
booths, inattentively hearing without listening to the songs they
had requested.

Jerry could not tolerate indifference. He played every type of
song he knew until he found a local favorite, and didn't mind
playing it again and again until the audience was satisfied. If
some were fans of Hank Williams and Jimmie Rodgers, Jerry was
prepared to lead them in "Your Cheatin' Heart" and "Carolina
Sunshine Girl." If he spotted some that looked like church-goers,
he sang "Old Time Religion" and "When the Saints Go Marching
In." To a predominantly older crowd, he sang "Goodnight Irene"
and "Silver Threads." Regardless of where he was and who was
present, he filled most of his set with country classics like "Born
to Lose" and "You Win Again." He played anything the audience
requested, usually a well-known ballad or the latest from Elvis,
but before the night was through, Jerry made sure "Crazy Arms"
and "End of the Road" had been featured.

From Brinkley, Arkansas, to Corinth, Mississippi, to Browns-
ville, Tennessee, Jerry, J. W. and Russ worked and reworked their
rockabilly road show. Returning to the studio with the public's

preferences fresh in his mind, Jerry recorded many of those songs so that Sam could decide which direction Jerry should take in refining his sound. Sun Number 259, "Crazy Arms" backed with "End of the Road" by Jerry Lee Lewis and His Pumping Piano was scheduled for release in December, at a time when Sam hoped Jerry would be opening for a Carl Perkins and Johnny Cash tour of Canadian hamlets. Both Perkins and Cash had recorded three hits, the last of each reaching the nation's top ten. A shared billing with Sun's hottest acts provided the perfect opportunity to test the performance of Jerry's new act and perhaps carry "Crazy Arms" into the charts on his stablemates' coattails.

As Jerry set foot on the threshold of his career, Elvis Presley, two years further down the same road, had three Number 1 hits in a row. Elvis dropped by the Sun studio to visit old friends whenever he was in Memphis, which became increasingly rare as his popularity forced him into hiding. Jerry wondered when the next visit might be; he wanted to be ready. It came sooner than expected, when Jerry had been at Sun hardly more than one month.

On the afternoon of December 4, Sam brought Jerry over to meet Carl Perkins, who was working in the studio with his band. Jerry heard someone playing the piano, walked into the room and recognized Elvis at the keyboard entertaining his girlfriend, Marilyn Evans. Elvis was singing "Blueberry Hill," a song not particularly suited to his voice and style. Noticing he had raised a small audience, Elvis stopped playing to exchange greetings with Sam, whom he still reverently called Mr. Phillips, and acknowledged the newcomer with a nod. Jerry mistook his aloofness for snobbishness. He maneuvered for a better view of the myth and sized him up as one might scrutinize an opponent in a fight. Aside from a large diamond ring on Elvis's right hand, Jerry found little to be impressed with—certainly not Elvis's ability on the piano—and had made up his mind not to like the superstar when Elvis invited Carl and Jerry to sing a few gospel favorites with him. Jack Clement, taking the invitation as a cue, stepped into the engineering booth to switch on the ever-ready tape recorder as Presley led the gathering in bits and pieces of twenty or more tunes. The trio sang "Peace in the Valley," "Down by the Riverside," "Blessed Jesus Hold My Hand" and other psalms common to their Sunday-school upbringing.

"You know 'Crazy Arms,' Carl?" Jerry asked, while Elvis was preoccupied with another song.

"Yeah, what key is that in?" Carl asked. "Is it A?"

"Yeah, that's the way I done it on piano. That's the one I done," Jerry repeated, hoping Elvis would take the hint.

Elvis picked up a guitar to strum the first few bars of "Crazy Arms" and stopped to ask if anyone had heard Pat Boone's newest, "Don't Forbid Me." "It was written for me," he claimed, then sang it instead of Jerry's request.

Johnny Cash arrived on the scene and the quartet struck up a pleasing harmony in a half-dozen hymns, including Johnny's favorite, "Will the Circle Be Unbroken." All the while, Jerry was itching to have a turn at the piano so he could show the hotshots how it's *really* done, but Elvis would not budge from the piano bench, even while picking the guitar, and Jerry did not know how to go about telling him to move. Elvis's last note was still ringing its sustain when Jerry slid into place and struck up a rollicking revival roulade entitled "There Are Strange Things Happening Every Day." It was practically the only selection he got to play, but his delivery was impressive.

"Say, Jerry," Carl asked, "would you like to play on my next session?"

"Sure," Jerry replied, flattered by the recognition.

Sam brought a photographer in to depict the "Million-Dollar Quartet," as it was to be called in days to come. As the legendary gathering was being recorded on film, Lois and J. W. Brown walked into the studio looking for Jerry. Lois was shy in acknowledging Elvis and turned down his invitation to be part of a picture. Marilyn Evans sat atop the spinet and posed with the quartet for two more photographs, and the party broke up as Elvis prepared to leave.

Jerry watched the king of rock 'n' roll drive down Union Avenue with one of his girlfriends in one of his Cadillacs. He wished he had a half-dozen hits to his credit. He wished network television was offering a king's ransom for two minutes of his talented time. He wished he had a diamond ring for every finger and a Cadillac for every day of the week. He wished for the day when Elvis begged him for piano lessons. He wished.

What Jerry wished and what he was granted left a wide margin between desire and reality. The day had yielded a picture taken with the top three acts in popular music, a tape no one would hear for twenty-five years and an offer to play piano in someone else's session for the royal sum of fifteen dollars.

Jerry thought that an opening spot in the upcoming tour was just what he had been waiting for, but as the time drew near, he became apprehensive. He was shy about making his first appearance on a grand scale, for he was unknown to the audiences who paid to see Carl Perkins and Johnny Cash. His first set on opening night was conservative and unusually constrained.

"Boy, you're gonna have to get loose out there or you're gonna die," Carl said to Jerry backstage.

"Get crazy," Johnny advised. "Go wild."

Jerry looked at the two men and wondered how they overcame the feeling of insecurity that washes over a performer as he first steps out onto a large empty stage. It was nothing like playing in a crowded club, and the audience was not much help, sitting quietly attentive until someone did something worth hollering about. Jerry watched Carl and Johnny work the crowd, marveling at the metamorphosis which changed them from bundles of butterflies into barnstormers. Where did these country boys find that kind of courage?

For Johnny Cash, the answer was chemical. From the professional drivers whose job it was to ferry Grand Ole Opry stars cross-country, John was educated in the use of amphetamines. Ten dollars bought one hundred white pillules prescribed by doctors as Benzedrine and commonly referred to as "bennies." It was a sure cure for the butterflies and whatever else ailed the body. Not only was the user briskly wakened, but timing improved, muscles relaxed and courage coursed into veins, producing a high without the telltale odor of alcohol which alerted friends and fans. The only drawback was that the high wore off harshly, requiring increased dosages with prolonged use.

In the past, when he had been tipped with pep pills from truck drivers, they had not done much for Jerry besides keep him awake. There had never been any shortage of self-confidence, only the assertiveness that experience brings. Taking Johnny's advice but not his example, Jerry walked onstage for his second set a different man. He loosened up and enjoyed himself, milking the crowd for a favorable response, and found that even the oldies could live again with a fresh application of his pumping rhythm. It was pure Jerry, with no chemical additives.

"Get crazy!" Johnny Cash called from the wings.

"Cut loose!" Carl Perkins enjoined.

He did as he was dared and the new Jerry Lee Lewis was born.

The next package tour that Bob Neal offered Jerry was a twin bill with Gene Vincent, ten days in Florida for one hundred dollars a night. Vincent's first recording, "Be-Bop-A-Lula," was written while reading a Little Lulu comic book in a drunken stupor and became a top-ten smash during the summer of '56. His follow-up, "Race With the Devil," hardly scratched the surface of the top hundred, but he was the sort of singer that had to be seen to be appreciated. Vincent, the Capitol Records answer to Elvis Presley, was a low-down and dirty version of the Big E. He slicked his hair back like Elvis, wore black leather jackets like Elvis and sang "Be-Bop-A-Lula" in the same way Elvis sang "Money Honey." The only difference was that Vincent brashly crossed over into areas that even Elvis, the wildest of the wild, considered taboo.

"I'm lookin' for a woman with a one-track mind, a-fuggin' and a-kissin' and a-smoochin' all the time," Vincent sang out in open defiance. Elvis might make sexual insinuations all night long with his bumps and grinds and couched suggestions as to what he meant by "Baby, Let's Play House," but Gene Vincent stated what was on his mind in no uncertain terms. Of course, Gene paid for it when the Virginia State Court found him guilty of public lewdness and obscenity and fined him ten thousand dollars in absentia.

Gene was Jerry's kind of guy, an assertive type worthy of emulation, cockiness in black leather. Jerry had to have a black leather jacket, too; his club colors. They held contests to see who could make up the filthiest and most ridiculous word, passing smutty lyrics to obscene songs back and forth like two schoolboys sneaking peeks at *Playboy*. The Killer had been initiated into the musical fraternity by guys who had learned the rules of the game and conveniently threw them away.

Christmas had already come and gone for Jerry when he returned to Ferriday to play Santa to his family; the nicest present he ever received was a black plastic disc with his name on it. Sam

Phillips fronted him three hundred dollars for the asking, and never had to give him another dime as far as Jerry was concerned. Thus he returned triumphant with grand stories for his parents and "I told you so's" for his wife. Mamie and Elmo were elated, the proudest parents on earth, but Jane's enthusiasm was tempered by having to remain down on the farm while her husband was off having high times in hot towns. Then, too, the bottom line had yet to reflect any significant gain in Jerry's tax bracket. He was still working for peanuts, waiting for his first hit record to make all the difference, and told his wife he was only able to make a go of it by living with his cousins rent-free. He was totally dependent upon the Browns and glad of it.

Jerry was anxious for his vacation to be at an end so he could return to work. His sights were set on the top of the record charts. On the day of his Lord's birth, Jerry reminded Him of their pact: glory to God in exchange for glory to Jerry Lee. He sat at his old Starck upright and filled the house with the joyful noise of "Silent Night," played on the black keys *and* the white keys.

Myra Brown wished Christmas could go on and on, or at least come more than once a year. Nothing waited for her in Memphis except a schoolteacher. Fortunately, there were a few days of vacation left before she had to return to the seventh grade, time enough to break in that new bike and have the girls over to try out her new portable record player, which Santa delivered along with all of Elvis Presley's hit singles.

On the first day home from her holiday at Grandma's, Myra roamed about the neighborhood visiting friends, only to find many still away. She returned home as her parents were leaving on errands. As soon as Myra walked into the kitchen for something to drink, a knock came at the back door. It was neighbor Woodall come to borrow something.

"Can I help?" she asked as Woodall walked into the next room, looking for whatever he had come for.

"Come 'ere," he said, a hint of surprise in his voice. "Wanna show you somethin'."

"What?" she asked, walking into the room where he took her by the arm down the hallway to her parents' bedroom.

He prompted her into position and withdrew his hand, taking a fistful of sweater. "Come 'ere," he repeated, his voice lowering. "I wanna show you . . . come 'ere . . . somethin'."

Myra stood in place, hands at her side, wherever Woodall moved her. The way in which he manipulated her with quiet forcefulness warned her that trying to escape would not get her very far. Woodall tugged at her blouse, which fell from her body as if each thread conspired to unravel in unison from its seam. Myra's eyes were fixed on Woodall's face, searching for an expression of anger or madness or jest. She saw reddened, lifeless eyes and a crooked smile picketed by mottled enamel. She heard soft, guttural sounds of pursuit.

Woodall waltzed her to one side and pushed her back on the bed. There was no one to rush into the room to answer the plaintive cries forming in her mind and ringing in her ears but unable to escape from her throat. What was he doing? And why?

All movement stopped abruptly. Woodall hid himself from view and hurriedly walked out of the room and disappeared. Myra gained her feet, tugging her clothing roughly into place, lunged for her bedroom and slammed the door. She felt no pain, yet her subconscious plumbed tears of solace into the open wound. Woodall had spoiled her, leaving what schoolboys laughingly referred to as "damaged goods."

"It happens to everybody," Myra said to no one. "This must be what girls are for."

Myra hid behind locked doors until she heard her parents return. She could not tell them. She did not know how to tell them or what words to use. She changed clothes, balled up her soiled skirt and hid it away, composed herself and tried to appear calm and collected. Her parents suspected she was not well in the way parents have of knowing when their children are sick simply by looking at them. Embarrassment prevented her from responding to her mother's questions about her feverishness. Thoughts of her father killing Woodall for revenge frightened her. She suffered silently, keeping the pain and worry and confusion bottled up inside.

Laying awake through many lonely nights, Myra wondered what man would want her in such sad shape. What chance did damaged goods have for happiness when all manhood reviled the deflowered maiden? Where is salvation and when will it come? She wondered. Who will rescue me?

3 *Whole Lot of Shakin'*

JERRY SAID GOOD-BYE TO HIS FAMILY AND friends at the end of his Christmas vacation not knowing when he might see them again. He had promised every one of them a share of his wealth should he find the pot of gold at the end of the road that led to Memphis. He promised a new house to his mother and a new car to his father. He promised cousin David Beatty a new car, too. Jimmy Swaggart decided then and there that if Jerry was going to be giving away new cars to remote cousins, one should be rightfully his. He was certain that Jerry would not deny an impoverished servant of the Lord the only means by which he could spread the gospel far and wide, confident that their childhood spent happily together would entitle him to a large legacy.

The last beneficiary to be dealt with was Jerry's long suffering wife, Jane. To her, he promised he would move her to Memphis before the month of January was over.

"Can I bring Junior?" Jane asked expectantly.

"Certainly," answered Jerry.

"Can I bring Ronnie?" she asked, trying her luck.

"No," said Jerry.

Arriving at the Browns' house on the third day of the new year, Jerry restored the first signs of life in his cousin Myra, who had been unable to put the tremendous weight of her personal burden behind her. Although moving out of her bedroom was a slight inconvenience, Myra liked having Jerry as a houseguest. In the afternoons, she brought her classmates home for him to entertain on the piano, and at night she would sneak into the living room with him to watch the late shows: *What's My Line, Playhouse 90* and Jerry's favorite, *Do You Trust Your Wife?* He flatly refused to watch talent shows on television. He could not bear to listen to other people sing. Jerry had a well-defined case of professional jealousy which creased his face with a frown whenever he saw a singing aluminum-siding salesman on Ted Mack's *Amateur Hour* or heard Myra playing her Elvis Presley records on her new phonograph.

With the first few dollars he made in Memphis, Jerry bought an old Cadillac. He now had a fleet of two cars. It did not matter that the grand old sedan was dented and lacked air conditioning; it was big and flashy and Elvisy. It was fun riding around downtown with the windows up, pretending to be cruising in cool comfort until beads of perspiration belied the fact. Myra's favorite drive was out along Highway 61 for hamburgers with lots of onions or a double sundae at the Dairy Queen.

Jerry was in the process of teaching Myra how to drive in his '56 Ford even though she could not reach the pedals and see over the steering wheel at the same time. She sat on the Memphis telephone directory or drew one leg under her like a stork and sat on her foot, spasmodically pressing the brake and accelerator with the toe of her shoe.

"Josie Mae, you need a ride home?" Myra asked the housekeeper one afternoon. "I can drive you whenever you're ready."

"Miss Myra, you can't drive," Josie Mae protested. "You only twelve years old."

"Yes, I can," Myra contradicted. "I been practicin'. Now, when you get ready to go, you let me know."

At five o'clock, Myra swiped the keys to Jerry's Ford and waited for Josie Mae in the car. She went over the ignition procedure several times to make sure she remembered everything. Josie Mae had strong doubts about Myra's capability, but got into the passenger's seat as she was told. On the way to Josie's house, Myra ran over three mail boxes, the front fender of Jerry's bumper car shouting assault and battery. Myra steered home by the grace of God and the seat of her pants, ignoring traffic lights of all colors, alarming pedestrians and spooking livestock. That evening as he was leaving for a night out, Jerry discovered the modifications to his prized possession. Myra confessed, and Jerry, much to everyone's surprise, had a big laugh. Nonetheless, Myra was grounded from further solo missions.

One afternoon as they walked along together, Jerry challenged Myra to a foot race. "I can run backward and still beat you," he chided, highstepping in reverse. Attempting to right himself in midstride, he turned his ankles and scraped along six feet of gravel on his belly, embedding his precious palms with bits of glass. For the next few days, Jerry played piano with his hands bandaged.

Handicapped Jerry was still the best pianist in town. Carl Perkins, Billy Riley, Warren Smith and Jim Williams invited him to sit in on their recording sessions during January. Jerry was paid fifteen dollars per session to record a few misses with Jim and Warren and hits for Billy and Carl. The hits were Billy's "Flyin' Saucers Rock 'n' Roll" and "Red Hot," and Carl's remake of Blind Lemon Jefferson's "Matchbox Blues."

Dewey Phillips was the first disc jockey to add Jerry's cover version of "Crazy Arms" to his playlist and, as a personal favor to Sam, pushed the song into the local charts. Sam gave a few copies of the record to distributors and radio stations, hoping it would be added to airplay rotation in other areas, but was not surprised few places outside of Memphis, Nashville and the "coonass" country of Louisiana paid any attention.

A few copies of "Crazy Arms" trickled into the record bins of New York City, where two girlfriends in particular had been East Side, West Side, all around the town in hot pursuit of a copy. Elaine Berman and Kay Martin had heard the song, or part of it, on the radio once, and it became a life and death matter to get a copy in their hot little hands and play it till its grooves wore slick. The girls weren't sure who the singer was, but overheard someone mention it was the comedian Jerry Lewis. Impossible, said Kay, whose high IQ had recently accelerated her into college at age sixteen. At long last, those crazy arms grabbed a firm hold of Elaine and Kay, and there was no end to what they went through to find out something about the mysterious singer. Through weeks of constant search, they could not even turn up a photograph, and only learned that the singer was from somewhere in Louisiana. That he was from the same stable as Elvis made Jerry desirable by association.

"I hope he records a lot more songs. I want to own everything he does," said Kay.

"I hope he's single," said Elaine, "because I want to own him."

* * *

The busy schedule of session work had stolen the month away before Jerry remembered his promise to Jane. He had completely forgotten about moving her to Memphis until Lois reminded him one night at dinner. "I can't understand it, Jerry. You've been up here goin' on four months without your wife, and you don't even call or write. Don't you ever get to missin' your family? Don't you think its time Jane joined you?"

"You're right, Lois, an' I been thinkin' mighty hard about that very thing, but with havin' a record out an' all the excitement an' everything, I guess I got sidetracked. There's nothin' I'd like better'n to have my fam'ly here with me, but, you know, I been stayin' here with y'all 'cause I can't afford a place of my own. Now that I got my first record out, maybe it won't be much longer."

"Well, if that's all that's botherin' you, they could stay here till you get settled into a place of your own. Rusty and Junior could play together and I could sure use Jane's help around the house, seein's how I don't get much help from a certain someone whose name shall not be mentioned," Lois said, looking in Myra's direction. "Call Jane and tell her to come up."

The Browns' house was filled to overflowing when Jerry's family moved in. Lois's idea proved not to be such a good one at that, but Jay, hoping his career as a musician was on its way, pleaded for his wife's understanding. Lois could only hope Jerry's record would become a hit, for everyone's benefit. When the men departed for the studio and Myra went to school, Lois and Jane were left at home with their toddlers, Rusty and Junior. Jane did nothing all day except wait for the Killer to return. She wasn't good at disciplining her son, who rode his tricycle through the living room, wreaking havoc and battering the furniture until Lois scotched him in the midst of his romp. Jerry took offense; no one reprimanded his son.

"You let my boy do whatever he wants," Jerry hollered at Lois. "That's my son, an' he can ride his bike in here if he wants to."

"Not in my house, he can't," Lois retorted, and it became obvious to one and all that Jerry Lee and company would have to soon make other arrangements. Ready or not, he drove around Memphis scouting for low-income housing and found a place on Koger Drive. He was forced to buy what furniture the Browns could not loan him, and by this point managed to forget all that Jay and Lois had done for him. Eviction cracked the foundation of Jerry's relationship with his cousins and immediately threatened his partnership with Jay. Lois was all for severing the relationship entirely. As far as Jay was concerned, the final decision rested on the success or failure of "Crazy Arms."

"What do I get outta this record anyway?" Jerry asked Sam at their next meeting.

"A hit, if you're lucky," said Sam. "Other'n that, three cents a record for royalties. But you'll get yours on the road. I expect you'll be makin' ten times what you're makin' now if this record goes anywhere."

"I hear diff'rent figgers," said Jerry. "I hear we sold ten thousand copies here, twenty thousand there. How many have we sold and where's my end of it?"

"I don't rightly know how many copies we sold, I'd have to check the figures. There's a lot you don't know about that I have to take into account—promotional copies, giveaways, returns, defects. You need money? How much? Couple hunnert? Here, take this," Sam said, handing a wad of bills to Jerry.

The bookkeeping department of Sun Records was comprised of Sam and his secretary, who made random entries in a loose set of ledgers reflecting whatever Sam wished to show. The logs of recording sessions were kept in the same manner, with dates carelessly guessed at, musicians freely substituted, added and deleted, and sums paid to union labor falsified. The fact was, no one knew, least of all Jerry, how many copies of "Crazy Arms" had been sold. His royalties, instead of being paid promptly twice a year, were portioned out slowly and piecemeal or whenever Sam wished to silence his complaints. Jerry, completely new to the business end of the industry, trusted the man who had given him his big break to treat him right. In the midst of all the excitement of having his first record out, Jerry developed a bad habit of overlooking the problems that beset him.

J. W. Brown forgot all about the Memphis Light and Gas Company as long as his checks were delivered on time. He was caught completely by surprise when he received a letter explaining that his compensation would be terminated unless he returned to work in some capacity. He held a debate with Lois, arguing the merits of life on the road playing music versus life on the road mending wires. Lois, who had entered the newer proposition with great skepticism, was cheering for the electric company. Jay was, in that sense, made to see the light.

"Jerry, I'm quittin'," Jay said one morning when his cousin came by to take him to the studio. "Got no choice. The comp'ny says I gotta go back to work or they'll cut me off, an' that's what's kept us goin' a good many years."

"You can't quit on me now, Jay," Jerry pleaded. "We're jus' fixin' to get things started."

"But I gotta do somethin'," Jay replied. "Music ain't makin' me no money."

"We gonna make it big one o' these times, Jay," Jerry insisted. "I tell you what: If you quit workin' for them, I'll give you half of everything we make. That's a promise."

"Deal!" said Jay, without looking in his wife's direction.

Jerry, sensing trouble with Jay's better half, followed Lois out to the kitchen. "Lois, I didn't hear you say anything in there about us keepin' on together. What's the matter?"

"Jerry, I got two kids to worry about, not countin' the big one in there that plays guitar in your band. How much is it you're makin' these days?"

"Hunnert, hunnert an' a quarter a night—"

"And Jay is gonna get half of it."

"Yes, ma'am."

"That's not a lot."

"Not now, but wait'll we get a hit. Then we'll be makin' more'n any of us ever dreamed, and, Lois, I assure you I'll split everything fifty-fifty all the way down the line if you stay with me an' help me through this thing. I know we're gonna make it, I can feel it. An' I need Jay in the band to look after the business."

Lois said nothing. Jerry interpreted her silence as approval.

Jay gave the power company his resignation with all the conviction of a man jumping from a sinking ship into a leaky lifeboat. In the studio, he tried to lose himself in his work. They were recording traditional songs, including "Lucky Old Sun," "I Don't Love Nobody," "Ole Pal of Yesterday" and upbeat versions of "Crawdad Hole" and "When the Saints Go Marching In," trying to cultivate an identifiable sound. They worked on titles by Jerry's favorite stylists, Jimmie Rodgers's "Carolina Sunshine Girl" and Hank Williams's "I Can't Help It" and "Long Gone

Lonesome Blues." Using Roland Janes, Jimmy Van Eaton and any musicians who happened to be hanging around the studio at the time, Jerry explored rhythm-and-blues standards such as Fats Domino's "My Blue Heaven" and The Dominoes' "Sixty Minute Man" for incorporation into his style. With Carl Perkins, Jerry taped one of Carl's compositions entitled "Turn Around," and Sam marked it as a strong possibility for future release.

In the spring, less time was spent in the studio searching for the right sound as Bob Neal had several interesting propositions for the trio to consider, the first of which was a poorly plotted tour of small towns for one hundred dollars a day. The band soon discovered the trip was costing almost as much as they were making, and after expenses and giving Russ his cut, Jerry and J. W. divided pocket change. Upon returning home, the boys sat down to have a long heart-to-heart with their agent. Bob began divulging further plans for the future with the good news that "Crazy Arms" had shipped thirty thousand copies and orders were still coming in.

"That's pretty damned good, especially when you stop to consider that Presley's first song didn't even sell twenty thousand copies overall. I tell you what," Bob said by way of apology for the tragic tour, "Johnny Cash is hotter'n a two-dollar pistol with the country crowd right now. How about openin' a coupla shows for him and Carl Perkins this summer? That'll give you plenty of time to work up some new material, maybe get another single out. Try out some new stuff and see what people like."

One April weekend, the trio was booked into a nightclub in Osceola, Arkansas, a small town due north of Memphis overlooking the Mississippi River. They arrived late in the afternoon at the same time that the club owner was sweeping out the site and moving new chairs inside.

"Welcome to the Rebel Room, the world's toughest nightclub," the manager greeted them.

"Jerry, Jay and Russ looked at one another with hesitant smiles.

"See these chairs? Metal. Bought 'em off a feller who got 'em from the state pen. Indestructible, he says. I just hope he was tellin' me the truth."

"Why?" asked Jerry.

"Well, you see that pile of kindlin' wood over yonder?"

"Yeah."

"That's what's left of the chairs I had in here."

Russ returned from a look-see inside the Rebel Room. "Hey, how come there's a chicken-wire fence in front of the stage? You keep animals in here or what?"

"You could say that," the owner responded. "Actually, the screen is for your protection."

"Now, hold on," Jay piped up. "What do we need protectin' from?"

"You'll see," was the owner's reply.

When the trio took the stage behind a floor-to-ceiling mesh of wire, they were glad to have it. Bottles and glasses and chairs were hurled in their direction as they began to play, as if the patrons had been waiting for a musical cue to trash the joint.

"I'm gonna kill Bob Neal when we get home," Jay said.

"You mean *if* we get home," Jerry corrected.

Jerry was able to keep the locals down to a dull roar by playing the same old requests and introducing his own songs at suitable points. The razorbacks weren't interested as long as he didn't play too loud to argue over. After the protective screen had been sufficiently tested for safety, the boys boldly played hoedowns for the choreography of fisticuffs.

"Hey, blondie," someone called, "play 'Big Legged Woman' for me."

"What was that?" Jerry said, squinting through the mesh.

"Play it, darlin'," the voice called, raising a few snickers.

Jerry paused.

"I said play it!" The voice rose, breaking a bottle for emphasis.

Jerry rattled the keys in search of the melody and rummaged through his memory for the lyrics he hadn't heard since he was a boy sneaking down to Haney's Big House. He recalled the first line, "Big Legged Woman keep your dresses down/You got somethin' up there make a bulldog wanna hump a hound," provoking hoots and hollers and an untoward remark at someone's girlfriend which spurred the Armageddon that cleared the Rebel Room of all contenders and twisted the shiny new metal chairs into Op Art. The law moved in and restored peace to the premises in time to accommodate a brotherhood of Shriners from Luxora. The troublemakers, honoring an age-old code of the west, paid the club owner for the damage so that there would be another roomful of furniture to break up again the next weekend. With restitution came complaints that the clang of metal chairs was not as satisfying as the crunch of wooden ones.

Along about midnight, Jay's face began to mirror the boredom of the crowd that filed in after the Rebel Room had been made safe again. "Hey, Jerry," he called during a lull in the action, "let's play that 'Shakin' Song' we rehearsed the other day, liven up this joint."

"I don't know that I can stand any more livenin' up tonight," said Russ, hiding behind his drum barricade.

Jerry couldn't remember the words that Roy Hall taught him in Nashville, lyrics Roy had written under the pen name Sunny David and recorded for Decca in 1955. Jerry sucked in a long, deep, deliberate breath, hit the keys a dozen times and sang out, "Come on over, baby, whole lotta shakin' going on!" improvising the lyrics as he went.

Heads turned. All conversation broke off in midsentence, some half-scared into attention, others completely scared by what had suddenly overcome the piano player.

> *I said come on over, baby, we got chicken in the barn.*
> *Come on over, mama, really got the bull by the horn.*
> *We ain't fakin', whole lot of shakin' going on.*

Glasses dropped. Hands drummed on tabletops, and as Jerry commanded, "Shake it, baby, shake it," the crowd did as they were told.

Jay's eyes lit up. For once, the sound of busting glass was music to his ears. It wasn't the start of another fight, it was the start of something big. By song's end, the crowd was standing, shaking, dancing and hollering for more.

"Play it again!" someone cried, and Jerry struck up the introduction to "Whole Lot of Shakin' Going On" once more, and Jay and Russ jumped in behind him. And the reaction became stronger. When the first encore ended, the crowd called out for another chorus.

And Jerry played "Whole Lot of Shakin'" again.

And again.

And again.

And twenty-one times after that, until the hoarse roar of the patrons fell to fatigue. Twenty-five encores of "Whole Lot of

Shakin'" had wrung the band dry of energy but filled their hearts with ambition.

They had found the Lost Chord.

When The Jerry Lee Lewis Trio returned to the studio in mid-April, the first order of business was to capture the wild "Shakin' Song" on tape.

"We'll get to it later," Jack Clement said, "but first I want you to listen to this song I wrote with you in mind. It's a honky-tonk tune called 'It'll Be Me.'"

"Yeah, okay," Jerry said, "but first we want you to listen a minnit. We played this song in Arkansas the other night and the people went crazy."

"C'mon, fellas, 'Whole Lot of Shakin' was no big thing when The Commodores released it two years ago. Besides, I keep tellin' ya, Elvis has it all sewed up. You gotta come up with somethin' different."

"I still like 'It'll Be Me' better," Sam said after hearing Jerry play both songs.

"Me, too," said Jack.

"You're makin' a big mistake," Jay protested. "This 'Shakin' Song' has 'em all beat."

Sam and Jack left the session unconvinced, the boys having failed to enthuse them with their discovery. "Don't worry," Sam told Jack, "your song will be Jerry's next single. Leave it to some kid from the sticks to tell me about the music business."

Recording sessions at Sun looked more like private parties than work to the casual observer. Friends dropped by to chat, refreshments were produced, and everybody got into the act. The band took breaks every ten minutes. Verses to the songs were forgotten, and Jack Clement gave up trying to get something intelligible on tape. Later in the week, on or about the fifteenth of the month, Jerry made more serious attempts to record "It'll Be Me" and "Whole Lot of Shakin'," employing Roland Janes on guitar and Jimmy Van Eaton on drums. J. W. Brown played electric bass, a prototype instrument, on the first takes of both songs, but Jack preferred subsequent takes without him. Sam pressed an initial run of promotional copies, insisting "It'll Be Me" was the A side. Dewey Phillips received the first copy of the new single and played both sides repeatedly in the first hour of his show. The telephone was ringing off the hook at WHBQ. Memphis was sha-kin'. The song was a hit.

"Looks like you got another winner, Sam," Dewey phoned in his congratulations. "We're gettin' a lotta calls on the new Lewis single."

"Hell, I knew it," said Sam. "I knew Jack's song was a hit the first time I heard the kid do it."

"Jack's song? I'm talkin' about the flip side, 'Whole Lot of Shakin',' " Dewey explained.

"Say what?"

"Yeah, the 'Shakin' Song' is getting all the response."

"Impossible. A cover version of a song that died two years ago?"

"Yep, it sure has a lotta people talkin', and not all of what I hear is good. Some say it's too suggestive, the lyrics are too sexy, especially at the break, where Jerry goes into his rap and tells the girls how to shake it. We may have some trouble with that."

"But you say it's gettin' a big reaction from your listeners?"

"It is doin' that, I'll have to admit. I'm not sure how long they're gonna let me keep it on my playlist, but the B side could take off."

Sam shipped promotional copies throughout the Southeast dur-ing the month of May, hoping the single would break wide open. The response in nine out of ten markets was negative. "Whole Lot of Shakin' Going On" was banned by most radio stations for being too provocative. Part of the problem arose over an uninten-tional interjection.

"Ever'body knows a whole lotta shakin' is what humpin' is all about," a distributor told Sam. "That's no secret. I had the same problem with the original version a coupla years ago, but we got away with it. The problem with your version is the cuss words."

"What cuss words?" Sam asked. "There ain't no cuss words—"

"At the break, don't the boy sing, 'Well, hell'?"

"What?" Sam listened more closely as the man attempted to imitate Jerry.

"Right before he starts singin' 'Shake it, baby, shake it,' don't the boy sing, 'Well, hell' or 'Well-a, hell-a'?"

"I don't know what the hell you're talkin' about," Sam said irritably.

"Go listen to your song," the distributor said. "It sounds like that's what Lewis is sayin'. He does it again right after the break. Now, you can't expect me to get my accounts to buy a song that has hell in it."

Sam played the song over and over, listening for the blasphemy, and upon giving up on the game, called Jerry into his office and asked his help.

"I know what the guy's talkin' about," said Jerry, "but all I'm doin' is singin' 'We-ell,' you know what I mean?"

"Well," said Sam, "we might have to edit it out, 'cause it sure has people up in the air about it."

"Just that one tiny part?"

"That and the fact that everybody thinks it's a dirty song. They think you're singin' about fuckin', not dancin'."

Jerry reddened.

"I tol' ya to stick with 'It'll Be Me' an' back it up with another country or rockabilly tune. Listen to me next time, will ya, please? Let me run my damn business."

When the single had been out six weeks, Sam had barely filled orders for thirty thousand copies. Not all of the complaints he received were based on the risqué lyric controversy. Some radio stations were refusing to play the song for segregationist reasons.

"We don't play songs by niggers on our station," a program director in Texas told Sam.

"Jerry Lee Lewis ain't a nigger," Sam informed him.

"If he ain't, he sure sounds like one. It's a nigger song and it sounds like it's sung by a nigger, so natur'ly we all thought he was a nigger."

"He ain't," Sam repeated. "He's a blon'-haired, blue-eyed son o' God from Ferriday, Lou'siana."

"Coulda fooled me," said the Texan.

The Bob Neal cavalcade of country music, starring Johnny Cash, Carl Perkins and Webb Pierce, was making its way toward Sheffield, Alabama, in late July when The Jerry Lee Lewis Trio was added to the bill. "Whole Lot of Shakin' Going On," banned by radio, had died on the vine and had been written off as a casualty by Sam Phillips, who figured the best thing to do with Lewis was farm him out for more exposure, find another song and try again.

Sheffield was home for Jud Phillips, one of Sam's big brothers. He had served in two wars as an army chaplain and was reported dead after being captured in Korea. Mom got the insurance money, his wife remarried, and Jud came home to zilch. He was discharged from the marines at a time when Sam was starting the Memphis Recording Service and needed help in making the new business a success. Jud replaced a partner who was fired for stealing, and pumped in enough new blood to own the body of Sun Records.

More than any other quality contributing to Jud's efficiency as a promoter was his ability to understand human nature and what lies deep in the hearts of poor country boys who come to the big city looking to make their fortune in the music business. He knew that these nobodies waking up one morning to find their names blazoned in the media could not be performers and businessmen, too. With a chaplain's compassion, he recognized the need for someone to take control of their reckless lives, someone to free the artists from the burden of management, someone to teach them what to say and when to say it, what to do and when to do it. When Jud was in the presence of these boys, he could be persuaded to join the party all too easily; that was his weakness. He did not understand the powerful forces that moved performers any better than they did, but he understood the men and their goals, and that was a rare feat in itself.

Sam carried the Sun banner; its heart and soul and mind was pure Jud. Sam was the company's president and figurehead, banker and accountant. Jud was head of the one-man promotion department and from time to time was consulted for his opinion of a new act. Since Jerry Lee Lewis was heading Jud's way, and because Jud was unfamiliar with the new act, Sam mailed Jerry's tape to Jud and asked him to appraise the show when it came through Sheffield. The tape convinced Jud that the boy had talent, and there was something about the "Shakin' Song" which warranted his going to see Jerry in person.

Jud arrived at the auditorium as Jerry was preparing to go on-stage. A feud had just been resolved and there was still ill will between the star of the show and the opening act. Carl Perkins, whose memories of the tragic car wreck which ruined his career always strenuously tested his nerves whenever the band traveled on the road, was fit to be tied.

"What's the matter?" Jud intervened.

"We was ridin' along in the limo playin' cards in the backseat when that little sonofabitch Jerry threw a damn cherry bomb under our car and scared the everlovin' life outta me, an' I'll tell you right now, it ain't a damn bit funny," said Carl, daring Jud to laugh.

"I tol' them boys not to do that," said Jerry, straight-faced, "but you know J. W. never listens to me."

As the Killer was introduced to the crowd, Webb Pierce approached Jud in the wings. "Watch that goddamn kinky-headed kid," Webb said, nodding at Jerry. "Watch the way he comes out on stage. Watch his mannerisms."

Jud moved out front and found the audience was being sung to sleep. This wasn't the act he came to see.

"This ain't no 'Little Green Valley' crowd," Jerry said to Jay and Russ. "Let's shake this place up a bit," Then he sang "Don't Be Cruel" and "Hound Dog," Roy Orbison's "Ooby Dooby," and "Ubangi Stomp," written by Sun producer Charles Underwood and recorded by Warren Smith. As Jerry launched into "Whole Lot of Shakin'," clapping filtered through the hall, and at his exhortation, the younger ones jumped to their feet and shook whatever would move. Jerry walked offstage to a thunderous ovation.

"I swear to God this'll never happen again," said Johnny Cash. "Jerry Lee Lewis ain't never gonna open for me after tonight."

"That's just what I wanted to hear," Jerry responded.

Jud invited the troupe to his house after the show for drinks. Jerry was included in the invitation, but not in the festivities. As everyone else made themselves at home at Jud's bar, Jerry warmed up to Jud's piano. Jud listened to him play and was more impressed than ever.

"Jerry, I bet I can take you to New York and put you on *The Ed Sullivan Show*," Jud said.

"Hey, why don't you do somethin' like that for me?" Carl Perkins interrupted.

"Yeah," Johnny Cash joined in like a little brother. "We been with you a helluva lot longer than he has. What about us?"

"You don't understand, fellas," Jud said diplomatically. "Here's a visual gimmick—this boy and his piano. Ever'body plays the guitar these days, but he's diff'rent. I can take him to

New York an' bring y'all right behind. It'll start a whole damn movement."

"We're the damn headliners," Carl and Johnny protested. "We the ones with the hits. We oughta be the ones to go first, then bring him along."

"I'm gonna go see Sam Monday mornin'. In fact," Jud paused, "I ain't gonna wait till Monday, I'll go tomorrow. I'm gonna take Jerry here to New York. You wait 'n' see. He'll do it for all y' all."

The Phillips brothers had widely opposing views on Jerry Lee Lewis, just as they'd had on Elvis Presley. Jud was not surprised that Sam was hollering no before his plan had been heard out.

"I tell you what I see," Jud envisioned. "I see somethin' new. I see a kid that can sell a song, anybody's song, I don't care if it's gospel or blues or country or rock 'n' roll. You take Elvis, he survives purely on good looks. He's got no talent for composing music or writing lyrics, can't play the guitar worth a shit and is only tolerable as a vocalist. Jerry Lee, on the other hand, sells music. I never seen anybody play the piano like this boy, and what's more, he can play anything and make it sound like he wrote it. He can even write a decent song when he takes the time."

"Fergit it," said Sam. "He's already had two chances."

"Give him another. He's the best shot we got at breaking big and pavin' the way for other acts," Jud insisted. "I can take him to New York and put him on national teevee, and from that point on, all you'll ever have to do is call Ed Sullivan and say 'I got,' and he'll say 'Send.'"

"It'll cost too damn much money for you an' Jerry to go runnin' off on a wild-goose chase," Sam said, holding his checkbook over Jud's head for leverage.

"It takes money to make money," Jud defended. "Dollars spent on promotion come back in the form of more sales, and if you didn't know that, then look at RCA and Elvis Presley and see what a big promotional budget can buy."

RCA and Elvis was a sore spot for Sam, who had quickly come to regret the deal that robbed him of millions. Jud had watched the clever maneuvering that took Elvis from Sun and was determined not to lose Jerry in the same way. Having lost their first and best shot at breaking Nashville's control over the southern market, Jud was determined that Jerry spearhead one last great push to put Sun on top.

"Do it or lose him like you lost Elvis," Jud threatened. "How many chances do you think you'll get, anyway? How's the old sayin' go, opportunity only knocks once? Well, you're gettin' a second chance, and his name is Jerry Lee Lewis."

"All right, all right," Sam conceded. "Take the sumbitch to New York, but it's his last chance."

Jud and Jerry flew to New York the next day. No sooner had Jerry absorbed the sensation of his first flight than he found himself becoming accustomed to his first luxury suite at the Delmonico Hotel. And Jud was making a personal call to Ed Sullivan. Standing in the center of the room with one hand on the telephone and the other resting on his protégé's shoulder, Jud bellowed, "Ed? Jud Phillips here. Got somethin' for ya, Ed. Another Elvis Presley—"

"Jud, don't bring me any more of that crap," said Ed curtly, and hung up in his face.

Jud chuckled. Instantly, the laughter turned to anger. "That bastard," he spat. "We went through this exact same thing with Elvis. We begged Ed to put Elvis on. He got a few complaints from li'l ol' ladies and refused to book him again, but he came back like they always do and begged for three shows which he gladly paid fifty grand for. Now he says he don't want no more ass-wigglin' nigger music. That bastard will never learn, boy, never learn."

Jerry was crestfallen. He had come all this way for a two-minute rejection over the telephone. As he began folding his shirts back into his suitcase, Jud stopped him.

"Now, hold on, son, don't go gettin' all down in the mouth. Ol' Jud ain't through yet. I got a few more numbers," he said, leafing through a little black book. "Operator, get me Henry Frankel over at NBC. He's the talent coordinator, if that's any help. An old drinkin' buddy," Jud said aside to Jerry. "Henry? Jud Phillips. Been a while, ain't it? Naw, I'm right here in town. Brought a boy to see you, a singer. Plays the piano like you never heard. Another goddamn Elvis Presley. Better, if you ask me. Can you see us today? Right. We'll be there. Thanks, Henry. Let's go, boy."

"Where?" Jerry brightened.

"Don't ask so many questions, son. NBC is waitin' on you."

At Frankel's office, Jerry sat to one side as he had been instructed on the way over in the cab. He leafed through a comic book, disconcertingly blowing large, lopsided pink gum bubbles while Jud attempted to sell NBC on his talent.

"I can make a call over to Jules Green," Frankel said. "Jules is Steve Allen's producer. He might be interested. He went for Elvis in a big way, and didn't run into the same flak Sullivan did with sponsors and spinster schoolmarms."

Green was receptive to anything Frankel took the time to personally introduce, so he agreed to meet Jud in his office immediately. This time, Jerry was made to wait in the reception area while Jud made his pitch inside.

"So, whatcha got?" Jules asked Jud.

"A kid that sings an' plays the piano like you never heard . . ."

"Well, I never heard of him," Jules interrupted. "How long has he had a record out?"

"His first one was released seven months ago, and the second has been out three months."

"How many copies has it sold?"

"The last one? About thirty thousand—"

"Have any pictures of him?"

"No, but . . ."

"I ain't never seen a salesman yet that didn't have a sample. Where's the record?" Jules asked impatiently.

"Hell, I brought my product with me," Jud said, pointing over his shoulder toward the waiting room. "This is an action artist. I want you to watch him perform."

"There's a piano," said Jules, pointing to the other side of his office.

Both men walked to the door and looked into the reception area for Jerry. No one was there except for a skinny kid blowing bubbles while reading a Superman comic.

"That's him," said Jud. "Jerry, you're on, son."

Jerry rose from his seat, folded Superman and stuck him in his back pocket, crossed the office and, without so much as warming up on "Chopsticks," went headlong into "Whole Lot of Shakin'."

Jules Green was stunned. He moved closer to Jerry and watched his hands set about the keyboard with lightning skill and precision. "I'll give you five hundred dollars if you take this boy back to his hotel room and not let anyone see him until nine o'clock tomorrow morning when we meet with Steve," Jules said. "I want him to sing that song on the show this Sunday night."

Before locking Jerry in his room for the night, Jud took him out to celebrate at one of New York's classiest restaurants, Jack Dempsey's on Broadway. The former heavyweight champ had retired from the ring to box lunches instead of contenders, and was there to greet Jerry and Jud personally. Jud introduced his singer to the fighter as "the guest star of the next Steve Allen show," and Dempsey called his photographer over before seating them at his best table.

"Mr. Phillips, what's a ten-ounce Delmonica?" Jerry nudged Jud.

"Delmonico, that's a cut of meat, son. J'ever eat steak?"

Jerry shook his head.

"Well, son, you're in for a treat. Waiter, bring us two of your best Delmonico steaks, medium rare," Jud ordered.

When the feast was put before them, Jud momentarily looked up to wave at an acquaintance and, upon addressing his plate, noticed that Jerry had already devoured his dinner. "I b'lieve you could eat another 'un, couldn't you, boy?" Jud asked, then ordered a refill. Jerry sharked that one, too, bent on fleshing out his lanky frame in one sitting.

"So, tell me, ain't that the finest food you ever did eat?"

"Mr. Phillips, I b'lieve if God had made anything finer, He'd akept it for Himself."

"You said it."

"Mr. Phillips?"

"Yes, son?"

"Can I have another?"

The next day, Jud met with Jules Green, Steve Allen and the show's staff, prepared to take advantage of Allen's ongoing dilemma of running head-to-head with Ed Sullivan, forcing Allen to book big-name talent to vie with Ed's star-studded lineups. But Allen did not have Ed's money to buy headliners, which meant he took chances on the up and coming, his biggest payoff coming with a gamble on Elvis Presley's first television appearance. Now was the chance to scoop Sullivan again.

"Elvis had a hit when we had him on." Steve hesitated. "Your kid isn't even on the charts."

"All I can say is, Jerry is an action artist, and the audience you have when he starts will be there when he stops," Jud guaranteed. "You won't lose anybody. And after his debut, the next time you announce he's gonna be on the show, you'll have the biggest audience you ever had."

Allen was convinced. The agreement was made. Now, all Jud had to do was persuade the radio-owned Broadcast Music, Inc. (BMI) to lift their ban on "Whole Lot of Shakin'" before Sunday. Technically, a banned title in the radio ranks was also taboo for television.

"I think the interests of all concerned would best be served by taking the song off the ban list," Jud advised BMI.

"Will Lewis continue to include the vulgar connotation that we object to?"

"Which one?"

"The one where he tells the girls to stand in one spot and wiggle it around just a little bit."

"Well," Jud said, stifling a laugh, "if NBC doesn't complain, what's your objection?"

The ban was lifted. Of course, NBC and Steve Allen had no idea the song had been blacklisted for obscenity. No one at the network had heard "Whole Lot of Shakin'," and they were unaware of the outrageous lyrics until they, along with the rest of America, saw the song performed live on Steve Allen's show.

Jerry called everyone he knew and told them to be in front of a television set Sunday night, turn the channel to *The Steve Allen Show* and get ready for a big surprise. Jay and Russ were sent packing for the long drive to New York while Jerry talked at length to Myra about airplanes, elevators, taxi cabs and luxury hotels. "They got meat up here with fancy names . . ."

". . . I'm gonna run down to the drugstore and buy film for my camera and take pictures of the screen so you can see what you look like on teevee," Myra said. "Don't forget to smile."

When the announcement was published in *TV Guide* that Jerry Lee Lewis would be among Steve Allen's guests on July 28, 1957, Kay Martin and Elaine Berman, Jerry's two biggest fans in New York City, began conspiring on ways to meet the singer personally. The best plan involved a direct attack on the NBC studio in Manhattan. They arrived early in the afternoon on Saturday, hoping Jerry would come sometime during the day for rehearsal. Immediately, the girls were faced with two minor problems: There were too many entrances to patrol, and they had no idea what Jerry Lee Lewis looked like.

On a gamble, the girls proceeded to the Steve Allen set with the intention of befriending a stagehand or usher and thereby gaining access to the object of their affections. There was no one around except for three guys standing about with nothing to do.

"Hi," Kay ventured. "Anybody here yet?"

"Like who?" one of the boys asked.

"Oh, any of the cast or guests."

"Nope, nobody we know."

"Look," Kay said with a certain amount of urgency, "I might as well lay my cards on the table. I'm looking for Jerry Lee Lewis, the singer."

"Why?" the young man asked.

"Because," she stammered, "I love his songs and I want to meet him."

"Oh," the boy said. "What's your name?"

"Kay Martin, and this is my friend, Elaine."

"Nice to meetcha. I'm Russell Smith, some people call me Russ, and this is J. W. Brown, some people call him Jay, and this is Jerry Lee Lewis and some people call him Jerry."

When next the girls found the composure to speak intelligibly, it was in an effort to find adequate words to express thanks for two passes to *The Steve Allen Show*.

At seven-thirty on Sunday night, Myra and Lois sat before the television set praying for a good reception and freedom from technical difficulty. Myra scoped the screen through the viewfinder of her Polaroid. It was half an hour before showtime, but Myra wanted to make sure that the television set was warmed up properly.

After what seemed like days of waiting, Steve Allen's face appeared on the screen, and Myra, who had become trigger-happy, took Steve's picture as he mentioned Jerry's name. "My guests tonight are Shelley Winters, Tony Franciosa, The Four Coins, songstress Jodie Sands, singer Jerry Lee Lewis, pantomimist Shal K. Ophir and, of course, our regular cast of crazies, Tom Poston, Don Knotts and Louis Nye," Steve announced.

"You don't think Steve Allen is gonna do somethin' funny to Jerry like he did to Elvis, do you, Mom?" Myra asked.

"Like what, dear?"

"Remember when he had Elvis on that time and dressed him up like a farmer and put him in a skit that made fun of him? Then they dressed him up in a tuxedo, and he sang 'Hound Dog' to a real live dog!"

"I don't know what they're gonna do to him, Sissy," said Lois.

They watched the show proceed through a comedy sketch between Steve and Tony Franciosa and an auto-driving skit with Steve and Shelley Winters reminiscent of Myra and Josie Mae, and the fear that Jerry was going to be made to do something foolish began to grow in Myra. Jodie Sands sang "With All My Heart" and The Four Coins sang "Shangri-la." With less than ten minutes remaining in the program, and down to the last two acts, Shal K. Ophir, the European pantomimic, was introduced next.

"They're never gonna get on," Myra cried. "There isn't enough time left!"

Then it happened. With a brief introduction of his newest discovery, a hopeful Steve Allen gave way to a nervous Jerry Lee, whose energy could scarcely be contained. He wore a bright striped shirt of a black and white vertical pattern, opened at the throat, and his hair was combed straight back, appearing darker than it actually was. Bits and pieces of Jay and Russ, dressed in coordinating outfits of black and white, were shown in the background and whenever the cameras panned the set. Midway through the song, Jerry jumped up from the piano bench and, by hooking his right leg accidentally, pushed it back with too much force and sent the seat skidding across the stage. He played while standing stiffly, pounding the keys with strikes and blows which pianists were not supposed to use. Viewers were shocked by the display—this boy appearing on national television and mistreating a fine instrument. He was out of control. And the studio audience loved it. Kay and Elaine, seated in the first row, jumped up when Jerry did and provoked the rest of the spectators into clapping along with "Whole Lot of Shakin' Going On."

Steve Allen, who usually watched his guests on a monitor while seated behind his desk, stood up and clapped along with the rest of the cast and crew. During the excitement of the last refrain, Steve picked up his desk chair and threw it across the stage, then hoisted Jerry's piano bench and threw it, too. He was reaching for a potted plant when Jerry brought "Whole Lot of Shakin'" to its thunderous conclusion and a standing ovation.

It had taken Jerry almost ten years to become an overnight sensation. Telephone calls jammed the NBC switchboard, letters and postcards flooded Steve Allen's office, and reporters were scrambling to be the first to interview the latest celebrity. In a matter of moments, the pianist debuting at the end of Steve Allen's show, a twice-married, draft-evading Bible school expellee from nowhere, became the dominating influence in the lives of thousands of impressionable youngsters. Here was a man, kids thought, who was tough enough to say what he thought, dress as he pleased and do what he wanted to do. There was no pretense, no showy finery to wade through, no stage persona which vanished when the show was over. Here was a rock 'n' roll hero.

The next day, Jud received a progress report from his brother. "I'll have to hand it to ya, Jud, you sure were right," Sam declared. "We've already got twenty thousand copies of 'Whole Lot of Shakin'' sold today, and orders are comin' in by the truckload!"

"That ain't nothin'," Jud bellowed. "Steve Allen's done signed Jerry to a return engagement in two weeks and he's payin' him five thousand dollars to do it. We'll be sellin' twice that many records, or I'll kiss your ass in the courthouse square an' advertise a month in advance to raise a crowd. Hell, Sam, Allen's got hundreds of telegrams from New York alone."

"How do you know that?"

"'Cause I sent 'em, that's how," said Jud. "A phenomenon don't just happen, you have to make it happen."

"Now don't start spendin' all my goddam money up there where I can't get aholt of you—"

"Easy, Sam, I'm on my way home. We got to get to work right away an' get this boy on some of these big shows."

"Don't go blowin' all my money in the meantime just because you got a brush fire started. You ain't made the big money yet."

"Brush fire, my ass, this kid is gonna burn 'em up! Allen's people are already talkin' a third show if the next one gets the same response we got last night. And they ain't talkin' peanuts, either. They're talkin' fifteen thousand dollars for Jerry to sing the one song. We're fixin' to take off, Sam. We'll sell a million copies of 'Shakin'' before September, just you wait 'n' see."

Jud returned to Memphis after sequestering The Jerry Lee Lewis Trio in a sleazy hotel where the rents were low. At Sun, offers for personal appearances had piled up into a stack within twenty-four hours of the debut broadcast. Alan Freed was on line one wanting Jerry for the coming Friday's *Big Beat,* a network program emanating from New York. Steve Allen was on line two reserving August 11, and Dick Clark, host of the Philadelphia-based *American Bandstand,* was on line three asking for the following Monday. Sam instructed his secretary to hang up on anyone not talking in multiples of thousands beginning with five. Exactly one week before, The Jerry Lee Lewis Trio had limped home from Alabama with barely enough cash to meet the rent after having worked ten days straight. Now they were being offered fifty times the amount of their largest previous paycheck for three minutes' work.

The single most important decision in launching a promising career had to be made immediately: what to do about management. It was obvious that Jay would no longer be booking dates at the Ice Cold in Brinkley, and that a larger, more efficient machine was needed to take control. Nightly receipts were going to become too large to be stuffed into a brown paper bag with a bottle of bourbon and hidden in the back of Jay's amp. As it was with Elvis, Bob Neal could carry the mail only so far, and then he, too, would have to be replaced.

"We got to get Jerry a manager," Jud told Sam. "Now, who are we gonna use? Hubert Long?"

"No," said Sam.

"Oscar Davis?"

"No, dammit, you know I don't want nothin' to do with any friend of Tom Parker."

"But the man is a heavyweight," Jud argued. "He's got a list of thousand-dollar one-nighters. He can do a lot for Jerry."

"He can take Jerry away from us and put him with a bigger label is what he can do," Sam contradicted. "No to Oscar Davis, and that's final. Look, I don't see where Jerry needs to be jumpin' into a management contract at present. It's not like he still has to go out and find a job somewhere for a hundred bucks a night. Deals are comin' in here by the bushel barrel. All we gotta do is make sure the boy gets where he's supposed to go. Anybody can do that, and for a helluva lot less than what a bandit like Oscar Davis charges. Why don't you be his manager?"

"Me?" Jud asked.

"Yeah, you. Jerry likes you, he trusts you. After all, you got him his big break. You know all the people we got to deal with. Why don't you go on the road with him for a spell?"

"Because I'm not a manager. I'm strictly promotion, not a babysitter. I can sell and that's about it. Now, I got us in the front door, an' I'm tellin' you, we need help keepin' this boy in line. He's gonna be a total hell-raiser when he gets some of this big money in his pocket. What you better do is call the circus and ask 'em if they know where you can get a lion tamer," Jud said, more in honesty than jest.

"All right, but let's not jump the gun. For now, you go out on these first few dates an' see where the problem lies, if any. You got to be in these places anyhow to promote the record. It'll gimme time to find someone to handle the dates. By the way, where did you leave them boys?"

"In a dive someplace." Jud shrugged. "I didn't see the sense in makin' 'em drive home if they gotta be in New York on the second for Alan Freed. Last I saw 'em, they had eight hundred in cash. It better last 'em till I get back up there."

Leaving Jerry in charge of the money was a mistake. Eight hundred dollars in the care of a poor country boy required his constant tally and proud display whenever making a purchase, regardless of its cost. There are people in big cities attracted by this vanity. Jerry appeared to be an easy mark. When settling the tab at the corner bar, Jerry impressed the barmaid by whipping out his wad and flashing big bills while hunting for smaller denominations. The boys made the mistake of returning to the establishment habitually, and on their third visit were served Mickey Finns instead of bourbon. The drug, intended to knock them out lightly, was too generously administered, producing a volcanic rumble in their stomachs causing the trio to bolt for the door in time to get sick in the gutter. The rest of the night was spent huddled over toilet, sink and tub, praying that God would spare them from horrible deaths.

Jud's arrival produced a quieting effect until the celebration began over the news that "Whole Lot of Shakin'" had sold one hundred thousand copies in less than one week. On Friday night, Alan Freed's devotees were treated to a performance of the new hit more incredible than its debut. The Four Coins headlined the *Big Beat* along with Mickey and Sylvia, Gogi Grant and Al Hibbler, but it was the rising star from Louisiana who made the deepest impression on the audience and caused an unprecedented amount of mail to flow into Freed's offices.

Freed's only regret was that Jerry Lee Lewis had not come along thirty days sooner, for from July 12 through August 2, Freed produced four rock 'n' roll spectaculars featuring who's who in popular sound. The lineup accurately reflected the public's varied interests in all sorts of musical styles, but there wasn't one act, with the possible exception of Chuck Berry, that had the stage presence of Jerry Lee Lewis.

Freed's first extravaganza starred Connie Francis, Ferlin Husky and The Everly Brothers, but no rock 'n' roll. On the night of Jerry's trial before Freed's television audience, Freed was across town promoting his last major concert production of the summer, featuring Andy Williams, Bobby Darin, Fats Domino, Frankie Lymon and The Teenagers, and Freed's personal favorite, Chuck Berry.

Andy Williams, whose career was inaugurated in the previous year, had already released seven singles on the Cadence label, and Bobby Darin had been working almost as long, with six seldom-heard and hard-to-find records to his credit, a prelude to the monumental success awaiting him in the next year. Both boys were crooners in the traditional black tux and bow-tie mold, standing stiffly behind a microphone with nothing in their hands but snapping fingers. The rest of Freed's bill was race music, rhythm to the blues. Fats Domino, to whom the emerging Jerry Lee Lewis would be readily compared, had by this time logged his twenty-second hit on the Imperial label. All but one had been in the R & B top ten, and beginning with "Ain't It a Shame" in 1955, most had been pop hits as well. Six of the Fat Man's titles were Number 1 entries, "Blueberry Hill" and "Blue Monday" being his most recent million-sellers.

The man whose career Freed had launched, and the act Jerry would have to dethrone for top honors, was Chuck Berry. Berry exploded onto the scene two years earlier with "Maybelline," and followed that one with seven top-ten singles, including the an-

them "Rock and Roll Music." As much as Freed loved the music
of rhythm-and-blues masters, headliners with black faces minimized his business. Freed needed what Sam Phillips had needed:
a white man with a black sound.

Freed's great white hope was across town in his television studio signing a piece of paper granting permission to Kay Martin
and Elaine Berman to found the Jerry Lee Lewis Fan Club. Kay
and Elaine had already set the wheels in motion for the manufac-
ture of buttons and cards, T-shirts and photos, and the publication
of a monthly newsletter. The first of a thousand kindred spirits
were enlisted, the core of Jerry's adoring public; he had succeeded in turning revolt into fashion.

On August 11, as Jud Phillips had predicted, Steve Allen's
largest viewing audience to date awaited the encore performance
of the hit single that was sweeping the nation, "Whole Lot of
Shakin' Going On." The studio audience got what they came for;
the reaction was electric. Jud, along with thousands of other
viewers, was on the horn to Western Union sending up raves to
NBC.

Reporters from United Press International were calling Jud for
interviews. The first article, nine inches long and two columns
wide, announced: "Record World 'Shook Up' by Piano-Poundin'
Singer."

"Does he shake like Elvis?" the reporter wanted to know.

"Doesn't have to," replied Jud. "When he feels like it, he just
jumps up and kicks the piano stool across the stage and plays
standing up. And his legs get real stiff. What's different about
him," Jud said, trying to steer clear of comparisons to Presley, "is
that he's got a beat, a rhythm, like you've never felt."

"Was it difficult getting him on television, as difficult as it was
getting Elvis on?"

"That's what was encouraging," Jud replied. "The same people
who turned down Presley at the start turned Lewis down. All of
the same people who told us Elvis didn't have anything have told
us Jerry Lee didn't have anything. I don't believe anybody will be
as fabulous as Presley has been, because Presley was standing on
the right corner at the right time. But I think this kid will be a
great artist."

"How many records has 'Whole Lot of Shakin'' sold?"

"Four hundred thousand copies in two months," Jud calculated.

"And we're shipping on the average of ten thousand copies a day. Yesterday, we shipped exactly sixteen thousand, six hundred seventy-one."

"Any plans to sell Lewis to a major company like you did with Elvis?" the reporter concluded.

"Hell, no."

In August, as "Whole Lot of Shakin'" leaped into the national pop charts to the Number 3 position, Jerry was besieged with offers. On August 19, he drove to Philadelphia to appear on Dick Clark's *American Bandstand*. Clark, like Steve Allen, wanted a return date as soon as possible. The William Morris Agency was preparing to add Jerry to its distinguished clientele on a trial basis, although most Morris inroads were into supper clubs and geriatric wards and their experience with rock 'n' roll was nil. At the end of the month, "Whole Lot of Shakin'" was Number 1 in the country charts.

On August 24, the newest Elvis Presley release, "Let Me Be Your Teddy Bear," was the Number 1 record in the rhythm-and-blues charts and was expected to maintain its standing for at least thirty days. One week later, all of the stuffing had been shaken out of teddy, and Jerry Lee Lewis ruled R & B. By October, sales had multiplied to two million units, spreading to Europe, where "Whole Lot of Shakin'" was Number 8 in England.

"Whole Lot of Shakin'" eventually sold six million copies worldwide before its initial phase of release was over, becoming one of the biggest-selling records in the history of popular music. Two minutes and fifty-two seconds of pumpin' piano boogie placed Jerry Lee Lewis next to the finest acts in the business, in spite of a complete lack of guidance, money or training. How did such a thing happen? It had something to do with raw talent and a measure of luck.

Jerry had the masterstroke that he had always wanted, persevered and prayed for. A newfound sense of pride in his accomplishment pushed him toward a higher goal, to be not merely great but *the* greatest. A handful of the elite—Presley, Berry, Domino and Holly—stood between him and headlines. The stars aligned in the heavens. The timing was perfect; the time was right.

There was a whole lot of shakin' going on.

4 *Great Balls of Fire*

THE SUMMER OF HER SEVENTH GRADE WAS marvelous for Myra. She was a local superstar, a celebrity in her cousin's right now that his record was achieving international acclaim. She boasted to envious friends that she, too, would be touring the South with The Jerry Lee Lewis Trio in August. She waited anxiously for the band to return to Memphis from Alan Freed's concert route through the Northeast, a homecoming which, unpleasant at the start, would alter the normal course of Myra's life.

An emergency telephone call from Mamie to her son demolished Jerry's delirious success. "She's at it again, son," Mamie shouted intercontinentally to Jerry in New York.

"Who? What?"

"Jane. She's at it again. Taken up with another man in Memphis while you're away."

"How do you know? Who told you?"

"Frankie. She jus' come home from her stay at your place. Said Jane's keepin' comp'ny with some o' them boys you work with down at the studio."

"I'll kill 'em," Jerry fumed. "Mamma, you sure about this? I mean, is Frankie Jean sure?"

"Your sister don't lie, boy. She seen it goin' on with her own two eyes. Drinkin', dancin', carryin' on right under your own roof."

"Lemme call Jane," said Jerry, then slammed the receiver down and stalked around the room while Jay and Russ stared, silently guessing at what Mamie had told him. They knew better than to ask Jerry personal questions, and waited for his call to Jane for an explanation.

"Jane? I want you outta my house. You know damn good 'n' well what this is all about. You think you're foolin' me, but you're not. I know all about your li'l party. I don't wanna hear it. I want you outta there before I get home. An' don't take my Cadillac, either. I'll call my ol' man an' tell him to come get you."

Jud walked into the room as Jerry began throwing his clothes into a suitcase, still ranting and raving and making threats. "What the hell is goin' on here?" Jud demanded.

"I'm goin' home," Jerry said without looking up. "I got trouble with my wife again. She's screwin' around with all them clowns down at the studio while I'm up here bustin' my hump tryin' to support her," Jerry accused.

"What clowns?" asked Jud.

"All of 'em. Hell, they're lined up outside my house."

"You can't go home," said Jud. "We still got a big show to do in Washington tomorrow for Alan Freed. You can't walk out. Now, before you go runnin' off to shoot up the studio, lemme call Sam an' find out what the hell is goin' on down there. I'm goin' back to my room. Jay, don't let him leave, hear?"

"Man, you can't trust them women," Russ commiserated. "You'd have to take one straight from her mamma an' raise her right by you to keep her true, jus' like a bird dog. Even then, you'd have to keep one eye on 'er all the time. First chance they get, boy, and wham, flat on her back in bed with some other bastard . . ."

"That's right, boy," said Jerry. "Then, wham, you gotta knock 'em flat on their ass."

"I ain't got that trouble, thank God," said Jay. "I never have to worry about Lois. I always know where she's at."

"Oh, really?" Jerry challenged. "You know where she is right this very minute?"

"I don't have to. I trust her."

"I trusted Jane. An' here we are up in Buffalo, an' there they are down in Memphis with nothin' to do but sit around the house all day. You don't know where Lois is," Jerry affirmed.

Jay grabbed the telephone. "We'll jus' find out right now, how about that? What the hell are you doin' down there?" he hollered at Lois when she answered.

Jerry sat back enjoying the company in his misery until Jud returned with his report. "Sam never heard about any kind of goin's on such as this, but I talked to the boys at the studio and they said it's true. Now, they say they ain't the ones doin' it, but they know it's bein' done. They say there's been some parties, but I didn't get a whole lotta details. What did Jane say when you talked to her?"

"She cried," said Jerry. "She's scared."

"So are the boys down at the studio."

The trio arrived in Memphis two days later as Elmo was packing Jane and Junior into his pickup truck for the trip to Ferriday. Jerry disappeared for five minutes and returned to Jay's car with his wardrobe.

"Where you goin'?" Jay asked.

"Home with you, okay? I don't wanna stay here by m'self. No sense in keepin' a house I don't need, is there?"

"Okay," Jay said out of pity for his cuckolded cousin. "Did you talk to her any?"

"Nope. Nothin' to say. She tried to deny it, but I wouldn't listen."

"What's she gonna do when she gets home?"

"I don't know and I don't care. I gave Papa twenty bucks to give her when they got there. When that's gone, I don't care what happens to her. It ain't my problem."

The homecoming at the Browns' took place in a strained atmosphere. Everyone tried to avoid references to the subject foremost in their minds—divorce.

"Tell us about your trip," Lois said brightly.

"Well, we played a coupla big shows for Alan Freed," Jay began. "But we had a bad time with the bookin's William Morris arranged. Somebody got the wrong idea about what kind of music we play, an' they booked us into supper clubs and tiny bars where everybody was forty years old an' guys had on jackets an' ties and women wore sparkly dresses."

"Oh, no," Myra moaned.

"Yeah, it was a mess. So I don't think we'll be doin' too much more with the Morris people. Some places they tried to book us into wouldn't take us 'cause they thought we was niggers. Hell, we had to take a picture in Chicago to send 'em. It was crazy.

"We made a lotta money, though," Jerry added, "jus' like I told you we would, Lois."

"What are you gonna do with it?" Myra asked.

"The first thing I'm gonna do is go out an' buy me a new Eldorado convertible," Jerry said without having to think.

"I'll bet Jane'll love that," she said, momentarily forgetting their breakup.

Jerry looked at her with hurt and surprise, then halted her as she began to apologize. "That's all right, don't worry about it. It's all behind me. She's gone and I'll never see her again. That's it. Finished."

"Just like that?" asked Myra.

"Just like that," Jerry echoed. "Look, I never loved her. I only married her 'cause I had to. We spent most of the time apart—"

"What are you gonna do now?" Lois asked.

"Stay here a spell, if y'all'll let me. As soon as we get back from playin', I'm goin' to an attorney. Looks like I'll be a free man again." Jerry smiled, and winked at Myra.

The day before leaving on the summer tour of the South, Jerry and Jay met with Sam and Jud to map strategy. Now that receipts were running into the thousands of dollars, good business practices dictated that a change be made from the brown bag in the bass amp safe to something more formidable. Acting under Jud's advice, a family corporation was drawn and chartered. The partnership known as Jerry Lee Lewis Enterprises consisted of Jerry as president, Jay as chairman of the board and Lois as treasurer and fan-mail respondent.

"You might use this to open up your new bank account," said Sam as he handed a check to Jerry. The instrument was written in the amount of $40,000 and represented Jerry's percentage on the sale of the first 1,300,000 copies of "Whole Lot of Shakin' Going On." Jerry was boggled by the zeroes. He looked at the amount and read it through three times, perceiving a larger sum with each study.

"This is more than four thousand," he muttered to himself. "Hell, this is forty thousand." A heat wave coursed through his body and his palms grew moist. "Forty thousand dollars! That's a fortune!"

"You realize that Elvis had to release eleven songs before he made that much money?" Sam added for emphasis. "This is only your second. Imagine what you'll be makin' when you've had nine more like it."

The Jerry Lee Lewis Trio returned to the road on August 22. Jerry and Russ took one car laden with instruments, and Jay piled his family into his car and led the way. As they steered toward Nashville, Myra turned around in her seat to watch her crazy cousin playing behind the wheel of his car, going into mock-hysteria every time he took both hands off the steering wheel to wave or hide his eyes. Jerry and Myra spent the rest of the hot afternoon playing in the motel swimming pool. They had a sandwich together in the dining room where Jerry cheerfully signed autographs for the waitresses and bus boys. As they prepared to leave, Jerry handed his forty-thousand-dollar royalty check to the cashier and asked if she wouldn't mind cashing it for him. It was his favorite prank. Jerry loved watching simple folk negotiate the astronomical amount with widening eyes.

"Aren't you gonna cash it?" Myra asked with concern. "What if it burned up accident'ly? What if somebody snuck into your room tonight an' took it? You better hide it someplace safe till you can put it in the bank."

"I ain't never had enough money to put in the bank," said Jerry. "I don't even have an account. I'll cash it sooner or later. Nothin's gonna happen. I jus' wanna have some fun with it first."

That night when Jerry took the stage, he was a colorful sight. His fair skin had turned lobster-red from the sun and, offset by his blond hair and white dinner jacket, made him look like the devil's teenaged son heading for the prom. He searched the crowd for Myra and spotted her easily in the front row, where she was excitedly bragging to those seated next to her that the man playing bass was her father and Jerry was her very own cousin. Jerry sat at the piano and waited for Myra to look at him before he began to play. They smiled as their eyes met, then broke into laughter upon recognizing each other's sunburned features.

It was the first time Myra had seen the celebrated act perform onstage. She watched Jerry constantly except for the few brief moments when she looked at her father. Halfway into his set,

Jerry stripped away his dinner jacket and string tie and rolled his shirtsleeves to the elbow. His formal black trousers rode up and over the tops of his black and white cowboy boots as he kicked and stomped the piano pedals. The white heat of the spotlight licked at his singed face which turned redder as he shouted the lyrics. Myra was hypnotized by his performance and amazed at the crowd's transformation into jiggling, wiggling jitterbugs. Never had she had so much fun.

After the show, the troupe returned to their motel, where hot and sweaty stage clothes were shed and Noxzema slathered on tender skin till the room reeked with menthol. Jerry returned to his room alone, secured the premises and went to sleep. He did not like staying in motels, especially in a room by himself, and took every precaution to guard against marauding fans and the unknown. He pushed a chair against the chained door and jerry-rigged empty Coke bottles into a snare-trap for burglars. Taking Myra's advice, he searched the room for a safe hiding place for his money.

Before beginning the long, dry ride to Mississippi the next day, Myra and Jerry went swimming. They were alone, playing and dunking each other in the icy blue, when Jerry hoisted Myra out of the water and, while her eyes were still closed, kissed her quickly on the lips. The splashing stopped. The ripples spread to the far sides of the cement basin and dispersed. The water was stilled again as quickly as the interruption had disturbed it. In a single, unblinking moment, Myra and Jerry were in love.

The excitement of the moment caused Myra's heart to soar, overwhelming thoughts of the meaning behind Jerry's playfully innocent caress. It was not until that night when he took the stage of a high-school gym in Philadelphia, Mississippi, that Myra understood the significance of the embrace. As the capacity crowd roared its welcome, Jerry searched for Myra and found her front and center. Playing the introduction to "It'll Be Me," Jerry looked into Myra's eyes and faintly said, "I love you."

Like her first kiss, the whispered message came as a surprise to the girl. She was sure he had been looking straight at her when he said it, and she was sure of what he had said—it's unmistakable —but she still couldn't believe it. He wouldn't want me, Myra thought to herself, as the secret crush she felt the first time they met resurfaced. Myra's timidity and self-abasement beat back the tides of pent-up passion brimming at her floodgate. She feared the unmasking of her feelings lest she suffer the painful rejection which was sure to follow.

Love was not mentioned again during the next few days, and Myra began to doubt that Jerry had ever said those three magic words. There was no change in his manner toward her, and as far as she could tell, the affair, if there was one, would only last as long as their vacation. Come September, she would return to school and Jerry would be off somewhere playing or recording. She had him all to herself for just one more week—and she hoped it would be a very long one. Try to find a way to make time slow up. Give her time to grow up.

The change in her daughter did not go unnoticed by Lois. She was certain Myra was only experiencing a schoolgirl crush and that nothing would come of it, but just in case, watchful eyes were kept on Jerry. Calf love, flirtation, fetish—regardless of what the endearment was called, Myra enjoyed playing at it. No one, not even she, bothered to ask Jerry how he felt about her admiration. She was careful not to act like a fan, for Jerry did not like the lunatics who interrupted his shows by rushing the stage and baying like bitches in heat. With the misogynistic mistrust of a man hurt by his wife's infidelity and the prudence of a Pentecostal preacher, Jerry railed against the female allegiants flocking to worship at his feet.

"It's downright shameful, the way some o' these girls carry on," said Jerry. "Kickin' an' screamin' an' grabbin' at my pants —some of 'em are married, and their husbands jus' sit there an' watch their wives clawin' at another man. I can't understand what gets into these women. They act like animals, an' that ain't no way for a lady to act. I sure wouldn't let my wife act thataway."

Myra listened carefully and steeled herself against any sudden urge to rip her cousin's clothes off. Standing next to Jerry created no such impulse in Myra, so she asked, "What would a girl want to rip your clothes off for?"

Jerry was flustered for a polite answer.

Lois and Jay smiled, and were reassured that their childly thirteen-year-old daughter gave them nothing to worry about.

On Sunday, the troupe visited Jay's family in Winnsboro. Jay was smitten with jealousy when his own kin trampled him underfoot to get next to their famous cousin. Jerry was delighted with the warm welcome but excused himself to attend his uncle Sun Swaggart's prayer meetin' at the Assembly of God Church. He wanted Myra to go, too, since she had never been to a Pentecostal service.

Jerry's arrival at the modest sanctuary fueled the fire and brimstone hailing down from the pulpit; his presence in church always had Sun and Jimmy Lee pitching hardest for the Lord. He was a highly sought-after convert, more so now that he was a celebrity. Many times Jerry had been on the brink of submitting his life to Christ, but blind ambition could not be moved. Uncle Sun was going to give the sanctification of Jerry Lee one more shot, speaking to him as well as about him.

"We're pleased an' honored to have amongst our number this mornin' a celebrity," Uncle Sun began, "a boy that grew up around here and whom you all know an' love, Brother Jerry Lee Lewis. I've knowed him since he needed a leg-up on a piano bench, and some of you may not know that Jerry was at one time an electrifyin' preacher 'fore he took up singin'. He's got a hit record out now and is doin' very well for hisself. God has smiled on this boy an' showered him with good fortune.

"But," Sun paused for effect, "they's also some not here today. In particular, a fair-haired young'un that was sittin' right where you're sittin' now a week ago but can't come back again. A tragic accident took his life, an' the plain dreadful fact of the matter is that he was too young to know enough about life to make a mess of it yet.

"The Holy Spirit come a knockin' at this young'un's door. He come a knockin' an' beggin' to come into this boy's troubled life an' save him from ruin, and the boy sat there in the back row with his hands grabbin' aholt of the bench an' wouldn't budge when I called the sinners to come forth an' be saved. I pleaded an' God pleaded, but the boy could not be moved. He was filled with the contrary spirit of the devil. The boy went home figurin' he'd get the call again next week or whenever. I see some faces here today that's been here before but never come to the altar," said Sun, covering Jerry in his gaze, "so I know they's some of us that knows what I'm talkin' about.

"So, when this boy that struggled with God left here an' resumed life in his worldly ways, he did so at great risk. He'd washed his hands of God, an' God withdrew His Spirit. And when that boy went down to the swimmin' hole last week, maybe God got to rememberin' that when the boy drank up too much pond water, sunk to the bottom an' drowned. He missed his chance to make his peace," Sun said, pacing and waving a white handkerchief soaked with sweat. "He missed his chance to get into the kingdom of heaven. Don't you miss yours. You may not get the chance to come back next week, either."

"And at the funeral for this boy, I saw such weepin' an' wailin', and his mamma an' daddy stood starin' into the open grave, askin', 'Why, Lord, did You have to take him away? Give us back our boy,' they screamed.

"It was pitiful," Sun said, wringing his witnesses dry, "the way these people have been made to suffer the loss of their only child. Who among us can guess what pains his soul suffers as he strains for a glimpse of the golden gates through the filthy black smoke that engulfs his hole in hell? Who among us is not in the same danger? The time an' place is here 'n' now for those of you who have not surrendered to the Holy Spirit knockin' at your door. Repent! Come forward, sinners! Receive the gift of everlastin' life! For all have sinned and fall short of the glory of God. Come forward!"

As Uncle Sun called the sinners to come forward for sanctification hoping Jerry would lead the way, he discovered that he had missed his mark slightly to the left, where Myra sat crying uncontrollably over the sad story of the boy that drowned and was banished to everlasting torment. Jerry was deeply moved, not by what Sun had said, but by Myra's display of emotion. Jerry, sitting on top of the world with a check worth forty thousand dollars, believed he already had God's blessing and plenty of time to keep his covenant. He was drunk with success. His deepest convictions lay with his own talent, and not with the blessing of a poor preacher. But he looked at Myra and thought here was a girl so good and kind that her heart was filled with compassion for the subject of Sun's sermon. He wanted to squeeze her and kiss the tears away. Here sat the girl he had always wanted; what a wife she would make when he would preach again!

Myra was not quite what she appeared to be. Granted, she was a fitting candidate for a preacher's wife, but more than anything else, she was scared to death. She was utterly frightened by her initiation into a religion that left little hope for those who had not experienced the mysteries of sanctification. Far beyond her Baptist upbringing was Sun's sermon-cum-harangue. Had she not been too petrified to move, Myra would have surrendered her life to Sun, Christ and things that go bump in the night. Her next voluntary action was to limp out of the tabernacle under Jerry's assistance.

Jerry was impressed by Myra's sanctity, her lofty spirit and unblemished soul.

Myra was impressed by fear.

Sunday evening, the visitors had no choice but to bed down at Jay's sister Grace's house. There were enough beds to accommodate the adults, but the kids would have to sleep on the floor. Lying down next to Jerry, Myra considered the risk that their puppy love might mature under such sleeping arrangements. She turned her face to the wall and spent a sleepless night worrying that Jerry would take the perfect opportunity to kiss her. She was relieved and slightly perturbed in the way only a woman in love can be to find that he was a perfect gentleman.

Jerry and Myra visited his family in Ferriday on Monday, and as he related the glorious story of the past nine months, Mamie looked wistfully out the window and complimented her son's new car, revealing her disappointment at not being the first person on his gift list to receive an automobile.

"I'm gonna buy you a new car just as soon as I get back to Memphis, Mamma," said Jerry. "Too bad I ain't got my money with me or I'd do it today. All I have is this big check I can't cash around here."

"Where do you keep all that money you make on the road?" Mamie asked.

"Lois has it."

"Lois? What's she doin' with your money?"

"Oh, I guess I forgot to tell you. Lois is the treasurer of my new comp'ny," Jerry said proudly. "Yeah, we got us a reg'lar corporation, Jerry Lee Lewis Enterprises. I'm the president, nat-chally."

"Lois keeps the money?" Mamie repeated.

"Well, yeah, Mamma, she is the treasurer. She's s'posed to. I get my share."

"Your share? What is your share?"

"Well, I get fifty percent an' Jay gets fifty percent, after we pay Russ an' the expenses an' the agents. Of course, I don't split my royalties with nobody."

"Fifty percent?" Mamie asked with surprise. "You should be gettin' more'n that, you bein' the star of the show. Jay don't sing on your records, does he? He don't write your songs, does he? He don't book shows no more, does he? What gives him fifty percent of your money?"

"Mamie . . ." Elmo began to interfere.

"Shut up. I'll handle this. Look, I don't like them handlin' my boy's money. If he needs somebody to look after his money, I'll do it. How can you trust anybody over your own mother?" she demanded of Jerry. "The Browns are jus' cousins. You send the money to me. I'll look after it. We gonna put a stop to this half 'n' half bizness right now."

"Yes, ma'am," said Jerry, turning to leave. He walked out of the room, grabbed Myra by the hand and led her out to his car. They jumped into the convertible and sped away from the mad crush of fans, friends and family trying to pet him into poverty. As the house vanished in the rearview mirror, the tension eased from Jerry's shoulders until Myra spoke.

"You know what I'd like?" she asked.

"What?" he snapped. "What is it you want?"

"A butterscotch sundae," she said dreamily.

Jerry breathed a sigh and redirected his course in search of a custard stand. He had to stop for gasoline first. The cashier behind the counter was an old familiar face who asked Jerry about his success. Myra watched their conversation and smiled when they looked at her. She could not make out what they were saying, but they seemed to be making mention of her. When Jerry returned to the car, Myra asked him what the conversation was all about.

"You," he smiled. "He asked me who you were, an' I tol' him you were gonna be my next wife."

Myra laughed. That was a hot one.

The trip was nearing the end as the troupe made their way along the Florida-Georgia borderline to spend the last three days on the coast at Fernandina Beach. It was there that the remaining days of Myra's romance were spent with Jerry, walking the bright white beaches, sometimes swimming, sometimes running, sometimes playing in the sand. The setting was perfect for the blossoming of her first love, but a pocket calendar in her purse reminded her that it would soon be over.

Myra had felt heartsease as her first kiss from Jerry obliterated the sordid assault of Woodall. Jerry was her salvation; it mattered not that he was an older, married cousin. On their last night together, they walked along a littoral path hand in hand, and Myra, despondent at contemplating that soft-boiled sentiment, clutched him tighter as tears formed a chaplet down her cheeks. He wrote "I love you" along the dunes and Myra answered with puerile hearts embracing their initials.

Love comes and goes, Myra thought, and this one has ended all too soon. She returned to Memphis to begin the rest of a life that would never again be as romantic as it had been during those few brief days in the August of 1957. When Lois took her to buy print dresses and pencils for school, Myra's summer of love was over. Stranded at her strandline, there would never be another summer such as that, Myra feared. And there never was.

"I want a divorce," Jerry said to Grover McCormick, attorney at law.

"I understand that, Mr. Lewis. I've talked to Jud Phillips, and he's told me about the separation. It's a start, but if you've made as much money as I think you have, you can count on her lawyer comin' after it. I'll have to have a lot more information to hang her. Let's start at the beginning. You were married when and where?"

"Hell, I don't know."

"Take a guess," McCormick prompted.

"All right, February fourteenth, Nineteen fifty-three," Jerry said, narrowly missing the correct date by seven months and three days, "in Fayette, Miss'ippi."

"Any children?"

"Yeah, one. Two. Well, one of 'em's mine an' the other one ain't."

"Tell me about it," McCormick said, pad and pencil poised for a juicy tale.

"Well, back when I was jus' startin' out playin' in clubs, I wasn't makin' much an' we was pretty bad off," Jerry recalled. "We had the first child, Junior, in November of fifty-four, an' I was workin' diff'rent jobs just to get by. Jane didn't like me workin' in clubs, an' we fought like cats 'n' dogs all the time. Then, around Feb'uary of the followin' year, she up 'n' left me an' went to live in Monroe. She even sued me for nonsupport, an' I had to pay her forty dollars a month for about three months."

"You did nothing to provoke her actions?"

"No. Hell, no. All I did was go to Nashville for a few days to try for a record deal, an' when I come back, she'd already been to court. While we was separated, Jane was runnin' around with this other feller an' got pregnant. She come back to me an' begged me to take her back an' swore up 'n' down that she'd never look at another man, an' I felt sorry for her an' took her back like a damn fool. When she had the child, she said she didn't 'spect me to raise him, an' sent him off to her sister Jewell to raise," Jerry said, continuing to project an air of innocence.

"Aside from the wild parties, were there any other acts of immorality or adultery, any examples of her bad character?" McCormick asked.

"She's got a temper, if that's what you mean," Jerry replied. "She uses cuss words. In the early part of fifty-four, when I was workin' in the clubs in Natchez, she knocked out all the windows of my car."

"Why?"

"No reason. Jus' mad, I guess."

"Go on, you said something about foul language—"

"There was the time she used the Lord's name in vain. She'd hung too many things on a flimsy curtain rod in the closet an' the whole thing collapsed an' she said G-D."

"And?" McCormick asked, with eyebrows raised.

"That's it," said Jerry. "That may not seem bad to you, but I was raised in a good Christian home an' I was taught not to use them words. I went to Bible school. I preached. My cousins are preachers. We don't use them words."

"All right, Mr. Lewis, I understand. Now, tell me, since your rise to fame, have you allowed Jane to share in your wealth?"

"Hell, yeah. I got her a nice house, bought her a Cadillac, give her whatever she wanted..."

"And that did not change her attitude toward you, make her more appreciative?" McCormick doubted.

"Hell, no," Jerry persisted. "She started runnin' around to nightclubs an' beer joints, which is another thing I don't allow. I might've worked in some o'these places, but I never hung out in 'em. Then she started havin' them wild parties at home, jus' to embarrass me in front of the people I work with."

"One last thing and I think I'll have just about all I need—what can you say in defense to allegations of your bad character that she might try to use against you?"

"There ain't none that I can think of," Jerry said without reservation. "I've never done anything to make her mad or jealous. Now, I know a lotta folks don't approve of the songs I sing or the places I work in, but I've also played in churches an' revivals. I don't run around with other women, don't drink, don't smoke, don't swear. It ain't my fault if I gotta travel a lot. I still take care of my fam'ly."

McCormick nodded. "You'll get your divorce all right, Mr. Lewis, but these accusations are gonna show Jane to be an unfit mother. The court is gonna want to know the extent of your concern for your son. Do you want custody of Junior?"

"Can I do that? I mean, can you take a child from his mother?"

"Sure, if you wanna play hard ball. But with your lifestyle, you won't appear to be a much better alternative."

"Well, I'd like to give Junior to my mother to raise. Can we do that?"

"Perhaps, but it'll take some doin'. I suggest we ask for custody and then go into it later with the judge," McCormick said with a wink, reminding Jerry of his former position on the bench. "In the meantime, young feller, I'll draw up the papers for you to sign and we'll get together again to review Jane's answer."

Jerry's petition for divorce was filed in the Circuit Court of Shelby County, Tennessee, on September 9, 1957. Jane employed a Natchez law firm with a Memphis affiliate for her defense and counterattack. Rather than admit to what Jerry alleged in his suit, Jane decided to file a cross-petition and fight him every inch of the way. "The stuff he says in here ain't true," she told her attorney. "He don't even have the correct date of our marriage."

"He goes on at length about cussin' and fightin' and one thing and another. Tell me your version of what the relationship was like," the attorney said.

"Well, we did fuss sometimes, but I never abused or neglected him like he says. He says I never loved him an' that I led my own life, but that ain't true, either. It wasn't as bad as he wants people to believe. I didn't break any windows in his car. I never made him work nights in bars to support me. He was doin' that before we got married."

"What about this instance in February of fifty-five when he says you abandoned him?"

"That's when I went over to Hazelhurst to visit my gran'father when he was sick," Jane remembered. "We was livin' in Jonesville at the time. I was only gone a few days. When I come back, I saw Jerry in a department store downtown an' he tol' me to pack up an' move to my sister's house in Monroe 'cause he said he didn't want me around anymore. So, I moved in with my sister, an' he ran off to Nashville for a month or two. He left me with no money, an' I had to go to court an' ask for support. The judge said I was to get forty dollars a month from Jerry, but he never sent it an' they put him in jail. In the three months we were separated, he only gimme about seventy dollars."

"And it was during this time that you were supposedly made pregnant by another man who is not named in the suit—"

"That's what he says. He says I came beggin' for him to take me back, but that never happened. When we had been split up about three months, he tol' me to bring Junior to his mother's house an' *he* s'gested we get back together. I moved in with him again an' he got me pregnant about a month later," Jane explained.

"He says he denied the child and that your sister cares for him," the counselor continued.

"He never did come right out an' say that Ronnie wasn't his. He paid the hospital bills an' everything. Jerry and his mother said Ronnie wasn't a Lewis 'cause he had dark hair, but, y'know, I didn't think they were serious."

"Why do you think Jerry says these hurtful things?"

"To keep from havin' to gimme money. He's been tellin' people that if he can prove Ronnie isn't his, he'll have grounds for divorce an' won't have to pay me any alimony or child support. He's got a guy workin' for him named Turner that he talked into gettin' up on the witness stand and admit that he's the father of our child."

"What about his charges of your drinkin' and runnin' around?"

"Lies, all lies. It's jus' part of his scheme. He'll say anything to protect himself."

"What about last July when he says you and two girls threw a party at your home where you committed an act of adultery?"

"This is the first I've heard of that crazy story," Jane refuted. "He's got that all wrong from somebody. What happened was, his sister Frankie Jean was stayin' with us, an' his cousin Myra come to visit one afternoon. Two of their boyfriends came by an' wanted to take 'em out. Frankie was separated from her husband, so she went out, but I wouldn't let Myra go, 'cause her mother don't allow her to date. She's too young. So, Myra's date left, an' me an' Myra stayed home with Junior."

"When Jerry called a few days later and told you to get out, what did you say?"

"I said that whoever tol' him the story about me havin' a party was lyin' an' that I hadn't been out with anybody, but he didn't listen an' I had no choice but leave when his daddy come for me."

"Has Jerry given you any money since then?"

"Twenty dollars on the day I left Memphis, an' that's it."

"Mrs. Lewis, the petition swears that Jerry gave you money, a new Cadillac and a nice house to live in. Isn't that true?"

"I should say not. He never gimme any money, not even for food. As for that Cadillac, it was his an' sometimes he lemme use it. It wasn't even new. It was about a hundred years old. And the house was rented month to month, the rent was always overdue, and if I hadn't left when I did, they'd've prob'ly thrown me an' my baby in the street."

"All right, Mrs. Lewis," the counselor consoled, "I believe you. Now that you've answered Jerry's complaint, let's get down to your cross-petition."

"Before we start, I guess I should tell you that Jerry wasn't divorced from his first wife when we married," Jane said.

"Did you know about the first wife?"

"No, my brother tol' me about a week after we married."

"That could present a problem. We'll have to show that Jerry misrepresented the facts to you, so that you will not be liable for knowingly entering into a bigamous marriage. In order to protect your claim, we'll have to state that he deceived you into marrying him."

"Whatever you say," Jane agreed, "but I really had no idea Jerry was still married to Dorothy."

"Good. Now, tell me, you mentioned earlier that you had a lot of fights. Did he ever leave you?"

"Many times he'd go off an' stay a night or two with his folks. There were only two times I can think of when he was gone for a long time. Once, when we'd been married about six months, he took off for two weeks, an' then after Junior was born, he ran off to Nashville for about a month."

"Did he leave you with money and provisions? Did he tell you where he would be or when he was coming back?"

"No, I didn't know where he was or when he was comin' back. He spent all our money on a car, an' left me with eighty-two cents an' six cans of milk. Me with a newborn infant an' no job or nothin'."

"All right," the attorney said in a tone which expressed sympathy and concern, "I'll draw up the papers and send them to Memphis before the eighteenth. We'll ask for a divorce on grounds that Jerry was still married to his first wife, and include harassment, humiliation, desertion and that he forced you from your home. I don't know why he filed for a divorce in the first place, since you were never legally married. The court could still throw the whole thing out. Let's hope for the best. Just be prepared for anything."

"I should be tellin' you that," said Jane.

On September 19, Jerry received an urgent telephone call from his attorney. McCormick was troubled by the answer to the divorce petition and Jane's cross-action, which revealed many facts which Jerry had neglected to tell him. "Why the hell didn't you tell me you were married before?" McCormick hollered at Jerry.

"You didn't ask me," Jerry retorted. "Besides, I didn't think it was important. Dorothy ain't got nothin' to do with my divorce from Jane."

"The hell she don't," McCormick said, still hollering. "You married Jane before you were divorced from Dorothy, right? It says so in the answer here."

"So?" Jerry asked with embarrassment.

"So, you don't need a divorce from Jane," McCormick railed.

"You weren't legally married to begin with. In other words, Jerry, you're not married, period."

"But we got a kid . . ."

"I don't care if you got ten kids. How long did you live together?"

"About four years, why?"

"Then you ain't even common-law married, accordin' to Louisiana. It takes five years to become common law where you come from," McCormick explained.

"You mean . . . ?"

"Exactly."

"And there's nothin' she can do to me?" Jerry asked with mounting joy.

"Nothing. You're completely and absolutely scot-free."

"What do I do now? I mean, about the suit an' all?"

"What you should do is drop your suit and get Jane to do the same, then drift out of the picture quiet-like," McCormick advised. "Go back to her and make up. Offer her money. Anything. Do whatever you have to do to get her to tear up that petition, and then you can tell her to go straight to the devil."

Jerry bit his tongue at the thought of having to reconcile with Jane. It took him nearly a month to work up to it, but nevertheless, he misplaced his anger and suggested Jane forgive and forget as he had and, as so many times before, she agreed to a reconciliation and dismissed her petition in anticipation of returning to Jerry's side to share in his rapidly mounting wealth and the spotlight growing ever brighter. When her claim had been abandoned, Jerry excused himself from their rehabilitated home recommending she remain with family, while he returned to a torturous tour and promised to come back for her in style with a brand new car and a pocketful of money. He didn't.

And so, Jerry and Jane did not get a divorce. They did not need one. At least, not right away.

"Whole Lot of Shakin' Going On" had sold into the millions, and orders continued to arrive daily at Sun in mid-September. Because Sam Phillips, who could find clouds on the clearest horizon, refused to advance-order a surplus for fear of losing an investment, the pressing plant complained that they could not fill orders for Jerry's single at the same time large orders were placed on products by Johnny Cash, Carl Perkins and Warren Smith.

"To hell with 'em!" Sam said. "Forget Warren Smith, shelve it. Fill the Lewis orders first!"

"Whoa, Sam," said Jud. "You better watch what you're doin'. Them boys ain't gonna like you cuttin' 'em off thataway."

"We don't got no choice, Jud. Jerry Lee is the biggest thing we got. This is a small comp'ny, funds are limited and we got to put everything behind the leader. We'll get around to the rest of 'em."

"If you're so hot on Jerry, let's discuss his management," Jud said, reviving an old argument. "This thing's gettin' outta hand. He's got a million-sellin' single and oughta have a big tour lined up by now. I keep tellin' ya we ain't in the management bizness, as much as you'd like for us to be. I know you're afraid of losin' this boy, but what he needs is a Tom Parker. Say what you want, but Parker's handled Elvis just right. He's manipulated the personal-appearance fee to top dollar, he's a genius at promotion and has marketed everything from buttons and photos to T-shirts, jewelry, bubble-gum cards, pens, notebooks, dolls—hell, they even got Elvis Presley cologne and lipstick now, for chrissake. At the core of the whole structure is a new single every ninety days and an extended-play record practic'ly every other month. You've seen what Lewis can do. He's in Elvis's class. Someone should be movin' him in the same direction. We need a strong individual to manage Jerry. I've asked around, and the man for the job is Oscar Davis, who's in Richmond with the Philip Morris tour. He's agreed to come down here an' talk to us."

"I tol' you before, I don't want him," Sam refused. "The last thing we need is some hotshot packin' Jerry's head with talk of bigger labels. It'll be Elvis all over again. At least with Bob Neal we're safe. He's my partner, and he ain't gonna do anything but book shows and leave the career decisions to us."

"That's just it, Sam," Jud argued, "Jerry needs more than that. He deserves more than that. Now, Oscar's comin' to see us. Pay him the courtesy of hearin' him out."

At the meeting between the Phillips brothers and Oscar Davis, the negotiators were at loggerheads within the first few minutes. Oscar, having met and liked Jerry, was prepared to book him immediately into a thirty-five-hundred-dollar-a-day engagement in New Orleans and a tour of Australia. Sam agreed to the proposition on one condition: that Oscar kick back half of his 10 percent commission to him.

"We have nothing more to discuss," said Oscar, and asked Jud to drive him back to the airport. "That's the craziest thing I've ever heard—taking half of a manager's commission."

"Look, Oscar, forget what Sam said, please. You an' I both know what we have here is a goldmine. I'll have Jerry sign a one-year contract naming you his exclusive manager, and let's pick up these dates you've lined up. I'll make sure Sam doesn't get in the way," Jud promised.

The contract was signed, and Oscar replaced Sam, Jud and Bob Neal as Jerry's manager/agent. For the first time, Jerry had the benefit of competent management, and Oscar, even if he needed a whip and a chair, was willing to tame the lion for 10 percent of a guaranteed fifteen hundred dollars a day. Jerry's faith in Jud was above reproach, and therefore the choice of Oscar was equally unquestioned. As far as Sam was concerned, he was not about to let Oscar replace him in Jerry's heart: Whenever Oscar gave Jerry ten thousand dollars for a week's work, Sam came behind him and cut a twenty, thirty or forty thousand dollar royalty check. "Don't forget who made you a hit, kid," was written all over it. When Oscar divulged plans for ten-day tours, Sam dangled a new release in front of Jerry. "Don't forget where your next hit is coming from," was written on its label.

Oscar had a hundred dates lined up, but how was Sam supposed to top "Whole Lot of Shakin' "?

"I already took care of that," Jud told his brother. "When we was in New York doin' Steve Allen, I took a copy of 'Shakin'' over to Hill and Range, the music publishers. They got a staff of songwriters workin' there, and what they did was they brought all the writers into the office an' played 'Shakin','' then asked which one could write a song like that for Jerry. A li'l colored feller named Blackwell jumped up an' said he could, an' they tell me he's sendin' us a song next week called 'Great Balls of Fire.'"

"Oh, yeah, Otis Blackwell," Sam recalled. "He wrote a coupla big ones for Elvis—'Don't Be Cruel' and 'All Shook Up,' I believe. He did 'Good Golly Miss Molly' for Little Richard, too. He's good. What else do we need to discuss at this point? Any complaints?"

"Just one, Mr. Phillips," said Jerry. "I'd like to make a change.

I don't like that corporation y'all set up. I don't like anybody holdin' my money. I want what's comin' to me after every show. No more accountin' an' puttin' the money away where I can't see it."

"What's the matter, Jerry, you don't trust Lois?" Jay asked indignantly.

"No, it ain't that, it's jus' that I like to know where my money is, an' I don't like havin' to ask for it. If I wanna go out an' buy a new car, I don't wanna have to come runnin' to Lois an' ask her for the money," he said, echoing his mother's complaint.

"You jus' bought a new convertible Cadillac," Jay accused. "You didn't have any problem then, did you?"

"No."

"All right, then."

"Look, I done made up my mind," Jerry said finally. "No more corporation. I'm takin' my money an' buyin' my folks a new house an' a new car. Another thing, I think we oughta talk about your fifty percent."

"Now, wait just a damn minnit," Jay spat. "If you ain't makin' enough to support your fam'ly, you ain't takin' it away from mine. You promised me on your word I'd get fifty percent—"

"Hold on, hold on," Jud stepped in. "Before we break up the act and Sam's office, let's talk peaceable about this thing. Jerry, if you don't like the corporation, we'll put it to bed. We only set the damn thing up as a convenient way to handle your money for you. If you think you can do better by some other method, then perhaps you should do so. We'll dissolve the enterprise, an' Jay will give you all your money an' you do whatever you think is best. I know what I got to do, and I best be gettin' on down the road."

"Where you goin'?" asked Sam.

"To sell some records," Jud said, walking out the door.

The highway was home for Jud during most of the year. All he needed was an old Greyhound bus and twenty grand to fix it up with bunks, stereo, television, lounges, kitchen and fully stocked wet bar, and Jud was prepared to take to the road on a trek to vend records door-to-door to distributors. Ten thousand copies of "Whole Lot of Shakin'" rode comfortably in the bay of the bus. Pulling up to a distributorship around lunchtime, Jud brought customers inside his rolling storehouse for a few drinks and a little shoptalk. He had been an understudy of Roy Acuff's promotional technique and was apprentice to Jimmy Durante at a time when the Schnozzola plugged radio stations. Jud's rap at times sounded like either mentor, and if the customer was unfamiliar with Sun's product, Jud could rely on any of a hundred tricks of the trade learned during his novitiate.

"Here, take ten copies of this record and a fifth of bourbon," Jud would tell a distributor. "Put these records in one or two of your juke boxes around town an' pass along a copy to the deejays, an' see if you don't have a hundred orders by Monday mornin'. Now, I can't be dealin' in no piddly amount. I start sellin' at a hundred copies—it's easier on the bookkeeper that way—but, I tell you what: I'll sell you twenty-five copies with a sell-or-return policy just to prove to you that they won't sit on your shelf."

Jud introduced the sell-or-return policy to the record business in order to introduce products to slumbering markets and places oppressed by prejudice, moral watchdogs and industry blacklists. Of course, as "Whole Lot of Shakin'" sold in the millions, Jud's work was made easier. Still, he had those offended by suggestive lyrics to win over. Jud had a knack for winning friends by catering to their private passions. Wherever he went, prospective business associates became his drinking buddies. This policy, which led to other friendly gestures such as cash gifts, became so prevalent in the incubating music industry that scarcely a newcomer could survive without it, and ultimately resulted in a U.S. Senate investigation into what became known as "payola." But in the early days, when a jackleg label out of Memphis went head-to-head with conglomerates, the underdog had to resort to some sort of equalizer, and in Jud's case, nothing worked so well as the pride of the distiller's art. Jud might walk into a target radio station with a bottle of bourbon and a copy of Jerry's record and leave an hour later with Jack Daniels on his breath and "Whole Lot of Shakin'" on the air. Deejays and those working on fixed incomes were impressed by Jud's generosity. They knew the Phillips boys did not have to be nice to anybody. Hell, they discovered Elvis Presley. People would stand outside Sun Records for three days in a hard rain just to shake Jud's hand. Still, Jud was quietly unaffected. He knew the big boss, but he never forgot the secretary, either.

"How the hell do you get in to see these people?" Sam was always asking his big brother.

"You get there by bein' nice to ever'body on the way in," said Jud. "Look, when you call a distributor on the phone, does he answer? No, his secretary does. She can tell you her boss is busy or out to lunch or go to hell. You have to take care of her if you wanna get to the head man, and whatever it costs in flowers or perfume can't begin to compare with what you get in return business."

"Great, but have you ever considered what happens to these accounts you've bought after you're gone? I mean, after you've left havin' made a lotta friends, what happens next week when I got another record to sell to these same folks an' you're down the road somewheres else? Somebody's got to come along behind you, or we can't effectively manage our territories and put all these bought 'n' paid for friendships to use. An' I can't afford to hire fifty more guys like you, either. I'd go bankrupt."

"I got hundreds of guys workin' for me for free," Jud said.

"I'm dyin' to hear how you pull that off," Sam retorted. "Where do you find all these eager souls willin' to work for nothin'?"

"The fire station."

"The fire station," Sam repeated.

"That's right. Every town has a fire department, and every station has fine young men that work for a small salary an' have plenty of free time. Every one of 'em jump at the chance to make five cents on every record they can sell as a local representative of Sun Records," Jud explained.

"That ain't legal, is it? To employ firemen?"

"'Course it is. An' I tell you somethin' else: People in small towns would rather do business with their neighbor than with a travelin' salesman. All I am is a country boy with a jackleg label sellin' songs by unknown artists. I got no money, no help and no connections. If you can figger out a better way to operate, I'm open to suggestions."

And so, in every whistle stop, Jud headed first for the fire station and then to his accounts to introduce the newest member of Sun's field staff. And firemen across America on their day off sold "Great Balls of Fire" for a five-cent cut to their local shops, distributors, bars and juke joints.

* * *

For every September morn that he was home, Jerry insisted on driving Myra to school in his new convertible. The custom began during a series of days when Myra had overslept and missed the bus because she had stayed up the night before to watch the late show with Jerry. The continuance of keeping company till all hours was affecting her schoolwork; that she kept company in provocative yet innocent baby-doll pajamas was affecting Jerry, driving him absolutely crazy.

Myra's arrival at school in a celebrity-chauffeur-driven Eldorado was an event rivaling the popularity of recess. Her classmates lined the driveway leading to the front entrance of the school and cheered as the coupe conveyed its precious cargo to the steps. Once the princess had arrived, classes could begin, and Myra's notability drove away with her carriage, leaving her melted into obscurity like Cinderella after midnight. For a few minutes each morning, Myra was somebody.

In the afternoons, Myra took the bus home and conducted private tours if Jerry could be heard practicing. After supper, Jerry devised one of a hundred different reasons for having to go somewhere, and Myra was always invited to go with him. On such a night, when wasting away for want of a Dairy Queen sundae had become an emergency, Jerry took Myra the long way around Coro Lake. He parked the car in a deserted spot with a view of the still water refulgent in a spoonful of moonlight.

"What are we stoppin' for?" asked Myra.

"Sit. Talk."

"About what?"

"Oh, anything," Jerry replied, somewhat annoyed at the dreamy mood being dismantled by her banter.

He watched her polish off the ice-cream treat, then set the empty plastic boat adrift on the black lagoon. She returned to his side and smiled vacantly, as if there were nothing on her mind and nothing to do. He kissed her. Without a warning or permission or an explanation of feeling or desire, he kissed her as if his touch related all he wished to say. In return, he felt a tremble which should have warned him that Myra was new to courtin' and sparkin'. He became carried away by her innocent willingness, her availability, and when matched with his newly acquired bachelor status and months of sexual starvation, the moment had the makings for burning, ravenous passion.

Before even Jerry was fully aware of his intentions, he had slipped out of his trousers and exposed his secrets to a bewildered concubine, hoping instinct might assert itself. In total misunderstanding of her cousin's advance, Myra thought she was the victim of a practical joke. Frustrated and bemused by her ineptitude, Jerry apologized until he began to laugh at her inexperience. He took her home, continuing to laugh away his nervous frustration, but before going inside, Jerry put a little something extra in his good-night kiss.

"Whole Lot of Shakin' Going On" reached the pinnacle of its success in mid-October. When Jerry realized that his first royalty check would not be his last, he finally cashed the faded and display-worn instrument. His new prosperity was evidenced by a new automobile parked in front of the new in-town address of Mr. and Mrs. Elmo Lewis. A new Ford and a rented brick house complete with indoor plumbing was high society in Ferriday, Louisiana, and the luxury of a ceramic bathtub was not lost on Frankie Jean, who soaked away as many as six hours a day.

Jerry spent his money as quickly as he could put his hands on it, confident that another earthshakin' single was somewhere in the vaults of Sun's tape library. He had finished sessions in which he covered every conceivable style, from the gospel strains of "Will the Circle Be Unbroken" and the ballad "Release Me" to "Shanty Town," "Mexicali Rose" and other blues and country tunes recovered from his childhood, when a package arrived postmarked New York City containing the Jack Hammer and Otis Blackwell composition "Great Balls of Fire," and the problem of finding a suitable encore to "Whole Lot of Shakin'" was solved. Early on the first Sunday in October, as the faithful were called to church, Jerry called Roland Janes and Jimmy Van Eaton to the studio and recorded the song, the first take being the best and the one chosen for release. Every educated ear that heard "Great Balls of Fire" knew it was going to be every note the hit "Whole Lot of Shakin'" had been.

To be safe, Sam Phillips selected Hank Williams's "You Win Again" for the flip side. Country was still Sun's biggest market, and he feared releasing two rock songs back to back would lose listeners. The finished product, known as Sun Number 281, sat on a shelf for a month, waiting for its predecessor to show the first signs of saturation.

Sunday, November 3, at eight o'clock in the evening, Jerry was the featured guest on Steve Allen's show, where "Great Balls of Fire" was presented to the public for the first time. On Monday, the band drove to Philadelphia to repeat the performance on *American Bandstand*. The response was staggering; the song became synonymous with its singer and Jerry became known to his audiences as the Great Ball of Fire. The single was released before "Whole Lot of Shakin'" ended its twenty-ninth-week stay in the charts, but due to Sam Phillip's cheeseparing policy of piecemeal release, a reluctance to give away promotional copies and disorganization in general, "Great Balls of Fire" slowly climbed into the charts.

At the same time, Warner Brothers was filming a feature-length motion picture entitled *Jamboree,* aimed at teen audiences and existing solely to promote a host of popular singers and their hit songs. Featured in the film were Fats Domino, Buddy Knox, Jimmy Bowen, Charlie Gracie, Frankie Avalon, Jodie Sands and The Four Coins, each singing one selection, many of which were written especially for the soundtrack. To attract the older generation, Count Basie and Joe Williams were included in the cast. Slim Whitman made a brief appearance on behalf of those who preferred country-western music, and Carl Perkins sang his newest, "Glad All Over." The most popular song to evolve from *Jamboree* was the latest rocker from Jerry Lee Lewis, "Great Balls of Fire."

The studio staff on hand for the recording of Jerry's segment of the film held an impromptu party when he pantomimed a lip-synched version of "Great Balls of Fire" different from the single. After director Ray Lockwood captured what he wanted on film, he pleaded for two encores of the real thing, and the set became a soiree as all work ceased for the remainder of the afternoon.

Jamboree was scheduled for release before the end of the year with premieres confirmed as far away as Australia, an area experiencing a rock 'n' roll boom in spite of its remoteness from the center of activity. Jerry attended a private screening and glanced at his wristwatch constantly to keep track of the precise moment when his entrance occurred. When he took Myra to see the movie, he refused to walk into the theater until moments before he appeared on screen.

"But I wanna see the whole thing," Myra complained.

"You don't need to," Jerry contradicted. "There's nothin' else in it you'd wanna see. There ain't nothin' to it but my song, anyhow. We'll watch me, then leave."

"But I won't know what the movie's about," she argued.

"It's about an hour an' a half too long," Jerry said flatly.

They witnessed precisely one minute and forty-seven seconds of *Jamboree* before Myra found herself back on the street blinking her eyes, which barely had time to adapt to the darkened theater. As exciting as it was to have seen Jerry and her dad on the silver screen, the thrill lasted about as long as a plunge from a high dive and left something to be desired.

"Now what do ya wanna do?" Jerry asked.

"See it again," said Myra.

"We'll hafta wait two hours for my part to come around again," he calculated.

"Forget it," she said. "Let's go home."

It was still early in the evening when they returned from their abbreviated date. Lois and Jay were gone, and Myra and Jerry found themselves alone with nothing to do. Myra put Jerry's music on the phonograph, casting Elvis aside, which she knew would gratify her cousin. He smiled. She smiled back. He placed her hand in his and led her down the hallway to her bedroom, his guest room. As he prompted her gently toward the bed, she recalled memories of Woodall when Jerry asked her, "Have you ever done It?"

She nodded, not meaning the way in which Jerry imagined, creating an everlasting misunderstanding between them. He believed her to be experienced, but never learned the nature of her darkest secret. She waited and watched his expression when she had admitted her flaw. Now that he knew, would he still want her?

Jerry asked no further questions. He smiled his nervous smile, curling the right side of his mouth into a sneer, embarrassed in attempting to be delicate. His nervousness shook her; he wasn't very good at seduction and she didn't know enough to help him. She could have scared him, scarred him, by running away, but the fear which she anticipated failed to appear. Worse for him was that she stood motionless as a mannequin, a mixed look of anguish and doubt tempering her silent plea for relief from the burden that had frustrated her for so long, neither encouraging nor guarding against his advances. It was either sweep her off her feet or ask permission, and succumbing to overpowering desire, Jerry drew Myra into a deep embrace. To the beat of his music, to the beat of two hearts, the house was filled with release, relief and restoration.

And Myra lay awake through many long nights, wondering, "What am I going to do now?"

In late November, concert promoter Doc Harris came up with a novel promotion which pitted reigning stars of different musical styles in a battle of the bands. In Boston and Hartford, no greater polarity existed than the battles staged between crooner Andy Williams, representing sweetness and light, the champion of chaperoned cotillions, clean cut and stuffed into a tux, and Jerry Lee Lewis, representing demons and darkness, the wild man of rock 'n' roll, the Great Ball of Fire. The experiment was supposed to reveal how Andy's fans would react to Jerry and vice versa, but lacking an equal distribution of tickets or sections reserved for partisans, it was difficult to judge the number of converts in the crowd. Jerry's fans suffered through Andy's set; bobby-soxers beat a path to the exits when shakin' chipped plaster off the walls. So much for science.

While holed up in Boston's Statler Hotel, Jerry contemplated the enigma of his loneliness. There must have been a million girls who would kill for the pleasure of his company. He could search the sea of faces surrounding his stage and choose from among them. Those with even the most basic familiarity with biology knew what the great balls of fire were and how to make that fire hotter and how to put it out. They lined up a hundred-deep backstage and refused to leave until each had kissed the Killer. His getaway in a brand-new Buick had been stopped by fans blocking all accesses, and when enough of them couldn't get to him through the windows, they covered the car till their weight caved the roof. They took his shirt or pieces thereof and whatever would come loose, from the chrome on his car to the hair on his head. His body they could never have.

Jerry loved his crowds collectively but hated the girls individually. He hated their winks and nods, the come-ons and bedroom looks. It was shameless and disgusting. There wasn't a mother in the lot. And by the time he had brought them to their feet, mobbing the stage and reaching out for his sanctification, the appalled preacher in him crushed upraised palms and kicked away crazy arms longing to hold him. Animosity toward his allegiants was the first of many amazing self-contradictions indicating the workings of a troubled mind.

Jerry decided that the third Mrs. Lewis would have to be more like Lois Brown. Lois catered to Jay's slightest wish, even putting him above their children. Jerry liked the way Jay got what he wanted whether he whispered or cracked the whip. Most of all, Jerry was impressed by Lois herself. She was a lady first and foremost, Jerry's highest compliment to members of the fair sex. She was quiet and reserved, always nicely dressed and her hair coiffed in a stylish fashion. Jay never had to ask for his dinner or hunt for clean socks, and whenever he returned to the road, Lois had his bags packed and waiting at the door. And while he was away, Jay never had to worry where his wife was or whom she was with, for Lois was always cheerfully attending to her housework, always listening for Jay's call. Yes, Jerry thought, the next Mrs. Lewis will have to be the image of Lois Brown.

Like Myra, for instance. She was, after all, Lois's daughter. Although she was thirteen, she had learned many of the uxorial skills and manners from her mother. Remembering the advice of his drummer, the best of all possible worlds would be to take Myra straight from Lois and raise her to become a faithful wife and mother. That notion was absolutely ridiculous: Not only was Myra just thirteen, she was his second cousin and his partner's daughter. Regardless, the more Jerry thought of Myra, the more he missed her, and rather than sit alone in a dark hotel room, he called her to say, "I'm feelin' far away from home an' wanted to hear a friendly voice."

During the next few days, Jerry's loneliness became so frequent that he called to talk to Myra four and five times a day, sometimes late into the night. In no time at all, Lois was on the phone to Jay telling him to put a stop to whatever was going on. "If this callin' doesn't quit," Lois threatened, "we're gonna have to send Myra away to boardin' school."

Jay, a man of few words, headed down the hall to have a few

well-chosen ones with Jerry. "What are you doin' callin' home like that all the time?"

"I'm jus' talkin' to Myra," said Jerry.

"What for?"

"Cheer her up about her schoolwork."

"She don't need cheerin' up at three in the mornin', does she?"

"Sometimes it's that late 'fore we get back to the hotel."

"She don't need cheerin' up ten times a day, does she?"

"Nothin' else to do." Jerry shrugged.

Dissatisfied with Jerry's attitude, Jay went to Jud's room and dragged him downstairs for a few drinks. It didn't take long to get around to what was on his mind, as queer as it sounded coming out of his mouth. "I think somethin's goin' on between Jerry an' my daughter."

Jud laughed. "Jay, you're drunk. You been on the road too long . . ."

"No, I ain't. I'm tellin' you what my wife said a li'l while ago. She said Jerry's been callin' at all hours to talk to Myra. Said one night she found her sittin' in the pantry past two in the mornin' whisperin' somethin' to him over the phone. Now, does that sound right to you?"

"He's just homesick, Jay," Jud reassured.

"All the same, I wish you'd take him aside an' talk to him. Find out what's the story here."

"Yeah, okay, Jay, don't worry about it. I'll take care of it."

Between shows the following night, Jud took Jerry for a spin in a hired cab. "I wanna talk to you about this thing that's got Jay an' Lois crazy," Jud said. "They say you're callin' the house too much an' botherin' Myra."

Jerry said nothing.

"They think y'all got somethin' goin' on."

Jerry said nothing.

"They're thinkin' about shippin' her off to boardin' school."

That statement produced a response. Slight as it was, Jud saw Jerry flinch. Still, he remained silent.

"So, I jus' thought I'd put a bug in yer ear," Jud said. "I mean, it would come as a surprise to me if a guy like you, in your position, would have trouble gettin' girls. It's not like you gotta hit on a child, for godsake. What is she, twelve, thirteen?"

"Now, hold on, Mr. Phillips, there's nothin' like that goin' on 'tween me an' Myra. An' she ain't a child, anyway. I don't care how old she is," Jerry defended, "she ain't no child."

"Well, whatever," Jud conceded. "Jus' cool it, will ya?"

"There's nothin' to cool. There ain't a word of truth to any of it."

"I didn't think so," and Jud said the same thing to Jay when, after the second show, they settled into the hotel bar. Even as Jud convinced Jay that the whole thing had been blown out of proportion, Jerry was on the phone ringing up Myra and her mother out of a sound sleep. His second call was to the reservation desk at the airport. The next morning, as the trio moved on to Cleveland for a show, Jerry was preparing to sneak away on another flight home to see Myra.

Jerry was not missed till late afternoon, when Jay, upon hearing further complaints of the same nature from Lois, stormed down the hall to Jud's room and demanded action. "Jud!" Jay hollered, "I want you to go down there an' tell Jerry to lay off before I kill the li'l sonofabitch!"

"What's up yer ass now, J. W.?" Jud asked.

"I tol' ya, he's foolin' around with my daughter an' I want a stop to it right now. Lois jus' called and said he's at it again with the phone calls."

"Well, you find him an' I'll talk to him. The promoter's been lookin' for him all day to show up for rehearsal an' I ain't been able to find him. If it'll make you feel better, I'll call Sam right now an' see what he says about all this."

"Call somebody," said Jay. "Do somethin'."

"Sam?" Jud said into the receiver, "I got a problem up here an' I wanna talk to you about it. It's Jerry. No, he ain't in jail, 'tho I couldn't swear to it right this minute. He's actin' funny. I know he always acts that way. No, what it is, see, he's been callin' Myra, Jay's daughter. An' Jay says he thinks there's somethin' goin' on. Jay, Sam says you're crazy. Sam, I think there's somethin' goin' on, too. Jay, Sam says we're both crazy. Well, that's all I had to tell you. We got a show tonight here in Cleveland for Bill Randall, then we'll be home. 'Bye."

"No help?" Jay asked.

"No help. Go find Jerry an' let's talk. If he ain't in his room, ask the front desk if they know where he is."

Jay was gone all of five minutes. He returned to Jud's room out of breath, repeating the bellhop's claim that Jerry had taken a taxi to the airport hours ago.

"The airport?" Jud asked. "Where the hell is he goin'? He's got a show to do tonight!"

Jud called the reservation counter at the airport. Yes, a Jerry Lewis had departed on an earlier flight to Memphis. No, it was a one-way fare. Jud called Sam, who was beginning to think the entire affair was some sort of joke, and told him to rush right over to the Browns', tackle Jerry and put him on the next flight to Cleveland. Sam refused to budge before he had the chance to expose the prank by calling the Browns first to see if Jerry was there.

Myra had been sitting in the living room talking to her cousin for a scant few minutes when Sam's call came. She did not know that Jerry was AWOL and that in three hours thousands of Cleveland's teens would be shouting for his show. Sam sped to Coro Lake still under the impression that Myra was part of the elaborate hoax and could hardly believe his eyes when he found Jerry pleasantly chatting away the afternoon. Without a word of explanation, Sam jerked Jerry out of his seat, into his car and to the airport, where he was loaded onto a chartered jet under Sam's personal supervision and sent back to Cleveland, with Sam hollering all the while, "This is gonna cost you, Jerry Lee! This is gonna cost you! It's comin' outta your royalties!"

Jerry's entrance was delayed long enough to have worked the crowd into a fevered pitch. Bloodshed was prevented only by Jerry's introduction the moment he entered the building. After the show, Jud and Jay cornered him in the dressing room, wanting to know what was the big idea in bolting for home.

"I jus' felt like it," Jerry set forth, and said no more.

"This is what I was afraid of," Jud said privately to Jay. "Jerry's gettin' a big head. He's findin' out what it is to be a star. He's findin' out how much power he has, how far he can push. He's tryin' to find the breakin' point, an' I guess the time has come for him to find out who's boss."

"Who is boss?" asked Jay.

"That's a good question," Jud said solemnly.

At home for Thanksgiving, Jerry called on an old friend named Glenda Burgess. "Glenda, I want you to do me a favor," he said.

"I want you to go with me to get a marriage license. It's not for us, it's for me an' someone else. She's too young to get a license, so I need you to fill in for her. Nobody knows I'm doin' this, not even her, so it's gotta be quiet-like."

Glenda was a big woman with a chubby, round face, and at age twenty-two did not look much like the girl she was impersonating. The clerk at the Health Department didn't care who she was. He did not ask for identification or proof of the falsified information Jerry supplied him. The clerk simply gave Jerry a license to marry whoever claimed to be Myra Brown.

It took Jerry several days to work up enough courage to move into action. On the tenth of December at seven o'clock, he reached the ultimate disastrous decision to marry his thirteen-year-old cousin. Myra was in the living room hammering out her homework when fantasy formed an immovable impression in Jerry's mind that here sat the love of his life. He'd been from Miami to Manhattan entertaining hundreds of thousands of eager, willing and able-bodied maidens of legal marrying age, yet all the while the one he had been waiting for was living under the same roof. As Myra put her books away, Jerry called her outside. "I wanna show you somethin'," he said. "It's in the car."

They climbed into his Cadillac. Instead of putting the key in the ignition, Jerry reached into the glove compartment and pulled out a folded paper. "It's a marriage license," he said. "It's for you 'n' me."

Myra looked at the florid form and was unable to read the words. "I thought you had to stand there and say somethin'," she cried, mistakenly thinking the document meant they were already married without benefit of ceremony.

"This is only a license, Myra, a permit. I wanna marry you," he proposed.

"But you're still married to Jane," she protested.

"No, I'm not. Judge McCormick said we never was married."

"But I'm only thirteen years old," she rebutted.

"You're almost fully grown," he observed. "You're a woman. Heck, my sister got married when she was twelve—"

"What about school?"

"You can quit."

"Let's wait three or four years," she said, feeling threatened.

"It's now or never," he replied.

Myra jumped out of the car and slammed the door. Jerry chased her up the front steps, leaping over a dog who was stirred by the commotion.

"Get outta my way, you damn dog," Jerry spat.

"Yeah, get outta my way, you damn dog," Myra repeated.

"Ladies don't talk like that," Jerry scolded. "Don't ever let me hear you say that word again."

"You ain't my daddy," she said, reaching for the doorknob.

"Hey, wait, Myra, don't go inside yet. I wanna talk to you some. I'm askin' you to marry me."

"Shhh!" she hissed. "Don't talk so loud. Mamma an' Daddy'll hear you."

"I said I wanna marry you. I love you."

"You're as old as my daddy," Myra whined.

"That don't matter one bit," he said, retreating into a rigamarole of rationale. "I got two hit records, dates booked up six months in advance, a hunnert thousand dollars—what else do you need?"

"Time to think," she answered.

"No time for that. It's now or never."

Myra retreated to her room and sat up all night in bed, debating whether or not to marry. Like most little girls, she wanted to get married and have a real baby doll. She wanted a real dollhouse to live in, too. She also wanted out of school. Among the dissentient points, of which there were many, she was reminded of her young years and her kinship to Jerry. Then there were her parents to contend with, not to mention Jane. It certainly would be rough going in the beginning, that is, provided there would not be a killing or two when the marriage was found out.

The controversial soliloquy came down to the last point, the deciding factor outweighing all other aspects: the disgrace of her despoiled virginity. Her ruination at the hands of good neighbor Woodall shamed her as if she were somehow to blame for the assault; she must have done something to deserve it, although she didn't know what. She was damaged goods, a curse which Myra feared but was too young to fully comprehend. But Jerry had been familiar with her flaw and it had not seemed to make any difference to him. He wanted her future, not an explanation of her past. Would any boy come along after Jerry who would have his same care and understanding? Probably not. Could she find compassion for her imperfection elsewhere? She could never tell. Who but Jerry could love someone like her? No one.

And with the cunning, self-deluding logic of a child, Myra arrived at a decision she should never have had to make, for which the world would brand her "Child Bride," and through which she was to find her greatest joys and deepest sorrows.

On December 12, 1957, at 1:10 P.M., Jerry Lee Lewis, twenty-two, married Myra Gale Brown, thirteen, in the wedding chapel at Hernando, Mississippi, before the Reverend M. C. Whitten. Hernando was a popular spot for eloping couples, those marrying without parental consent and the underaged. The bride wore a new red dress her mother had picked out as part of her school wardrobe.

The chapel was located twenty miles south of Memphis in the old Spencer house, a white clapboard structure with green shutters and a sign which read, "Where your sacred hour of today becomes tender memories of tomorrow." What was once a dining room was now the chapel, consisting of makeshift wooden pews and six small pots of fresh flowers. The windows had been replaced with a pale blue pattern of stained glass which chilled the rosy glow of young brides.

The Baptist ceremony was over in a second and sealed only with a kiss; the groom did not have time to buy a ring. Having nowhere to go and nothing else to do, the newlyweds drove home, Myra dreading what was to follow so that she wished she could pretend the whole affair had never happened. Dinner was partaken uneventfully, and at bedtime Jerry and Myra still had not worked up the nerve to mention their marriage to Lois and Jay.

The bridegroom was anxious for the honeymoon to begin. Cornering his mate, he pawed the buttons of Myra's blouse with thick fingers, causing her to panic when she heard her parents stirring a few feet away. He had come for the connubials and would not be stayed.

"What are you doin'?" Myra whispered to her husband.

"Whaddya think?" the Wildman mimicked.

"We can't," she said, slapping his hands away. "Not till they know."

"Well, when you gonna tell 'em?" he asked, nervously jiggling about. "Can't you do it now?"

"No, I wanna do it my way. By tomorrow night, I promise."

Escaping the darkened bedroom before her clothes were clawed away, Myra sat up till dawn outlining a plan of action. Black circles beneath her eyes convinced her mother when she said she was too sick to get out of bed the next morning. She couldn't very well go to class if the board of education forbade married children to attend elementary school.

Jerry spent the entire day at the studio hoping the storm would have blown over in time for the family to sit down to supper. When he arrived home, the place was tranquil. "Did you tell 'em?" he asked his wife.

"No, I didn't tell 'em," Myra whispered.

"Why not?"

"I didn't get the chance. I left the license out on my dresser where Mamma would see it, but she didn't notice."

Neither did she get the chance the next day or the next, until there was a good chance that both of them would be institutionalized for nervous frustration before the truth was out. To gain time and ease the tension, Myra trudged off to school after convincing herself that no one knew she was married and that she might get away with it for as long as it took for her folks to find out.

"There's some people actin' mighty funny aroun' here," Jay said. "I think Jerry's up to somethin' with Myra again. It might be worth the drive to Hernando to check a few records an' find out if there's been any marriages lately that we oughta know about."

"It's a mistake, Jay," argued Lois. "Jerry an' Myra could not possibly—"

"Maybe, maybe not, but there's a helluva lot goin' on aroun' here I don't like. Now you get dressed an' we'll go see for ourselves," Jay said.

Lois disappeared into her bedroom while Jay went into Myra's room to hunt clues. He checked her clothes closet, going through her pockets for a marriage license but found nothing. What's this? Uncooked rice in the pocket of a coat? Jay tore the jacket from the hanger and shook it. Josie Mae watched from the doorway.

"Mister Brown, is you really fixin' to go to Miss'ppi to check on Miss Myra an' Mister Jerry?"

"Yes, I am, Josie Mae."

"Well, Mister Brown, you don't has to," Josie Mae said, reaching into Myra's dresser drawer for the license. " 'Bout three days ago, Mister Jerry an' Miss Myra went to Hernando. The chile didn't know nothin' about it, it was all Mister Jerry's doin's. She didn't know how to tell you."

Lois was in a state of utter disbelief. Jay went into shock, his eyes opening wide and his face reddening. Josie Mae thought it was a coronary coming, but instead of keeling over, Jay jumped up and ran out of the room.

"Jay, where you goin'?" Lois called after him.

There was no answer, only Jay running from the bedroom to the front door with a loaded pistol in his hand.

"Jay? Jay!" Lois cried out.

"I'm gonna kill that li'l sonofabitch!" he hollered, jumping into his car and screeching out of the driveway in a direction toward town.

Lois raced to the telephone. "Sam? Lois Brown. Where's Jerry? Grab him up an' hide him 'cause Jay's on the way over with a gun an' he's gonna kill him. He married Myra. We found the license. He's comin', so hurry," she cried, and dropped the receiver.

"Whoaa, Jerry Lee!" Sam shouted, and Jerry came running. "Boy, the dam has done broke loose an' there's all kinda hell gonna hit here any minnit. Jay's on his way to shoot yer ass fulla holes. We gotta get outta here!"

"They found out!" said Jerry, the blood draining from his face.

"Listen, you can leave today for that radio show you're supposed to do in Alabama tomorrow. I'll take you to the airport right now, an' you can take the next flight out."

"I ain't got my clothes."

"You're lucky to have your hide, boy, now let's move!"

Jerry didn't wait for Sam. He hopped in his car and took off for the airport in a cloud of exhaust. Jay pulled into the lot moments later and leaped from his car, leaving the engine running and the door open. Clutching his pistol, finger on the trigger, he blew past reception and drew a bead on the first person he sighted as bystanders fainted all over the studio.

"Come out, you rotten bastard!" Jay called at the top of his lungs.

"Is that you, Jay?" Sam called from behind a closed door. "Put the gun down, Jay. Ain't nobody here."

"Where is that bastard?" Jay demanded.

"Who do you mean, Jay?" Sam pacified.

"Jerry Lee!" he screamed.

"Don't you remember, Jay? He had to go make that promotional tour today. He'll be gone several days . . . maybe weeks."

"Did Myra go with him?"

"No, Jay. Jay, come on in here an' let's talk about this thing."

"Ain't nothin' to talk about," said Jay, walking into Sam's office where the whited executive poured two glasses of bourbon. Jay sat down with the pistol firmly gripped and resting on his knee. "I'll kill him, I'll kill him," he repeated.

"Looka here, Jay, you know you can't kill the boy. There are ways to handle this thing. Call the distric' attorney an' discuss it with him. Maybe there's somethin' legal you can do, but ease up on that trigger 'fore someone gets hurt."

Jay could not be pacified. He took Sam's phone and told the operator to place an emergency call to the DA's office.

"Come on down, Mr. Brown, and we'll execute the necessary papers," the district attorney told him.

Jay picked up Lois and made straightaway for the courthouse. In the district attorney's office, Jay was fuming with renewed anger.

"Kidnappin', bigamy an' incest," he declared. "Write 'em up an' I'll sign it. Put that bastard away the rest of his life."

"All right, Mr. Brown, it can be arranged," said the DA. "But I want to warn you that once we put this action in motion, there's no going back. Now, I don't know how close you are to Jerry Lee and I don't know how much you care for your daughter, but you don't know if she's gonna have a baby or what."

"A baby?" Jay exclaimed. Lois swooned. "She's only thirteen years old."

"No matter, Mr. Brown, it's happened before. And you know somethin', Mr. Brown, who's to say things won't work out between them? They may have a good life together and maybe not, but you'll have to live with your actions for the rest of your life, 'cause you can put this boy away forever. Now, you can do it if you want to or leave the kids alone, but like I said, once we get started, there's no going back."

Jay sat back for a moment and sorted his thoughts. "Lemme see, he's outta town an' she's at school. We can go get her an' make her get a divorce."

"You could, but once again, sir, you just don't know whether or not they'll make a go of it. I've seen this happen a hundred times before. Sometimes they'll surprise you."

"Thanks for your help, but don't throw them papers away," Jay cautioned. "I might be back."

Myra walked in the front door of her house and could feel that something wasn't right. Josie Mae was waiting for her.

"Oh, chile, you better get ready."

"For what? What's happened?"

"Yo' mamma an' daddy done found out 'bout you an' Mister Jerry. They left here fust to go shoot him, then to put him in jail."

Terrified, Myra ran to her room. She heard her parents drive up in front of the house. Her first impulse was to turn off the lights. She jumped into bed, pulled the covers over her head and pretended to sleep. Jay crashed into the room, turned on the lights and whipped off his belt. With tears streaming down his face, he cut her sheets to ribbons with stinging slashes.

"How could you do such a thing?" Jay cried as Lois came running to save her child's life.

Catching the backlash of his whip, Lois pulled Jay off Myra. He backed away and she pushed him out of the room, leaving Myra quaking in the middle of her bed. No words were spoken till Myra returned from school the next day after withdrawing from the rolls.

Her notice was given to Bertha Forrest, principal of Levi Elementary School. Mrs. Forrest had received news of this nature in times past, but had never become used to the shock when learning a child would be quitting school to assume the roles of wife and mother. She could not have been colder, her cruel remarks focusing on Myra's youth and complete inability to perform the duties of a wife. "You don't even know what it is you're supposed to do," she scolded with hands on hips. "I think you'll be surprised and most unwilling to do the things which will be required of you by your husband. You are throwing your life away."

Myra left school feeling her lowest. That same afternoon, Mrs. Forrest called an assembly for all students in grades one through nine, the purpose of which was to lecture on moral decency. Her illustrative example of indecency was Mr. and Mrs. Jerry Lee Lewis.

"I know why Myra *really* got married," Dottie Carr told her friends. "She had to. She's gonna have a baby. I know." Dottie made a far greater impression on her classmates than Mrs. Forrest, and by the time students reached home that day, word had reached the Browns. Lois marched Myra to the Carrs' house and barged into their living room.

"I'm Lois Brown. I b'lieve you know my daughter, Myra. We understand Dottie has been spreadin' the word that Myra married because she's pregnant. It's not true and I want it stopped. I expect Dottie to return to school tomorrow and admit to everyone it was a lie. And if I hear another word about it, action will be taken. Why my daughter married and who she married is none of your business, so why don't we just leave it that way."

The long, slow healing process had begun as Lois fought for her daughter rather than against her. Perhaps now everyone could discuss the entire affair calmly. It took two days of talking before making any progress. Jay was swamped by the fact that his cousin, a boy he helped build a career, had stolen his only daughter, a child of thirteen. Lois had not yet developed that special mother-daughter relationship before she found motherhood at an end. Myra, in the eye of the storm, awaited instructions from all sides.

Jerry had not been heard from in three days. When the telephone rang that evening, it was the long-lost lover calling for a weather report. Lois answered. Jerry did most of the talking.

"Lois, you mad?"

"Not anymore. Just hurt. Surprised, is all."

"Good. Listen, Lois, I jus' called to say that I love Myra an' I'm gonna take real good care of her."

"Jerry, she's just a child."

"Maybe in years, but not inside where it counts. She ain't like any other thirteen-year-old. She's been drivin' a car two years, an' that's pretty grown up, idn't it? She can cook, an' kids don't do that, do they? And if it's money you're worried about—"

"I'm worried about my little girl," Lois sobbed.

"Don't," said Jerry. "She's my little girl now, an' I love her an' she loves me. So, I hope you'll unnerstand an' Jay'll unnerstand an' that he'll keep on now that we're makin' all this money."

Jerry and Jay did not speak. The next morning, the Browns packed for the trip to New York. The Jerry Lee Lewis Trio was to open at the Paramount for Alan Freed in three days; there was some doubt as to who would appear onstage.

"I suppose you'll be drivin' up with Jerry," Jay said to Myra. "Y'all have a safe trip. I guess we'll see y'all up there." He walked out of the room without looking at her and joined Lois and Rusty in the car.

Myra suddenly realized that for the first time in her life she was alone. She wanted to run after them. Too late. They were gone.

There was nothing to do but return to her room and prepare for a new life. Her chore was simple: She sorted out the few dresses she owned and folded a small stack of jeans, socks and undergarments. She did not have a suitcase, so she searched for a suitable replacement. Her only choice was to use the red cardboard dollhouse which Santa had brought her last Christmas. Myra turned the dolls out of their pasteboard apartment, moved the miniature furniture, balled her clothing into the compartment and closed the rooftop shut. All of her worldly goods were packed away in her dollhouse, the few things with which to set up a dollhouse of her own. She sat alone in her room crying, waiting for her husband to come for her. It was bound to be bad luck, all those tears falling on a bride's possessions.

5 *Rockin' Jerry Lee*

MYRA AND JERRY'S HONEYMOON CONSISTED of a two-day drive from Memphis to New York. They were joined by Jerry's drummer, who sat in the front seat with the newlyweds, smushing Myra in the middle. Jerry took the first available private moment to instruct his wife that she should sit closer to him, avoiding all physical contact with Russ. The first rule of marriage impressed upon the young bride was: No touching of or by unauthorized personnel. And that meant everybody.

Listening to the radio was the only form of en-route entertainment. The noticeable lack of liquor and fireworks had Russ longing for the good ol' days when road trips were rolling parties. Keeping track of how many times Jerry could be heard on the air was the only amusing aspect of an otherwise long and dreary drive. They monitored election results deciding who was king of rock 'n' roll. The voters of Richmond, Virginia, picked Jerry Lee Lewis, and suddenly Myra realized hers was no ordinary lot in life. That her husband's voice could be heard on every radio station lining the Eastern Seaboard gave Myra the feeling that Jerry's music was ubiquitous; that she possessed the source of universal appeal was beyond her comprehension. She was married to the Great Ball of Fire, and therefore everything he came into contact with automatically had great sentimental value, a pathetic fallacy which turned ordinary objects into treasures. Matchbooks, swizzle sticks and toothpicks were packed into Myra's purse until they could be permanently added to her collection. Keeping photographs was a foregone conclusion. She was fanatical for newsclippings, maniacal for doodlings on loose scraps of paper. Leave behind the cellophane wrapper to a memorable packet of crackers? Never.

Jerry dreaded the first face-to-face encounter with his in-laws. Lois and Jay were no more eager for a confrontation. So many questions crowded Jay's mind that the frustration of deciding how and where to begin kept him from saying anything at all. For Jay, the answer to the question "Why did you marry Myra?" was more important than Jerry's answer to "Do you love her?" Pregnancy weighed heavier upon Jay's thoughts than whether they were happy. Jay was also ready at the attack with federal statutes on kidnapping and scriptural commandments barring incest and bigamy, and perhaps it was best that he and Jerry not meet one moment before stepping onto the Paramount stage before thousands of screaming fans.

The twelve days of Christmas that Alan Freed booked for his Holiday of Stars at the Paramount Theatre were all sellouts. It was the biggest show held anywhere to date and featured fourteen acts crammed into two hours and played back-to-back six or seven times a day. Most of the performers were allowed only five or ten minutes onstage—just long enough for a big break to take place—and those who did not play instruments were backed by Freed's Rock 'n' Roll Orchestra.

Opening night, Jerry was backstage bitching about the billing. He was scheduled to appear before Fats Domino, who had been given the honorary top of the bill.

"I'm the king of rock 'n' roll," Jerry claimed.

"Yeah, says who?" asked Freed.

"Richmond, Virginia," answered Jerry, with a poll for proof. "I can blow Fats Domino off the stage. Why do I hafta go on before him?"

"Because he's had six Number One hits and you've only had two in the top ten," Freed recalled.

"Yeah, but who's got the hottest song right this minute?"

"You," Freed acknowledged.

"My point. He should go on before me."

"Can't." Freed shrugged. "It's in his contract: Fats on top."

"We'll see," said Jerry with a glint in his eye.

Buddy Holly also felt his name should appear at the top of the roster, and with half a dozen hits to his credit, his claim was even stronger than Jerry's. But Freed found out Holly was maneuverable in money matters and was motivated more by the dollar sign than prestige, and paid The Crickets to keep quiet and stay put. It wasn't much more, but Holly was the highest-paid act in the show. Jerry, on the other hand, was already making more money than he could imagine. What he wanted was for the world outside Richmond, Virginia, to know he was the undisputed king of rock 'n' roll.

The stage was set for the showdown. By eight o'clock, the Paramount was crammed to the rafters with fanatics who had rushed to the theater for tickets at the first mention of the show. Outside, attendants for the late show had already queued around the block. The orchestra struck up Chuck Berry's "Rock 'n' Roll Music" and the crowd roared as Alan Freed made his entrance wearing a tartan jacket that Bill Haley had made stylish.

"Hello, New York," Freed shouted into the mike, "and hello all you old friends of WINS. Great to see all of you out tonight. We've got the biggest, the brightest, the hottest rock 'n' roll show you've ever seen. I'm not gonna waste another minute, so if he's ready, please put your hands together and welcome Terry Noland singing 'Patty Baby.'"

Noland walked out to a warm reception, and polite applause continued through the brief appearances by Lee Andrews and The Hearts, the Twin Tones and Jo Anne Campbell. Freed introduced each act with a big send-up, bringing them on to ovations that increased in volume as their reputations increased in status.

With the preliminary acts out of the way, an unfledged and unripe Paul Anka ran out to center stage to sing his benighted songs of love, a virgin venturing onto virgin soil. Anka was the world's toughest fifteen-year-old performer to follow, and Freed wisely shifted the mood to the boppin' sounds of Danny and The Juniors, whose rousing rendition of "At the Hop" sent hundreds of patrons pouring into the aisles to dance. Buddy Holly played his twenty-minute set next and was the first of two performers to receive encores. The Everly Brothers sedated the crowd with their folksy harmonies and clean, uncluttered style. They were young and bright and innocent, twinned in appearance down to matching guitar straps, feeling far away from their old Kentucky home and the Opry stage which reared them. They were the calm before the storm.

"All right, kids, here he is as I promised, from Ferriday, Loui-

siana, the one and only true king of rock 'n' roll, Mr. Jerry Lee
Lewis," Freed announced, bringing the multitude to its feet as the
thin blond decked out in red pants, wine sharkskin jacket and
white shoes strode onstage. Evincing the same taste for garish
clothing as most country stars, but not going quite so far as to
emulate Presley's passion for pink, Jerry had invested a sizable
portion of his first paycheck in Lansky Brothers men's shop, catering to its black neighborhood in Memphis. He was a sight to
behold, this gaudy Ball of Fire, this veloured Vulcan whose tastes
ran negroid, whose dispositions harkened to the country and
whose talent was matchless.

Having hardly twenty minutes to work his magic, Jerry wasted
no time on warming up. He hammered the keys until his fingertips were bruised by the barrage. He jumped to his feet, kicking
the piano stool into the wings, grabbed the mike positioned between his legs and pounded the keys with his fist. He played the
piano with his elbows, his bootheels, and ended the song by sitting on the keys. A single curl unraveled over his forehead, and as
the heat wave rose, his long blond hair streamed into his face and
over his eyes. Withdrawing a silver comb and whipping his
tresses back in place provoked screams and cheers; tearing his
jacket off was the sign for the faithful to come forward to the
altar.

"Whole Lot of Shakin'" started a riot. Girls fainted. The crowd
mobbed the stage, hands held high, grasping for the pianist whenever he moved too close to the edge. For his final selection, Jerry
waited for the pandemonium to subside, then hit the keys four
times briskly:

> *You shake my nerves and you rattle my brain.*
> *Too much love drives a man insane.*
> *You broke my will, but what a thrill.*
> *Goodness gracious, great balls of fire!*

Urged on by the mob, Jerry pulled out all stops. When cheers
overwhelmed the sound of his music, he jumped on top of the
piano singing and dancing as Russ and Jay played rhythm and
bass. The balcony emptied, ushers ran for the exits, and policemen waded through entwined arms and legs, trying to stay the
tarantella. The song was over and so was the show.

After waiting ten minutes for the din to die down, Fats Domino appeared, having been patronizingly introduced by Freed as the king of rhythm and blues. Some of the people had already left and others were preparing to leave as the little fat man with the soft, drawling voice attempted to hold his own with his four-fourths timed laments and Lydian measures, a whispered aftermath of the storm that had wrecked the theater. After the program was officially over, Fats told Alan Freed that he would prefer not to follow Jerry Lee Lewis again.

The next morning, while New Yorkers hustled and bustled toward downtown department stores in search of Christmas-stocking stuffers, Alan Freed interrupted the flow of sidewalk traffic as he summoned crewmen to the front of the theater with a ladder long enough to reach the marquee. "See where it says Fats Domino and then Jerry Lee Lewis?" Freed pointed out. "Well, switch 'em. Jerry Lee Lewis first, then Fats Domino, The Everly Brothers and Buddy Holly."

Jerry had made a believer out of Alan Freed. Throughout the next eleven days, the Paramount surpassed all prior box-office records established by Johnnie Ray, Dean Martin and Jerry Lewis, and Frank Sinatra, making believers out of teenaged New York, Jerry Lee Lewis was surpassed only by his performance the following night.

The triumph in New York assured Sam Phillips that "Great Balls of Fire" would equal and perhaps surpass the fifty thousand copies a day sales mark set by "Whole Lot of Shakin'." Jerry's taking the headliner title by storm was a timely benefit to Sun Records, a boon that could be doggled by huge record companies hungering for the latest craze. It was contract-signing time for Jerry, and Sam could picture him going the Elvis route with the big boys; it was certain that Jerry would never sign another standard contract meting out a measly 3 percent on 90 percent of retail sales; the kid didn't have to be a genius to know he was worth more than that. Sam had been lucky to have released two multi-million-selling singles under the terms of a minimal contract and to have fifty or sixty songs with musicians such as J. W. Brown who had no idea they were entitled to union wages for session work. Sam could only hope that sudden success had made none of them the wiser, and that Jerry, in the midst of signing stacks of autographs, might put his signature on a long-term contract.

"I want you to sign Jerry to a five-year deal," Sam instructed Jud. "I don't care if you have to give him another percentage point to do it, just get him to sign. Four percent is as high as I'd go on any artist, but Jerry is the hottest act we've ever had an' I figger he's worth it. Also, I wanna lock him into a publishing company I've got set up. Jerry'll get half, an' me, Oscar, and Jim Denney will get the other half. This is gonna have to be handled smoothly and tactfully, at the right place, at the right time. You got ten more days in New York. Don't come home without that contract."

Backstage before the evening performance of the twentieth, spirits were running high and there was drinking and joke-telling going on in the star's dressing room. Not a cross word had passed between Jay and his son-in-law. They were finding it easier to adjust to their new relationship while basking in the spotlight of celebrity. It seemed to Jud like the right time and right place to work his unconscionable hocus-pocus.

"Say, Jerry, can you believe it's been more'n a whole year since you came to Sun an' cut your first record? Boy, we sure have come a long way, ain't wc? Your new song is gonna be another big hit, an' you can look forward to albums, movies, maybe even a trip to Europe."

"Yeah, Mr. Phillips, I have a lot to be thankful for," Jerry agreed. "God's been good to me."

"I was jus' noticin' the other day," Jud said, "it's that time again—contract-signin' time."

"Is it, already? Time sure flies, don't it?"

"Ain't it the truth," Jud said warily. "Y'know, I've loved you like you were my own kin. I took a personal int'rest in you, an' that's somethin' I never done for nobody. 'Member that fuss Perkins an' Cash kicked up when I tol' 'em I was gonna take you to New York an' put you on the teevee an' make you a star?"

"Yeah," Jerry nodded, wondering what all this was leading up to.

"And here you arc, jus' like I promised, a star."

Jerry Lee ain't sayin' nothin', en Brer Phillips, he lay low.

"And to show you jus' how much we think of you as an artist, we're gonna move you up from three to four percent of the gross record sales on your next contract," Jud announced.

Jerry Lee stay still, en Brer Phillips, he lay low.

"Lemme tell you somethin' else. I've always believed that if you spend ten thousand dollars to make a record, you oughta spend ten thousand to promote it. So, I'm pledgin' an equal amount to what's spent on releasin' your material for promotion," Jud said, sweetening the pot.

Jerry Lee, he sot dar, he did, en Brer Phillips, he lay low.

"So, what do ya think you might like to do?" Jud asked finally.

"About what?" Jerry asked.

"The contract—"

"Oh, I'll sign it, Mr. Phillips," Jerry said disarmingly. "Jus' show me where to put my name."

Surfacing from the depths of his devious sales pitch, Jud's blood flowed again through ice-watery veins warmed by the light of trust and faith in the boy's face. All traces of fear and doubt were erased as Jerry accepted the papers and asked for Jud's pen in the same voice he asked fans wanting a note inscribed in their autograph albums. Jud was embarrassed by his moment of doubt —this kid knew nothing about business—but pressed on with his task.

"It's the same deal as last time, idn't it?" Jerry asked, apparently neither hearing or caring to understand what Jud had said.

"Basically, but like I said—"

"Want me to sign here?" Jerry interrupted, without reading the fine print.

"Yeah," said Jud.

Had he known he was signing a five-year agreement without salary or guarantees, Jerry would have probably been just as happy as if he was signing what he thought was a one-year contract. Figures, percentages and promotional budgets did not concern the young man who walked onto the Paramount Theatre stage during Christmas 1957 as king of the jungle. He trusted Jud implicitly, and as long as Sam cut off a hunk of cash for him every so often, he didn't care if it was less than the proper amount; it looked to be endless. He made his way toward the footlights leaving Jud with an ironclad lien on his life which knowledgeable stars of Jerry's status would have found laughable. None of it mattered to Jerry when New York was on its knees at his feet. As the tumult for the leopard-trimmed shaker washed into the wings, Jud had the uneasy feeling of having won the prize at the cost of betraying a confidence.

* * *

By the time Jerry finished the sixth or seventh performance of the day, his fans had all exits manned and womaned with pen and paper at the ready for highly prized autographs. Jerry, hands trembling from strain, was not in the mood to oblige hundreds of hounds. The cunning and the daring who made their way backstage as far as his dressing room might get a punch in the eye as quick as a pat on the back.

Wild-eyed harpies who screeched throughout Jerry's show waited in small covens to ambush him like so many penis flytraps. With lipstick thick as lacquer and dark as blood they tattooed his face with kisses, the traces of which rubbed into his face before rubbing off on his handkerchief. When he stumbled into his suite, whatever hasty ablutions made in the elevator hardly disguised the favor of his fans from his bride. A dozen painted puckers melded into a deep blush on cheeks reddened with embarrassment.

Each day of the two-week stay was the same for Myra. She was forbidden to go to the shows, partly because of the policy which forbade Mrs. Lewises on the job, partly because Jud was afraid of the reaction to the secret that Jerry was married to one so young. So Myra stayed in the suite watching television except when she went downstairs to buy magazines or window shop with her mother. She had nothing to look forward to other than Jerry's sporadic visits and dinner together alone in their room. She moved about her gilded cage fearing the panic of suffocation. But before she worried herself into a state of agony, Jerry came back to spell her loneliness.

When Jerry came in from a show with his libido in high gear and intent on getting a little sugar, he didn't have to beg, coax, whine or wheedle. Myra simply submitted to the chore, a silent surrender to the imposition she allowed to happen without her effort or enthusiastic cooperation. Still uncomfortable in the act of love, she most often pretended to be asleep while he took his pleasure, numb to Jerry's powerful urge.

Sometimes Myra remained awake, watching Jerry sleep and remembering summer when she wished to revive romance. How hard it was to love a man who shared himself with millions, who gave his best to the rest and left for her the depleted remains. How hard it was to be possessed by a man who left most of her unused. How hard it was to be proud of a husband whom she was married to secretly and forbidden to claim in public. She watched him sleep, his long hair in disarray, his cheek leaving the last of kisses from other girls on his pillow, and she wondered how many of those girls would like to be in her shoes now.

There were two girls in particular who would have traded places with Myra in a second, the co-presidents of the Jerry Lee Lewis Fan Club. Kay Martin and Elaine Berman were somewhat chagrined that for more than a week they had sat in the hotel lobby waiting for an audience with the king. Kay called Jerry's room without answer, left notes without reply, waited without reward. Into her tenth nonproductive day, she cornered Jud Phillips, who told her in strictest confidence of Jerry's secret marriage. Kay was flabbergasted, and Elaine, who for almost five months had devoted a significant part of each day toward conducting the affairs of the fan club, hoping her reward might be Jerry's favor, was crushed. The prize had been won by another, loyalty flew out the window, and the shame of it all was having been undone by a mere slip of a girl.

Not a creature was stirring in the Hotel Manhattan on the night before Christmas. There was no tree, no decorations, no stockings hung by the chimney with care. There was no chimney. And there were no presents. On the morning of her thirteenth Christmas, Myra learned conclusively, regrettably, there was no Santa Claus.

Back in Memphis, however, Jerry made up for Santa's loss.

"What's red, has four wheels and belongs to you?" he riddled Myra.

"I dunno, what?"

"Your weddin' present," he said, swinging open the Browns' front door to reveal a candy-apple-red convertible Cadillac waiting in the driveway.

With a squeal of delight, Myra dashed outside to gush over her new toy. Although she had to stretch in order to toe the pedals while straining to see over the dashboard, nothing, nobody, could stay her from taking a solo inaugural ride around the block. Neighbors ran hysterically to the telephone to inform police that a child had stolen someone's brand-new Cadillac. The Memphis mounties converged upon Myra from all directions and hastily concluded that they were asking the driver for a license which she was not old enough to possess.

When Myra returned from her joyride with a police escort, Lois and Jay were waiting on the front porch wondering what was going on. "Are you the parents of this little girl?" the officer asked.

"We are. What's the trouble, officer?"

"Found her out drivin' around in this car . . ."

"Yes?"

"Says it's hers . . ."

"Yes?"

"Says her husband give it to her . . ."

"Yes?"

"And she says her husband is Jerry Lee Lewis, the singer."

"Yes," Jay said, waiting for the charge.

"You mean . . . ?"

"That's right." Jay smiled. "If you don't b'lieve me, either, you can ask her husband if it's her car," and with that modest introduction, Jerry came out on the porch, hands in pockets and a wide grin on his face.

"Well, baby, how does she handle?" Jerry asked.

The police left the premises, having asked Mr. Lewis for autographs and Mrs. Lewis to restrict her travels to the end of her driveway for the next four years, after which she would be legally entitled to use the public thoroughfares. To avoid a repeat panic among the neighbors, they were told of Myra's marriage and the gift from her husband. The explanation created more problems than it solved. Those who had suspected the Browns' kinship to the Killer all along now accused Lois and Jay of promoting the match in order to get to Jerry's money, using the new Cadillac, which everyone knew Myra was too young to own, as evidence. It was not a suspicion restricted to casual observers; Mamie Lewis shared it as well.

In his telephone call home at Christmas, Jerry broke the news of his marriage and his mother responded with a blessing out that boiled down to her belief that those scheming Browns had plotted to have Myra impregnated by Jerry, forced him to do the honorable thing and marry her, then pay in restitution that which they had not already stolen for room and board while he lived with them. Never one to argue with his mother, and possessing a murky perception of sex and its causal relationship to things natal, Jerry was unable to refute the speculation that Myra was indeed pregnant. No mention of this conversation was made to Myra or her parents, contributing to their continual amazement at Mamie's unexplained hatred for them.

Upon returning from New York, it appeared that Jerry and Jay had simply picked up where they left off before the elopement. Still, it was an extremely delicate subject for Myra's parents, and the change in family relationships was too difficult for them to bear. They would never be able to sleep under the same roof with Jerry in Myra's bed. The only solution was for the newlyweds to find a place of their own, and until that time they would have to revert to former sleeping arrangements—Jerry in Myra's room and Myra on the sofa.

Jerry would not have it. On the first Sunday of the new year, he and Myra went house-hunting in the same suburb of Memphis where Elvis Presley made his home. They stopped at the very first "For Sale" sign they saw and told the agent on duty they would take the house without a second thought. The three-bedroom dwelling on Dianne Drive looked like every other house on the block and cost $14,500. Jerry financed the purchase even though he carried enough cash in his pocket to pay for it on the spot.

On Monday, armed with signed blank checks, Myra drove to a furniture warehouse and walked its six floors pointing out what she wanted to a clerk who wrote up the long list after making sure it was not some prank that a co-worker had put her up to. Myra had the same difficulty with an appliance dealer who humored her purchase of a stove and washing machine. The last stop of the day involved choosing sheets and towels, pots and pans, dishes and glassware, all of which were considered adorable by condescending sales ladies until a quick call to Sun Records verified that the little lady meant business.

On Tuesday, a procession of delivery trucks trundled the purchases to the Lewis residence, where the mistress of the manor marshaled installations and directed placement of furnishings. In three days time, Myra had an instant house. She marveled at the thought that a month before, as a kid catching the school bus, she had dreamt about the vision which materialized thirty days later —a husband, a home and a shiny new car. Yet in the middle of this marvelous mystery, doubts undermined her happiness. Never having to go to school again was every child's wish, but was she too young to live out the rest of her fantasy?

"What am I doing?" Myra asked of her kitchen and the array of pristine implements waiting to be scorched. A few messy experiments that made slopwork out of supper had her running out to buy a library of cookbooks to facilitate her on-the-job training. Myra cussed over everything she cooked—raw chicken simmering in water sauce, more potato in the peeling than in the pot, and for dessert, "oh, fudge." At the tragic end to her debut dinner, Jerry was comforted by the thought that he had to return to New York on January 8 for the *Big Record Show,* allowing Myra to practice the culinary arts in peace.

Two months after its release, "Great Balls of Fire" had become the Number 1 song on the country charts, runner-up in the pop polls, Number 3 in R&B, and was well on the way toward becoming Britain's favorite rock tune. Jerry's appearance on the *Big Record Show* with songstress Patti Page featured his newest hit and a minor disaster; as he sang the titular lyric, technicians operated a gas valve which optimally manufactured flames from the inner workings of the grand piano, but the device malfunctioned, singeing Jerry's eyebrows, lashes and forelock.

While Jerry worked, Jud Phillips was across town at the Musicians' Union disposing of the new contract recently filed. Upon learning the terms that his brother pledged, Sam demanded another contract with Jerry be signed, eliminating all clauses pertaining to exorbitant promotional budgets. Jud feared the union had discovered theirs was a substandard contract which guaranteed Jerry next to nothing in exchange for having signed his life away. Sam had every intention of keeping his golden boy in the spotlight by releasing a new product every ninety days, but should trouble arise somewhere along the five-year term of the agreement, the contract hedged against huge losses by limiting Sun's liability to two sides a year. Although Sam found it easier to admit to Jerry's talent after he had become successful, he could never be sure another monster hit was in the vault or that Jerry could outlast the trends, in spite of owning two of pop music's biggest songs back to back. This contract, this conniving breach of faith, at its worst could foreclose on Jerry's recording career, a likelihood so remote in January 1958 that the legal papers were lost among a stack of fan mail.

Oscar Davis, as Jerry's manager, was in a position to rectify the predicament that the contract could conceivably create by steering his client into a sound settlement with Sun or by plucking a bonus contract with another label out of the daily mail. His effectiveness was minimized by Jerry's devotion to the Phillips brothers. As Jud had assured Sam, Jerry was their boy and nothing or no one could take him away from Sun.

Oscar had a hard time with Jerry in every other area. His star was manageable only by suggestion. He was spoiled. He habitually complained, enjoyed being demanding and liked to make people jump. If he did not like the tone in which he was told to prepare for departure for an engagement, Jerry might lock himself in the bathroom and comb his hair, forcing his entourage to sit and wait for as much as an hour. Onstage, in the middle of his hottest numbers, Jerry destroyed momentum by stopping abruptly in midstanza and taking long pauses to pull up his socks or turn his back on the audience to converse with Russ and Jay. Oscar made futile attempts to groom the wildman from the swamps into a class act; the audience screamed no matter what he did.

Oscar, Jay and Russ necessarily had to suffer through Jerry's moods, and opening acts learned to steer clear, but some fellow travelers refused to be intimidated. Warren Smith, whose seniority with Sun entitled him to a degree of respect, quickly tired of placating the star. In every town on their brief tour, the same fierce photograph of Jerry Lee leered at Warren from the placards which bloomed overnight. Lewis relegated Smith, the opening act, to filler space at the bottom of the card. And in every roadhouse they stopped at, Jerry poured fistfuls of coins into the juke box and punched his songs in succession, ignoring Warren's listings. In a fit of pique at the last of Jerry's boorish insults, Warren left his meal to cross the street to a record shop where he purchased every last copy of "Great Balls of Fire" and ceremoniously smashed them to pieces.

The newlyweds had spent one night alone in their new house when they were visited by their first guest. Jerry's ten-year-old sister Linda Gail was Mamie's spy, sent to Memphis to find out and report back on the state of the union, the house, the furnishings and whether Myra was going to make the grade as the newest Mrs. Lewis. For Myra, still in her untutored apprenticeship as mistress of a household, entertaining Jerry's kid sister was an added, unwelcome burden, and Jerry was vexed at not being able to take his wife on the road. Hospitality, therefore, consisted of a strained politeness.

For her part, Linda Gail was eaten up with jealousy within moments of her arrival. Here was little ol' Myra, hardly three years older than she, driving a new Cadillac and lounging around a big house filled with anything and everything her heart desired. What a setup! Myra began to feel threatened by Linda's habit of going on about how lucky Myra was to have all this neat stuff for free.

Linda Gail decided that music was the life for her, and hoped her brother would put her in business. Until that time arrived, she did not hesitate to share his success by going on shopping sprees with his money. At check-out counters all over town, Linda Gail looked at Myra with that hand-over-my-brother's-money look and Myra paid her way. When Jerry came home from the studio, Linda took every opportunity to score points with him while the competition for his affections was slaving over another sad supper. In the battle for the bulge in Jerry's wallet, Linda was not above hitting below the belt.

"Guess what Myra did today," Linda said to Jerry. "She took me for a ride in her new car. Boy, you shoulda seen her. She had a cigarette in one hand, a beer in the other, and she was flirtin' with a sailor."

Jerry's face went red with rage at the telling of the three deadly sins. He stalked into the kitchen where Myra meditated over recipes, and at the moment she looked up to adore her husband, he slapped her with such brisance that the blow could not have been harder had he hit her with his fist rather than an open palm. She ran to their bedroom in fear of what would happen next, searching her memory for some wrong she might have committed. Finding none, she trusted Jerry to tell her what she had done to deserve punishment, but when he came to bed, he said nothing. The incident was not mentioned again.

Myra was used to that sort of thing: People get to drinkin', a fight starts, someone gets hurt and it's over. The next day, the liquor is gone, so is the fight, and it isn't mentioned again. That's the way it happened in the Browns' home and Myra supposed that's the way it was going to be in hers. Husbands did not need reasons to hit their wives, it was a matter of right as far as Myra could tell.

The last stroke to Jerry's personality portrait was a dark line, a jealous streak that moved him to violence over the pettiest offenses, real or imagined. The infidelity of his mate was the greatest injury to his pride. With his new wife, his third and he hoped his last, Jerry sought to erase all signs of trouble from the very beginning. The inability to trust the love of his life required constant reassurance that he shared her with no one, not even her parents. In that sense, Myra was made to pay for the original sin of her predecessor.

In the middle of January, Jerry was all day at Sun working on a pair of tunes by the severed songwriting team of Otis Blackwell and Jack Hammer. Each had submitted separately a likely candidate for Jerry's next single, targeted for release during the first week of February. Blackwell's "Breathless" had the edge over Hammer's "Milkshake Mademoiselle," and in the same sessions Jerry worked up Roy Orbison's "Down the Line" as a possibility for the flip side. It was then that Oscar entered with an interesting offer to join Buddy Holly and Paul Anka on a tour of Australia. Jerry's only reservation was flying a great distance over water, a fear assuaged by a contract worth fifty thousand dollars.

On the afternoon that he packed to leave his bride for the first time over an extended period, Jerry peeled a hundred-dollar note from a ball of bills and gave it to Myra for necessities. No one had ever handed her more than ten dollars at one time, and she expected some sort of ceremony to accompany the presentation, as if a man giving his wife that much cash should make a speech. She did not trust memory enough to put the bill down, so she helped her husband pack for the ten-day trip with Franklin firmly clutched in either hand.

As soon as Jerry departed, loneliness began to creep over Myra. She did not feel like cooking for one, so she busied herself around the house and settled in for a night of television. According to some unwritten law, the scariest movies air on nights when no one else is home. Myra watched *The Hand,* a story about a pianist whose severed limb scrabbles about crablike until it finds and strangles its detractor. Trust Myra's luck to have married a pianist. As memories of the movie crept into bed with her that night, she ran out of the house, selected from the stable a new white Cadillac and drove to an all-night eatery for breakfast. Before her order was prepared, she remembered that the hundred-dollar bill was all she had.

"Don't fix the food if you can't break a hundred," Myra told the waitress.

The waitress took a long, hard look at the child. "Wait here a minnit an' I'll see what I can do."

She walked into the kitchen and spoke to the manager, who came to the door and looked at Myra, at her new car, then at her again. "I'm sorry, we can't break no hundred," he said.

"That's all right, I'll just go home," said Myra.

"No, no," he insisted, "jus' set here an' have a cuppa coffee on the house."

Meanwhile, the waitress was informing the police that the woman involved in a bank robbery earlier that day was in the restaurant. "It was a man an' a woman in a white Cadillac, wadn't it? Well, the woman is here. She wants to pay for breakfast with a hunnert-dollar bill. No, she ain't got no gun. She ain't even got a pockerbook. We'll keep her here long as we can. Hey, y'all ain't gonna shoot up the place, are ye?"

The desk sergeant dispatched an alert which sent six cruisers to surround the greasy spoon. Roadblocks were erected on all access roads. Myra thanked the manager for his kindness and headed for home. At the end of the block, red lights began to flash and high-powered spotlights blinded her vision. She was ordered out of the car with her hands up.

"Drivin' without a license can sure get you in a lotta trouble around here," she said as she got out of the car and stood before a dozen troopers.

Officers descended from all directions and ransacked the auto, searching under seats, rummaging through the trunk and dash, and ripping up the carpet. Myra watched in silent disbelief as Jerry's prized possession was systematically dismantled. The treasure hunters gave up and asked Myra for a clue to where the money was hidden, the officers holding her by the arms tightening their grip till she coughed up the hundred-dollar bill.

The chief of police arrived in time to oversee the arrest and recovery of the stolen money. He bellied his way through the badged shirts and sidled up next to the officer in charge and his quaking quarry. "What have we got here?" he bellowed.

"Chief, this here is Myra. Says she's thirteen. No license or ID on her. Only thing she got is this hunnert-dollar bill."

"Fine. I'll take over from here. Now, Myra, tell the chief where you got this money."

"From my husband."

"You're married? To who?"

"Jerry Lee Lewis. He's a singer. He gave me the money while he's gone to Australia."

"And where do you live?"

"In Whitehaven. Forty-seven fifty-two Dianne Drive."

"Check it out, boys, and find out who owns what's left of that car," the chief said, then calmed Myra so that she stopped crying.

"The address checks out, Chief," an officer reported. "The Cadillac is registered to Jerry Lee Lewis. This little girl belongs to Mr. Lewis, too."

Myra accepted the chief's invitation to ride home in his car, and before the night was through she received an explanation, a very long apology and the chief's assurance that Jerry's car would be restored and that not one word of the incident would be mentioned in the newspapers. A houseful of coppers cleared the premises of ghosts, and Myra had no further trouble getting to sleep that night.

The Jerry Lee Lewis Trio had flown to Los Angeles after a doctor had been summoned to the boarding gate to give them vaccinations which they did not know were necessary before embarking to Australia and which made them sick as dogs. In California, they were reacquainted with Buddy Holly, Paul Anka and Jodie Sands. On board the airliner bound for Waikiki, Buddy sat next to Jay and Jerry found himself paired with Paul, whom he did not like in the least. Paul, sensing the strain of maintaining a conversation with the Killer, busied himself writing lyrics. Occasionally, Jerry gave him an expressionless look, to which the kid always returned a big, friendly grin. After three minutes in the air, Jerry had all of Paul Anka he could stand.

At the age of fifteen, Anka was already a veteran singer/songwriter of four singles and hoped to impress Jerry with a sample of his work. Handing Jerry lines which he thought highly of, Paul awaited his reaction. Jerry shrugged, then flipped the page to read "Diana," Paul's second attempt at songwriting, which had become one of the best-selling records of the decade. "Don't make sense. Write somethin' else," Jerry said, shoving the sheet back at its deflated composer.

Spurred by Anka's incessant scribbling, Jerry began to assemble ideas for his own songs. His difficulty with writing lyrics was not so much a matter of inability as impatience. It had become too easy to sit back and wait for the best lyricists in the business to deliver his next hit. So when Jerry dabbled with composition, he had a propensity for relying on patented phrases, and his rhymes were predictable: moon, spoon, June. He could get three lines of a stanza down easily, but was invariably stuck on finding the fourth rhyme, resorting to a conventional way of detecting the missing word by placing each letter of the alphabet in front of the root syllable and considering all of the possibilities. For instance, to rhyme "luck," Jerry wrote "auck, buck, cuck, duck, euck" and so on, till he found what he was looking for. Odd how sometimes nothing else seemed to work as well as a vulgarism and how many passages simply wouldn't do without, in fact cried out for, dirty words.

Jerry's second attempt at songwriting was like his first, an autobiographical lyric built around his watchwords and inspired by every other song of its type. Appropriately titled "Lewis Boogie," it was intended to be sung by its composer exclusively.

> *My name is Jerry Lee Lewis, I'm from Louisiana,*
> *I'm gonna do a little boogie on this here piano.*
> *Doin' mighty fine, I'm gonna make it shake,*
> *I'll make you do it and make you do it until you break.*
> *It's called Lewis Boogie, in the Lewis way,*
> *I'm gonna do my little boogie woogie everyday.*

> *Well, now cruise on down to old Memphis town,*
> *that's where that Presley boy says you ain't nothin' but a hound.*
> *But now you take my boogie, it keeps you in the groove,*
> *until your sacroiliac begins to shiver and a-move.*
> *It's called Lewis Boogie, in the Lewis way,*
> *Lord, I do my boogie woogie everyday.*

As Jerry pondered over poetry and sidestepped around plagiarism, sneaking peeks at Paul's paper to check the progress of his competition, across the aisle the pairing of Holly and Brown was doing no better. After complimenting each other on their successes, they decided not to discuss show business. Jay felt like telling jokes, Buddy didn't feel like laughing. Jay felt like having a few drinks, Buddy was a teetotaler. Under such conditions, twelve airborne hours can seem like a prison term.

Losing interest in tune-crafting, Jerry became lost in thoughts of Myra and the incident which Linda Gail had provoked. He regretted having hurt his wife and worried whether she was capable of temptations he found impossible to resist. Arriving at the Hawaiian Village Hotel on Waikiki, Jerry promptly reached for the coral-pink stationery and wrote out his thoughts and fears in one long, continuous and barely punctuated stroke:

My dearest dearest dearest Darling,

How is the most wonderful girl in all the world, fine I hope. Darling I sure do miss you, because I love you so so so much. How is everybody fine to I guess. Darling please take care of your self if anything was to happen to you I'd die and that's no joke. Oh Myra I love you with all my heart. Baby we're going to have such a beautiful life together, we're going to be so happy too. Myra if you ever done me wrong it would kill me, well I'd rather you would kill me. Well I no you woulden do me wrong would you darling. Myra I've let myself fall in love to much with you, don't break my heart. Darling this is the most beautiful place you ever seen But I can't enjoy it without you. I'll be home soon. May God watch over you, pray for me,

your husband,

Jerry Lee Lewis

He autographed the letter underscoring his name three times, then prepared the envelope with a return address which read "Jerry Lee Lewis, A Rolling Stone." The recipient, after memorizing the message, folded it in half and placed it in the dresser drawer with her most valued possessions.

Over the next seven days, concerts were scheduled in stadia situated in Sydney, Newcastle and Melbourne. Although each venue seated thousands upon thousands, second shows were added at every site to accommodate bushmen coming from the most remote areas of the continent. It was possible that these performers would never see crowds of such proportions again, a sobering thought which called for a fifth of sour mash—a hard commodity to come by in Australian bars. The boys would have to settle for lager.

Watering holes in Sydney consisted of rude barracks where patrons filed past a window at which a bartender filled buckets with beer from a hose tapping a large tank of brew. The foamy lager gushed in a steady stream, sloshed over the edge of the pails and dripped a spotted trail to long, wooden, sudsoaked tables and benches where groups of Sydneyites discussed life on the docks and sang hick ditties. In the center of activity sat Jerry, Jay, Russ and Cricket Jerry Allison. Paul Anka, not being a drinking man, had come along to be with the boys.

"I never hadda beer before," Paul commented to his friends.

"Do tell," said Jay, winking at the others. "Well, you'd like it."

"Looks good," Paul said thirstily.

"Is good," said Jay. "I think we can find you a glass."

"Oh, no," Paul protested, "I gotta sing tonight. I'm the headliner, you know. I'll just have a Coke."

"The headliner?" Jerry hollered from the end of the bench.

"That's right." Paul flashed his toothy grin.

"No Cokes," said Jerry. "They ain't been invented here yet. Alls they serve here is beer."

"How about milk?"

"Sure, if you can stomach the stuff. It comes from kangaroos."

The boys cracked up over that one. Warming to the occasion, Paul decided to join them in just one beer.

"Go on now, Paul," Jerry prompted. "Ain't nothin' in it to hurt ya. They give it to babies."

Paul took bird sips at the mug, managing to suck down some of the suds. Finding nothing objectionable about the taste, he took a long, steady drink.

"Like it?" Jay asked.

"Yeah, boy," Paul squeaked.

"Good. Have another. They got plenty."

"I feel pretty good," Paul braved after finishing his first beer.

"Loosens up the vocal cords," Jerry stated.

"It does?" Paul asked in amazement.

"Absolutely. Wouldn't go on without a coupla beers first. Right, Jay?"

"Right. J'ever notice how sometimes you'll get up there to sing an' your throat gets tight an' you can't hit them high notes? Beer fixes all that." Jay smiled, getting up to fetch another bucket. After two more trips to the window, the boys were glad all over, having led impressionable Paul down the path to blue ruin.

"Come on, Paul," Jerry said. "I'll drive you around a spell so you can sober up. You boys go on back to the hotel an' I'll look after Anchor here."

Jerry poured Paul into the rental car and took off into the Australian countryside. Paul clutched his stomach and doubled over. When next he opened his eyes, he found himself in the middle of nowhere. There was no recognizable landmark, only dense brush and few open spaces.

"What're we stoppin' for?" Paul asked dizzily.

"We're stoppin' here 'cause I'm gonna kill you," Jerry joked with a straight face. "No one will ever know what happened to Paul Anchor. They'll never find you, there'll be no one to blame. They'll jus' think you've run off with the kangaroos."

Paul began to cry. "Lemme go, please. I haven't done nothin'."

"Don't matter, Paul, it's the perfect crime. No body, no witnesses. I've always wanted to do it. Now's my chance. Didn't you know about headliners, Paul? I've always hated headliners," Jerry said quietly.

Paul got sick. It was time for the prank to end. Jerry drove Paul to the hotel, where he ran upstairs to his room and stayed there. That night, the emcee informed the capacity crowd that the headliner was unable to perform due to illness. For the rest of the week, for the rest of his life, Paul Anka kept a great distance from the Killer.

At Brisbane's Cloudland Ballroom, a disparaging remark likening lager to urine inspired Jerry to another practical joke beyond the bounds of practicality. He siphoned off recycled beer from his own hose into an empty bottle and placed it among a dozen bottles of uncontaminated lager on the bet that an inebriated Aussie couldn't tell the difference between piss and pilsner. The butt of the joke, a feisty little man with a big thirst, drained long draughts of essence of Jerry, spat out the last mouthful and cursed, "I'll kill the man who did this!"

"An' I'll help you, brother," said Jerry.

Jerry's fourth Sun single, "Down the Line" backed with "Breathless," had been released on February 1. Compared with earlier releases, less of a distinction could be made between the two sides, reflecting Sam Phillips's desire to concentrate on the rockabilly market which drew evenly from fans of pop and those who preferred country. "Down the Line" had been "Go! Go! Go!" in a former life two years before as the B side to Roy Orbison's "Ooby Dooby." "Breathless," written with Otis Blackwell's magic pen, was sure to be Jerry's third million-seller, but something was amiss and the single wasn't getting any airplay. Jud asked Sam about the mystery.

"How come the stations ain't playin' the new single?"

"I don't know." Sam shrugged. "Maybe they ain't got it yet."

"When did the samples ship to the stations?"

"They haven't, and they ain't gonna be. Jerry is hot. If the stations wanna play his record, let 'em go out and buy it like everybody else."

"Are you crazy?" Jud blew his top. "There ain't a station in the nation that buys its own records."

"Too bad, then. Let 'em explain it to the public when they get all them phone calls."

"For the price of a box of records you'd let the single die?"

"It ain't gonna die. It'll sell a million as soon as the kids hear that a new Lewis single is out."

"Not at this rate, they won't," Jud argued. "Is the record in the stores yet? Surely you've shipped to distributors—"

"Not if their accounts ain't up to date," Sam said. "And even then, they ain't gettin' any free copies."

"Sam, you're cuttin' our throat. We can't do business thataway. Those people don't need us, we need them. You treat 'em like that an' they'll drop us like a hot potato."

"We don't need anybody," Sam negated. "We got Jerry Lee and Jerry Lee is hot. They'll come beggin' for the new single."

"What's the problem with distributors?" Jud backtracked.

"You know how they are. Some of 'em won't pay for a record till the next one is out. They won't pay us for 'Great Balls of Fire' till they get 'Breathless' and see how it does. They're afraid of gettin' caught in the middle of a moneymaker and a loser. But Jerry is a winner, and I ain't sendin' 'em nothin' till their accounts are up to date."

"Where does that put us?" asked Jud.

"Hell, I don't know, Jud. Ask my girl in the office."

"You mean I got to ask some whore what shape our business is in?"

"She's able—"

"I know what she's able at," Jud retorted, "but I'm askin' you when's the last time we billed these distributors."

"Two, three months ago, I dunno."

Jud was breathless. The single would never succeed in the vicious circle created by a small company being caught up in its own incompetence and tricks of the trade. It was not a matter to be discussed with artists on the label, so Jud had another story to tell Jerry when he wondered at the slow start his single was experiencing.

"Y'know, Jerry, 'Breathless' does lack that dance beat which the other songs had," said Jud. "It's got the rock tempo, but then along comes the break where you stop an' breathe an' it ruins the rhythm. And 'Down the Line' ain't what you'd call brand new, so maybe this single ain't happenin'."

At a time when "Breathless" needed exposure most, an invitation was issued to Jerry to open the television premier of *The Dick Clark Saturday Night Show* on February 15. From its new home at the Little Theatre on Broadway, Clark launched his sponsorless network experiment with fingers crossed, hoping five hundred warm bodies would brave a blizzard to watch Pat Boone, Connie Francis, Johnnie Ray and The Royal Teens lip-sync a favorite song. He was surprised to find fifteen hundred kids standing behind police barricades knee-deep in winterbourne gutterwash one hour before rehearsals were to begin. Inside, a heated debate warmed the hall as Clark's crew were having a difficult time explaining to Mr. Lewis, replete in black tux with leopard lapels and two-tone shoes, that it would not be necessary for him to rehearse in the traditional manner.

"I know it ain't necessary, I jus' wanna try out the place," Jerry said, sitting down at a bright white baby grand.

"No, you don't understand," the technician tried again. "You won't be playing. You'll be mouthing the words to your recording."

"I'll be damned. I ain't sittin' up here like a damn dummy and ..." Jerry finished his refusal to lip-sync by silently opening and closing his mouth like a goldfish.

"But, Mr. Lewis, we're not set up for live performance. Everybody will be doing pantomime."

"I don't give a damn what everybody else does. I ain't no puppet, and I didn't come all the way up here to play charades."

That night, Pat Boone mimed "Everybody's Gonna Have a Wonderful Time Up There" and Connie Francis convincingly faked "Who's Sorry Now?," but Jerry Lee Lewis played and sang exactly as he always had, straight from the heart and his own vocal cords. He was introduced by Kay and Elaine, co-presidents of his fan club, which had grown to more than five thousand followers, many of whom contributed to a viewer response unparalleled by anything Dick Clark had experienced before, doubling previous ABC ratings in the 7:30 time slot.

As a result of Jerry's performing "Breathless" on Clark's show, the single sold one hundred thousand copies. But with minimal exposure elsewhere caused by Sun's incompetence and Sam's refusal to cooperate with the rest of the industry, the disc appeared destined for a quick and untimely death until another avenue was opened with a call from Dick Clark three weeks later.

"I've got a new sponsor who isn't very happy with the show," Clark told Jud Phillips. "Beechnut is afraid they won't sell any spearmint gum, and if they pull out, that's it. I need to come up with something fast. I was hoping you could help."

Jud's mind began to click. Somehow there was a way to save Jerry's song and Dick's show at the same time, but only if Jud could gain the cooperation of the sponsor in a chancy promotion. "Tell me what you think of this idea," Jud said to Clark. "Jerry's got this song out that isn't movin' very fast and you ain't movin' enough gum. What I propose we do is have the kids send in five Beechnut gum wrappers and fifty cents for the new Lewis single. We'll plug it on your show and maybe get Beechnut to tie in a new ad campaign that goes somethin' like, 'Beechnut leaves you Breathless.' Maybe get Jerry to sing a jingle—"

"I like it, I like it," Clark rejoined. "But, Jud, you know you'll have to sell the idea to Bud Kloss and the ad men at Young and Rubicam who handle the Beechnut account."

"If you like it, I'm sure they'll give it a shot," said Jud.

"Go with it, then," said Clark. "And, Jud, if this works, I'll owe you one. I really will."

The powers that used to be at Young and Rubicam, the professionals whose job was to invent ways to prod the public into purchasing new products, thought Jud's idea was too involved. Nobody will go out and buy a pack of gum and mail the wrappers and fifty cents to Dick Clark for a lousy record, they said. Besides, sending money through the mails is a pain in the ass, and then there's the problem of splitting the proceeds.

"Then I tell you what I'll do," Jud said to Bud Kloss. "I'll give you a fifty-thousand-dollar performance bond guaranteeing Beechnut won't lose one cent." Even as he spoke, time was running out. Jud could not find anyone to back his bet. Without surety, his last resort was to call the president of the bank where Sun kept its accounts and asked him to set aside fifty thousand dollars in escrow to serve as Beechnut's guarantee.

TV Guide listed Jerry Lee Lewis as Dick Clark's lone guest on March 18, and as Clark's last chance took the stage, the sponsors waited in the wings with one hand on the plug. Jerry sang "Breathless" and "You Win Again" while Clark beat his Beechnut drum. Jerry closed the show with "Whole Lot of Shakin'," and Dick begged America to take him up on his once-in-a-lifetime offer. Within three days, Clark's office was littered with tens of thousands of Beechnut gum wrappers and enough loose change to ballast a battleship. Beechnut, which was to the chewing-gum trade what Sun was to the record industry, sold more chaw in one week than it had since its inception, forcing the plant into overtime to meet the demands flooding in from the nation's candy counters.

"Breathless" sold a million copies.

Dick Clark kept his *Bandstand*.

Jerry Lee Lewis had saved the day.

"You have my everlasting gratitude," Clark thanked Jud. "I'll never forget what you and Jerry have done for me."

During its fifteen weeks in the pop charts, "Breathless," because of its odd syncopation and a glut of competition, reached no higher than Number 7. The R & B appeal was even less, charting for seven weeks but peaking at Number 6 in early March. Again, the greatest gain was made in the true blue country ranks, where it rose to Number 4. Entering the marketplace at a time when The Champs had the hottest hit with "Tequila," Chuck Berry rocked with "Sweet Little Sixteen" and The Monotones sold millions of copies of "Book of Love," the most unlikely entry to top Jerry in the hit parade was by Laurie London, a one-hit wonder who scored with a gospel singalong entitled "He's Got the Whole World in His Hands."

At the conclusion of a week-long tour of Florida, The Jerry Lee Lewis Trio was to fly to Los Angeles from Miami to film a cameo appearance in a movie produced by Alfred Zugsmith for MGM. The film was *High School Confidential*, starring Russ Tamblyn, Jan Sterling, John Drew Barrymore, Mamie Van Doren and Diane Jergens. "Not since *Blackboard Jungle* such shattering drama of the tough, troubled teenagers of our time!!" read the ads for the exposé about drugs on campus. "No recording star of the American scene could have brought to a movie what Jerry Lee Lewis delivers" read ads for the theme song, "the very pulse-beat of American teen life." And in the first three minutes of the movie, as the credits rolled, The Jerry Lee Lewis Trio rolled in front of a typical high school and sang the title tune from the back of a flatbed truck as the tough, troubled teenagers of the time gathered around; the only part of the film Myra was permitted to see.

Jerry, Jay and Russ flew to Hollywood immediately following the second show at Ft. Lauderdale's War Memorial Auditorium. The trio hated long trips, and before departing they stocked up on all the necessities required to pass the time in amusement. Jay spent an hour getting primed in the terminal lounge while Jerry purchased a rackful of comic books and Russ found souvenirs. The prize find was a jointed wooden snake which was good for a laugh even though it had not the slightest resemblance to a real one. By takeoff, the boys were feeling no pain. As the airliner moved north over the everglades, flight attendants passed out complimentary tenth pints of liquor and mixers. Jay, who could gargle with what was in the itty-bitty bottle, was trying to filch Jerry's allotment while the Killer was absorbed in another adventure of Superman, and Russ was rooting through his shopping bag for something to play with.

"Where's my snake?" Russ said to no one. "I can't find my snake. Jerry, have you got my snake? J. W., you got it."

"No, I don't," said Jay. "It's prob'ly on the floor somewheres."

Russ got down on his hands and knees and proceeded down the center aisle in search of his souvenir, looking under seats and asking other passengers if they had seen his snake.

"What are you looking for, sir?" a stewardess asked Russ.

"My snake. He's brown an' got a stripe an' yaller eyeballs like this," he said, looking at her with a googly expression.

The stewardess quickly headed for the front of the cabin. The seat belt and no smoking signs were illuminated and Russ returned to his seat, where he found his simulated serpent squirming between the cushion and armrest. The plane made a wide arc and headed back toward Miami.

"What the hell is goin' on?" Jay asked.

"Beats me," said Russ.

"Maybe we left the pilot in Miami," said Jerry, looking up from his comic.

"Ladies and gentlemen, this is your captain. We have to return to base momentarily. There is no cause for alarm. There is nothing wrong with the aircraft. We hope to have the problem under control immediately and be on our way again soon."

When the plane returned to the terminal, the passengers remained seated, the hatch was opened and three uniformed security guards came aboard with a plainclothes officer. The stewardess pointed Russ out to the posse, who then stalked down the aisle to where The Jerry Lee Lewis Trio was seated.

"Okay, Chief, where is it?" the officer said.

"Where's what?" Russ asked.

"The snake."

"The snake? Oh, right here," Russ said, reaching into his bag for his toy.

The officer stared at Russ without speaking for several minutes, apparently deciding whether to put him under arrest or off the plane.

"If you want one, you can get one inside," Russ said, trying to be of help.

The flight was resumed. The boys had lost their buzz and asked for drinks. They were served coffee only.

High School Confidential was scheduled to be released at the same time Jerry's single would be reaching the stores in June. The song had been written by Ron Hargrave, a novice whose inexperience allowed Sam Phillips to wrangle a piece of the publishing royalties for Jerry by insisting he be listed as co-writer. Because Jerry's vocals and arrangement guaranteed the song would sell a million, Hargrave gladly gave up part of his song in exchange for instant stardom; because "High School Confidential" was Hargrave's only claim to fame, it was not a fair trade. Perhaps his inability to become a writer of renown was due to his dependence on the groundwork of others. Had it not been for "My heart's beatin' rhythm and my soul's singin' the blues" from Chuck Berry's "Roll Over Beethoven," Hargrave would have been stuck for the last line of his second stanza. Insuring the song's success was a return to the bright rock tempo which had fueled Jerry's earlier hits and which had been sacrificed at Sam's insistence so as not to alienate Sun's country cousins, who preferred more hillbilly than rock in their rockabilly.

With the triumph of "Breathless," the promise of a fourth smash hit, the completion of a second film and a tour during which he had stolen the show from Holly, Haley and The Everly Brothers, Jerry was ready for a showdown with Elvis Presley. As much as he admired Elvis, he was that jealous. In return, it was known by very few that Presley was in awe of Jerry's musical ability. Jerry wanted the world to know he was superior, period.

"No question Elvis is king," Jud said in a debate with Oscar. "He's got the looks, the voice and a certain mystique because he stays off in that mansion by hisself. Jerry, on the other hand, is tops on piano. A kid from the swamps with a mastery over the keyboard makes a strong case for reincarnation. And the girls are hot for him, too. But he shows up in joints all over town and puts his business in the street. That's why I'm sayin' if this thing about him marryin' Myra gets out, he's had it. At least Tom Parker makes sure nothin' about Elvis makes the papers unless it's supposed to."

"Jud, there are a lot of critics looking for a place to stick the knife in rock 'n' roll and I think Elvis is the prime target," said Oscar. "They'll come huntin' him, not Jerry."

"That's where you're wrong. You'll never find a bum rap about Elvis in print," Jud warranted. "He could run for office. If we could keep that wild-ass Jerry out of trouble, he'll be bigger'n Elvis."

"Hardly seems possible, Jud."

"I don't know why not. At least Jerry can write his own songs when he wants to. Elvis does only what he's told, he's a puppet. He never wrote a line in his life, and whatever carries his name has been bought an' paid for. Elvis can't write music; Jerry doesn't write more than he does 'cause he doesn't choose to. Both have every songwriter in the country sendin' 'em material. But, given time, Jerry will hand you a dozen more like 'End of the Road' and 'Lewis Boogie.' And when it comes to showmanship, nobody can follow Jerry, includin' Elvis. And to prove my point, I'm gonna call Alan Freed and get him to book Jerry and Elvis together and we'll see once an' for all who's king of rock 'n' roll."

For the asking, Alan Freed quickly pieced together a thirty-day concert tour pitting Jerry against Elvis. It was to be touted as the battle of the century, and negotiations had entered into the final phase when the disappointing news came that the promotion had been scrapped.

"I knew it would never happen," said Oscar. "Tom Parker would never run the risk of having his boy upstaged by another act."

"It ain't just that, haven't you heard? Elvis is goin' in the army at the end of the month," Jud announced. "Which will make Jerry top dog—"

"How you figure?"

"People will forget Presley in two years. Without a record out and unable to make movies, he'll die," Jud vowed.

Those same thoughts circulated through Elvis's camp, that two years of military service looked to outlast the collective public memory. But the colonel mapped a campaign that, with the army's cooperation, could be routed into a publicity-stunt-cum-recruitment program. By the time Elvis was to board the bus for boot camp, ads for his latest film, *King Creole,* would already be in full swing to capitalize on the news coverage his enlistment was sure to create. And prior to his departure, the colonel would make sure Elvis had enough songs in the can to continue releasing a new single every ninety days. Lastly, Parker reached an understanding with army brass that regulations regarding off-duty activities would allow Elvis time to hightail it to Memphis to TCB; no army colonel was cleverer than Col. Tom Parker.

Toward the end of March, as Private Presley prepared for induction, Jerry spent his spare time at Sun working up new material, concentrating on an arrangement of "Frankie and Johnny." Sitting at the piano with his back to the door, Jerry hadn't noticed that he had a visitor, but when the general hubbub turned to complete silence around him, Jerry looked up from his work and was surprised to find Elvis watching him from the doorway. Before Jerry could speak, Elvis tearfully renounced, "Take it, just go on and take it. Take the whole thing."

Elvis was gone. The throne had been abdicated. The crown worn by the first king of rock 'n' roll had been relinquished and awaited the claim of his successor. To a tournament at Brooklyn's Paramount came hopeful Buddy Holly, Paul Anka the Younger and Chuck Berry, the Black Prince. The search for an heir among the houses of Chart, Checker and Chess had begun. In the rising generation, who could compare with the champion of Sun, the Great Ball of Fire?

To the kingmaker came Jud Phillips, to beseech his blessing and to tempt him with a one-third ownership of a publishing company controlling Jerry's catalogue. With Tom Parker's participation, Jerry's songs would be pushed on every up-and-coming performer, earning a tremendous revenue from royalties. Into the concord came Sam, a tight-lipped tightwad, creating a breach which would cause the fortunes of his house to totter.

From a mortmain military outpost in Bremerhaven, Germany, the exiled king continued to reign. A new line of novelties coursed down assembly lines—Elvis dogtags and T-shirts with PFC Presley stenciled across the chest. A rash of novelty songs broke out, including "Bye, Bye, Elvis" by Gennie Harris and "Marchin' Elvis" by The Greats. A team of writers created a musical play about a singer leaving for the army, which later began a two-year run on Broadway as *Bye, Bye, Birdie*.

The reviews for *King Creole* were the kindest Elvis ever received. Patriotic critics could not bring themselves to blast a teen idol whose induction into the army placed him above contempt. Elvis was now part of the Establishment. Alas, the press was forced to find not a new king, but a new scapegoat, someone to bear the brunt of syndicated malice and shoulder the blame for having corrupted his contemporaries. Scandalmongers in correspondents' clothing had begun a search of their own. The quest ended as quickly as it had begun, for in the very same issues that praised the patriot Presley were the first accounts of a deliciously newsy divorce between Mr. and Mrs. Jerry Lee Lewis.

Comes now the complainant, Jane Mitcham Lewis, and sues the defendant, Jerry Lee Lewis, for an absolute divorce on March 10, 1958. Having heard from her former mother-in-law of her husband's remarriage, Jane realized it meant Jerry would not be coming back for her as he had promised six months previously during the feigned reconciliation. Still, with Jerry she could never be sure, so Jane had the sheriff ask, "Which wife will you live with?" To which Jerry replied, "This one," placing his arm around Myra's shoulder. His decision made, Jane was not clear what relief she was entitled to, and called Jerry to ask him what she should do. Jerry, whose attitudes toward divorce were unique, advised her that they were never legally married, that a divorce was unnecessary but to get one if she wanted, and please do him the favor of keeping it quiet.

And quietly Jane proceeded to reactivate her suit, recapitulating her original complaints of cruelty, abandonment and nonsupport, updating her charges to show Jerry had reneged on his promise to buy her a house, that the two-year-old Ford he gave her had been repossessed and that his idea of sharing his phenomenal wealth was to dole out two hundred dollars a month for her and her two children to live on. She further alleged that on or about January 1, hardly three weeks after secretly marrying Myra, Jerry had again tempted Jane with a real and lasting reconciliation, but that a few days later he had changed his mind again. Premises considered, Jane asked that Jerry make a full disclosure of all property, earnings of every type and the details of all contracts which produced income so that an equitable alimony and child-support payment could be negotiated, all of which was above and beyond Jerry's patience and understanding.

Jerry had a choice between attacking Jane's suit as superfluous or acquiescing to her claim and paying her off to get her out of the way. He entrusted the decision to Sam Phillips and Oscar Davis, who looked ahead to a forty-five-day tour and advised him to pay off the indiscretions of his past rather than jeopardize his future.

The process of discovering the extent of the defendant's wealth consisted of the court asking Sam what Jerry's recording contract was worth, to which he could only guess after losing listeners in a roundabout explanation, then asking how much Jerry had been paid on the contract, another amount Sam could only guesstimate, keeping the figures low for Jerry's benefit. From Oscar, the court was helped immeasurably by learning Jerry was earning anywhere from fifteen hundred to ten thousand dollars for every night he worked, but from that principal sum was whittled away fines, fees, commissions and expenditures. In the end, Jerry came out looking like the poorest man ever to sell a million records.

The final decree was handed down on March 26, granting Jane full custody of the children, six hundred fifty dollars per month alimony and one hundred dollars per month child support. Additionally, Jerry was made to pay thirty-five hundred dollars for Jane's attorney's fees and four hundred dollars for other expenses.

"Chicken feed," Sam bolstered his star. "You'll make enough by June to pay Jane off for the rest of her life."

Still, Jerry did not like the court facilitating Jane's theft of a percentage of his earnings which she had no part in making nor any right to share. He went home cussing, then put the whole affair out of mind, having only minutes to pack himself and his wife off to New York to begin an infamous tour which remains to be equalled in scope, size, impact and importance.

The spring of 1958 was a time when the greatest names in rock 'n' roll were performing their best works. Alan Freed's Big Beat Show touring the northeastern and midwestern United States and parts of Canada from March 28 through May 10 starred Buddy Holly, Chuck Berry and Jerry Lee Lewis. Beginning with five performances at the Paramount in New York and extending for sixty-eight shows in thirty-seven cities, more than three hundred fifty thousand people heard Holly's latest hits, "Maybe Baby" and "Listen To Me," Berry's "Johnny B. Goode," and the boppin', hoppin', rockin' fool from dear old Confidential Hi, Jerry Lee Lewis.

Chuck Berry had been Alan Freed's favorite performer and headliner of Big Beat shows since 1956, and once again, Berry was billed as the star. Freed should have known better than to schedule an act to follow Jerry; he knew good and well it made Jerry mad.

"I thought Alan Freed would've learned by now that I don't play second to no livin' human bean," Jerry spat. "Chuck Berry, what makes him the star?"

"The man's had a dozen hits in the top ten, Jerry," said Oscar. "Even you play a couple of his songs now and then. Now, Freed told me Chuck's got to close the show, and I hope this'll be the end of the argument."

"Who's arguin'? I shouldn't hafta argue. I should close the show," said Jerry, determined to make Freed a believer all over again.

Night after night, he destroyed the pianos he played, first by wringing the last tones from steel-wire strings snapped and mis-shaped by the warp of felt-covered hammers, then by kicking the carcass and dancing atop its closed-lidded casket. Audiences thought the Louisiana Piano Pounder had lost his mind; Freed was convinced of it. News of the devastating spectacular swept the country, striking fear in the hearts of promoters who were next on the list, titillating the greed of those who could afford to invest a piano in what would have to be the instrument's finest hour and forcing others who could not bear the loss to purchase junk for Jerry to demolish. Jerry accepted the stingy sacrifices, insulted at the inability to produce decent sound but thrilled at ripping out the keys, throwing them to the fans and watching the pandemonium that resulted. A promoter in Cleveland was prepared with two pianos, one for each show. When the first instrument survived the onslaught, the promoter threatened not to pay Jerry unless he wrecked the second. Jerry wondered who was crazier, he or the man telling him to turn Mr. Steinway's six-thousand-dollar mas-terpiece into kindling, then raped the eighty-eights and pushed the damaged goods into the front row. The other acts were pushed to the peak of their capacity as word spread to the rest of the enter-tainment world: Do not attempt to follow Jerry Lee Lewis on-stage.

The Big Beat was scandalous; it was front-page newsworthy in every city it visited. Aroused by Jerry's appearance on Dave Gar-roway's *Today Show*—possibly the only time he would ever play "Down the Line" at 7:30 in the morning—the news media met the tour at every stop along the route, and on the day Freed pitched tent in St. Louis, *Look* published a feature on the rock 'n' roll frenzy. In the issue of April 15, an essay entitled "Revolution in Records" appeared, complete with photos of Jerry splashed across the center spread with a caption that read: "Once a student in a Bible institute, Jerry Lee Lewis howls a hit aptly titled 'A Whole Lot of Shakin' Going on.' Regarded as the ultimate in rock 'n' roll frenzy, Lewis makes parents mourn for the comparative quiet of Presley."

The remainder of the article was equally condescending toward rock 'n' roll, quoting a description by one musicologist as a "reversion to savagery." Its author, Richard Shickel, who would later become a critic for *Time,* labeled Jerry's sound "a musically illiterate blend of driving beat, monotonous elementary chord structures and simpleminded, often sexy lyrics." Mitch Miller, then director of pop artists for Columbia Records, said rock 'n' roll was dangerous because "kids see the way some of these guys behave on stage, and think that's what sex is really like."

From Archie Bleyer, president of Cadence Records, came rock's defense and the reason for its popularity: "As our society has grown more complicated, there has been a growing desire to get back to nature. Rock 'n' roll is part of this drive for simplicity."

With the delicacy usually reserved to the handling of laboratory specimens, Shickel wrote off the entire movement as a "teen-age fad." For *Look* readers who by that point needed assurance that rock music would not cause a second fall of Rome, Shickel had it on good authority that after sixteen years of age, the kids stopped following the crowd and exercised personal taste—"the serious jazz of either the Brubeck or Dixieland variety. After college, they are likely to discover the virtues of more widely known performers like Sinatra, Perry Como and Doris Day—artists whose popularity is impervious to fads."

"But this is no reason for optimism," Shickel concluded. "Even if rock 'n' roll dies, you can be sure another teen-age musical fad will soon follow it. And there's no telling what it will be."

To rock's rescue came Vic Fredericks, who compiled facts, photos and fan gossip about two hundred stars in a who's who booklet. A chapter was reserved for Elvis, another for Alan Freed, two pages were devoted to how to break into the big time, and a dictionary of hep talk explained that "crazy" meant "very good" and "bad" meant "excellent," and to be "cool" was "the greatest achievement." Fredericks's biography of Jerry Lee Lewis was a thumbnail sketch compiled at a time when 'Whole Lot of Shakin'" was his only hit, depicting him as "a quiet, pleasant, modest young man in spite of his popularity," and his father was credited with being the "inspiration behind young Jerry's desire to climb the ladder to success."

"'He plays to packed houses wherever he appears,'" J. W. Brown read aloud. "'He insists that the fellows in his band and his fans have had a tremendous bearing on his success.' Jerry should see this book," Jay added. "Apparently, he's forgotten this bit of information."

Success had created changes within the family. Jerry became sensitive to the differences between himself and Jay and Russ. They were only his support; forget friendship and the long haul to the top. It was Jerry that people paid to see. The fact that Myra now traveled on the road with Jerry and her father did nothing to bring the family closer together. To the contrary, her presence made Jerry flex his muscle and inspired him to the ultimate vindication: To sever the partnership with Jay and relegate him to hired-hand status. Fifty percent of the net was too much for a bass player to earn, campaign promises notwithstanding. What Jerry needed was an argument to provide him with a reason to demote his father-in-law, and out of respect for Myra's marital bliss and domestic tranquility, Jay refused to dignify his partner's insults with a response.

"You think you made me, don't you?" Jerry nettled Jay. "You think you got me started. Well, you didn't."

"Whatever you say, Jerry." Jay nodded.

"I been thinkin' about makin' a few changes," Jerry goaded, "and the first is in the money department. No more fifty-fifty."

"You weren't at all concerned with money in St. Louis when that new Buick broke down and we abandoned it on the side of the road," Jay recalled. "You couldn't even remember where we left it. You jus' went out an' bought another."

"Well, we gotta make it up somewhere, don't we? I'm cuttin' you back to forty percent."

"That's all right with me," said Jay, reaching into a brown paper bag for the receipts and counting out twelve thousand dollars for Jerry and eight thousand dollars for himself.

"That's still too much for a bass player to get," said Jerry, and Jay, reaching the end of charitable patience, exploded.

"Take it all!" he shouted, flinging the bills in Jerry's face.

Jay decided to quit. His investment of time and money and love and care, the hospitality of his home and the sacrifice of his daughter, all neatly placed at his cousin's disposal, was yielding verbal abuse and a cut in pay. Jay gave notice to Oscar who, powerless in dealing with emergencies, frantically called Sam Phillips for help. Sam's first call was to Jay, and after asking what all this quitting nonsense was about, turned the receiver away from his ear as a steady stream of frustration poured over the line. Sam made another approach and persuaded Jay not to hock his guitar until he had a chance to straighten Jerry out.

With much haggling, Sam was able to win Jay 25 percent of the net profits from performances, half his former guarantee. It was not a lot of money, but more than the 10 percent Jerry wanted him to have. Taking nothing from record sales and denied union wages for session work, Jay's reward hardly compensated his efforts; resolving the dispute was more important, so Jay surrendered another slice of King Contentious's ransom.

The Big Beat toured the Midwest in April, and after a show in Bartlesville, Oklahoma, on the twenty-first, a day off gave The Jerry Lee Lewis Trio barely enough time to fly home for an essential recording session, with the soundtrack to *High School Confidential* as the main objective. The trio also recorded Jack Clement's "Fools Like Me," Roland Janes's "Put Me Down," and "It All Depends," a tune too old for anyone to remember its composer. According to plan, Sun would release three extended-play records and Jerry's first long-playing album before the end of summer, taking advantage of a busy concert calendar including a trip to England in May. Only the imagination could contemplate how many millions of Lewis records would be sold.

The master plan involved the devastation of domestic concert venues before embarking on the invasion of England. Rejoining the Big Beat in Wisconsin, the tour was ten days away from reaching its zenith in Boston. Envy and professional jealousy had twenty acts wringing audiences for ovations, the big three — Holly, Berry and Lewis—claiming victories in every camp. The word was out: Rock 'n' roll is coming to a theater near you. Advance notice in Boston caused thousands without tickets to march to the site and demand added shows, while the secret force that unites parents, preachers, principals and police warned them to expect the worst.

An unbroken string of million-selling singles, the impending debut of another movie, a stage spectacle unlike anything ever witnessed and, perhaps most important, a predominantly white turnout convinced Alan Freed that Jerry Lee Lewis was entitled to close the show. Jerry rewarded Freed's vote of confidence with full-tilt boogie, the venom and viciousness of his attack nearly splintering the keys, the long blond curls cascading into his face as he taunted the crowd with screams of "Go! Go! Go!" Charging into a medley of "Whole Lot of Shakin'" and "Great Balls of Fire," the kids jammed the aisles and converged upon the stage. In the white heat of the frenzy, the house lights went up and the crowd ceased chanting and dancing, wondering at the cause for the intrusion. Boston police had come for a look-see, streaming down the aisles in pairs with flashlights and nightsticks at the ready. Alan Freed cursed and raked his hands through his hair, then charged out onstage.

"Hey, kids, take a look at this," Freed cried. "The cops don't want you to have a good time!"

Catcalls and boos spread until the entire house groaned its resentment. Officers in riot gear froze with muscles tensed in anticipation of an attack, looking at one another for a cue to clear the premises. A sergeant signaled retreat, and the bluebellies turned and filed out to the triumphant jeers of the teenagers. In the street, where thousands had hoped and prayed for a command performance, the accumulation of pent-up frustrations was aggravated beyond restraint when police closed the box office and confiscated the receipts. Rocks and bottles filled the air in front of the theater. Clenched fists and claws, the protesters divided into factions and a melee of hand-to-hand combat jammed the metropolitan streets of Boston.

A warrant was issued for the arrest of Alan Freed, citing him with "anarchy and incitement to riot." It had not taken very long for those hackneyed Hollywood movie plots to become reality.

England had anticipated the arrival of Jerry Lee Lewis since January, when the first notices appeared in *Hit Parade*, *New Musical Express* and other British fanzines. "Great Balls of Fire" topped the charts, and Jerry's appearance in *Jamboree*, renamed

Disc Jockey Jamboree for foreign distribution, had given Great Britain its first glimpse of Jerry and a foretaste of things to come.

"From all we've heard of Jerry's personal appearances in the States, it will be a unique day in the history of British show business," wrote *Hit Parade*. "More shattering than Liberace's first visit here in 1956. More shattering than Bill Haley's arrival on the rock 'n' roll express. Perhaps even more shattering than Johnnie Ray's first trip here way back in 1952."

With a classic British sense of propriety, rave reviews of Jerry's music and banner headlines welcoming his arrival were tempered by snipes and jibes characteristic of free-lance journalists hoping to win a column by berating the scourge that was rock 'n' roll. As was the case with one self-righteous scribe who summed up his dislike for Jerry :

> There is some doubt about the reason for his three-bar-reled monicker. The name of Lee has a certain attractive distinction down in the southern states. But more likely, the singer's handlers saw fame acoming and stuck the "Lee" tag in as an identification. With all his comic antics on-stage, the more moronic section of an audience might have believed they were watching the other character of the same name.

One editorial transcending statements of personal taste addressed its readership with a far more significant question: "Can Jerry Lee Lewis Steal the Presley Crown?" In the article, which established a number of parallels between the careers of the two singers, the writer realized that the answer to his query depended on whether Elvis's enlistment would cause a lull in the popularity he had enjoyed for the past two years. "There is one way in which Jerry Lee does differ from Elvis, however—he will be making his debut in this country," the editorial surmised. "So when you start arguing about whether Jerry Lee can ever take the place of Elvis Presley, remember that you'll soon have the opportunity to judge for yourselves."

At long last, the recognition Jerry wanted had come. This was the chance he had prayed for, the break the Phillips brothers had waited to exploit. Seizing the once-in-a-lifetime opportunity with both hands, Sun released the single "High School Confidential,"

Jerry's first album and three extended-play records, each containing four songs from the album. With spotlights converging as he stepped from the wings, the question of Jerry's readiness to take it all had already been answered. Nothing stood in his way.

6 Love Made a Fool of Me

AS MYRA PACKED EVERY ITEM OF CLOTHING she owned for the six-week tour of England, Jerry called home to ask his parents if they would change their minds and come along. Elmo and Mamie, whose collective airborne experiences were nill, decided against earning their wings on a ten-hour flight overseas, but if it was all the same, Jerry could take his sister Frankie Jean instead. Jud Phillips was preparing a proper send-off, arranging for Jerry to appear on *The Dick Clark Saturday Night Beechnut Show* before leaving for London.

Jud chaperoned the expedition to New York, not out of a desire to savor lavish tributes from Clark and the account executives at Young and Rubicam but out of a nagging suspicion that a sensitive subject, if handled without the utmost discretion, might create an embarrassing situation for Jerry. The potential hazard lay in the discovery of Jerry's marriage to Myra, a secret that had remained successfully hidden from the media for six months without incident. But the Hotel Manhattan lobby was overrun with hounds barking at Jerry's heels for a bit of news and he was in a talkative mood. Jud was frightened by the possibilities.

"Jerry, this thing is fixin' to break," Jud worried. "I don't think this is the time for you to be stirrin' things up by tellin' everyone you're married to Myra."

"Mr. Phillips, the public demands me," Jerry said with authority, putting his foot on the king-sized bed of the master suite. "The people want me. No one or no thing will ever be big enough or bad enough to kill Jerry Lee Lewis. In fact, I'm gonna break the news on Dick Clark's show so the whole country'll know I'm married to Myra."

"Jerry, Oscar don't even want you to bring her to England—"

"An' I tol' Oscar either Myra goes or I don't."

"Jerry, listen to me," Jud pleaded. "I don't expect you to keep her in a closet for the rest of her life, but don't make a scene now. The tour of England is too important."

"Too important for a li'l thing like my marriage to ruin it," Jerry interrupted. "Wait 'n' see. People won't care if I'm married."

"That's not what I mean," said Jud, hesitating to bring up Myra's age.

Jerry addressed the mirror and combed his hair. "I might even bring Myra on the show, put her on teevee an' sing a song to her," he said, complacently.

Jud was placed in a difficult position: He could not let this happen, nor did he want to anger Jerry by stopping him. The boy was blinded by the spotlight, and this was a time for reason. At a critical moment, Jud called Bill Backer at Young and Rubicam, hoping to scare him from sponsoring a controversial show.

"Why wouldn't you want Jerry to go on?" Backer asked.

"Because he wants to bring his wife on the show," Jud said, divulging the secret under strain.

"That's okay. I'm sure the viewers will get a big kick out of seeing what she looks like. When did they marry, yesterday?"

"No, last December," Jud said, concealing his concern for Myra's age. "It's important that we keep it a secret a while longer. You know how all these girl fans will get when they find out their heartthrob is taken—"

"Then tell Jerry to shut up. If he doesn't mention it, Clark won't."

"You don't know Jerry. Nobody can tell him nuthin'."

"You are on the level, aren't you, Jud?" Backer coughed.

"Trust me. It's a little too complicated to go into at the moment, but, b'lieve me, it could embarrass a lotta people."

Backer hung up, saying he would talk the situation over with his superior, Alex Crowe, and Leon MacNamara, agent in charge of the Beechnut campaign.

"It's bullshit," Crowe said. "Jud's just trying to up the price. He wants more money now that his kid's hot."

"What if it isn't a buildup?" Backer asked.

"Well, we can't take that chance. It might not be to Beechnut's advantage if Lewis gets his head handed to him after having done the 'Breathless' co-promotion. Better call Clark and tell him."

"Tell him what?" Backer asked.

"Tell him . . . tell him it's in his and our best interests if he cancels all shows Lewis is scheduled to play," Crowe said.

Jud had already taken care of breaking the news to Dick Clark. At three o'clock in the morning, Jud called Clark at home, disguising his voice to avoid a confrontation. "Dick? You don't know who this is. You don't have to say anything. I jus' wanted to tell you to watch out. Jerry Lee Lewis married his thirteen-year-old cousin and all hell's fixin' to break loose. You're promotin' the daylights outta him, so you'd better be careful."

The next day, Clark discussed the tip with his associates, who were confounded by the news. Taking his own troubles with the network and sponsors into consideration, Clark's decision was obvious, even though Jerry's marriage was still a secret and an unfounded rumor. Regardless of Clark's reasons, to give Jerry the axe seemed to be a coldly calculated resolution, hardly fitting recompense for the man whose talents had contributed so much to Clark's success.

Jud was content to let Clark take the fall. Jerry was bewildered by the unexplained notice that he had been dropped from the show, and Jud matched him bitch for bitch about Clark's ingratitude. "Judas," Jerry's most damning curse for disloyalty, became interchangeable with Clark's name. The catastrophe which would have resulted from exposing Jerry's child bride had been averted for the moment, leaving Jud wondering whether he should continue on to England to run interference. He had other pressing business though, and the responsibility of keeping Geronimo Lee Lewis out of harm's way was entrusted to Oscar Davis.

So they set out in full sail, Jerry and Myra, Jay and Lois, Frankie Jean, Oscar, drummer Russ and Myra's brother, three-year-old Rusty, expecting to capture England without opposition. He who would be king led his retinue without fear even of death —until the Number 2 engine of their aircraft erupted in flames, forcing an emergency landing in Ireland. After breakfast, a sturdier craft made the hop to London Airport, where hordes of reporters and photographers from England's primary presses as well as the lesser publications and scandal sheets stood in one great clot awaiting the party in the terminal. Attention momentarily turned to a pair arguing the merits of modern music, one a young Turk who believed all music prior to 1955 was played on a clavichord, the other a defender of the Percy Faith who would have Jerry's sceptered head.

"I hate this duty, covering arrivals," said the older gent.

"I didn't hear you complainin' when it was Liberace," said Turk.

"See here, you're not suggesting that an artist of Liberace's stature can in any way be likened to the boogie-woogie of a country bumpkin—"

"All I say, sport, is that natural ability uneducated has more often made a success of a man than of an educated man without talent," said Turk.

At that moment, natural ability uneducated personified was ushered into the terminal with a pop of flashbulbs. Oscar introduced Jerry to the press, leaving Jay, Russ and the ladies behind. Oscar tried to keep his crew moving, and those reporters who felt nothing worth quoting would be said moved or were pushed away by the mad crush. To one side, the girls stood unnoticed until they caught the eye of a rogue reporter blocked from access to the star. He approached Lois, then asked Frankie her name and relationship to Jerry. Myra turned away, hoping the reporter would leave if ignored.

"And who are you, miss?" the reporter asked, tapping Myra on the shoulder.

"Jerry's wife," Myra muttered.

"His wife? I didn't know he was married," the newsman said, sensing a lead. "Mind if I ask you a few questions?" And before Myra could answer, Oscar came to the rescue and pushed her toward an exit and a waiting car.

From the moment Myra and Jerry set foot on Britannic soil, it was apparent that their visit would create a culture shock, not only for them but for Britons never before in contact with common folk from Louisiana. Judging Jerry by his accent, Londoners looked at him as if he had just fallen off the back of a turnip truck. Likewise, Jerry had a difficult time understanding the Cockney clip of bellboys and chamber maids.

"Oy'm one of th' skivvies, sah," a maid said to Jerry, who thought it odd that hired help should be called the same thing he called his underwear. "Now, over here we have your telly," she said, placing her hand on the television, "the loo," she said, pointing to the bathroom, "and, oh, don't mind that, mum, it's for the dumbwaiter," the maid added, referring to a cubbyhole as Myra looked around for the servant she'd insulted. Later in the day, Myra discovered with embarrassment that the water in the finger bowl was not for drinking, and Jerry learned that "Keep your pecker up" was not meant to be personal.

At their hotel, The Westbury, in the fashionable Mayfair district of London, a pair of reporters from the *Daily Mirror* and the *Daily Mail* flitted about the lobby from person to person trying to gain an audience with rock's royal family. Boldly, Paul Tanfield from the *Mail* and his photographer went around to the Lewis suite and were admitted by Myra, who thought she recognized Tanfield as the man who had approached her at the airport.

"You're married," Tanfield said to Jerry, by way of introducing Myra into the interview.

"Yeah," said Jerry, surprised that the word was out.

The two men stared at each other, waiting for the other to speak. Jerry was cautious, having sensed something in Tanfield's manner which made him wonder whether his curiosity about his wife was friendly. Myra sat on Jerry's lap and appeared as anxious to discuss the most intimate details of their personal affairs as Tanfield was curious.

"How long have you been married?" Tanfield began.

"Two months," Jerry hedged, testing the water.

"And how old is Myra?"

"Fifteen," said Jerry, playing it safe by making her a more respectable age.

Tanfield attempted to hide his amazement with the same widening eyes with which one might spy a pair of aces.

"Gee, it's fun bein' married," Myra began her first interview. "The girls back at school were mighty envious when I married Jerry."

"Really." Tanfield smiled politely, then turning to Jerry, said, "I recall your having been married before."

"Yeah, but I'm real happy with my third wife," Jerry said. "Yes, sir, real happy indeed."

"But, Jerry, when do I get the wedding ring?" Myra teased.

"It's on the way, honey," he said in a trying-to-discuss-business tone.

"Could we go back to your former marriages a moment?" Tanfield requested.

Jerry began to comb his hair nervously. "I married first at fifteen," he said, mixing fact with fiction. "Too young, I guess. We divorced. Next time I was seventeen. Still too young. We were divorced after a year, but we had a son, Jerry Lee. He stays with my mother. Myra was a fan of mine, of course. We met through the drummer in the band."

"Do you have any worries about marrying a girl so young?" Tanfield asked, bringing the subject back to Myra.

"Nah," said Jerry. "I guess you got to get married when you're ready. And I figure any girl is capable of marrying at fifteen, whereas a boy is still too young under twenty-two. Besides, look at her. She's a grown woman."

"Are you," Tanfield said to Mrs. Lewis. "Tell me what you think of matrimony."

"What I like best is cookin' and housework," Myra began diplomatically. "My favorite dish is spaghetti. But I can't fix it very well yet. Jerry gave me a red Cadillac for a weddin' present. Sure wish I had a weddin' ring, though. We didn't get time to choose one."

"I want two girls and a boy," she added, figuring a comment of that nature was expected of a mature married woman. "But it sure is awkward. You see, Jerry wants three boys—"

Into the room walked Oscar, to notify Jerry that a press conference had been set up in the lobby to accommodate the horde of newsmen wanting interviews. He was surprised to find Tanfield busily scribbling on his pad, and told him his time was up. "You can join the rest in the lobby," Oscar told Tanfield.

"Thanks, I will," he returned. "How about Myra? Will she be coming along?"

"No. Why?"

"Well, we didn't expect her. I'm sure everyone will be interested . . ."

"Look, *I* didn't even know they were married," Oscar said, pulling Tanfield into the hall. "Why don't you keep it to yourself, huh, buddy, and let them have their privacy."

Jerry followed the men to the lobby, combing his hair and straightening out his scquin- and velvet-trimmed stage clothes. He buffed the tops of his two-tone loafers on the back of his trouser legs and posed for pictures.

"Was that your wife with you earlier?" came the first question at the conference, and Jerry, who by that point believed it was a well-known fact, admitted it was.

"She may look young and be young, but she's grown," said Jerry.

With that, John Rolls from the *Daily Mirror* turned and hurried to the Lewis suite, where the real scoop waited to be uncovered. Myra answered his knock, believing it was Jerry returning for his key. She was alone, watching television and sipping a Coke, having also ordered a bottle of milk for her husband which was cooling in a champagne bucket, a detail which did not go unnoticed by the reporter's keen eye.

Introducing himself, Rolls said, "We've just heard all about you from your husband. You are . . ."

"Myra."

"Right. And you've been married how long?"

"Two months," she said, remembering what Jerry had told Tanfield and followed his lead in misleading the press.

"Aren't you a bit young to be a wife?" Rolls remarked.

"Gosh, no. Back home you can get married at ten. One girl got wed at nine," Myra informed him.

"How did you meet? Were you a fan of Jerry's?"

"See, it all happened one night on the way to see Jerry's movie," she said, warming up to having fun with the reporter. "He said, 'Let's get married.' It was a bit of a surprise, but I said, 'Let's go!' It was all a secret. I didn't tell my parents for three days. When they found out, they had a fit—Daddy particularly. See, I was Daddy's little girl. Mamma was for us. She tried to get Daddy to settle down. He was gettin' hasty, as you would call it," she said, affecting a British accent. "But everything is all right now."

Everything was not all right. The next morning, the entourage assembled in the master suite and laid out copies of the early editions of the London newspapers. From the bed, sofa, dresser and floor unfolded two-dimensional accounts of the scene at the Westbury Hotel. No one combed the copy carefully. Myra, for

Left: The Black River Stallion as a colt. 1948–49. *Right:* The Million Dollar Quartet at Sun Studio: Jerry, Carl Perkins, Elvis Presley, and Johnny Cash. December 1956. **(Courtesy Murray Silver)**

Dennis Quaid as "The Killer" Jerry Lee Lewis in *Great Balls of Fire*. **(Orion)**

Jerry Lee Lewis (played by Dennis Quaid) performs for cousin Myra Gale Brown (played by Winona Ryder) and two of her girlfriends. **(Orion)**

Jerry and Myra. 1957.
(Courtesy Murray Silver)

Trey Wilson (*left*) as Sam Phillips, Dennis Quaid as Jerry Lee Lewis, and Stephen Tobolowsky as Judd Phillips in *Great Balls of Fire*. (**Orion**)

Front page of England's *Daily Sketch*. Dennis Quaid and Winona Ryder as Jerry Lee and Myra Lewis in the lobby of the airport on their London trip. (**Orion**)

Jerry and Myra. England 1958. (© *London Express*)

Dennis Quaid as Jerry Lee Lewis and Winona Ryder as Myra Lewis in *Great Balls of Fire*. (**Orion**)

Jerry Lee Lewis (played by Dennis Quaid) and Myra (played by Winona Ryder) get remarried. **(Orion)**

A romp with Phoebe. 1965.

Dennis Quaid as Jerry and Winona Ryder as Myra. **(Orion)**

Dennis Quaid as Jerry Lee Lewis. **(Orion)**

Jerry and Myra. Memphis 1961.

Myra Lewis Williams today.
(Louis Cahill)

The Great Ball of Fire. 1982.
(Phoebe Lewis © 1982)

one, was intrigued with wading through stacks of her likeness plastered under bold headings: "Meet Myra From Memphis— Wife at 15!" and "Jerry Brings Wife No. 3, Fair and 15, Like a Well-Scrubbed Fourth-Former!"

"What's a fourth-former?" she asked.

Oscar and Jerry were arguing on the other side of the room. Myra's question was unanswered.

"How come I'm not mentioned?" Frankie Jean pouted.

The telephone rang. Lois answered. It was the hotel operator with thirty-two messages requesting interviews, all for Myra.

"Listen, this isn't the kind of greeting I expected," said Oscar. "I didn't think we were going to mention Myra."

"What's the big deal?" Jerry asked irritably. "People are gonna find out anyhow, so who cares? I don't see anything wrong with these articles."

"Yeah, but they're all about Myra," Oscar complained. "No mention of your music, the new single or the concert dates."

"So what? The tour's a sellout, the song's a hit. 'High School Confidential' is Number Twenty-one in the pop charts today. A few pictures of Myra ain't no big deal."

"This *is* a big deal, Jerry," Oscar ranted. "You're on the front page of the biggest daily newspaper in the universe. They gave you more space than General de Gaulle's takeover of France and the revolution in Tunisia, for god-sake, and it's all about Myra."

"Say, who is this de Gaulle fella, anyway? He seems to have gone over bigger than us."

Oscar ignored Jerry's ignorance of world affairs and the feeble attempt at humor. "We oughta be open about this thing. The straightforward approach might be an advantage—"

"I dunno," Jay piped up. "Some of these reporters didn't seem to cotton a whole lot to the idea of Jerry an' Myra bein' married."

"That's because a lotta girls are gonna be real upset when they read I've been taken," Jerry joked.

"What's a fourth-former?" asked Myra.

All interviews were denied for the rest of the day. Oscar kept his charge indoors, waiting to see what the response would be to the news that Jerry Lee Lewis was married to a fifteen-year-old girl whose ponytail and plain, unpainted face was featured on the front pages of England's leading newspapers. Papers which missed covering the arrival were starving for a word, a photo, anything. Getting no help, one smaller publication paid through the nose for a culled print of Myra and quoted her as having said, "I was a fan of Terry's [sic] for fourteen months before we married. My parents didn't mind—they liked Terry [sic]," which is all anyone could expect for five pence.

In every other report, the primary point of interest was that Mrs. Jerry Lee Lewis was just fifteen years old. Apparently, the lie about her age was not big enough to quell the curiosity in her juvenility. The entire affair might have ended there had not the foul-mouthed trumpet of fame sounded a call awakening the emotional appeal in Iain Smith, a reporter for the *Daily Mirror*. Smith heard the shrillness of sensationalism in the whispering campaign circulating through Fleet Street and decided that the mystery of Jerry's secret marriage required further research on his part. Before the courthouse in Memphis closed on Friday, Smith learned that not only was Myra the daughter of Lois and J. W. Brown, but that she had married Jerry five months before he divorced Jane and, last but not least, that Myra was actually *thirteen* years old. Hurrying to meet his deadline, Smith rang Oscar Davis.

For the hundredth time that afternoon, Oscar claimed to know nothing about Jerry's marital affairs. "All I know about is the divorce I was a witness to a coupla weeks ago," he said, a verification that would have been better left unmentioned. "I've been Jerry's agent since the middle of last year. He didn't tell me about his third marriage. But I found out for myself. I thought it was asinine. It was the first time he let me down."

Piecing together parts of the puzzle, Smith asked if Jerry had remarried Myra since his divorce from Jane, addressing the issue of whether their marriage was valid.

"I can't say," said Oscar. "So help me. Neither of them have told me so."

Without comment from the principals, Iain Smith quickly tapped out a brief statement of his recent discoveries and was awarded the upper right-hand corner of page three in Saturday's *Mirror*. It appeared that the details of Jerry's private life were to supercede accounts of his concerts, which were being regarded as history-making events in the minds of spectators.

On Sunday morning, following Jerry's opening at the Edmonton Regal, crowds milled through Mayfair and loitered in front of the Westbury hoping to catch a glimpse of walking, talking front-page news. Oscar was relieved that police were on their way to disperse the crowd. But the officers came inside the hotel without saying a word to bystanders. Moments later, the front desk called to say the bobbies were on their way to talk to the Lewises.

The officers summoned the guest register. Mr. and Mrs. Lewis had been clearly and boldly inscribed. They inspected Myra's passport and found everything in order. They asked diplomatically phrased questions concerning the status of the marriage, and explanations were offered in defense of its validity. The officers departed and filed a report with the Home Office secretary, who was authorized to deport undesirable aliens. What had caused this inquisition, Jerry demanded to know.

"Haven't you heard, sir, it's in all the papers: 'Jerry Lee's Bride is Thirteen.'"

From the *London Sunday Pictorial:* "Child Bride Is So Young," cried inch-high headlines. In an interview with Mamie Lewis by a correspondent in New York, Jerry's mother allegedly exclaimed, "I'm crushed, just crushed. We didn't even know anything about his second wedding . . . now there's this one." And the *Evening Standard* printed a three-columned calumny of Ramsden Grieg entitled "Mr. Lewis (22) Talks of His Three Marriages," wherein a staged cab conversation disgusted its readership:

> Driver: "And there, sir, is Buckingham Palace."
>
> Mr. Jerry Lee Lewis: "Buckingham who?"
>
> Driver (tactfully changing the subject): "What would you most like to see in London?"
>
> Mr. Jerry Lee Lewis's fifteen-year-old sister, Frankie: "Ah jus' gotta see a real live London werewolf."
>
> Mr. Jerry Lee Lewis's wife, Myra (who will be fourteen on July 11): "Yeah, we saw one once in a movie."

"The entourage then moved to the Westbury Hotel where Frankie and Myra sat down to watch children's TV while Lewis talked, in a Louisiana drawl, about his life," Grieg continued. "He sure was tickled pink to be in London but, shucks, he hoped England wouldn't think it odd that his wife was so young. Why, shucks, he was just fifteen himself when he married his first wife."

The *Express* published quotes from all concerned regarding the questionable status of Myra's marriage to Jerry. "I'll marry him a million times if necessary," Myra said. "I am now waiting to hear from Mississippi whether the marriage is legal. If it is not, I will live apart from Jerry until we have gone through the ceremony again."

Seconding Myra's statement, Jerry added, "The news that my divorce wasn't final has come as a great surprise to me. The lawyers said the divorce had gone through. People may think I'm in the wrong over all this business, but I must leave that to God because my intentions all through have been sincere."

"Myra is now married with my permission," J. W. Brown explained to the *Star* reporter wanting to know how the marriage could be legal if it had taken place without parental consent. "I did not know about the wedding when it happened. There wasn't anything I could do about it. I just tried to go along and make the best of it. I could probably have put Jerry in court, but it would have ruined both their lives."

Aside from the unresolved questions of legality, notable citizens of London were becoming incensed over the deplorable scandal taking shape. "Something should be done about this disgusting example to British teenagers," a member of Parliament was quoted. And from the home secretary, who was being pressured to deport the undesirables, came no comment until the couple's landing papers arrived from London Airport on Tuesday. In the meantime, the home secretary was apprised of the archconservative viewpoint in a twenty-two-column-inch tirade entitled "Clear Out This Gang!," complete with a photo of Jerry captioned "Bigamist" and one of Myra labeled "Girl Victim."

Recapping the entanglement, the writer hacked away at Jerry and his "shameless gang," demanding deportation. "But nothing like that is likely to happen to this teenage idol. Instead, he is living in luxury at London's swanky Westbury Hotel, all ready to clean up with one night performances all over the country," the writer inflamed.

Jerry said nothing, referring all inquiries to Oscar, who brushed them off, saying, "Don't ask Jerry any personal questions. His private life is his own affair. It's his performance that counts."

"We say that the baby-snatching antics of this bigamist are very much the affair of Britain's teenagers and their parents," the writer concluded. "And we hope the whole rabble will have the decency to clear out of this country while there's still time. If they don't and they have the effrontery to carry on with their tour, we can promise them a none-too-friendly reception. Here's a chance for Britain's teenagers to show that even rock 'n' roll hasn't entirely robbed them of their sanity."

Could scare tactics scare the crowds away? That was the question Oscar asked show promoters Sunday afternoon. The hour before going onstage at the Gaumont in Kilburn was spent in silent prayer asking for a full house. All efforts to lighten the mood fell flat. Contempt chilled the air, reflected in the eyes of strangers who stared silently at the infamous celebrity. Contempt which caused weariness to sap the power from Jerry's performance, the desire from his heart, the longing from his soul. A certain discriminative disapproval, not of musical style as it had once been, but of private lifestyle, poisoned the public. Alien alienated, Jerry walked onstage to a none-too-friendly reception, hoping to make progress within the realm of uncertainty.

"We're in trouble," Oscar said to a stagehand in the wings. "Twenty-two hundred no-shows, more than half the house. We're in big trouble."

"*We're* in trouble?" asked the bystander. "*We're* in trouble? Look at this," he said, nodding toward the stage where Jerry sat slumped over the piano stroking the keys.

The first two numbers were competently completed without effort. The magic was gone. Ten times during his twenty-minute act, Jerry ran a comb through his hair. Calculated to make the girls swoon, the only response was barracking from the balcony. Unable to understand Cockney curses, Jerry pretended not to hear.

"Baby snatcher!" came a call from the back of the hall. A few snickers, then another cried, "Cradle robber!"

Jerry squelched the taunts by tapping out the introduction to another number. Walking his hand down the keyboard and following it with his eyes, he stole a glance at rows of expressionless faces which looked as though they were witnessing an execution. Melodic magic, black as he could make it, only provoked insults.

"Go wheel your wife in a pram!" a cheerleader shouted.

"Put a lid on it," Jerry returned.

"What? What was that, sport?" the heckler persisted. "Eh, kiddy thief?"

"Will somebody please lower the lid on this trash bin," Jerry repeated, then ran into the wings.

"What are you doing?" Oscar asked. "Get back out there."

"You go out there," Jerry rebounded, as Jay and Russ remained frozen to their places, staring blankly back at the audience. "If they don't wanna hear me, I don't wanna play."

"It's just a few troublemakers," said Oscar. "There's a lotta other folks out there waiting to hear your hits."

"I don't care who's out there. I don't have to put up with that."

"We'll have to refund the money," Oscar called after Jerry.

He turned and walked onstage to scattered applause and continuing derision. He bowed to a claque of supporters, turned toward the troublemakers and, resisting a strong impulse to give 'em the finger, shook his curly head in answer to the arrows. Support was not strong enough to warrant an encore.

"The sounds he made were frantic," said a critic from the *Express* of Jerry's show. "But there was little action to go with them. And while he squawked lyrics like 'I'm all shook up,' the teenage audience sat stonily composed. Those who stayed away missed nothing."

Jerry's following was entranced, moved and convinced, not by his performance, but by the damning denigration of a press warning that rock 'n' roll is more than just a song and dance.

"Wonder if it'd make these bastards happy if you and Myra remarried," Oscar said to Jerry, throwing a newspaper across the room. On the front page of Monday's *Daily Sketch*, a five-by-nine-inch photograph of Myra, "the girl at the center of all the fuss," appeared over headlines announcing: "Police to Act in Case of Mrs. 'Rock' Aged 13."

"Police on both sides of the Atlantic may act today to end the bigamous marriage of rock 'n' roll singer Jerry Lee Lewis," said the report. Accompanying the update on what the Home Office, the Ministry of Labor and British child welfare organizations were doing to tear asunder that which God had joined together was an underscored editorial ordering, "Get out, Lewis!"

Now that he is known to be cohabitating with a thirteen-year-old girl following what appears to have been a biga-mous marriage, we say he has no business to stay in Britain. We call on the Home Office to take a closer look at these people. They should have no difficulty in finding grounds for sending the whole outfit back to where they came from. British teenagers want no part of Lewis and his lot. How soon can they pack their bags?

Jerry's response to the attack was his claim that the marriage mixup was a "technical hitch."

"Do you think you've committed bigamy?" a reporter from the *Daily Mirror* asked.

"I cannot discuss it. I think my divorce is a matter for God," said Jerry, going over the home secretary's head to a higher authority. "I used to preach at one time, but I don't now. I believe a preacher is a preacher and a rock 'n' roll singer is a rock 'n' roll singer."

A chain of events happening within the next few hours changed Jerry's attitude from reluctance to discuss his private affairs to eagerness to make a full confession to newsmongers. The first event causing complications came in the form of a directive from the American Embassy denying Oscar's request that Jerry and Myra be remarried immediately. Citing a conflict with British law and the inability of stateside jurists to sort out and solve the strange case of Mr. Lewis, the embassy literally deferred to the opinion of British magistrates. The second crisis arose over a cancellation of a show in the West Country. Harry Foster, the booking agent for the tour, feared that the deletion of one date would cause others to follow. Oscar looked further ahead and, upon hearing that the debut of the movie *High School Confidential* was suffering from reactions to the bad publicity at home, feared a drop in record sales and possibly the end of Jerry's career, although that was an unmentionable horror.

Jerry took each bit of bad news in stride, intent upon riding out the storm. It was not until he received an overseas phone call from Jane that his mood blackened. In exchange for her threats that he would never see his son again, Jerry decided to preserve the truth as he knew it in every newspaper in England. In that way he hoped to get even, perhaps win a few votes in the lagging popularity poll.

"I was a bigamist at the age of sixteen," Jerry confessed to a class of yellow-journalists in his hotel room. "I have not told the full truth about my marriages before, but I got an abusive phone call from my second wife, Jane Mitcham. I decided that if she wants to play it that way, so will I. Jane said on the phone, 'You're giving me lots of publicity over here, but you won't see your son when you come back.' So let me tell you how it really is.

"When I met Jane, she was as wild as the wind. I married her one week before my divorce from my first wife, Dorothy. I never went through another ceremony with Jane afterward. So, you see, I was never married to Jane at all. I only allowed her to get a divorce from me to try and avoid publicity. It doesn't seem to have worked out that way," Jerry smiled darkly.

"If youth and inexperience were your excuses for the failure of your first marriage at fourteen, why did you marry again so soon after?" the *Daily Mirror* wanted to know.

"She said she was going to have my child," Jerry said blankly. "I was real worried. Her father threatened me, said I had to marry her. Her brothers were huntin' me with hide whips, said they'd whip me if I didn't. Remember, I was only a kid of sixteen, and I was scared—so we got married. It was really what we call a shotgun wedding—'cept there were no guns. But we didn't stay together more than one month in six during the three years or so of our married life. Though Jane divorced me, she didn't need to. She never was my wife."

Jerry looked at Myra. "I was a young fool when I married at fourteen and sixteen. My father should have put his foot on my neck and beaten a worm out of me. Everybody thinks I'm a ladies' man and a bad boy, but I'm not. I'm a good boy and I want everybody to know that.

"This is real love," he said, squeezing Myra's hand. "Myra and me are married for good. I'll marry her again ten times over if they want me to. But there's six lawyers said our marriage was legal. I guess they can't all be wrong."

In further response to the scabrous remarks made by his detractors, Jerry appeared onstage at the Granada Theatre in Tooting, sporting a spicy mustard-colored suit with black-sequined trimming, and exhorted the crowd to join the party. "You don't have to sit quiet here," he taunted his sober judges, "this is a rock 'n' roll session, so you can let your hair down. It'll be all right."

The less than capacity crowd was less than enthusiastic. Those who had come to heckle were restricted to sounding wolf whistles during brief breaks in the action when Jerry stopped to comb his hair, for he steamrolled through a barrage of blistering rock 'n' roll. Patrons attending the late show were of a tougher ilk. They stood on queue harboring hatred, saving the cruelest cuts for when they were inside where they could amuse themselves and their friends by shouting down the beleaguered singer. What a singular trait, Jerry thought, that Britons pay to see a show they want stopped.

"Y'all seem awful quiet out there," Jerry said, when his best attempts at "Lawdy Miss Clawdy" and "Good Golly Miss Molly" received little response. "I'm alive. I sure hope y'all ain't half as dead as you sound."

"Go home, baby snatcher," someone shouted.

"Get home, you crumb," booed another.

From that point forward, the show was a disaster. Never had twenty minutes passed so slowly. At the end of each selection, Jerry glanced at his watch, anxious to finish.

"We've had enough of you, too," cried a malcontent, filing out with others to gather at the stage door, chanting the chamade "We hate Jerry Lewis."

"Watch him wheel his wife out in a pram."

"Baby snatcher!"

The demonstration did not please Victor Chapman, general manager of the Granada Theatre chain, and executives from the Rank and Grade organizations. They were all in agreement: The tour must be stopped. Early in the morning of the following day, Oscar Davis was making a last-ditch appeal to the American Embassy to come to Jerry's rescue. It was too late.

Oscar returned to the hotel and woke Jerry with the bad news. "You're all washed up, kid. The British tour is over. They don't want you here. We'd best just go home, so I've booked you on the first flight out to the States tonight."

"What if I don't wanna go?" Jerry said, working himself into a prime fit of pique.

"Why the hell would you wanna stay?"

"I might like to sight-see. Then, after all this dies down . . ."

"Forget it. Our reservations here are up and can't be extended. We were supposed to move on to Birmingham today, and the manager says he needs these rooms. No other hotel will take you.

We're under siege," Oscar said, pointing to the window. "Not even Scotland Yard can guarantee your safety."

Myra rushed to the window. Looking to the avenue below, she saw hundreds of Londoners streaming toward the Westbury; bands of teens wanting autographs, others wanting nothing more than to see the Child Bride. Some were simply caught up in the flood and whisked down New Bond Street not knowing if Guy Fawkes had arisen or if Lady Godiva was at it again. Every attempt to leave the room was met with a crush of reporters wanting to cash in on the scandal of Jerry Lee and his ladykin. Police were called to clear a path through the streets when the entourage was forced to depart for the airport and a plane that would not take off for nine hours.

Constable barracks in Mayfair sounded the alarm, and quadrants of young starchily suited bobbies locked arms at the elbow and bulldozed bystanders twenty yards downfield before the tide surged and the line buckled and broke. It was a regular field day. The bobbies huddled for another scrimmage and, like so many uniformed teammates, rejoined the fray and pressed into the mob once again only to be repelled far from their goal line.

Upstairs, the Lewises and Browns were tossing six weeks of provisions into wide-mouthed steamer trunks yawning open in the midst of disarrayed suites. Myra dressed inconspicuously in a navy-blue sailor suit and covered her face with large dark glasses. Jerry threw on a jacket, ranting and raving about the bastards who were still busy dismantling his career with headlines like: "Tour Bosses Sack 'Baby Snatch' Jerry," "Lee Lewis Is Kicked Out For Good" and "Jerry and Myra Fly Off Home."

A limousine idled curbside awaiting persone non grate making plans for their escape. "I'll go out the front and draw their fire," Oscar said. "Y'all go out the side door and jump in when I give the signal. I'll meet you at the airport with the luggage."

The group braced for an unpredictable reception from the crowd. Were the onlookers mad? Was London filled with hate, or curiosity?

Oscar appeared on the steps of the hotel before a mob numbering in the thousands. Silence overcame the throng as he announced that Jerry and Myra were already gone. The crowd groaned and turned away. Oscar beckoned his group to advance when the coast was clear. They piled safely into the car when a group of stragglers cried out, and before the limo could pull away, the mob converged on all sides. Hands pounded the glass as kids piled onto bonnet and boot. The crowd thickened to thirty deep at every point and rocked the car from side to side, pitching the terror-struck passengers to and fro.

"We're gonna turn over!" Myra cried, as Jerry held her tightly on his lap.

"They're tryin' to get in!" Frankie Jean screamed.

"What do they want?" Jay hollered at the driver.

"I don't know, sir, it's hard to tell," the chauffeur said with fear. And it was indeed difficult to discern whether the rioters were friend or foe. The few faces that could be seen registered pain and stress at attempting to avoid being crushed to death. Waving palms mashed flat against the windshield under the weight of piling bodies. Daylight could be seen only where pushing and shoving allowed glimmers to filter through the movement.

Lois expected to suffocate under the blanket of humanity. Rusty was crying and Myra began to whimper, too. Police pulled people away from the outer perimeters as the chauffeur sounded the horn and revved the engine, inching out from under the hundreds blocking the way. As black marias tootled down the street, scattering scavengers bearing off antenna and door handles, the plagued and beset tourists fled for the safety of the airport.

Iain Smith, the *Daily Mirror* scribe whose homework accelerated the scandal, was among the many reporters assigned to cover the retreat and described the scene at the airport: "For eight hours —while the Home Office officials were still looking into their papers—they wandered forlornly around the lounges and bookstalls, and gazed at the rain through the windows."

"I don't wanna see no more of Britain," Myra said in response to Jerry's offer to take her sight-seeing at Windsor Castle. "I just wanna go back home to Memphis. I did want to stay long enough to get a wedding ring," she added, changing a pink amulet from her right hand to the ring finger of her left hand.

"Are you disappointed at not being permitted to finish the tour?" a reporter asked Jerry.

"Sure, I'm disappointed at not finishing the tour. I don't like to disappoint my fans. I would've made a hundred thousand dollars in the next six weeks. I've got contracts—but I'm not going to press for payments for a tour I haven't made."

"Then the financial burden is not entirely yours—"

"Whoever's losin' money on this, it ain't me," said Jerry. "I've lost nothing. I'm being paid for not working. I got guarantees. I'm not going to sue anyone, and I'm not pressing for payments for performances I haven't given."

"Surely you won't receive all of the money to which you were entitled had you completed the tour—"

"Look, I make money, not lose it, see?"

"Jerry, looking ahead, don't you think your popularity will be diminished at home?" another reporter ventured.

"There's plenty work back home," he insisted. "I don't have to worry about money. I'll be glad to get home. I didn't need this tour. I earn twenty thousand dollars a week back home. I don't think I've lost anything in reputation or anything else by this."

"Jerry, a word about your fans here. How do you feel about the shouts of 'go home'?"

"You British are nice, on the whole. I've had a wonderful reception. And those people who yelled at me were just mixed-up teenagers. I didn't mind that. You get these slobs at performances from time to time. The audiences were great." And in an attempt to erase the quizzical looks that his airless optimism created, Jerry aimed a barb at the critics among his fans and the press: "Look, no matter how good you are as an artist, or how clean you are, there's always some smart-ass who likes to shout out."

"They're just jealous, plain jealous," Myra chipped in. "I've got nothing against the British. The audiences were just fine— there were just some mad ones who wanted to make a fuss. It's just jealousy."

"So, you're saying you believe the tour has been canceled because of disapproval of your marriage and not because your fans have turned against you," one writer debated.

"They canceled my tour because of what has been said about my marriage to Myra. I've been beaten up pretty hard by this publicity. Back home they take a different view of this sort of thing. I expect to get a great reception when I get back. I'm not worried about my reception in the States. My fans will understand. Look, we love each other and we want it to stay that way,"

Jerry finished, squeezing Myra's hand. "Other people should mind their own business."

In the aftermath of anathema, promoters of the British tour tried to bleach Jerry's crimes of the blackest dye by continuing with the supporting act, The Treniers, and a replacement, Terry Wayne, a sixteen-year-old guitarist from Plumstead. "He's good! He's clean! He's wholesome!" proclaimed advertisements for the salvaged show, and in support of that claim, newspapers carried a quote from Terry: "I never met Jerry, though I collected his records and liked them. But I think all this has been—well, disgusting."

"Had we known beforehand of his private life, we would never have agreed to use him," said Victor Chapman of Jerry in a terse disclaimer from the Granada Theatre chain. Apparently, Mr. Chapman's research into the background of the supporting act, The Treniers, was conducted with a similar careless disinterest. While none of The Treniers had done anything in their private lives as shocking as marrying a thirteen-year-old cousin, they had achieved notoriety by recording a cheap and nasty tribute to lust entitled "Poon-Tang!," hardly fitting fare for the affable vaudevillian theaters of England.

Repercussions of the Lewis Incident reached major proportions when Minister of Labor Iain MacLeod was called upon to answer a protest lodged by Sir Frank Medlicott, representing the Independent constituency of Norfolk Central in the House of Commons.

"Is my right honorable friend aware that great offense was caused to many people by the arrival of this man, with his thirteen-year-old bride, specially bearing in mind the difficulty that others have in obtaining permission to work here?" Sir Frank puffed. "Will he remember also that we have more than enough 'rock'n'roll' entertainers of our own without importing them from overseas?"

"This was, of course, a thoroughly unpleasant case, which was ended by the cancellation of the contract and the disappearance of the man," said the minister of Labor. "But at the time the matter was before my officers, it was purely a question of a permit for employment, and his case was treated under the ordinary arrangements which apply to everybody."

In the *Daily Express* of May 28, accompanying the article "The

Exodus of a Fallen Idol"—appearing above the daily horoscope predicting for Jerry and Myra a splendid day for home affairs and engagement announcements—Cyril Stapleton penned an essay on the power of public opinion entitled "The Fans Who Make Them Discover They Can Break Them."

"I think we're witnessing an interesting social phenomenon," Stapleton said. "The kids who turn nonentities into overnight stars have just discovered their power to blast them into oblivion. If the fans begin to get tough with the clay-footed idols, they are in for a one-way ticket back to their home town. The singing stars of the future might even be forced to learn their trade first."

Not every review of the Lewis Incident was ablaze with fire-words, as in the case of one Charles Govey who, in his paean titled "Jerry Lee Lewis Was the Wildest," not only lauded Jerry's performances but went as far as to accuse the press of overplaying the facts. Other inveterate provincial performers had toured England before less than capacity crowds similarly unenthused, said Govey. And there were other space-available free-lance contributors who shared Govey's opinion that if Jerry Lee Lewis wasn't the greatest musical entertainer to hit their shores, he was certainly the wildest. But the insertion of testimonials was embarrassingly scant, pigeonholed in back pages where they existed at all.

The marriages of Mr. Lewis became secondary to a warming debate whether the reaction of the public spurred by a vengeful press had been warranted. To what extent are the private affairs of a public figure fair game for scrutiny and criticism? There were no lords of the fourth estate to argue in the affirmative that the secret life of Jerry Lee Lewis should be concealed. Rather, the prevalent position among publishers of the news upheld the narrower negative view that he who seeks publicity must endure public opinion—"a compound of folly, weakness, prejudice, wrong feeling, right feeling, obstinacy, and newspaper paragraphs," as stated by Sir Robert Peel one hundred years before the Lewis Incident.

The line between censorship and disapproval was never less distinguishable than by remarks published in the *Daily Sketch* written by an anonymous editor pen-named Candidus. "Let This Be a Warning to Others!" Candidus cautioned.

So Jerry Lee Lewis and his malodorous little circus have been given the old heave-ho by Britain's theater managers. The rock 'n' roll performer who makes a reputed five hundred thousand dollars a year in his native America won't be taking much home from this country . . . except a batch of blistering press cuttings. Never before, to my knowledge, has a visiting variety star taken such a pasting from the newspapers—or a more richly deserved one.

I'm wondering now if this latest instance of vigilance on the part of the press is being regarded as an "intrusion." Meanwhile, it becomes increasingly plain that there is a limit to the amount of private misbehavior which the public will put up with in performers' private lives. To say—as Mr. Lewis's manager was reported to have said—that a star's private life is his or her own affair is just not true. Once performers begin living on public applause, it matters very much what code of morals they subscribe to. It will be no bad thing for British show business—or for our young rock 'n' roll fans, either—if the unsavoury saga of Jerry Lee Lewis ends up as a cautionary tale.

His faith questioned, his marriage belied, his talents trampled on, Jerry returned to the United States despondent and disheartened. Here was a man made for people to hate; not only did he live beyond the letter of the law, but beyond the spirit as well. With all he had done thus far in his turbulent lifetime, how ironic to have been undone by his only private pleasure—love for his wife. His professional life was put in jeopardy not by acts or ideas, but by the words "Child Bride." After parrying British press inquiries for the final time, he boarded the midnight trans-Atlantic flight confident that folks at home would catch a falling star and set him gently on his feet.

America provided no bridge of gold for the retreating rogue, although what was scandalous front-page news in London appeared under small and inoffensive headlines in Memphis. "Jerry Lewis Blames Mixup On Lawyers—British Riled," was the way in which the entire fiasco was summarized in a mere fourteen column inches without photographs on page 20 of the *Commercial Appeal*. The attorney general of Shelby County, Tennessee, explained to newsmen that bigamy charges would have to be filed in Mississippi, where the marriage to Myra took place, but Mississippi ruled that no law had been violated, since Jerry had not lived in that state with either wife. Therefore, Jerry was not liable for bigamy despite having married twice without benefit of divorce. Legalities aside, the Lewis Incident was still the harshest indictment that Anytown's League for Decency had to prosecute and persecute the plague that was rock 'n' roll. America was shocked that England was shocked; everyone was shocked by Jerry Lee Lewis.

Annealed by the batch of blistering British press cuttings, Jerry and Myra calmly appeared before a small huddle of reporters waiting at Idlewild Airport in New York. If Jerry was to be painted as a public enemy, he wasn't going to pose for the portrait; he would lie to protect himself and his family; he could never trust the truth with anyone again. He was prepared to lend meddlesome reporters an earful of colorful copy when he was screened by Steve Yates, a publicity agent employed by Oscar Davis to keep the Killer as quiet as possible.

"I was homesick—that's why I'm back so soon," Jerry told reporters with a straight face. "We weren't deported or anything like that. We could have stayed in Britain and made our home there if we'd wanted to."

"Aren't you angry, Jerry?"

"I guess I'm not sore at anyone." He shrugged. "I'm a pretty happy boy."

"Just how old is your wife?" a confused correspondent queried.

"Sixteen," Steve Yates interrupted.

"No, you can't get away with that one." Jerry smiled. "All Britain knows she's thirteen. She's comin' up to fourteen in July. But she's all woman, I can tell you that."

"Tell us about the reception you received Monday night—"

"What about it?"

"The booing."

"I never heard any boos. I've never been booed in my life. The English are a real nice audience," Jerry claimed. "They don't scream, like our gals and boys—just sit quietly clappin'. Three thousand people did demonstrate outside my hotel, though, shouting 'We want Jerry.'"

"Could we get a shot of you kissing your wife?" a photographer requested.

Jerry clutched Myra and kissed her on the forehead.

"No, no, on the lips, please."

"We never kiss that way in public," Jerry said—then rattled her roundly with a loud smack on the mouth.

"Oscar warned me not to let him talk," Steve Yates moaned. "They'll crucify him. They'll ruin his career."

They went nowhere unnoticed. Although few bypassers spoke, the pair caught every eye. What were people thinking?

At the end of the gangway leading into the Memphis airport terminal, a motherly woman spotted the Lewises. "That poor child," the woman said as Myra passed. The sorrowful look on the woman's face and the tone with which she expressed her pity formed a lasting impression on Myra's memory. Yet the recognition factor kept Myra from withdrawing into herself. Perhaps there is a certain pride which springs forth from infamy, when the cause can be justified.

Jud Phillips was the only familiar face in a crowd of one hundred people, mostly airport employees, that met Myra and Jerry in Memphis. An informal press conference was staged in the terminal coffee shop, where the weary couple related the oft-repeated comments for the benefit of the local papers. En route to Memphis, Myra decided that her name was not glamorous enough to suit one in her position, so she instructed reporters to refer to her as "Gale," since it looked smarter in print. The game was nearing its end, and she felt entitled to some small satisfaction at the media's expense.

When the tale had been retold, Jerry begged to be left alone, taking Myra by the hand and leading her to where one of their Cadillacs, the light blue one, waited to take them home. There were no crowds to impede their progress as they drove to White-haven, a remarkable contrast to the surly send-off Londoners had given them not too many hours before. Hoping the city would swallow them, Myra and Jerry were reminded as they drove past the gates of Graceland and saw fans milling about that more newsmen and spectators were probably hovering around their home. They decided to spend the night with Myra's parents, wanting company and protection. They were not surprised to find the Browns' telephone ringing off the hook. The next morning, they drove to Ferriday to lay low until it was safe to come out again.

"What's the latest from Oscar?" Jud asked Sam when they met to discuss the handling of these urgent affairs before the troublesome trend became irreversible.

"He's asked the British promoters to fork over Jerry's full salary," said Sam. "He says Jerry didn't cancel or violate the contract and wasn't even given a reason as to why he was canceled, and therefore is entitled to his money."

"What's their reaction?"

"They jumped all over him. The Grades say Jerry has already been paid more than he was due to receive for the number of shows he performed, and they say the cancellations were due to his decision to air his private life before the press. Now they're threatenin' to sue."

"Has the press let up yet?"

"No. Oscar sent back a few clippin's, not all bad. One says dozens of fans raided the hotel where Jerry stayed, wantin' to buy or steal everything in his suite—ash trays, sheets, anything he touched. Never seen anything like it, the hotel management said. They've hosted royalty from all over, but never had a reception quite like the one for the king of rock 'n' roll. So, what do we do now, Jud?"

"It's a little late in the game to be askin' my advice, idn't it? Why the hell didn't y'all listen to me a month ago, when I warned you an' Oscar somethin' like this was fixin' to happen?"

"I never dreamed . . ."

"Y'all shoulda known the papers would make a federal case outta all this legalistic crap. Our problem is we're takin' this thing too serious. I think we oughta make fun of it, too, just like everybody else. It's a joke. We oughta take advantage of all this free publicity and get a few more laughs. Let Jerry wheel a baby buggy onstage—"

"No," said Sam. "You can't flaunt this in people's faces. They won't stand for it. This ain't funny—they're laughin' at us, not with us."

"People have always laughed at us—the critics, the big shots in New York. Lookit the hillbilly cat, ain't he a hoot. I tell ya, I like Jack Clement's idea. He and a local deejay put together a gag record, a novelty item that'll sell like there's no tomorrow. It's a reporter, see, meetin' Jerry at the airport on his return from London, and he asks Jerry all these silly questions. Jerry answers him with lyric extracts from his hits. The announcer asks Jerry how he feels about bein' back home and Jerry sings, 'Feels good,' taken from 'Great Balls of Fire.' Then he asks where Myra and Jerry met, to which Jerry sings, 'Boppin' at the high school hop,' from 'High School Confidential.' Oh, it's great."

"Cute," said Sam, "but I think a lotta people will be outraged on top of outrage."

"There's nothin' you can do about that kind 'cept apologize an' disappear," said Jud. "For those who want an apology, let's apologize. For those who see the humor in the situation, let's give 'em a laugh. If you don't like either of those ideas, let's put Jerry on the damn bus and carry him around to every damn deejay in the country and let him talk to 'em man to man. Let the deejays see the monkey in the cage."

Sam ignored the suggestion. "We already have a problem with the stations refusing to play 'High School Confidential.' After hittin' Number Twenty-one last week, it dropped clean off the charts. It's just beginnin' to make a move in rhythm an' blues, but it won't last. Parents are callin' up the stations threatenin' to boycott sponsors' products if they don't quit playin' Jerry Lee Lewis. That's it for the album."

"Not if you get behind him," corrected Jud. "Look, parents have always boycotted rock 'n' roll, that's nothin' new. You'll just have to spend a li'l more to get over this hurdle, that's all."

"Jud, you got to know when to hold on to that money," Sam refuted. "You threw away two, three hundred thousand in the last year on promotion. We ain't got enough money to buy off everybody that's sick of Jerry's shenanigans. Nobody's got that much money."

"You're wrong," said Jud. "Too many owe us favors. Grease the wheel and you get a hit, same as always. Gimme twenty-five thousand and 'High School Confidential' will be top ten by the end of the week."

"You jus' don't get it, do you, Jud? The record ain't sellin', it ain't gettin' played. Oscar's got a list of cancellations as long as my arm. And you think I'm gonna turn over my checkbook an' let you throw good money after bad? I ain't spendin' another cent on Jerry Lee Lewis till the slate's clean. If you can't get his records played without payin' somebody, shame on you. A lotta people owe us and owe big. You can start with your pal, Dick Clark, who wouldn't be where he is today if it wasn't for you and Jerry."

Sam and Jud rigged a recovery program designed to overcome adverse publicity and restore Jerry's music to its former prominence. The first facet of the plan was an apology in the form of an open letter to the music industry, a plea for compassion penned by Sam and Jud, signed by Jerry and published in trade magazines *Billboard* and *Cashbox*:

Dear Friends:

I have in recent weeks been the apparent center of a fantastic amount of publicity, none of which has been good.

But there must be a little good even in the worst people and according to the press releases originating in London, I am the worst and not even deserving of one decent press release.

Now this whole thing started because I tried and did tell the truth. I told the story of my past life, as I thought it had been straightened out and that I would not hurt anybody in being man enough to tell the truth.

I confess that my life has been stormy. I confess further that since I have become a public figure, I sincerely wanted to be worthy of the decent admiration of all the people, young and old, that admired or liked what talent (if any) I have. That is, after all, all that I have in a professional way to offer.

If you don't believe that the accuracy of things can get mixed up when you are in the public eye, then I hope you never have to travel this road I'm on.

There were some legal misunderstandings in this matter that inadvertently made me look as though I invented the word indecency. I feel I, if nothing else, should be given credit for the fact that I have at least a little common sense and that if I had not thought that the legal aspects of this matter were not completely straight, I certainly would not have made a move until they were.

I did not want to hurt Jane Mitcham, nor did I want to hurt my family and children. I went to court and did not contest Jane's divorce actions, and she was awarded

$750.00 a month for child support and alimony. Jane and I parted from the courtroom as friends and, as a matter of fact, chatted before, during and after the trial with no animosity whatsoever.

In the belief that for once my life was straightened out, I invited my mother and daddy and little sister to make the trip to England. Unfortunately, Mother and Daddy felt that the trip would be too long and hard for them and didn't go, but Sister did go, along with Myra's little brother and mother.

I hope that if I am washed up as an entertainer, it won't be because of this bad publicity, because I can cry and wish all I want to, but I can't control the press or the sensationalism that these people will go to to get a scandal started to sell papers. If you don't believe me, please ask any of the other people that have been victims of the same.

Sincerely,
Jerry Lee Lewis

From the other side of their mouth came the second phase in redemption—release of "The Return of Jerry Lee," the novelty single by Jack Clement and disc jockey George Klein. Response to advance copies was encouraging enough to prompt the twosome to work up a sequel, but as with all jokes, it was only funny when heard the first time. The flip side was "Lewis Boogie," Jerry's second original composition, which had been sitting on a shelf for several months.

The third stage in the Phillips plan of attack was more deliberate, calling on friends in high places to pay IOU's. The brothers were surprised to find out how short some memories can be. Some who had been given a leg-up at the beginning of blossoming careers did not think they owed Sun so much as to rally behind a universally denounced sinner and scoundrel. Others wanted nothing to do with Jerry Lee Lewis, period. Jud pinned his last hope on the most powerful figure to emerge in popular music—disc-jockey-cum-television-toastmaster Dick Clark.

"With this marital mess and the parents all upset, Jerry's single ain't gettin' any support, Dick," Jud said. "We need help lining up support for the boy. We need to get him a coupla shots on teevee. A guest spot on your show would go a long way in helpin' to start things off right."

"Mr. Phillips, if it was left up to me, I'd have Jerry on my show every week. But you know my sponsors are my harshest critics, and I don't think they'll back me up on this. Jerry's too hot for me to touch right now. I'd love to help, I really would, but I'm in an impossible situation here. The network just won't go for it unless you can create a demand for Jerry again. So far, it's just not happening. We don't get letters asking for Lewis like we used to. Maybe later in the year . . ."

"Dick, we need help now. There may not be a later on for this boy. Now, are you with us or not?"

"I wish you wouldn't put it that way, Mr. Phillips. You know how much I value our relationship. It isn't my decision and I think you know that. I'm terribly sorry."

Jud's report touched off an explosion which had Sam calling Dick Clark to cuss him out. At that precise moment, the brothers felt the icy sting of isolation. The line was clearly drawn separating the Protestant Ethic and rock 'n' roll, saints and sinners, us and them. Back to the beginning, in an effort to build support from the grass roots, the brothers implored Oscar Davis to schedule bookings for his ailing act as soon as possible, preferably in areas of strength. When at last Oscar was located, he and fifty thousand dollars in receipts from the abandoned tour were honeymooning in Paris and Madrid, having so angered Lew and Leslie Grade that the promoters filed a complaint with the Musicians' Union. All questions, said Oscar, regarding the performing future of that has-been could be addressed to Steve Yates in New York.

Yates, the PR man who attempted to prevent the return of Jerry Lee from becoming another media ordeal, had secured a four-week booking for his new act at a Manhattan supper club. The Café de Paris, located on Broadway, was renowned for providing diners with a frothy cabaret pianist and a bleached-out chanteuse united in songs sung low enough to burp over. Sequins and cummerbunds were not Jerry's kind of crowd, and the engagement was terminated in record time, beating the old mark established in England by three days.

Money. The last alternative in solving the dilemma of putting Jerry back together again came down to buying his reprieve. Sam's position on the issue was absolute—there would be no perks or bribes emanating from his bank account, and Jud's money was Sam's money. Without a friend left in the business to bail them out of the hole Jerry had dug for them, Sam and Jud turned to brother Tom. In the formative years of Sun, Tom was a talent scout and sound engineer, and from those vantage points observed as much of the business as his brothers allowed him to see. The money he managed to squirrel away was there if his family needed it, and briefly, Tom was brought into the business to underwrite the Jerry Lee Lewis revival. Before he had scratched the surface, his bank account was wiped out.

More money. To the old homestead in Alabama the brothers went in search of funds to further finance the recovery. Four wealthy physicians anted one hundred thousand dollars apiece into a war chest which was plundered by waste, misappropriation and futility. And more money. When the doctors went belly up, Jud went into hock, pawning off his prized possession, the grand tourismo Greyhound, to music publisher Bill Lowery.

When at last it became apparent that no amount of cash could save Jerry's career, the Phillips brothers reached an impasse. Jud returned home to pursue other interests, including the proprietorship of new and used car lots, as another investor, losing all he was worth, took his own life.

In the backlash of reconstruction, promoters in Britain won a hundred-thousand-dollar judgment against the scandal-ridden singer, friends fled like rats from a sinking ship, and Jerry was the target of an industry blacklist. A boycott was in full effect: No records were played on the radio, no television appearances, no bookings, and stores shipped hundreds of returns back to where they came from.

Hardly two years had elapsed since the unknown itinerant piano player had first stepped into a studio, then ascended in June of 1957 with one of the biggest-selling singles in pop music history. When next June appeared on the calendar, Jerry's star had dropped below the horizon. The good ol' days, of which there were exactly 569, were over.

7 *Big Blon' Baby*

MYRA'S MARRIAGE, OF A FEW DAYS AND much trouble, had been doomed from the start. Hadn't the censure of the incident in England been warning enough of its impropriety? To the contrary, Jerry never conceded that she caused the ruination of his career. As if his love derived new vigor from the opposition, he vowed publicly and privately his love for her was genuine and their marriage valid.

Admitting mistakes might have been made in counseling Jerry in his affairs, his attorney advised him to remarry Myra to remove the taint of bigamy. On June 4, the Reverend J. P. McKeithen performed a brief ceremony before Jerry's family at home in Ferriday. As far as these occasions traditionally go, it was not a happy affair, owing to the sheer inconvenience and perplexity suffered at having to repeat that which the parties had already affirmed. At a time when no one in the entire world would have blamed them for separating, with full knowledge and in the face of all detractions, Jerry and Myra chose to remain man and wife —luckily, for, as yet unknown even to Myra, she was with child.

Returning to Memphis in late June following a second honeymoon, Jerry believed the scandal had run its calamitous course and the matter of his marriage to Myra forgotten. He was prepared to pick up where he had left off, supposing a new tour had already been mapped out, when Jud broke the bad news.

"I'll just come right out an' tell you, boy, there's been some changes," Jud began. "It ain't gonna be like it was for a while. This incident still has to die down some."

"Where we playin'?" Jerry interrupted the speech. "The Paramount?"

"No. No Paramount."

"The Metropole in Boston?"

"Not yet, Jerry."

"The National Guard Armory in Cleveland?"

"No."

"How 'bout the damn Ice Cold in Brinkley?"

"If . . . you'll take three hundred dollars," Jud said, bracing for the shock to reverberate.

"What do you mean?" Jerry demanded. "I ain't changed. I'm the same guy singin' the same songs, same ever'thing. What's happened?"

"It's them, Jerry—the papers, the promoters, the program directors, sponsors, parents, teachers, preachers . . . I'm not sayin' they ain't some still willin' to work with you, but Fred Humes and Jack Ward are the only promoters we can find right now. Them, and little guys like Leon Walden and Eddie Crandall. I figger you got to pick up on a few dates where your strength lies and get some good publicity for a change."

"Like where?"

"Down around my ol' home town, Sheffield, Alabama, where we first hooked up a couple years ago, your old stompin' grounds, small towns like that. We'll build an entire new show around you usin' local talent every place we play. That'll win some folks."

When anger subsided and his pride had been displaced, Jerry reluctantly agreed to start over from the beginning in Sheffield. It was not a difficult town for Jud to deliver, but just in case, he would insure a packed house greeted Jerry's return to the stage even if he had to give the tickets away. For a solid week preceding the date of the show, the town was smeared with placards advertising Jerry's second coming. The show was a bona fide sellout, two thousand tickets at a buck and a half a head, and enough people wanting seats to add a second and third show.

"I don't think my fans will let me down," Jerry told a reporter before stepping onstage. "I've had offers from the movies, but I like these personal appearances better."

"How much you figger on makin' this year?" the reporter asked, more out of curiosity than for his story.

"Couple hunnert thousand," Jerry claimed. "Maybe more."

"I hear tell you changed your style some in England. You don't jump around no more, just sit quiet-like—"

"I jump on the piano if I feel the music. If not," Jerry added with sinister emphasis, "I sit real still. And you can print this, too: I love rock 'n' roll about as much as a hog loves slop. I sing for anybody that likes my music. And I always keep my show clean."

With that, Jerry stormed onstage supported by a trio which now included Roland Janes on guitar. Sporting a yaller suit and two-tone loafers, the new, improved model reached down deep for the boogie bass that echoed in Water Valley and rumbled in Sulphur Dell. Halfway through the first number, Jerry's feet were on the keyboard; eight bars later, they were on the music rack.

The *Commercial Appeal* in the early morning edition of the following day reported, "A packed paid attendance welcomed Jerry Lee Lewis back to the entertainment stage. His fans screamed with an abandon matched only by certain forms of religious ecstasy. Half the audience was male. The usual answer is that their wives insisted on going. But women can make men go, but not stay and yell as these did."

"Nice," Jud said of the report.

"Nice?" Jerry disputed. "What's so nice about it? When it's bad news, I get headlines. When it's good news, I get a spot on the back page."

"It's a start," said Jud.

"Another start," said Jerry dejectedly.

The first week in July took Jerry through the heart of the Southland, from Waycross and Columbus, Georgia, to a very important date in Atlanta. There was a chance that before his concert at the Ponce de Leon ball park Jerry would perform a remote television pickup for Dick Clark; that chance eliminated with a resounding *no* from the boardroom at ABC.

The newspaper in Columbus heralded Jerry's arrival, announcing: "Coming here with Lewis will be his thirteen-year-old wife, Myra. It was Myra who caused Jerry Lee's contracts to be canceled in England." Thereafter, it seemed that every time Jerry's name appeared in print there was always mention of his child bride, his curse, the jinx that sank his ship as he ventured up the Thames.

"The marriage to his thirteen-year-old cousin Myra Brown was the talk of the town in London recently," was the way in which a Fort Benning chronicler described the scandal. "Consequently, the rest of his engagements were canceled."

"Jerry Lewis Is Here Without His Myra," the *Atlanta Journal* hollered from its headlines. And throughout the seventeen-town, three-week tour, Myra received as much, if not more, attention than her husband. Jerry could not sidetrack reporters; Jud could not stop it. Myra went home and remained hidden away for the remainder of the itinerary.

"We're buildin' a swimmin' pool," Jerry told newsmen. "Myra stayed at home to attend to the details."

The reporters forgot Jerry completely. They went to Memphis for their stories, to Mrs. Lewis for the real scoop.

"If anything, our marriage helped Jerry," Myra was quoted less than ten days from her fourteenth birthday. "Everywhere we go, people holler at us and say hello. Every single letter we received about the treatment we got in Britain has been favorable. They say: 'We're sorry they did that to you—don't pay any attention to them.'"

"What if Jerry's career were to end suddenly? What do you think he'd do with himself?"

"Farm," said Myra. "He bought a two-hundred acre farm near his hometown in Louisiana about six months ago. I'm a city girl, but a farm would suit me fine—anywhere Jerry Lee is would suit me."

In figuring ways to steer press attention away from Myra and back to Jerry, Jud recommended he do something notable, charitable and praiseworthy—a surprise benefit performance for the hospital at Fort Benning, for example. The impromptu show before five hundred patients and dignitaries was delayed two hours due to heavy rains and slippery highways, but Jerry performed a medley of his hits, then hurriedly changed for the contracted appearance in town. The human-interest angle was lost in a reporter's efforts to relate the seedier side of Jerry's story.

"So what do ya think of the English?" the reporter asked while watching Jerry change clothes.

"I don't think they like Americans," he replied, trying to avoid the wearisome subject.

"What do ya think of your wife?"

Jerry paused. "She's a good cook but would rather eat out."

"What do ya think of Elvis?"

"He's a real good boy," said Jerry, and stalked out of the room, leaving the reporter with his incomplete checklist.

Another reporter in Atlanta began, and ended, his interview by asking Jerry if he recommended marrying a girl as young as Myra.

"If she's a woman," sneered Jerry, then instructed J. W. Brown to get rid of the guy and hereafter keep all reporters away from him. "Don't send 'em back to talk to me no more. England this, Myra that, Elvis . . . I swear they're gonna drive me crazy."

"Look, just tell 'em the incident ain't hurt your career none, we're booked solid and there's no cancellations," Jay advised. "Tell 'em Myra's a good wife, a good cook and a smart girl. Maybe in time they'll put the scandal behind 'em and leave us all alone."

Ignoring the logic in Jay's suggestion, Jerry refused all requests for interviews when the show moved on to Macon. As a result, offended journalists gave the opening act more than the usual passing reference in their write-ups. Sweetie Jones, a local one-hit wonder who played a guitar with one broken string, was credited by a local critic as "the crowd favorite, as he carried the ball the greater part of the show."

Nevertheless, Jerry was riding on the crest of a dozen sellouts in small but friendly venues when the tour hit Sulphur Dell and its first washout. Six months earlier, Sulphur Dell's ball park had been the scene of three thousand jubilant fans surrounding a makeshift stage at home plate, cheering Jerry wildly. As Jerry drove out to the stage in a chauffeur-driven Lincoln, he was dismayed to discover less than four hundred locals loitering about, nonchalantly awaiting his return. The gathering greeted him as his hard-core following always did, with cheers and prolonged applause, only on this occasion the fewer voices rattled around the infield with less enthusiasm than displayed at a little league baseball game. Jerry took the stage, tested the microphone with a rumbling belch and began his show, a shorter set than usual. After playing the obligatory hits, he jumped from the platform and fled to his car.

"I don't understand it," he said to the show's promoter. "Where is everybody?"

"Jerry, you're too good a showman for this to continue," the promoter comforted. "You'll make it back. We'll have you back real soon."

What Jerry had difficulty in understanding was summarized simply and accurately in the small notice his production received: "The problem? Apparently marriage to Myra Brown of Coro Lake, Tenn., which seems to have sharply reduced his popularity here."

Jerry couldn't get arrested, and neither could Myra. As the tour migrated to Florida unnoticed, Myra was front-page news in Memphis for having wrecked her red convertible Cadillac while driving to the dry cleaners. All kinds of dust was kicked up about her not having a Tennessee driver's license, and more of a fuss ensued over her Louisiana license, which she was not old enough to legally possess. Accorded every consideration with which Memphis treats its misdemeanant celebrities, Myra was permitted to return home unhampered as long as she promised to report to the Highway Patrol office with her husband as soon as his tour ended. A *Press-Scimitar* staff writer was assigned to follow up on the wreck story and inform anxious readers whether Jerry was mad about the incident, exhausting six paragraphs explaining "Myra Forgiven, Flies to Jerry" to spend the rest of his tour in relative safety.

After Birmingham, where he played to his largest turnout— seventy-five hundred people—Jerry received wild receptions in New Orleans and Springfield, Missouri, where the Civil Defense Auxillary Police were called out to restrain five thousand fanatics, some of whom tore Jerry's discarded clothes into scraps of souvenirs, then grabbed the cable to jerk away his microphone and kept it, too. Wearing what remained of his trousers and socks and the cuff of his right sleeve, Jerry was helped backstage by a wedge of uniformed guards and treated for red welts clawed into his pale skin.

Jerry was rejuvenated by the favorable public sentiment in seventeen southern sites. Instead of tricking and treating his way back up the ladder as the Phillips brothers vainly attempted, Jerry managed to succeed simply by giving people what they wanted; exciting performances and flashy showmanship. Had Sam and Jud been too hasty in surrendering?

At home, Jerry tested his newfound good fortune by going into the studio to tape four songs, including material to be released as a new single in August. Three of the titles, "Break Up," "It Hurt Me So" and "I'll Make It All Up To You" had been written by a newcomer to Sun, Charlie Rich. Rich was a promising jazz pianist when he came to Sam Phillips bearing a demo tape. Sam played the opening strains of technical perfection and switched off the recorder, disappeared momentarily and returned with several songs by Jerry Lee Lewis.

"Listen to these," Sam said, "and when you've learned to play as badly as that guy, come back and see me."

Following the unprecedented success of "Whole Lot of Shakin'," every musician hoping to record for Sun was expected to sound like Jerry Lee Lewis. Jerry was the new standard, and Ray Smith, Cliff Thomas and Jerry's cousin Carl McVoy were among the first acts who attempted to fit the Lewis mold and found marginal success. Charlie Rich went to work for Sun's musical director and arranger, Bill Justis, and played around town in Bill's band. Bill tried to undo all that Rich had managed to accomplish and rebuilt him from "Lewis Boogie" up. He returned to Sam with a new tape fashioned in Jerry's rockabilly style, and one of the cuts, "Lonely Weekends," became a classic for Rich, who was destined to become a major recording act in his own right.

Jerry was one week away from making further headway by contracting with MGM to take an acting role in a movie. Before departing, he belatedly remembered Myra's fourteenth birthday by giving her a white miniature poodle, appropriately named Dinky, which Jerry had shelled out two hundred dollars for on the seller's warranty that the dog's grandsire was owned by Elizabeth Taylor. The dog's days were numbered; Liz's grandsire's kin or no, Dinky ruined everything in the house, teething on what was low enough to reach and peeing where he pleased.

On Friday, July 18, the *Press-Scimitar* scribe assigned to the Child Bride watch caught up with the entire Lewis clan at the airport shortly before Jerry and Jay departed for El Paso and several dates in Texas, from where they would proceed to Hollywood.

"What about the traffic ticket your wife got two weeks ago?" the writer asked Jerry.

"I just didn't have the time, man," said Jerry. "We got in Tuesday morning and only had a day and a half at home."

"You mad at Myra for wreckin' that car?"

"No. It wasn't her fault. She's a good driver. They can't put her in jail, y'know."

"Where you off to in such a hurry?"

"I'm on my way to Hollywood," said Jerry. "Gonna get an actin' part in a new movie. Not just singin' this time. MGM has me under contract."

Elmo and Mamie, having spent the past two days visiting their son, had come to see him off. The reporter was bemused by the tearful departure. Everyone was crying. Mamie was crying. Myra was crying. Dinky was crying.

"We drove up from Ferriday to visit Jerry Lee durin' his two-day stopover," Elmo told the reporter. "I used to be a carpenter, but now Jerry takes care of us—"

"In the Elvis Presley tradition?" the reporter interjected.

"Yep. That boy sure is good to us—too good, in fact. He bought me a farm outside Ferriday, a home in Ferriday, livestock, ridin' horses, and he's gonna buy me two hunnert an' five more acres that we've picked out down there. He bought me a new truck and give his mamma a eighty-four-hunnert-dollar baby-blue Cadillac. Jerry also gives me two, three thousand dollars ever' time he sees me," said Elmo proudly. "He's sure some boy."

Myra listened to Elmo boast about his son and sympathized with the way in which he had to lie away the hurt he suffered silently. The house, the farm, the cars and the money had all been given to Mamie. Elmo lived in the lap of luxury without sharing it. He never asked anything for himself—the truck and the livestock, sure, it was nice, but Elmo wanted those things so that he could work to earn a few dollars for himself. He never had more than ten dollars in his pocket, and then only if Mamie had given it to him. But Myra never heard Elmo complain. And he wasn't about to tell the world that Jerry wasn't every inch the thoughtful son Elvis was.

Mamie, on the other hand, did not have to ask Jerry's permission to spend his money, just ordered up what she wanted and sent him the bill. As Jerry explained to Myra, "If I had a dime, a nickel of it would be my mother's, unless she wanted the whole thing." No sooner had Jerry shelled out eighteen thousand dollars for the first farm, his mother had her sights set on another. While Mamie went on spending sprees, Elmo could be found at work in the fields, clad in threadbare blue jeans and a gray T-shirt which rode halfway up his back. And, like Elmo, Myra asked for nothing and received little more.

If Jerry was to continue supporting his family in the Elvis Presley tradition, then hopefully he would earn money in the same manner. Motion pictures were the likely avenue, and MGM was considering Jerry for the lead in a comedy entitled *Rally Round the Flag, Boys*. One close-up view of Jerry's blondined-curled, snaggletoothed puss and a sound check of his bayou brogue had MGM continuing the talent search. The role was awarded to another blue-eyed blond with neat rows of even choppers, Paul Newman.

Trying to get the truth of the movie matter out of Jerry was something else. He didn't want to return home without a part in a film as he had announced in the paper, so he stuck by his story. "I'm gonna make movies," he told everyone. "Maybe not the one I went out to Hollywood to talk about, but they got others that are gonna be even better. Don't know how I'm gonna find the time to take off from tourin', though." And the moveable dream of motion-picture stardom was kept alive indefinitely by stringing everyone along.

With or without a movie contract, Jerry was still sensational copy for tabloid newspapers and fanzines. *Modern Screen* had an interest in publishing Jerry's story, only they had no concern for his purported film career. Their interest was purely prurient, the focus of their exposé Jerry's now-famous quote: "Myra's only thirteen but she's all woman." America's Greatest Movie Magazine revealed—or rather, invented—"The Shocking Story of Jerry Lee Lewis and Little Myra."

The writer responsible for what amounted to soldered press accounts and publicity releases confused and distorted details of how the infamous couple met and married—that was the only shock to his fictionalized story:

"Well," Jerry Lee said, gallantly, "the feeling is mutual, Cousin Lois, because I like Myra, too. In fact, if she wasn't my cousin, I might even end up marrying her someday."

Everybody at the table laughed heartily at that one—except Myra. Myra was blushing now, suddenly and hard.

"How old you be, anyway, little gal?" Jerry Lee asked.

"I'm thirteen," Myra said, her voice suddenly trembling.
"Mmmm," Jerry Lee said.

And from no less a gossiping personage than Louella Parsons, the same issue of *Modern Screen* published her scoop that comedian "Jerry Lewis may take legal action against Jerry Lee Lewis, the latter a singer who was booed off the stage after he married his thirteen-year-old cousin. Our Jerry is sick of being confused with this 'kissin' cousin.' "

Modern Screen's milieu was milk and water compared to the poison-pen approach of *Confidential*, whose four million monthly copies were published under a "Tells the Facts and Names the Names" masthead. "We will respect the respectable, love the lovable—but detest the detestable," warranted its editor, and keeping those ideals foremost in mind, *Confidential* dispatched Renee Francine to New York to: interview the Lewises for "the first intimate, inside story of what it feels like to be the child married to America's No. 1 Rock and Roller—singer, Jerry Lee Lewis." Entitled "Grade School Confidential," Francine's description of a day at Coney Island began:

> Myra Gale is such a little child. Just turned fourteen, she is a bright child, who, like other children, might be spending the summer at a girl scout camp, or at a day camp away from the city. By rights she should be in bed at 8:30 P.M. after watching TV or catching up on her reading of *Black Beauty*. But not Myra. Myra is a housewife.
>
> The child becomes aggravated when people call her a child. She doesn't like jokes such as, "Jerry Lee Lewis had a double-ring ceremony—with a wedding ring and a teething ring."
>
> "I don't feel like a child," she says. "I feel like a happily married woman."

And in spite of Myra's feelings, Francine and other penny-dreadful journalists continued to exploit her plight. Francine's story was not published until October, and the scandal which should have petered out in June was stretched into its sixth month of compelling coverage.

Myra and Jerry were also a popular topic for televised forums.

On the CBS-TV debate *Right Now!*, Alan Freed, answering a remark made by the moderator about the responsibility of rock singers, particularly Jerry, argued that examples set by Hollywood stars and jazz musicians were no better. Elvis Presley, home on emergency leave to be with his mother at her death, commented on Jerry's expulsion from England at a press conference: "Jerry's a great artist. I'd rather not talk about his marriage, except that if he really loves her, I guess it's all right." A fitting remark, since Elvis would soon become enamored of his future wife, fourteen-year-old Priscilla Beaulieu; though having learned a valuable lesson from Jerry's experience, Elvis would wait ten years to marry her.

It was Jud Phillips's opinion that as long as Jerry was a hot topic he should hunt up all the free publicity he could get, although Jud wanted to change the angle to a positive slant and impress upon the public that Jerry was doing as well as ever—artistically, professionally and financially. With the widespread attention that Elvis's comments received, Jud decided to capitalize on it while Jerry was on an autumn tour of Texas with Carl Perkins. Jerry returned home to find his name in headlines. "Jerry Lee May Buy Elvis's Mansion, $200,000 Price Tag," began the story, relating how Jud, in Jerry's behalf, had negotiated a down payment on Graceland with an undisclosed salesman representing Presley. Tom Parker said it was the first he'd heard of the deal; Private Presley was even more surprised than his manager.

"They wanted somethin' to talk about, so I gave 'em somethin' to talk about," laughed Jud, and everyone laughed right along until the punchline was heard in Louisiana, where Jerry's ex-wife Jane, a humorless girl, hauled the Killer into court for being in arrears with alimony and child-support payments. At the same time, a court order was handed to Sun attaching all royalties paid to Jerry until a judgment of $4,159 was paid on the '58 Buick he had given to his parents. Jud's publicity stunt backfired as creditors came out of the woodwork looking for a piece of the fortune with which Jerry was to buy the most prized parcel of land in Tennessee—the fortune Jerry no longer had.

In the court of Judge W. Edward Quick, Jane complained that her ex was late with the checks to the tune of eleven hundred dollars. He had been prompt with his payments in the beginning, but came late and then were reduced as his cash flow dwindled to dribs and drabs. Jane's attorney, whose figures on Jerry's earnings were more accurate than his own, showed he had earned eighty thousand dollars in the first five months of 1958, from which he appropriated funds to buy a farm, a swimming pool, Cadillacs all around and a tutor for his child bride. In the plaintiff's opinion, there should have been enough left over in petty cash to cover her monthly award.

In Jerry's defense, his counsel admitted the complaint was true, but that upon returning to the United States from England Jerry had lost a hundred thousand dollars and his record royalties plummeted to nine thousand dollars for the second half of the year. Nevertheless, the judge ordered Jerry to come up with the back alimony. He was flat broke until the end of the month, when a tour would take him to Michigan for five days. An advance from Sam was out of the question; he'd have more luck selling blood.

Jerry demanded his attorney find a way to reduce the size of Jane's alimony and fix it so his parents got custody of the children. In support of a crosspetition seeking those ends, Jerry lodged a list of complaints against Jane, all of which were beguiling and untrue. He accused her of all kinds of crazy acts, including one occasion when she got in an automobile in her pajamas and took a bottle of whiskey to a man, was involved in a drunken brawl with a different man in a Natchez rooming house, and once got so drunk that she passed out for two days. In support of these malicious lies, Jerry obtained the sworn testimony of a seventeen-year-old fan who jumped at the chance to serve his idol, legally or otherwise. It was Jerry's mistake to have threatened Jane that he had such a friend, willing to swear he had been intimate with her even though it was not true. Such was his maneuvering and the depth of his deception.

The judge found Jane innocent of these shenanigans, but allowed she had done too much "social drinking and frequenting of night spots, not to her credit, but not so as to warrant a change of child custody." Further, since Jerry denied the paternity of Ronnie, the court could not in good conscience award both children to Jerry's parents, because of the awkward situation which would be created. Jerry won a marginal victory in the battle over alimony —his payments were shaved to three hundred dollars a month, but was docked for expenses and attorneys' fees which he refused to pay and which became the foundation for further legalistic hostilities later in the year.

Thus, the press, having relied on Jerry for filler copy for most of the year, had nothing further to report on scandals, divorces and rock 'n' roll. There was a temporary lull in further installments of the ongoing saga of the Killer and the Child Bride until the end of 1958, when Myra reemerged in a dramatic new light.

Mamie had seen this sort of thing before. Elmo had, too. Lois Brown feared the worst. Even Jerry knew his wife was going to have a baby, but Myra wasn't able to figure out why she awoke every morning and threw up. By midday, she felt fine, wasn't feverish and sat down to a big lunch, but every morning it was the same sickening routine. For the first few days, Myra believed it was simply a sneaky virus. Coincidentally, she began to recover when all of a sudden her period stopped. If it wasn't one thing, it was another. Only now did she begin to worry, and still no one confirmed her suspicions.

When at last Myra accepted the obvious, she found it difficult to break the news. She wasn't exactly sure, but if she was pregnant, she didn't want to talk about it. She fretted over her fate, remembering her mother's vivid description of the deathlike pains of delivery. The pain, the pain, the pain—all Myra could think about was the pain. Having no one to comfort and console her, to counsel away those self-destructive doubts, the tiny mother-to-be silently suffered a fear of death in the torturous throes of childbirth.

A trip on which Myra accompanied Jerry to Florida was marred by her advancing case of motherhood. When she began to gag at the sight of meat or the smell of onions, she was packed off to Ferriday and taken to Doc Ratcliffe, the wise old family physician who had singularly administered to the aches and pains of the Lewis clan for twenty years. With Myra, Doc Ratcliffe would need a great deal of patience and understanding.

"Ever have any trouble, like nausea?" Doc asked.

"No," Myra said innocently, "but could you gimme somethin' for this upset stomach?"

Doc Ratcliffe felt around in private places and prodded his expectant patient this way and that, then predicted he would attend to a new generation of Lewises by March 6, 1959. The news was regarded by Mamie as a hunch confirmed rather than a surprise. That the child would not be his first tempered Jerry's excitement; life with a pregnant wife is not always a joy. Myra began counting the days of the rest of her life.

At home with his parents, Jerry outlined a plan. "I think Myra should stay here on the farm with y'all. I don't want nobody but Doc Ratcliffe seein' her, an' travelin' back 'n' forth to Memphis will be too hard on her. Besides, I want the boy born in Lou'siana."

Myra had no choice but to accept the arrangement, including the part about having a boy. But she had one question: Why was it so important that Doc Ratcliffe supervise the production exclusively?

"Because he saved my life when I was a baby," said Jerry. "I had a case of enlarged stomach muscles. He put me on Co'-Cola an' it saved my life. Besides, I don't want anybody else to see you nekkid. Doc Ratcliffe is like fam'ly. I've known him all my life. An' he's an ol' man."

"Mrs. Jerry Lee Lewis to Croon Lullabye—14-Year-Old Bride of Singer Expecting a Child in March," announced the *Memphis Press-Scimitar*. Asked if she were afraid to have a child, she replied, "No, why should I be? It happens every day," then proceeded to worry why the reporter would ask. Myra said she planned to join Jerry on a tour of the Carolinas where she would break the news to her parents, if they hadn't already heard. Ten days later, they were to return to Memphis so that Jerry could go to Hollywood to begin work on his first acting role in a movie, *The Big Bongle*.

After closing up their home on Dianne Drive, Myra moved to the farm in Clayton to prepare for the birth of her son and the end of her life. Nights when her husband was away, she sat by the window light and cried for the racking pain that would kill her. She gazed up in wonder at the bright white eyelash of a moon and picked a patch of the Bible-black heavens where her light would take its place among the illuminated souls. She kept her sadness to herself, never mentioning her condition or bothering to ask questions as she contemplated the gut-wrenching torture that awaited six months away.

Jerry hadn't a clue to his wife's misguided sensitivities. He was not an empathetic man. His own problems, those concerning his rollercoaster career, were much more immediate. The boycott had reached far and wide, destroying his last release and severing off whole legs of his tour. Network television shows waging bidding wars for him four months before now flatly refused his services. The country's top promoters, men whose pockets were lined with fortunes from Jerry's concerts, were investing in other talent. And then the word came from Hollywood: There was no room for him there. His inability to act was never considered as the reason for refusal; it had to be the blacklist.

Support from die-hard fans did not appear to have been diminished by the continuing adverse publicity. Kay Martin reported receiving at least three hundred letters a week, sometimes as many as five hundred, many of which came from England, and all but two or three were supportive. Kay's only problem, aside from being unable to answer the fan mail, was funding the club's expenses. Her difficulty in gaining financial and promotional assistance was indicative of a greater problem, the fact that support for Jerry from his producers had come to a standstill.

A letter Kay wrote to Oscar requesting $11.50 for fan-club expenses was never answered. Oscar, who was trying to put Jerry as far behind him as possible, had his hands full with an Internal Revenue audit into some forty thousand dollars of unreported income. Jud was at home in Alabama establishing his Judd Records label to harbor fugitives from Sun, and Sam was barricaded in his office with problems the size of Jerry's fourfold.

What happened to the bargain with Johnny Cash, Carl Perkins and the rest of the Sun roster, whereby Jud was to take the newcomer Lewis to New York, make him a star, then bring the others behind to start a whole movement? What happened to the promise that each in turn would enjoy a promotional campaign to equal Jerry's, taking them around the world and to the top of the charts? What happened was the money promised to Johnny Cash was spent on Jerry; when Cash asked for a royalty increase to match Jerry's, Sam refused. Pressings of Carl Perkins and Warren Smith singles were minimized or shelved to make way for the newest Lewis release. There was no substance to Jud's Big Deal; there was nothing left for the boys in the back after the Lewis Incident washed ashore. If Sun's brightest hope could have his riches ragged, Sam had no confidence that Cash, Perkins and the rest were anything more than a passing phase.

"I quit," said Johnny Cash.

"I quit," said Carl Perkins.

"I quit," said Roy Orbison.

"I quit," said Warren Smith.

"There goes Sun Records," said Jud from an armchair in Alabama.

"Oh, I wouldn't say that," Sam controverted. "I own hundreds of unreleased songs by each one of them boys that I can put out whenever I want. People'll never know they're gone. Besides, I still got the best of the lot—they can't blacklist Jerry forever, and there's five years left on his contract."

On August 15, Sam released what he hoped would be Jerry's lucky single Number 7, "Break Up" backed with "I'll Make It All Up To You," covering all angles by coupling a dance tune with a country ballad. The great majority of popular radio stations discarded it without so much as an audition, but of greater encouragement was the strong reaction to the flip side by the country crowd—people who would continue to enjoy Jerry's music as they always had, unswayed by scandal and impervious to fads.

The experiment ripened in September. The results: "Break Up" ranked Number 52 in the pop charts after five weeks of limited exposure. "I'll Make It All Up To You" lasted one week in the pop charts, where it struggled to Number 85, but rallied to Number 19 in the country sector. Sales volume was down drastically from the million-selling "High School Confidential." It was the first attempt since Jerry's initiation that failed to strike the golden gong.

"What happened to me?" Jerry asked Jack Clement and Bill Justis, the men who recorded and arranged the Sun sound.

"Who knows what makes a hit?" Clement replied. "I don't know. Remember the song I gave you, 'It'll Be Me'? That was a hit, but you'll never believe where I got the idea for that lyric. I was sittin' on the pot takin' a shit," Clement continued, much to Jerry's amusement. "I was sittin' an' thinkin', and the topic of reincarnation crossed my mind. Then the words came: 'If you see a lump in the bowl, baby, it'll be me, and I'll be lookin' at you.' I changed the lump of shit in the toilet bowl to a lump of sugar in a sugar bowl, and I had me a hit and ten thousand dollars. So, son, as far as I can tell, hits come from the can in more ways than one."

"Jack, why don't you go take another one o' them ten thousand dollar shits?" Bill Justis joked in Jerry's behalf.

During the first week in November, Jerry recorded a trio of tunes from the days of his youth—"Drinkin' Wine Spo-Dee-O-Dee," Gene Autry's "You're the Only Star (In My Blue Heaven)" and Moon Mullican's "I'll Sail My Ship Alone"—harkening to the ways of the ancients, hoping to rediscover the secret of the popular song. The session represented a radical departure in the nature of Jerry's sound. As if the Killer no longer trusted his own ability, Charlie Rich not only arranged the music but played the piano, both formerly Jerry's exclusive rights. And on "I'll Sail My Ship Alone," a saxophone was added to the instrumentation for the first time, a significant change in Jerry's rockabilly signature.

From these sessions, "I'll Sail My Ship Alone" and "It Hurt Me So" were combined to create the next single, which shipped in mid-November. The handling of "It Hurt Me So" was a further departure from Jerry's traditional style: In addition to his understudy taking over on piano, Roland Janes's guitar dominated the instrumentation and a male chorus backed Jerry's vocals. The release was so unlike the best of Jerry's music that those stations not involved in the boycott refused to play the record purely on critical criteria. For one week late in January 1959, "I'll Sail My Ship Alone" was listed at Number 93 in the top hundred and was never heard from again.

"I'll Sail My Ship Alone"—how appropriate a title for a Jerry Lee Lewis song. Mutiny had robbed him of his following, and piracy among his producers rotted the planks beneath him. J. W. Brown took his leave, having had enough of the road, ridicule and bickering—and Jerry, he'd had his fill of him, too. Jay invested what money he had managed to save in a business that built and restored pianos. Jerry accepted Jay's resignation as he had on so many prior occasions, confident he would return once he had gotten over whatever had upset him. His retirement was not as brief as Jerry expected; it would be one year before Jay was persuaded to join Jerry onstage again.

Jerry was set adrift. The blacklist had taken its toll, ending an eventful year on a sad note, with a bleak forecast for the next.

An ugly rumor spread through the music industry at the end of 1958 which cautioned against hard times for record companies, promotion men and disc jockeys. There were rumblings about an investigation into bribes—"payola," as perks to deejays for playing new records were called. If the government decided to launch an investigation, whole companies could be put out of business if their files were confiscated and bank accounts attached.

"I'm not sayin' we got anything to hide," Jud told Sam, "but I think you and I ought to part comp'ny. Make a clean break. So if the investigators find any unaccounted-for expenses, you can just lay if off on me. I'll say the money came to me, and the most we'll stand to lose is a tax penalty. But the important thing is they don't come in here an' wipe us out. We play the game that you and I ain't gettin' along, see, and I'll go home and start my own label. Who knows? I might even sell a few records."

"What about Jerry?" Sam asked.

"He's yours for at least four more years under the contract. I don't want him. Hell, I can't do nothin' with him."

"Neither can I. And I ain't about to keep spendin' money on puttin' out his songs if no one's gonna play 'em on the radio," said Sam, checkbook in pocket.

"So, I guess it's up to me to tell the boy."

"What are you gonna tell him?"

"I dunno. He ain't gonna understand most of it, and I'll guarantee he ain't gonna like any of it."

When Jerry had heard enough of boycotts, resignations, investigations and slackening releases, he surprised Jud by announcing none of it mattered, he just wouldn't sign up with Sun for another year. Recalling the previous December when Jerry signed a contract in a Paramount Theatre dressing room, Jud confirmed the fear he had all along that Jerry did not know what he had gotten himself into.

"Jerry that was a five-year contract you signed last year," Jud said.

Jerry stared at Jud. "No, no way. It wasn't for no five years. You tol' me it was jus' like last time, the same deal as before. You didn't say nothin' about no five years."

"I thought you read it."

"What for?" Jerry asked of his trusted friend. "You said it was just like the first one."

"Look, would it have made any difference if you'd known it was for five years instead of one? You were on top then. There was no England, or any of that mess."

"But if Sam ain't gonna put out no more records on me, what's he want me for? What am I s'posed to do for the next four years?"

"Try to make it back. It's not like he ain't gonna put out your records, it's just that you won't be gettin' the push you got before. You won't be makin' the money you used to."

"What about all the money Sun owes me for my hits? I ain't seen all of that yet, have I?"

"Who knows? Sam's got two girls down there tryin' to make heads or tails outta his books. Neither one of 'em can add. He ain't got a company fulla accountants an' bookkeepers like RCA. They got a ledger that sometimes they write in and sometimes they don't. Right now, nobody could tell you how many copies of anything Sun's sold. There's no way to find out how much you've earned or how much you're due. You got just about all that's comin' to you, 'cept maybe foreign royalties."

"What," Jerry asked in complete ignorance, "are foreign royalties?"

It wasn't the money that concerned Jerry; Sam may not have paid him all he was due, but he was way ahead of the game because of Sam's having taken a chance on a poor boy from Ferriday once upon a time. What Jerry began to understand for the first time was that his recording career as he had once known and enjoyed it was over. He was finished. No more hits, no more royalties. He was under contract to a company that could not sell his product yet would not let him go in case he was miraculously resurrected sometime in the next four years. Jerry couldn't sell a record anymore. And if he couldn't sell a record, would anyone want to see him perform?

"What do I do now?" Jerry asked his mentor.

"Do what you've always done. You got more talent than anybody I ever seen. You did it once the hard way and you can do it again. And, Jerry," Jud said in parting, "if there's anything I can ever do, call me."

*   *   *

Clayton wasn't the end of the world, but it was very close to it. Myra was lonely, even when surrounded by Jerry's family, and labored under a constant undercurrent of resentment. Alone and depressed, she fretted away the last two months of pregnancy, wanting kindness and sympathy and a friend in whom to confide.

Elmo was Myra's closest ally. His complaint was as constant as hers, stemming from a total lack of respect from his wife and family. He had seen affection vanish into passive resistance, and had long since surrendered his place in Mamie's bed to Linda Gail. He, like Myra, suffered silently, and idled about till one of the women in his life dispatched him on an errand. He could do nothing to lessen Myra's burden without increasing his own.

In her calls and letters home, Myra never spoke of unpleasantness, nor would she share her sorrows and complaints, fearing it would only prove she was unfit for marriage and legitimize the gossip that poisoned public opinion. She wanted to be thought of not as a good wife but a great one—a gourmet cook, a doting mother and a rock upon which her husband's erratic career could support itself. Her parents were defeated by the distance between them and their daughter. Without witnessing events of the day firsthand, and without a discouraging word from her, Lois and Jay had no cause to suspect Myra was miserable. Knowing Jerry must be in financial straits, Jay offered his son-in-law an honorable means of supplementing his income by endorsing a line of pianos, promising to divide the proceeds of every sale equally with Jerry in exchange for permission to stencil his name on the key cover. When Jerry learned of the promotive gesture, he refused.

"Ain't nobody makin' another dime off my name," Jerry swore. "If I want my name on pianos, I'll put it there and take all the money. I had enough of leeches."

One look from his mother's eyes reminded Jerry that those thieving in-laws had lived off him in style too long. So powerful was Mamie's suggestion, so complete her control over her family, that she even had Myra believing her father was a cunning cheat. Jay, whose every effort to aid his cousin was twisted by the Lewis jealousy and greed, was the unsuspecting victim of Mamie's deep-laid scheme which hurt no one but Jerry. Recognizing Mamie's treachery for what it was, Myra never trusted her mother-in-law again.

Kay Martin, president of Jerry's ailing fan club, became

Myra's pen pal and confidante. As time passed, their correspondence, which began when Kay invited Myra to contribute a few lines to the club's newsletter, became more personal to serve Myra's need for companionship. A closeness between the two could not begin until Myra was sure Kay wasn't after her husband, and her earliest letters probed for ulterior motives. Kay's deep devotion to her idol and running his fan club kept her from a career and had even gotten in the way of her romances, but if her interest in Jerry was something other than professional, Myra never detected it. Myra's first letter at Kay's request was a hundred-word essay on "Why I Like Jerry Lee Lewis," creating a dream-hole in the tower Mrs. Lewis erected about her husband:

> I like Jerry Lee Lewis because he's so understanding, soft-hearted, sweet, adorable and talented. Jerry can play any kind of instrument from an organ to a harp and he can play them all very good. He has a wonderful voice, he can sing any kind of song like it was written just for him. Jerry is kind to everyone and anyone. You can't help but just love and adore Jerry even if you're only around him for a few minutes. There is only one thing that I regret and that is that there isn't another Jerry Lee Lewis so that another woman can be as happy as I am!

Kay must have appeared to be the only friend Myra and Jerry had in all the world. Because she continued to steer a flagging fan club without assistance, monetary or otherwise, Myra sought to keep Kay's loyalty at a time when Jerry himself could not have cared less for his following. Thanking Kay for her continuing efforts in Jerry's behalf, Myra cheered her with hopes that the struggle would soon be over.

When Myra was three weeks away from giving birth, a news flash on February 3 brought the shock of the airplane crash that killed Buddy Holly, the Big Bopper and Ritchie Valens as they traveled between dates for the Biggest Show of Stars. The tragedy heightened Jerry's anxiety when flying, and the loss of his friends and costars was considered an omen by his family. February performances were scheduled closer to home so that he was only a short trip by car from Memphis or Ferriday.

Myra longed to see Jerry once more before the end, for the end was near. She was frightened of facing her fate without her husband, who phoned every once in a while from a roadside station far away and would still be on tour when she was due to give birth.

Without Jerry, there was no one to take Myra's mind off her condition. So much of her day was wasted away in anxious anticipation; with every kick of a tiny foot inside her belly, she was reminded of the pain, the pain, the pain of death in the delivery room. From her window she could follow a wagon trail from the farmhouse to where it passed alongside the family cemetery, the only shady oasis on the eighty-acre farm. Mamie's parents were there, visited only on occasions when another member of the clan was interred. The cemetery had once been Jerry's favorite place to play, where his son would play. Then, with another kick of a tiny foot, Myra was reminded that it would not be long before her place was staked out among her ancestors; the kid had a great beat.

Since Baton Rouge was hardly 125 miles away and she was not due until March 5, Myra decided to drive to Jerry's show with his parents on February 26 rather than sit at home with nothing to do but worry. It was Mamie's idea, and Myra thought it strange that she should seem insistent on her going. What Myra did not know about was a scene that took place earlier in Dothan, when a friend of the Lewises, a Bible salesman, had gotten drunk at Jerry's show and was arrested. Jerry not only saw the man's wife safely to her motel but tucked into bed as well. As Jerry was showing his concern for the lady's welfare, a shadowy figure appeared at the foot of the bed and called Jerry by name, saying it was time to go home. It was Mamie, come to retrieve her errant son, and she dragged him out of the room half-naked; he, protesting all the while, "Mamma, we was only talkin'."

The secret bond between mother and son insured that not a word of his indiscretion would be mentioned, especially to Myra. Jerry's most embarrassing moment remained a little secret between him and Mamma for twenty years. Mamie hoped to prevent repeated sins by carting Myra about to satisfy her insatiable husband's needs. When he first laid eyes on Myra that afternoon before his show, Jerry had to have her then and there, little knowing she was only hours away from giving birth.

Jerry expected to find his family seated ringside for his late show but could not spot them. They had been awaiting his return to the club during his break when, precisely at fifteen minutes after midnight, Myra felt the first of what had to be labor pains, no doubt initiated by the invigorating interlude at the motel. She clutched Elmo's arm in reflex to her spasms.

"I think we better go now. I'm feelin' somethin'," said Myra.

Elmo, who had delivered all four of his children, was not the least bit shaken, nor was Mamie, who was just a little put out with Myra for such poor timing. "No need to stay in Baton Rouge," Mamie said with asperity. "The pains are comin' too far apart. We got plenty of time to get home."

Elmo left word for Jerry and hurried Myra into their Cadillac. She sat in the front seat next to Mamie and held on to the door handle with a death grip, gasping for air. She felt faint, knew death was at hand and began to sob. When they had sped fifty miles along Highway 61 into the remotest southwestern corner of Mississippi, the pain deepened and Myra panicked. There was only a whistlestop named Woodville between them and the hospital at home. If Myra had to stop, she would have to depend on Elmo and Mamie to deliver the baby in the backseat of the car on the side of the road in the swamplands of Mississippi.

As Myra cried in correlation to her contractions, Mamie elbowed her husband. "Elmo, you gotta knife? I don't think this child is gonna make it."

Wild-eyed with terror, Myra blanched white at the thought of dissection with Elmo's whittlin' knife. Waterbrash wambled in her stomach as the infant squirmed. Elmo put the pedal to the metal, pressing the car beyond 110 miles per hour. In Baton Rouge, Jerry received news of the emergency and was thirty minutes behind them.

Elmo blazed a trail through Natchez and across the Mississippi River Bridge in a way which would have made Cecil Harrelson green with envy and possibly with fright. The car carreened through town and skidded to a halt at the front door of Ferriday's clinic, and Myra was rushed inside. It was almost 2:30.

The eight rooms for patients opened onto the main hallway where the entire Lewis family convened to watch what was happening inside. They stood silent and expressionless as the tiny fourteen-year-old child prepared for motherhood or the hereafter, screaming in gut-wrenching torture while clinging to the bed. Doc

Ratcliffe came running into the building, his necktie blown back over his shoulder, and ordered Myra into the operating room immediately. A nurse placed a mask over Myra's mouth and she sucked hard for the gas that burned her throat. Off came the mask. The nurse pulled her into a sitting position and gave her a spinal block, knocking her out before she could draw another breath. Myra's last thought, as she sank lifelessly to the bottom of a dark pool, was the great sorrow to have died without seeing her baby.

Out of the child came a child, a son, born at 6:43 on the morning of February 27. Myra was restored to life several hours later, roused by a cheering section which included the Associated Press and a reporter from every paper in the hundred-mile radius of Ferriday. With eyes half-opened and still groggy from the experience, Myra was handed 7 pounds 11 ounces of baby boy abask in the afterglow of arrival. The proud papa waltzed in leading a parade of fourteen photographers who began blasting away with a barrage of flashbulbs.

"Jerry, move in closer, that's it, good."—Flash—"Myra, hold his head up a little, fine."—Flash-flash—"Now, smile, please." —Flash.

Myra felt she was still in the middle of a crazy dream, one which had begun some nineteen months before. She didn't know where she was or when she would wake. It wasn't until she saw her photograph in the paper that she fully comprehended the events of the day. The same photo traveled around the world bearing copy that hailed a son born to the Rock Singer and his Child Bride. Myra noticed the baby wasn't named.

What is his name?

She had never considered it; all of her thoughts had been consumed by visions of death, never a thought as to what it might be like to make it to the other side of motherhood in one piece. Myra was a mom, of all things, and had lived to tell about it.

Now, what *is* his name?

Jerry had already taken care of that—Steve Allen Lewis, named for the man who had given him his big break in show business. Myra had never heard the first mention of that intention, but accepted it agreeably.

Two days later, thriving child and mother still limpsy left the hospital, although Myra wasn't sure if she had been discharged by her doctor of if Jerry had simply come to fetch her home. Her parents! No one had called her parents! They had read about their grandson in the paper, but no one had thought to call them. So, a call to Jay and Lois was the first order of business upon returning home.

Myra met motherhood with a fanaticism not unexpected of one so young and inexperienced. She had the help of two private nurses, who were subject to the same rules imposed on all visitors. Rule 1: No one breathes on the baby. And over the protest of Mother Mamie, Myra boiled everything that came into contact with Stevie for the first nine months of his life. After every feeding, Myra went into the kitchen, donned rubber gloves and dusted off the pressure cooker. Everything had to boil for twenty minutes, that was Rule 2. When Myra tired of the joking from her in-laws about her persnickety habits, she restored to sneaking into the darkened laboratory to conduct her experiments in the dead of night. When folks in the parlor heard the clinking of boiling glass, they fell about in fits of laughter.

There was no shortage of help with the baby—two sets of parents, two aunts and two nurses. Stevie was easily the best-kept kid in town, which was fortunate since Myra returned to the hospital on the first of March, complaining of severe cramps. She was given injections for every possible complication and a big bottle of glucose for good measure. Doc Ratcliffe ordered her to stay put for a week, and Stevie returned to the hospital to be with his mother. Jerry returned from touring Texas to find his wife still undiagnosed and feeling no better, and decided if the treatments weren't working, Myra might as well come home. Following husband's orders to the exclusion of her doctor's learned advice, Myra went home still experiencing the mystifying pains.

Songwriter Otis Blackwell had gotten into a jam and came to Jud Phillips for financial help at the first of the year. When Jud refused to make a loan, Otis offered to sell him a pair of his latest tunes, one of which, by fate or coincidence, was entitled "Big Blon' Baby"—a natural for a certain singing expectant father.

"You're under contract, Otis," Jud remonstrated. "You can't sell the publishing rights on a song when you're under contract."

"I know this," said Otis. "But looka here, I wrote these songs under another name and you can have 'em free 'n' clear. One's called 'It Won't Happen With Me' and the other I call 'Big Blon' Baby.' Both got Jerry Lee wrote all over 'em."

"How much we talkin' about dollar-wise?"

"Four-fifty for the pair."

"Lemme do my homework," said Jud, and upon checking the titles discovered a fault either in Otis's memory or honesty. "Big Blon' Baby" had already been published and the copyright secured. "It Won't Happen With Me," attributed to one Ray Evans, was still available. Jerry accepted an arrangement to divide the publishing rights on the second song and record the first. As the Killer began work on the tribute to his unborn son, Jud asked Sam's secretary to claim the copyright on "It Won't Happen With Me"; either through incompetence or neglect, she failed to do so. Later, when Johnny Rivers turned the song into a hit, Jud inquired as to the whereabouts of his royalties and was informed that a Mr. Blackwell owned the copyright and all monies had been paid to him. That's show biz.

Released twelve days before Stevie's birth, "Lovin' Up a Storm" backed with "Big Blon' Baby" received excellent reviews. *Billboard* selected it as "Spotlight Winner" for the week of February 23, *Music Reporter* plugged the record as its "Super Scoop" and *Cash Box* named it as the "Disk of the Week" for March 7.

A logical conclusion would be that Jerry Lee Lewis was back. No matter how great the personal criticism, no matter how severe the sin, good works gain acceptance. Perhaps the birth of a baby would elevate Jerry's marriage to Myra to a plane higher than scandal, in the same way that Elvis's enlistment made him more the all-American boy and less the leather-clad punk. After all, everyone is entitled to a fresh start, from impeached public servants to freed prisoners. Everyone except Jerry Lee Lewis. Jerry's ninth single, a celebration of life and the reaffirmation of a singular talent, sat unplayed on many shelves, completely ignored by the judge and jury that is the popular radio station program director. The "Big Blon' Baby" promotion was a cute idea that simply didn't work. Imagine that, a fourteen-year-old mother; it was crazy to many, pathetic to some and disgusting to those who had been offended by the original sin.

Ironically, British critics greeted Jerry's new single with rave reviews.

How was it possible for a Lewis single to go uncharted in America while rising to Number 20 in England? Were Americans so repulsed by Jerry's offenses, were stations so stiff-necked, that he should remain banished from the airwaves even after he had been reclaimed by the country that wanted his deportation? That was not the case. "Lovin' Up a Storm" failed to become Jerry's fourth million-seller for no other reason than the fact that Sun Records had fallen apart. With Jud's departure from the label, Sam developed an ego clash with producers Jack Clement and Bill Justis, culminating with their dismissal in March. They had been working in the studio with Charlie Rich one night when Sam entered with a party of drunken revelers. Justis told them to leave, and Sam fired him because he didn't like the tone of his voice, then fired Clement for laughing at the sad scene.

Clement and Justis had seen it coming; Sam had earlier proclaimed that he was now a millionaire controlling radio stations and mineral mines in addition to the little studio which he was no longer interested in. Releases became scarce as he cut away to avoid expense. Singles were pressed on a daily need, and if no orders were called in, Sam didn't bother to drum up business. Mailings of promotional copies came to a halt. Other labels made hits by covering Sun material in larger quantities, as in the case of Imperial borrowing Bill Justis's "Raunchy" and outselling the original two to one. When he could be located, Sam was usually found in Florida searching for land deals or celebrating the un-earthing of a vast vein of zinc in one of his Arkansas mines. Who needed grief and aggravation, boycotts and scandals, rock 'n' roll and rednecks, when retirement to a life of leisure was possible at age thirty-six?

Several men attempted to replace Clement and Justis as general manager of what was left of the label: Onie Wheeler, Ray Smith, Ernie Chaffin, Vern Taylor, Alton and Jimmy, Jerry McGill and The Top Coats, and Jerry Lee Lewis. Jerry Lee Lewis? He had his day in the Sun, said Sam, I owe him nothing. He had a good thing going and he killed it, not me. Nobody wants him, so he can just stay put four more years and I'll do him the favor of putting out a record on him two, maybe three times a year, for old times' sake. Jerry Lee Lewis? To hell with Jerry Lee Lewis.

Jerry was out; Cousin Mickey saw it was a way in.

* * *

J. W. Brown's piano company did a great business, but there wasn't much excitement in buying old pianos and fixing them up for resale. As difficult as life on the road had been, he never really wanted to retire from rock 'n' roll. He would join Jerry in a minute if he would only call, but that was not likely to happen unless he was in trouble. It was a pleasant surprise, then, when Mickey Gilley came to Memphis at the end of January 1959 to find Jay and ask for his help.

"I want you to do for me what you done for Cousin Jerry," Mickey asked of Jay. "I can sing jus' like him an' play like him, too. I could use your help in gettin' my first record out. We can pick up where Jerry left off, if you get what I mean."

"Well, let's see what you got and whether I can do anything with it," said Jay.

At the first rehearsals, Jay was surprised that Mickey was as good as his claim. In fact, Mickey sounded too much like Jerry, which had its good and bad points. Similarities were good in that Jerry had created a popular style, and if Jerry wasn't getting any airplay, radio might be receptive to Mickey as a suitable replacement. On the other hand, a mimic had a hard time carving a niche with a borrowed style, and there were many listeners who would accept no substitute for the real thing. Nevertheless, Jay thought Mickey was good enough to take on the road, plotting a thirty-day tour of Florida as a test. Mickey kept patrons from walking out on him, so Jay brought him to Los Angeles at the end of February to woo the Vegas boys.

In the midst of negotiations for a three-week debut at one of the Strip's smaller clubs, Jay began to feel exhausted. What was worse, his glands were swollen and he experienced a different kind of sore throat. Jay had the mumps, no laughing matter for a man his age. The doctor recommended he not move out of bed until after the first week in March.

The deal which would have taken Mickey to Vegas fell through and he went home to Texas to wait several more years before attempting to move up in the entertainment world. When he recovered, Jay returned to Memphis to find his car repossessed, his mortgage foreclosed and his business on the verge of bankruptcy.

Jerry had no sympathy for his father-in-law and former friend. "You thought you were really pullin' somethin', you an' Mickey," Jerry chided Jay. "Yeah, y'all thought y'all were gonna do

somethin' big, make a hit record and take over. I guess you
learned your lesson. Ain't nobody ever gonna replace me."

In mid-March, proud Mamma brought Stevie to Memphis to
meet his maternal grandparents. It was during this visit that Myra,
who had been out of touch with her husband's business affairs,
learned of several pending lawsuits dealing with unpaid car notes
and canceled show dates. Cancellations became frequent upon
finding smaller turnouts in Jerry's old strongholds, spawning a
don't-give-a-damn attitude in him. A steady stream of complaints
flowed to the Musicians' Union, which levied fines and threatened to revoke Jerry's card.

Before Jerry was to leave on a long road trip through Texas and
New Mexico, Myra joined him in a business discussion. In her
role as head of the household, she politely inquired about bills
which he was supposed to have paid and shows he was supposed
to have played. What Jerry needed was a manager, which he had
been without since returning from Britain, and a strong one, at
that, which he'd never had. The few who were willing to apply
for the position were not capable of handling one so contrary.
Jerry was his own manager, and he didn't want his wife worrying
with his affairs. There are plenty of big-paying jobs in the offing,
said he, not to worry, which was Myra's specialty:

March 31, 1959
Dearest Kay,
   You'll forgive me for answering your two letters with
such a short one. But honestly, Kay, I feel like I'm on the
verge of a nervous breakdown. It seems like fifteen people
have law suits against poor little Jerry. I'm so worried, I've
bitten my fingernails off to my elbow. I always was the
worrying type. I feel so depressed.
   Jerry has an offer to appear on Steve Allen's show for
eight thousand dollars and the same on Dick Clark's show.
That's one thing to be happy about. So you'll be seeing
Jerry pretty soon. That is, if he makes the appearances.
The union is giving Jerry a lot of trouble. He is scheduled
to leave for Australia April 17. I hate to see him go so bad.
I just know I'll die.
   With all our love,
   Myra and Steve Allen

With Jerry's anticipated departure on the seventeenth and enough dates to keep him busy till then, Myra would not see him again until May unless she abandoned her six-week-old son to fly to Texas for a few days. It was Jerry's hope that Myra would leave Stevie with Mamie permanently and return to his side as his constant lover and companion; there were too many temptations. It turned out to be a bad idea—poor planning forced Myra, Jerry and band members Russ Smith, Roland Janes and bassist Leo Lodner to leave late one night after a show and drive all of the next day in order to cross the twelve hundred miles between engagements. Two flat tires and a dead battery caused them to just miss a three o'clock show by almost twelve hours. Having missed one show on April 5, they raced to the next booking and huffed into Albuquerque shortly after midnight for a late show only to discover they had overshot their destination by some three hundred miles. At that point in the tour, there could be heard many a discouraging word on the topics of show business, automobiles and broken air conditioners. The same dirty words were repeated in calls and letters from club owners to the Musicians' Union.

Myra made the wise decision to hop the next flatcar home before she was blamed for the whole chaotic catastrophe. Her motherless infant provided the perfect excuse for cutting her trip short, and she returned to the farm to find Gran'ma Mamie at wits end having to play Mommy for the first time in a long while. Mamie required three days' rest in recovering from Stevie's five A.M. aubades. Jerry had enough of touring himself, and canceled a trip to Australia with Sammy Davis, Jr., for two weeks of uninterrupted fishing and fathering.

A typical day off at home with the Lewises in the spring of 1959 began by sifting through the mail—offers and rejections and the latest batch of tapes from would-be songwriters. Jerry had a trunk filled with tapes, hundreds of songs with lines like "Myra mine, you're so fine," written by talentless but well-meaning fans who wanted to attract Jerry's attention and believed their chances were better if Myra was the subject.

Never a day passed without Jerry practicing the piano. It might be the minute he got up, still clad in pajamas and hair creased where he had slept on it, or in the middle of a boring television program. Whenever the dub of a new single was brought to the house, he stood before the record player, usually barechested and barefooted, hands in pockets, head slightly cocked to one side, listening to the cut over and over. No one was allowed to talk while the record revolved on the cheap phonograph, noticeably out of place in the home of a recording star. "Most of my fans own a crappy record player," Jerry justified. "I wanna hear it just like they do. If my song sounds good on this set, it'll sound good anywhere else." When the hearing was through, Jerry never failed to remark, "If that ain't a hit I'll quit the bizness an' go back to farmin'." The scene was repeated again and again during all the years they were married, but Myra never became a farmer's wife.

Once again Jerry's name was mentioned in connection with feature films going into production. A sequel to *High School Confidential* entitled *College Confidential* was in the works, but the role intended for Jerry was awarded to Conway Twitty. Producer Alfred Zugsmith had Jerry in mind for another project, *The Beat Generation,* in which he would play the part of a musician in a way-out coffee shop frequented by bongo beatniks and weirdos in sweatshirts spouting poetry that didn't make sense. It was a chance for Jerry to sing half a dozen songs, but he balked at the idea of going bohemian. Hollywood decided against using Jerry for the part anyway, and for once, rejection worked in his favor. *The Beat Generation* failed to attract a popular singer for the musician's role, and in the end, the only person willing to take the part was trumpeter Louis Armstrong, who seemed oddly out of place as a lone black beatnik. The film was returned by exhibitors so that Zugsmith could reconcile the inconsistencies of casting Armstrong opposite blond bombshell Mamie Van Doren and Vampira, a beach bunny whose only credits consisted of hostessing a late-night horror movie on a local Los Angeles television station.

It was fortunate Jerry had been denied the role, since the film went on to become a dismal failure. Nevertheless, Jerry was wounded by what he believed was a prejudice continuing to work against his private life. From his wife, his Number 1 fan and best friend, came unwavering support. Like the lines from the age-old anonymous poem, "It's when things seem worst that you must not quit."

A one-sheet mimeographed monthly newsletter titled *The Rollin' Stone*, published by the Jerry Lee Lewis International Fan Club originating out of Kay Martin's home in New York, contained a special message at Myra's request. It was a call to arms for loyal fans to get behind a big push to put their hero back on top.

Released in June, "Let's Talk About Us," an Otis Blackwell composition backed with Charlie Rich's "The Ballad of Billy Joe," was a complete bust. Rock fans despised the female chorus backing Jerry on the A side; stuck their fingers in their ears or down their throats upon hearing side B, which relied on listeners having heard Johnny Cash's song about a murderer named Billy Joe. The record never charted, but Myra, whose heart was in the right place even if her hearing had become distorted by bias, praised Kay for her effort to push the record on fan clubbers.

Also included in Myra's letter to Kay was a request from Mamie for a copy of Chuck Berry's newest release. "Mrs. Lewis said that she would be thrilled if you would be so kind as to send her the record," Myra wrote. "I suppose you know that next to Jerry, Chuck Berry is her very favorite"—and his mother's preference made Jerry crazy with professional jealousy. It was bad enough her admitting a penchant for Berry's music, but being wakened every morning with Chuck's greatest hits at a time when he couldn't get a record played was more than Jerry could bear. Jerry did not want to share his mother's admiration with anyone, much less the black boogieman.

All victories had been blasted out of Jerry's life. No one wanted to hire a man with his history. There was nothing to look forward to with hope: The Steve Allen appearance never materialized; neither did the Dick Clark date, nor the sixteen thousand dollars that went along with them. Myra began to think such plans were the product of her husband's own fertile imagination and his desire to shelter her from worry and financial concern. From time to time, Jerry raised the hopes of his dependents with half-truths and whole lies: Success was just around the corner, he guaranteed, and for every disappointment there was a new and better promise of a brighter tomorrow. The growing frequency of Jerry's self-deluding prophecies wore away Myra's nerves. At last, the cause for those mysterious abdominal pains was discovered when attacks began to accompany each bit of bad news.

When he had run out of luck and ideas, Jerry found other dreams to follow, a moving dream of living simply as a country pastor with loving wife and crop of kids, offering hymns to heaven all the livelong day. "One o' these days," he often began, "I'm gonna get me a li'l church somewhere an' preach, do some farmin' and jus' be with my fam'ly. All I need, Lord, is jus' one more hit record." This was Jerry's favorite vision, a new deal for his God of bargains made over and over again in the next ten years and another ten, without conviction and with a snowball's chance in hell of happening.

Jerry started talking about a church of his own shortly after having been to hear Jimmy Lee Swaggart preach again. Jimmy was quick to remind his congregation of his kinship with the famous singer and used recollections of their childhood together to illustrate his sermons. Jerry was the perfect pagan, the God-given talent who had forsaken his calling as a preacher to walk streets paved with gold in the ways of the world. Jimmy, as a servant of the Lord and Jerry's antithesis, triumphed over his celebrated cousin at the end of every discourse because he walked in the ways of righteousness. His congregation, albeit small and needy, gathered twice every week. And where were Jerry's followers?

"Are the consolations of God too small for you?" Jimmy asked the gathering, meeting his cousin's stare. "Why doth thy heart carry thee away?"

Jerry lowered his eyes. There he sat all by himself in those expensive clothes. Lord, ain't he a sight? This time last year he was playing the devil's music in a den of iniquity, profaning the sabbath to his personal profit. And where was he this time last week? Committing the same sin, but much had happened to change his good fortune. Lord, how many are his adversaries become. Many are they that rise up against him. Many there are that say of his soul: There is no salvation for him in God. And those who flocked to Jerry for autographs before Jimmy's sermon were that much afraid of him, were that much sorry for him, after the demon that tortured his soul had been exposed.

"'Because ye have offered, and because ye have sinned against the Lord, nor walked in His law, nor in His statues, nor in His testimonies, therefore this evil is happened to you,'" Jimmy quoted Scripture. "'And Obadiah said to one gone astray: Thou are greatly despised. The pride of thy heart hath beguiled thee, o thou that dwellest in the clefts of the rock, thy habitation on high; that sayest in thy heart: Who shall bring me down to the ground? Though thou made thy nest as high as the eagle, and though thou set it among the stars, I will bring thee down from thence, saith the Lord. All the men of thy confederacy have conducted thee to the border; the men that were at peace with thee have beguiled thee, and prevailed against thee; they that eat thy bread lay a snare under thee, in whom there is no discernment. For the day of the Lord is near upon all nations; as thou hast done, it shall be done unto thee; thy dealing shall return upon thine own head. And the kingdom shall be the Lord's.

"'This is the thing which the Lord hath commanded,'" said Jimmy. "'When a man voweth a vow unto the Lord . . .'"

"Let me make it one time in my life an' I'll do Your biddin' ever after," Jerry renewed his pledge.

"'. . . or sweareth an oath to bind his soul with a bond,'" Jimmy continued.

"Gimme jus' one more hit record an' I'll take the money and set up a li'l church somewhere an' dedicate the rest of my life to You in Your service," promised Jerry in his prayer.

"'. . . he shall not break his word; he shall do according to all that proceedeth out of his mouth,'" Jimmy concluded.

"That which I vowed I will pay," Jerry bargained, "that the Lord may once again have compassion with me."

After prayer meetin', Jerry and Jimmy walked along together to where Jerry's Cadillac was parked. The sermon was still leaning heavily on Jerry's conscience as Jimmy said, "Y'know, Jerry, the offerin's have been mighty slim pickin's these last few months. If we lucky, we might take in thirty dollars a week. Lookit what we got today, pocket change. I got to travel these parts spreadin' the Good Word, an' my ol' jalopy fin'ly up 'n' quit on me. This just ain't gonna take care of it."

"I asked you to come to Memphis an' record at Sun, Jimmy," Jerry responded. "You could make a lotta money with a gospel album."

"No, it just wouldn't be right for a preacher to go there with all that I heard goes on in places like that," Jimmy said. "I prayed for help, y'know. Had my car break down on the side o' the road once, an' you know I don't know shucks about machin'ry. Well, brother, I laid hands on its hood an' ast the Holy Spirit to make 'er whole again so I could get about His bizness, and lo an' behold, the Holy Spirit filled the vehicle and she was as good as new an' didn't need them new cylinders like they was talkin' about down to the garage."

"Well, why don't you lay hands on it again," said Jerry. "I'd like to see that m'self."

"Oh, but, brother, you can't ast the Lord for any more help than you're willin' to help yourself. He got me this far, I got to do the rest."

Jerry didn't seem to be getting the picture: distressed car, distressed collection plate, wealthy cousin, pennies for heaven.

"'If there be among you a needy man, one of thy brethren, within any of thy gates, thou shalt not harden thy heart, nor shut thy hand from thy needy brother,'" Jimmy fell back on Scripture as they drove past a new car lot, "'but thou shalt surely lend him sufficient for his need in that which he wanteth.' Looky there, brother, my prayers have been answered."

Jerry bought a new Oldsmobile and gave it to Jimmy. He surrendered the cash in conscience money, a sacrifice to God and a guilt offering to indulge his sins. At a time when he could scarcely afford a car of his own, when he soothed his wife's money worries by convincing her that their last new car was actually a cheaper used model, he cheerfully gave God's servant that which he wanted without hesitation, concern or regret. It was an easy pardon purchased with easy money; it did not last nor was it adequate to absolve Jerry of the chain of transgressions he had forged as a disciple of the devil's music; no amount of money enables a man to run from God.

Jerry consented to an interview with Helen Bolstad, who had introduced him to *TV Radio Mirror* readers during the heyday of 1958. Bolstad was one of the first feature writers to take a friendly interest in the beleaguered couple and, as Myra told Kay Martin, the first to treat her like a lady instead of a child. If motherhood could confer no other benefit on a fourteen-year-old girl, it went a long way toward making a woman out of her in the eyes of the public. Helen Bolstad, expecting to meet the Child

Bride, recognized Myra's maturity instead, yet not to the fullest extent of her pure and candid soul. In supposing what her friend Kay Martin was like, Myra revealed much of herself:

> You're the little girl down the street that was always bossed by your older brother and made to do everything he said do. And you're the poor one who missed out on all the fun because your mother didn't want you to be hurt by doing things that she thought would maybe hurt you. You never joined in with kids your age and really enjoyed yourself. Am I right? I'm sure your mother loves you and always wanted the very, very best for you and always done what she thought was best, not knowing that all the time she was hurting no one but you. But maybe now that you're grown you can piece your life together as you wish.
>
> If you feel like you want to ride down Broadway with the top down on your car in December, do it. It makes you feel more human if you do a few crazy things sometimes.
>
> I know at times I do foolish things like—be cleaning house and all of a sudden run out of the house like I'm crazy and jump right in the middle of the swimming pool clothes and all. Then climb out and go get dressed again. Well, that's what I call enjoying yourself. Just let go.
>
> I never had a childhood. By the time I was ten, I was as mature as I am now. By the time I'm twenty-five, in my mind I'll be fifty.
>
> Today Linda and her class had a picnic about twenty-five miles from here. All the mothers was taking a few children in their car, so I volunteered to take a few, too. Frankie was with us. When we got to this place, we all went exploring and we ran upon this lake where there was mud. UH-OH . . . So we had a mud fight. After we was black as Little Sambo, Frankie pushed me in the lake. Then Linda helped Frankie in the water, too, she had on a real nice dress. Then a few more kids joined us in a sand fight. Right now, if I shake my head, sand flies out. I have an appointment at the beauty shop (as if it could help me). I even have sand in my ears. But to make matters worse, all the mothers came down to the lake to scold their children for doing such a silly thing. Gosh, you can imagine how I felt . . . Stupid, silly and like a child. I enjoyed it anyway. It's been a long time since I had a mud fight, I was nine."

That was Myra—a parent before she stopped being a child. On May 25, Myra wrote Kay:

> Thanks loads for "Little Queenie." Mrs. Lewis is just mad about Chuck Berry. You know how I feel about him? S N B A. Ever since he tried to beat up Jerry, I haven't liked him a bit. If I'm not mistaken, Jerry wrapped a chair around his head. I wish he would have knocked his head off. Don't get me wrong, I think Chuck is a very talented Negro. Have you ever seen him put on a real live show? Well, WOW if you haven't. That is one Negro that can flat put on a show. But he doesn't "get it" half as much as Jerry. There will NEVER be another performer half as great as Jerry.

Would that his mother thought so. Chuck Berry's "Little Queenie" was standard airfare for Mamie morning, noon and night. After three days, Jerry could no longer stand to hear his mother play his rival's music and called a session at Sun on the twenty-eighth for the sole purpose of recording "Little Queenie." If Mamma liked the song so much, her son was going to sing it. Henceforth, copies of the original were nowhere to be found in the Lewis household.

Mamie followed Jerry and Myra to Memphis for a two-day visit. For some unknown reason, she brought Jane Mitcham with her. Tax time had come and gone, and Jerry was tense. With a despised ex-wife under his roof at his mother's invitation, Jerry was past tense. He was cordial toward Jane, never uttered a cross word to his mother, but rained frustration on Myra. She was sitting at her desk in the den typing a letter to Kay when in rushed Jerry, snarling like a wet cat, picked up her typewriter and smashed it on the floor.

"I don't"—smash—"like"—smash—"you writin'"—smash —"Kay Martin about me"—smash—"all the time," he yelled, picking up the keyboard and slamming it down again.

Jerry was a notoriously poor accountant. He didn't believe in banks, and if he needed a readout of his current financial condition, he only had to count what was in his pants pocket and the wads stashed around the house. He hadn't sent the government their percentage yet; he didn't know how much he made; he didn't know how much to send. Nineteen fifty-eight was the first year he earned enough income to tax. The Internal Revenue in Memphis understood that his hectic schedule kept him on the road and that he wasn't able to meet his return on time. They gave him a sixty-day extension in that understanding way they have, hoping he would not require another one. Jerry called one of Jud's friends in Florence to come over and help with the arithmetic. Myra was convinced that taxes weren't the real problem with her husband and characteristically reproached herself:

> Kay, if I thought it would put Jerry back on top, I would kill myself. I blame nobody but myself for Jerry's downfall. I suppose I should have never married him because of his career. Please tell me the truth. It was me that hurt Jerry more than anybody, wasn't it? Have you ever hurt someone you loved? If not then you cannot imagine how I feel.
>
> I was young and wild and in love when we married. I didn't realize what our marriage would cause. How can I ever make it up to Jerry? Or can I? You know and I know that Jerry's music is his life. Oh, God, will he ever forgive me?

And in June, when "Let's Talk About Us" was released to total lack of interest on the public's part, Myra's persecution complex worsened:

> Oh, if only I could call back two years ago. I *wouldn't* marry Jerry again for anything in this world. I've hurt Jerry more than you'll ever know. I've destroyed *his* world, *his* music. There's no use blaming anyone else because I know it was me.
>
> I remember how happy he was—Steve Allen Show, Patti Page Show, Dick Clark. Oh, I wish I was dead. Well, you know Jerry *is* dead, dead, dead. The disc jockeys are the ones, along with me, that need to be shot. I hate their guts.

July was booked solid with one-nighters: a record hop in St. Louis on the third, a concert before four thousand in Halls, Tennessee, on the fourth and a few nights in Lake Charles, Louisiana, before taking off for a week in New Jersey and Coney Island.

If Myra remained in Memphis while Jerry toured, Mamie, Frankie and Linda, with Elmo in tow and sometimes Junior, packed up and moved in for a spell. Testing her memory, Myra was not surprised to discover she had spent only three nights at home alone with her husband in twenty months of married life. Oddly, Myra was alone on her fifteenth birthday, forgotten. The Lewises blew into town, raided the house for a week and headed home with a sack of Myra's groceries and whatever else wasn't nailed down. They had taken a sofa on the previous visit. In between diaper changes and letter writing, Myra aided Jerry's career by calling radio stations in a variety of voices and requesting "Let's Talk About Us." The single had moved onto the local charts at Number 35, moved up four notches the next week, then disappeared. She deduced that the whole affair was a Communist plot. She didn't know what a Communist was, but she knew they were responsible for everything bad that happened without reason.

During the first week in August, Jerry made two side trips from his base at Coney Island's Rip Tide Club to appear on Alan Freed's local New York television show. On the eighth, he was without a bass player, an emergency he had never anticipated. There was no one else to call but J. W. Brown. Jay, with trusty bass, was at work on the ninth. On the fifteenth, he returned to Memphis to close his piano business. It was as if he had been in the band all along, all grievances forgotten.

There were other advantages to bringing Jay out of retirement. He could be instrumental in helping Jerry break his contract with Sun, since Sam owed and had never paid him thousands of dollars in union wages for Jerry's sessions. Not only could Jay support Jerry's action, but he could also facilitate the taking of Sun's license. Before Jerry and Jay could activate the plan, Sam nullified their complaint by paying Jay fifteen hundred dollars for seventeen sessions and apologizing for the oversight.

Let no one forget Jay's innate ability to handle all manner of emergencies on the road. Jerry, having left Memphis's Baptist Hospital after being treated for what doctors believed to be food poisoning, experienced a second attack while performing in Kiowa, Kansas, a week later. Jay came to the rescue with a sure-fire laxative, then called a doctor when the cathartic brought Jerry close to death. Appendicitis was a more accurate diagnosis, and the Lewises and the Browns spent Thanksgiving at Jerry's bedside as he recovered from surgery, then returned home to celebrate Stevie's first Christmas.

Nineteen fifty-eight was the last year for vintage rock 'n' roll —Danny and The Juniors' "At The Hop," Buddy Holly's "Rave On," Elvis's "Hard Headed Woman," Chuck Berry's "Johnny B. Goode" and Jerry's "High School Confidential." Within the next year, Holly, the Big Bopper and Ritchie Valens were gone and an auto accident had killed Eddie Cochran ("Summertime Blues") and disfigured Gene Vincent. Chuck Berry began a long legal battle ending in his two-year imprisonment for transporting a minor across state lines for immoral purposes. While Elvis served the remainder of his military sentence, Jerry began a long, frustrating exile.

The rising stars of 1959: The Kingston Trio, inaugurating the folk music boom, Ricky Nelson, Fabian, Frankie Avalon, Bobby Darin and other fresh, clean, wholesome, white male teenaged singers. John, Paul and George, ages eighteen, sixteen and fifteen, respectively formed a basement band called The Quarrymen. The sixties would be the Beatle decade, when America rediscovered its music attractively repackaged with English accents. fashions and hairstyles; and when England rediscovered Jerry Lee Lewis, mentor to Lennon and McCartney, a man of sorrows struggling to satisfy the demon inside him.

8 *Baby, Baby, Bye Bye*

FRANKIE JEAN REMARRIED AT AGE FIFTEEN IN the summer of 1959 and was expecting her first child in March of the next year. She had moved one hundred fifty miles from Ferriday to Lafayette, where her husband, Wayne, worked, and the stress of motherhood went to work on Frankie's delicate nerves. She developed an annoying habit of constantly clearing her throat and a fetish for cleanliness, in herself and her surroundings, and could not sit still without straightening things. She spent endless hours rubbing salves and ointments into her skin till her body glowed with oil, then turned her attention to the furniture for the same careful treatment. Mamie worried that her daughter was unattended much of the time, and instigated a plan whereby everyone—Elmo, Linda, Gail, Jerry, Myra and Stevie—would move to Lafayette to wait out the last six weeks of Frankie's pregnancy. Wayne could not come to Ferriday because of his job, and Frankie would not leave him behind, so everyone else was made to come to Frankie, and the move was made at Jerry's expense.

It was February, and Jerry drove the clan to Lafayette to house-hunt. Starting from Frankie's residence, they circled the neighborhood till they found a larger house for rent. The agent could not have been more helpful once he found out who the prospective buyer was.

"We didn't intend to rent this little beauty," the agent told Jerry. "We aim to sell it outright."

"I don't wanna live here forever," Jerry said. "I jus' need the place for a li'l while. Lemme rent it."

"I'm sorry, but we wouldn't want to be in the same situation another six weeks from now," the agent said.

"All right, I'll take it," said Jerry.

"Fine. Now, about the arrangements—"

"I wanna finance the whole thing."

"With your references, I'm sure the bank will have no objection to whatever terms you'd be comfortable with, Mr. Lewis. But we'll need some sort of down payment."

"How 'bout two hunnert?"

Myra pulled Jerry away from his business to ask how he could possibly afford to buy a house that he only intended to inhabit two months.

"Simple, baby, I give 'em a small down payment, and when we're done here, we'll jus' move out an' not pay no more. The bank'll foreclose and resell, an' all we'll be out stacks up to rent money. It's an old trick my daddy taught me."

Few provisions were taken to Lafayette when the clan moved in like so many attending storks. There was little in the way of furniture, so the place more closely resembled a gypsy camp than hearth and home. At the end of the first month, Myra and Stevie returned to Memphis for Stevie's first birthday on the twenty-seventh, a celebration for the honoree and fifteen playmates and their moms.

Myra did not intend to return to Lafayette. She was toying with the idea of returning to school to complete her education, provided she could find the perfect situation whereby classes would not interfere with mothering her baby. Stevie was always her first consideration. She enrolled at the Miller Hawkins Secretarial School, where two evenings a week she attended courses in shorthand, typing, business English, spelling and personality. Because of Jerry's changeable schedule, she was unsure how long self-improvement would continue, but planned to attend while he was gone most of March and April.

Jerry signed with a new agent, Henry Jaffe, who immediately placed him in Lee Gordon's Supershow and found a hot new movie property for him to star in. Talk of featuring Jerry in the title role of *The Hank Williams Story* gave way to a chance for him to star in a murder mystery entitled *The Young And The Deadly*. Jerry was to play the part of a nightclub owner, a dramatic role which would also allow him to sing three or four songs which would then be released on an extended-play record. Jerry recorded several songs from which E. M. Productions were to select the movie soundtrack and Sun would release the next single. Two of the cuts were instrumentals, "In the Mood," the Glen Miller hit, and an old honky-tonk piece entitled "I Get the Blues When It Rains." But at the same time Jerry was to begin filming, a movie strike halted production. By the end of March, E. M. Productions had run out of money, time, patience and hope, and *The Young And The Deadly* died in its infancy.

The January sessions were the last to be recorded in the original Sun studio as a new facility opened at 639 Madison in the summer, but from those tapes came the single released on March 7, "Old Black Joe" backed with "Baby, Baby, Bye Bye," both attributed to Jerry. "Old Black Joe" was a traditional spiritual, the type of plantation melody which Jimmie Rodgers popularized in the thirties but which offended the black struggling for social and economic equality in the sixties. Here was a completely new twist to the Lewis boycott—a ban on his music for being racist. The flip side fared no better, a tune which harkened to another traditional folksong, "The Old Grey Mare." The single did not chart.

Lee Gordon's Supershow toured Australia at the end of March. Tommy Sands, who began his career as a country artist for RCA, then came to Capitol in 1957 to record a dozen pop hits, coheadlined the extravaganza with Neil Sedaka, who had hits with "Calendar Girl" and "Oh! Carol." Also featured were rising star Freddie Cannon, Ace Records ace Jimmy Clanton, "Teen Angel" Mark Dinning, "Running Bear" Johnny Preston, Jack Scott, and one-hit wonders Rod Lauren, Chan Romero and Marv Johnson. The first of the few great instrumental groups, Johnny and The Hurricanes, were spotlighted along with Dion and The Belmonts singing their dozen hits. With all this talent, it must have seemed strange to some and insulting to others that Jerry Lee Lewis should be the only performer to receive not one but three encores at every show, at the end of which he was invited to spend ten weeks touring New Zealand by himself. He refused, saying he only wanted to go home and do some fishin'.

Much was made of a misunderstanding between Jerry and an Aussie interviewer who confused a description of Jerry's private life to mean he and Myra were separated and living apart, he in

Ferriday and she in Memphis. What disturbed Myra more than these odd accounts was not having heard from her husband in more than a month. It was unlike him to allow three days to pass without a phone call, and it had already been ten times that long. When the band returned to Memphis without Jerry, Myra was anxious to know why he remained in Los Angeles. She couldn't believe that after having been gone so long he would choose to stay away another three days. It couldn't be business that kept him if his band had come home; maybe it was talk of another movie.

With a little help from Kay Martin, Myra learned Jerry had dined with a comely fan at her apartment in Los Angeles. Her name was Lynn and she was a West Coast correspondent for the fan club. In her mind's eye, Myra envisioned her husband, a young man void of understanding, passing through the street near Lynn's corner and went the way to her house. In the twilight, in the evening of the day, in the blackness of night and the darkness, there met him a woman with the attire of a harlot and wily of heart. So she caught him and kissed him. And he knew her, in the biblical sense. Cupid's hot minion could not get home soon enough for his wife, who cut him off in Ferriday before he could make Memphis.

"Where you been, Jerry? How come you stayed an extra three days in LA, Jerry? Who's Lynn?" she asked.

He reddened and stammered nonsense, amazed by his wife's psychic ability.

"I bet you got her phone number on you," Myra accused. "I bet it's in your wallet."

"No, it ain't," Jerry denied, then ran after her to snatch his billfold from her grip and locked himself in the bathroom.

"Come on outta there, Jerry." Myra hammered on the door. "Let's see the wallet."

The toilet flushed, and Jerry opened the door. "Here ya go, look all you want."

"What kinda fool do you think I am? You already flushed it down the commode."

"Look in there, I said. Go on, it ain't in there. See? I tol' ya," he said when the snipe hunt failed to turn up that which was floating somewhere in a cesspool.

The argument turned into a mental shoving match, testing one

another on treacherous new ground. Jerry swore his innocence,
and for the moment Myra believed him. He never swore a lie; it
violated one of his few absolute principles. But there were still
three days in California unaccounted for and destroyed evidence
hinting at betrayal.

"That's it," said Myra.

"What? What's it?"

"I'm through. I had enough."

"You mean you want a divorce?" Jerry asked.

"Do you?"

"I ast you first."

"I jus' can't take it anymore."

"Whaddya mean?" Jerry pressed.

"The weeks on the road without hearing from you," she started,
then poured out the frustrations of the past two years, "the papers
and the lawsuits and the ex-wives and other women—I jus' can't
live like this."

Jerry was silenced as he watched the only person who had
remained steadfast throughout his ordeals fall to pieces. "Okay, if
you want a divorce, we'll go see a lawyer tomorrow. But it ain't
all my fault, y'know. Some of it's you, too. You're not the same
girl I married, you're diff'rent. Much diff'rent."

"What are you talkin' about?" Myra cried.

"Well, you never travel with me anymore. I need you with me.
If you'd been with me where you belonged, this whole thing
would've never happened."

"I can't leave Stevie," she sobbed, and knew if he could be so
insensitive as to let another raise their child maybe she was better
off without Jerry.

When they appeared before an attorney the next day to outline
a settlement, Jerry did all the talking for both of them. "We want
a divorce nice an' quiet," he instructed. "We done figgered it out
an' we both agree to the follerin'. First, she don't get no alimony,
but she gets two hunnert a month child support. Second, she don't
get the house. Third, no car. She can keep whatever she owns,
clothes an' furniture-wise."

The counselor observed Myra closely and saw no response.
When faced with trauma, she could be counted on to go completely blank, moving in whatever direction she was pushed.

"When did you decide on this divorce?" the attorney asked.

"Yesterday," said Jerry.

"And for what reasons?"

"We ain't got along for the past six or seven months."

"How much of that time were you home, Jerry?"

"Maybe half, maybe less."

"I see. And what is Myra supposed to do without shelter, without transportation, or a job or money to live on?"

"That's her problem," said Jerry. "She's the one doin' this, not me. This is all her idea."

"I see. Well, then, you should know that by law I can't represent you both, and that Myra will have to bring the action and that she will be entitled to much more than you and she have apparently agreed to."

"That don't matter," said Jerry. "This is what *we* agreed to, an' this is all she gets."

"Myra, do you have family you can stay with?" the attorney asked.

"No," Jerry answered. "They don't want her."

The attorney looked at Jerry, saw no sign of life from Myra, then agreed to draw up the papers. "It'll take about a week," he said, "but if it's okay with you both, you can go ahead and sign—"

The attorney slid a sheet of blank paper before them and asked each to sign their name. They stared at the sheet for the longest time, realizing they had come too far to turn back. It was a country lawyer's unconventional way of restoring harmony between quarreling lovers. Sometimes a backwoods barrister can spot when husband and wife get carried away and find themselves instigating actions they do not wish to take effect. A faked formality can release a wave of regret which turns an attorney's hard work into birdcage lining, so it is considered a work-saving device to second-guess the plaintiff's intentions.

Mr. and Mrs. Lewis returned home to their farm together. At bedtime that night, as they headed off in the same direction, Elmo stopped them. "Wait a minnit. You can't be sleepin' in the same bed no more."

They smiled sheepishly and Papa laughed. The appointment set to consummate the formalities was not kept, and although the couple had not kissed and made up, some of the starch had been taken out of the lawsuit.

When Jerry left on tour again, Myra had much on her mind. Having come so close to separation, she wondered whether it wasn't the best thing to do after all. Perhaps the incident in California was not isolated, as Jerry claimed. Maybe he was on his best behavior at home, disguising the alter ego assumed when traveling from town to town. The Reverend Mr. Killer. The Black River Stallion. The Great Ball of Fire. First one, then another, sometimes all three at once. There was still so much about him Myra didn't know. That scar on his arm, for instance. How did it get there?

"I got it in a knife fight," said Jerry, flexing the whited blemish and stretching the truth to hide the fact that he had sustained the injury as a child by falling into a rain barrel. The history of the wound, like most points in his past, was beguiled by his desire to romanticize his illusory image. He had a marvelous memory for events that never happened, likewise a poor one for facts he wanted to forget. If some of those great stories did not actually happen, they should have; legends suited his lifestyle. So it could be said that Jerry was to Myra whatever she was gullible enough, or in love enough, to believe.

Jerry considered it his duty to raise Myra into the type of woman he wanted her to be, in a mold fashioned after his mother. At the first sign of independent action, he cracked the whip to regain complete control over her. As much as he wanted her to become a lady, he was even more protective that no one notice his handiwork, for Jerry was a jealous husband. He consumed Myra's every thought and dominated her every move. His ravenous desire for her secluded her from the outside world, alienating friends and family.

Jerry pushed Myra to see how far he could go before she would break. He tested her capacity, as in the case of the California cutie, then promised never to commit the same offense again. Suspecting her of his weakness, he erased her self-esteem by ridiculing her appearance and, by convincing his piteous bride she was the ugly duckling she had always perceived herself to be, hoped her careworn countenance would keep courtiers away. If Myra's blouse was not buttoned to the neck, Jerry accused her of baiting other men with a come-on. She might change a dozen times before finding something he approved of, and often nothing would do except a dark blouse with high collar and long sleeves;

exposed flesh was a sin in the Pentecostal Church. Before her fourteenth birthday, Myra had cleared her closet of anything with style or color, replacing girlish fashion with a neat row of dowdy dark suits and dresses.

Cosmetics, too, were a prideful sin. "Any woman who wears rouge is only tryin' to entice a man," Jerry preached. "You already got a man, an' I don't need enticin'. Jezebel wore paint. When she died, the dogs ate her body 'cept for the cheeks and lips where she wore that wicked paint. I'll grant you ain't very pretty, but paint don't cover up ugly. I hate to tell you, baby, but I see people laugh at you behind yo' back when you walk out of a room. They feel sorry for you. They say, 'Uh, uh, uh, ain't she pitiful?'"

Myra was broken, yet Jerry's upbraiding was relentless. He kept her in poor style and embarrassed her because of it. The modicum of pride that his name lent her was negated by his refusal to share the rest of his wealth, and what bordered on mind control took the charm from the girl and bleached the beauty from the woman. In time, Myra learned to greet whomever she was introduced to with her eyes at their feet, never looking up lest she be accused of luring a lover. She did not allow herself to feel emotions. She ignored everything to the exclusion of Jerry and waited for him to spoon life to her in small sips. Those who did not know her wondered at her terrific shyness. Some guessed it was a mental affliction.

"I'm so much in love with you I want you all to myself," Jerry would say once in a while, and Myra could brook his abuse at its worst. She strived for perfection in every thought and gesture. As a reward, he only encouraged her to purify her soul at the church of his choice twice a week, even when he couldn't go with her, which was the usual case.

Myra never questioned Jerry's dictates under threat of abandonment. As he often warned, "Anytime you don't like the way I run this show, you can go back to yo' ma an' pa. But they don't want you. They were only too glad to get rid of you. So jus' remember that next time you think you got someplace to run off to. There's worse places to be, like back home with that crazy bunch." Thus, Jerry was not only Myra's salvation but her last resort. "You weren't no virgin when I married you," he accused, taking every opportunity to remind her that she was damaged

goods when he came along. "Who do you think would take you
now? An' speakin' of which, how come you weren't no virgin
when I met you? We never did get that straight."

By this point in these frequent tirades, Myra was in utter disbelief of how cruel her husband could be. She reasoned that he
could not say things so terrible unless they were true, and therefore had no choice but to believe him. What began as the education of a young bride disintegrated into the imposition of one will
over another. Myra became mentally, physically and emotionally
dependent on a husband who was sometimes gone a month or
more and who made life pure hell when at home. She had no
defenses, free thoughts or contrary suggestions, only reflexes.
She had married before she was able to formulate her own opinions; hence, she was, for better or worse, nothing more than an
extension of Jerry's tastes and attitudes.

Jerry preferred that Myra accompany him on the road, never
much fun for her since she was forbidden in nightclubs and confined to their hotel room for afterhours amusement. She chose to
remain home with Stevie, which Jerry quickly came to resent. As
soon as he was gone, the party began, retrieving the Elvis records
from under the sofa, then dashing to the drugstore for the latest
magazines, the type of godless gossip and romance confessions
Jerry abhorred. She spent hours in front of the television watching
programs which he denied her the pleasure of viewing. She im-
ploded with hysteria rather than laugh at suggestive jokes in
Jerry's presence and be accused of appreciating smutty humor;
sluts laugh at smut. So Myra feigned shock at television comedies
which, according to the restrictions of the day, could not manage
to offend little old ladies in Boston yet kindled indignation in a
man who once preached that the devil's tail was shaped like a
television antenna. Myra could watch only a very few shows in
Jerry's company—Steve Allen, for instance—and feel completely safe.

Taking advantage of Jerry's absence, Myra was in the mood for
one of her private parties. The house was uninhabited except for
Johnny Frank Edwards, Frankie Jean's ex-husband who was employed as Jerry's lackey. Johnny Frank had long harbored a crush
on Myra and saw the golden opportunity to come forward. He
plugged in the record player, set a stack of singles on the spindle
and sat down next to Myra with two glasses of bourbon. They

danced, and when the first slow number plopped into place, Johnny lifted Myra's chin and kissed her without a struggle.

"What do you think you're doin'?" she asked.

"Nothin'," he said. "Now that you're gettin' a divorce, I got as much right to you as Jerry does. You are gettin' a divorce, ain'tcha? I mean, y'all ain't gettin' back together again, are ya?"

Myra began to think. She was reminded of her baby asleep in the bedroom. And she thought of Jerry: Their problems were no easier on him than they were on her. Divorce? Divorce would destroy Jerry's career once and for all, as it nearly had done once before.

Myra snapped out of her trance. She raced to the record player and raked the needle across Hank Locklin as he sang "Please Help Me, I'm Falling" and pulled the plug out of the wall. She shoved Johnny Frank out the door, sending his bottle after him, then raced around the house till glasses were washed, dried and shelved, and everything restored to perfect order. In a fit of conscience, she dialed Dallas and told Jerry what had happened before he heard it from someone else. He was furious, until Myra stopped him cold with news that she was pregnant. Johnny Frank, never one to underestimate the wrath of the Killer, was never to be seen or heard from again.

It was 2:30 in the morning when Jerry checked into the Cardinal Inn across from Sheppard Field in Wichita Falls, Texas. The door to his room opened with a kick of his boot, and he fell back on the bed paying no attention to the man trundling in with his bags. It could have been ten minutes or two hours before he opened his eyes again to look beyond his boot tips at the desk. Was he in Pine Bluff or Opelousas? It could have been Natchitoches for all he could remember; motel rooms were all the same.

He reached for the packet of complimentary stationery and bore down on the notepaper with deliberance, briefly resembling Mrs. West's failing fourth grader attempting to squeeze simple phrases out of a pencil. "My Dearest Myra, I love you very much and miss you more than any thing in the world," he began, then settled back self-satisfied, as if a love sonnet were close to complete. From that point on, all of his letters were alike, running in circles of undying love and eternal faithfulness.

. . . Remember our vows we made don't let me down.
Will be looking forward to seeing my Darling, and Darling
I no you told me everything. I believe you and trust you
from now on, and will write you every week and won't go
out to Calif. without you Darling well take care of your self
be good take care of my man, I miss you too much Darling. I love you with all my heart and soul will see you
sooner than you think, your husband the guy that loves
you.

At the letter's end, Jerry felt much the same as any boy who
had completed a chore and wanted his reward. He folded the note
and mashed it shut in an envelope addressed to Myra Lee Lewis.
"That'll do 'er," he said, flipping the letter across the room like a
playing card at an upturned hat, then answered a gentle tap at the
door.

Upon receipt of Jerry's love letter, Myra knew their troubles to
be at an end, and in summing up the entire misunderstanding to
Kay, she wrote: "It took someone else to make us realize that we
really love each other. I'm glad it's over. Everything is wonderful
between us now and it's going to stay that way. Nothing or no one
will ever come between us again." And, fortunately, her pregnancy turned out to be a false alarm, having served its purpose in
diverting Jerry's anger over Johnny Frank to concern for her welfare.

The California Affair was over and done with exactly two days,
when Myra received a photograph of Jerry and Lynn together.
The sight of her rival vexed her sore; now Myra had a face to
hate. "I must admit I feel better since I've seen her ugly mug,"
she wrote. "She looks like a pile of crap! Ha! Ha! I have a surprise for Jerry. The picture of he and Lynn is going to turn up in
Jerry's billfold. I want to see his expression!"

And as if photos weren't enough proof, Kay engaged Lynn in a
lengthy telephone conversation and sent Myra a transcript of
Lynn's revelation that Jerry had filed for divorce with the intention of making her the fourth Mrs. Lewis. Out of the abundance
of Myra's complaint, the affair ulcerated again as she went from
practical jokery to revenge aimed at humiliating her husband and
annihilating her competition. Was this any way for the wife of a

celebrity to act toward an amorous fan? Sure, if she was fifteen years old.

May 7, 1960
Dear Kay,

I received the script this morning. I read it thru and after a little consideration this is what I've decided, and not yet determined, to do. I'm going to leave Jerry while I still love him. I know that sounds absolutely stupid, but let me explain. As you know by now, Jerry has lied to me about that girl from the start, so he undoubtedly loves her or he wouldn't lie, would he? Every time I think about Lynn I get mad, and when Jerry's around we argue about her. If we keep on arguing, soon we'll hate each other. So right now, BEFORE I'm hurt any more by Jerry, I'm getting out. I'm not the kind to hang around when I know I'm not wanted, like Jane did. You know what a time he had getting rid of her. When Jerry wants a girl, like he wanted Dorothy, Jane, me and now Lynn, he doesn't stop until he gets what he's after, meaning marriage. Jerry has done me dirty. And I'll never forget it but it's one thing about it, I'll never say anything to hurt Jerry's career or his personal life. I'm not the kind to go around hurting people just to get back. When I file for divorce, I'm going to say that I just don't love Jerry and that I don't want to live with him anymore. And after I do that, he can see Steve anytime he wants to, but I hope to God that I never have to lay eyes on him again. As for Lynn, she'd better never cross my path, for I had just as soon kill her as look at her.

One of these days Jerry's going to be hurt the way he's hurt me and then he'll know what it's like. I hope I'm around when it happens, because I think he'll apologize to me. Don't think I'm trying to get you to feel sorry for me, because I'm not. But you don't know what it's like to be hurt this way.

About me touring with Jerry—the only reason I stopped was Steve. Jerry asked me to give Steve to his mamma and travel with him from now on. But, God help me, I can't. I can't give my baby away. I love that little doll something terrible (here I go crying). But I love Jerry just as much. Tell me, what am I going to do?

Right now Jerry thinks he loves me, but in six months
it'll be Lynn. He thinks he can drop me and then come
back whenever he wants to, but he's badly mistaken. Once
someone does me dirty, I'm thru for good. I'm really sorry
I'm that way, but in a way I'm glad, too. It's not pride, I
just know that Jerry doesn't love me, he thinks he does. I
also know that if I went on and lived with J L L, he'd do
me like that again and then I'd hate him. It might be twenty
years from now, but I'd be expecting it any day, and you
know, Kay, we couldn't be happy that way. Don't ever fall
in love or marry anyone, because it's for sure you'll be
hurt. You might be an old gray-haired woman, but you'll
still feel the pain.

Myra prepared for her exit with a well-rehearsed farewell
speech and had her bags packed and waiting by the door when
Jerry returned a week later. His stress detector sounded a warning, and within minutes of his arrival he was packing his bags,
too; only, he planned on taking his wife and son on a vacation.
All the fight drained out of Myra, and before embarking on another honeymoon, she zipped off a few lines to Kay, promising,
"I'm dropping that bull about Lynn right now before it causes
more trouble. So, forget I even know a girl named Lynn."

What appeared to be a lasting truce between the loving couple
was entered into during the holiday in Louisiana. The days were
spent fishing together, the nights as young lovers; the sour turned
to sweet. Before Jerry took leave of her again, Myra tucked a note
into his suitcase which he answered as soon as he arrived at the
Hotel Horsley in Albertville, Alabama:

Dearest Myra and Darling Steve,
    Just a few lines to let you no that we made the trip just
fine, Darling I miss you already and I haven't been gone
one day and night. How's my little Stevie kiss him for me.
I love you and him very much. I read your little note Darling it made me feel real good, to no that I've got a good
wife back home that's true to me and loves me very much.
Darling drive careful when you go up town. I don't want
you or Steve to get hurt. If anything would happen to you
all, it would kill me to, I coulden live without you I love
you too much Darling I don't care what happens if I never

get back on top, I know I have a wonderful wife and son and I'm thankful for that. Well Darling we had a good show last night, looking for a good one tonight. Well Darling I'll let you go. Be sweet be good be kind, and watch my baby I love you with all my heart and soul you no that. But Myra if you don't want to live with me please let me no and I'll get out Baby. I don't want to tie you down if you don't love me and can't be true to me it's just not right. But remember Darling I love you love you love you love you love you,

> Your husband,
> Jerry Lee Lewis
> P.S. I'm true to you.

As the summer of 1960 dragged on interminably, Myra wasted away beneath the oppressive heat and the disillusionment of marriage. As she confided in Kay:

> Every time I look at Jerry I think about him and Lynn, then naturally I get upset. I've told Jer to leave at least twenty times, that I wanted a divorce and that I *did* love him but I couldn't get my mind off *that*. Then I'd tell him that I was sorry. That I didn't want a divorce. I'm absolutely miserable. I would have left Jer long ago but he acted like he *really* loved me and was going to do right. People would have said that I walked out on him just when he needed me. Times are rough now, I mean rough.

And rather than make it that much rougher, Myra would remain at Jerry's side, "for as long as I live, but whenever he does me wrong just once more (I know he will), I'm afraid I'll kill him.

Even while on his best behavior, Jerry ran afoul of his wife and, upon remembering Myra's sixteenth birthday thirty days after it had passed, hoped to gain her forgiveness by spending his last dime on new furniture and a new car, the news of which was forwarded to Kay. As Myra hoped, Kay included the particulars of her joyous celebration in the August fan-club newsletter and made sure Lynn got a copy. "I'll bet it burnt her up!" Myra wrote Kay. "She was so sure Jerry was divorcing me! Ha!" The months-old affair had become ancient history for the participants when it developed into a daily battle of one-sided one-upmanship whereby Myra accumulated points, reported the score to Kay, who then published the results in the newsletter. By the end of August, Myra announced she was returning to the road with her husband, especially for the California dates.

Myra readied herself for war by beginning a quest for perfection. She checked out three or four books from the library weekly, reading fifty pages, then returning them for more. Her first selections included poetry, *The Crown And The Cross*, and *The Life of Adolf Eichmann*. She returned to church, and at all other times was the embodiment of Pentecostal practices. For the pièce de resistance, a new black negligee.

"Jane told me one time that she was going to get Jer back and I told her 'may the best one win,'" Myra wrote Kay. "I'll tell Lynn the same thing. I won over Jane and I think I won over Lynn, too. Don't you think so?"

J. W. Brown rejoined the Brother Lewis Traveling Salvation Show in his role as performer and agent as well as manager and parent when there was no one left to attend to the endless details that had been ignored for more than a year. Although Jay again placed his fortunes in jeopardy by underwriting a tour, Jerry could not resist riding him about the Mickey Gilley fiasco. Jay tried the first few times to make explanations and grew tired of not being heard, so he allowed Jerry the pleasure of getting in a few digs.

Promoters were few and far between, no money was forthcoming from Sun, and Jay saw the only way out was to withdraw ten thousand dollars from the bank—money he had stashed away for his family as a promise to his wife—and create their own bookings in St. Louis and Kansas City. Even with working capital provided, no one could be found in those cities to lend a hand. It was Jay's mistake to ask assistance of an old friend, Oscar Davis. He forwarded the entire sum to Oscar and asked him to get the ball rolling—rent the hall, buy up radio and newspaper ads and plaster the place with posters.

Hopes for a do-it-yourself comeback were riding high when the gang rode into St. Louis. They looked for Oscar, who could not be found. They scanned the papers for announcements, and found nothing. They searched around the dial for radio spots, and heard nothing. They walked onstage before no one.

"I found them more receptive in Kansas City," Oscar told the band after the show. "The people around here, I don't know, they're kinda funny, so I didn't want to waste my time and your money. But I can assure you a better turnout in Missouri."

Hopes were riding high when the gang rode into Kansas City. They looked for Oscar, who could not be found. They scanned the papers for announcements, and found nothing. They searched around the dial for radio spots, and heard nothing. They walked onstage before no one.

"Where is everybody?" asked Jay.

"I don't know," said Oscar.

"Where is the money?" asked Jay.

"I don't know," said Oscar.

"You're fired," said Jay, and turned and walked away. Twice he rolled the dice and twice he crapped out. The business was bankrupt. The troops retreated to Memphis.

It was a happy day in June 1960 when Jane remarried and Jerry was free from alimony which he neglected to pay. The court, siding with Jerry for a change, recognized that his earnings were now virtually at a stop due to trouble with the Musicians' Union, and absolved him of arrearages and decreed that child support was to be paid only when his earnings permitted him to do so, dismissing the citation for contempt and adding that Jerry was not to be held in contempt on the same charge in the future.

Nevertheless, a petition citing contempt was entered in October and again in November of the next year. Jerry's earnings for eight months in 1961 were slightly in excess of $8,800, from which the court concluded he should pay $150 a month in child support. Jerry was so angered during the course of these proceedings that twice his counsel made motions to require Jane and Ronnie take blood tests to disprove paternity; twice the petitions were denied.

Jerry's financial condition was not helped by the songs he chose to record—an upbeat remake of the traditional folksong "John Henry" and the Chuck Willis hit "Hang Up My Rock and Roll Shoes" coupled to create his thirteenth Sun single released in August 1960. They were good renditions in spite of the sax solos and Jerry's hoarse, unpolished vocals which sometimes slipped into the style he and Elvis traded back and forth. Both sides sounded as if they were recorded at one of Sam's parties. The message, for the few that heard it, was clear:

> *Mama she done tol' me,*
> *She don't like this rock and roll.*
> *I said, "Oh, Mama, please, you just don't know*
> *I don't wanna hang up my rock and roll shoes."*
> *Well, I gets that feelin' every time I hear those blues.*

Mamma done tol' Jerry somethin' else: next time you go down to the studio, take your sisters; maybe they'll help Brother find a hit. Acting on Mamma's advice, Jerry carried Linda Gail and Frankie Jean to the studio to tape a coltish version of "Good Golly Miss Molly" which was wisely buried in the vaults of Sun.

Jerry continued to have difficulty with the union and his label. Jud, in between selling Judd Records and dodging payola investigations, had gone to bat against Brother Sam in Jerry's behalf. If Sam would not honor Jerry's contract by promoting his releases, Jud asked that Jerry be allowed to step up on the auction block and vend his wares elsewhere.

The major obstacle, Sam defended, was Jerry's disfranchisement by the union and not Sam's dereliction of duty: Jerry could not be considered in good standing with Sun if he was at odds with his union. Until Jerry paid off one hundred thousand dollars in default judgments for no shows and caught up on his dues, he could not record, perform in union-sanctified venues or sign with another label. Sam, in his inimitable way, would not consent to an advance to pay the fines.

Jud, meanwhile, sought a reconciliation with the union. He spent weeks sorting judgments and making appeals that cases be reopened to examine gross injustices. Owners of hundred-seat clubs were claiming ten thousand dollars in damages due to Lewis cancellations. The union saw Jud's point, but reminded him that Jerry had ignored the claims and all judgments were final. Jud appealed to the union's spirit of cooperation, pleading that their primary interest should lie with the artist and his effort to record music rather than in hitting him with fines while taking away his means of paying them. Once Jud pointed out that Jerry could get even with a hit single, the union agreed to accept a weekly installment, but would not fully reinstate him until the entire amount had been satisfied. At that rate, Jud calculated, Jerry would not regain his card for twenty years.

Alan Freed's days as a concert promoter were over following the payola investigation which convicted him of commercial bribery. Chuck Berry was on trial for a violation of the Mann Act, and Holly, Valens, Cochran and the Big Bopper were gone. Elvis, newly discharged from the army, had put rock 'n' roll behind him, shaved off his sideburns, packed away his black leather jacket and appeared on a Frank Sinatra special wearing a tuxedo. Presley and Sinatra sang each other's hits, then performed a duet of romantic ballads which critics universally panned as "merely awful."

Who was left to rock 'n' roll? Surely not Percy Faith, whose "Theme From A Summer Place" was the biggest hit in 1960, or The Everly Brothers or Mark Dinning. The top ten in September included The Ventures, The Safaris, Brook Benton, Chubby Checker's "Twist," Bobby Rydell's "Volare" and Brenda Lee's "I'm Sorry"—not a rocker in the bunch. Top-selling albums included comic Dave Gardner's "Kick Thine Own Self," jazz clarinetist Pete Fountain, The Kingston Trio, Paul Anka, Chet Atkins and The Platters. A kid would have to search far and wide for rock 'n' roll, and just about the only place it could be found was wherever Jerry Lee Lewis was playing on those fall evenings. Rock 'n' roll had been a woefully brief chapter in the history of music, having begun in 1957 and ending a year later.

The time was ripe for another rockin' Jerry release, but the union forbade it and there was no point in pressing another "John Henry" or "Old Black Joe" as far as Sam Phillips was concerned. Perhaps the best idea was to release a single that didn't even list Jerry's name on the label.

"Instrumentals are the rage right now," Sam said, looking at the charts. "Look at that 'Walk Don't Run' by The Ventures— Number One again this week. The mood is right for instrumentals. You oughta put one out."

"Yeah? Under whose name?" asked Jerry.

"An alias," said Sam, "a mystery vocalist. An' we could really fake out the union by releasin' it on the Phillips label instead of Sun."

"The whole idea stinks," said Jerry, insulted at having to hide his identity in order to sell a record.

"Wait, now, hear me out. What we do is put out this record by this mystery man, see, an' get a lotta publicity. Ever'body'll rush out to buy it, and you'll pay off your debts with the royalties. Then we say, 'Surprise! It's Jerry Lee Lewis!' An' that's it."

"That's what?"

"A hit."

"No, it ain't. They'll stop playin' it. They'll know who it is inside of two minutes, anyhow," Jerry argued.

"Then we stick to the instrumental idea, like I wanted to in the first place," said Sam. "We'll use the two you taped in January."

Before the mystery record shipped in August, Sam made everyone swear under penalty of death not to reveal the true identity of "The Hawk," lest the union be upon them like locusts. Kay Martin first heard "I Get the Blues When It Rains" in New York on the twentieth and immediately zipped off a letter to Myra demanding an explanation. "No one plays piano like Jerry," said Kay, "you can't fool me." Within two weeks, Myra received six more notes from Kay begging to be let in on the secret, and Myra admitted the plan: "Yesterday I called every record shop in Memphis and more than 50 percent said it *was* Jerry Lee Lewis, and Dewey Phillips announces that it's Jerry on WHBQ when he plays it."

Members of Jerry's fan club were wise to the plan almost as quickly and were writing Kay asking for photographs of The Hawk. According to Sam's scheme, once Jud had made the arrangements to repay the union with proceeds from the record, The Hawk would be in demand and the publicity stunt would blossom into the promotion of the century. Unfortunately, most radio stations were tipped off, and those who weren't had little or no interest in an anonymous unknown pecking out "In the Mood" on the piano, which lost something in the translation sans horns. The Hawk promotion hit the industry with a dull thud, giving Jerry the satisfaction of saying to Sam "I told you so" while suffering the failure.

As Jerry's twenty-fifth birthday rolled around, Myra made plans to fly to Atlanta to surprise him. She found him alone and depressed that no one cared enough to call or send a telegram wishing him happy birthday, with the exception of true-blue Kay Martin. Kay also decided The Hawk needed a helping hand, and the Jerry Lee Lewis Fan Club fostered a separate entity, The

Hawk Fan Club. Members of the parent organization balked at the idea of being billed for an additional membership fee, and the new club failed.

A reaction to The Hawk was expected from the union, but their message was bewildering. The newest interpretation of their rules prohibited Jerry from playing the piano on a recording, but he was not enjoined from singing. Sam decided that his next move would be to release a ballad which would not require Jerry's handiwork on the keyboard. And what kind of record would that be?

At the close of 1960, Sun Records shipped a limited number of Number 352, "When I Get Paid" backed with "Love Made a Fool Out Of Me," by Jerry Lee Lewis. As decreed by the union, Jerry did not play the piano. He did not even attend the session, coming to the studio late one night to add the vocal. The single was unlike anything he had done before. "When I Get Paid," recorded at bossa nova tempo, blared with horns and was interrupted by a guitar break instead of the trademark piano solo. Side two, a she-broke-my-heart-and-stole-my-car lament, had Jerry singing in duet with a female vocalist who nearly drowned him out. This was the lowest point in a career which many in the industry considered finished.

Jerry spent most of his down time in a favorite hangout of his youth, the pool hall in Ferriday. Fittingly, it was where he was reunited with his oldest and dearest friend, Cecil Harrelson.

Jerry noticed the change that hard work in the oil fields had made in Cecil. In those steely eyes, he saw the reflection of trouble, of a marriage gone wrong, of breaks that had all been luckless. And Cecil studied the red, remorseless eyes of his friend and listened as the renowned voice fraught with anger spoke of vintage years which went dry as dust, snared in an evil time that suddenly fell upon him. There in the dimly lit hall, two in need of understanding came to be brothers again, resolving to share whatever the future would bring.

When next the Jerry Lee Lewis group took to the road, it was like the good ol' days. The original trio with Russ Smith on drums and Jay Brown on bass was together again, and Cecil was apprentice road manager at a salary of five dollars a day. Jerry's parents went with them sometimes, but rarely together. Elmo pre-

ferred life on the road to staying at home. Mamie favored Holiday
Inns, and would opt for another two-hour drive rather than stay in
a town not accommodated by the Nation's Innkeepers. "No matter
where you are, the rooms is always the same," said Mamie of the
decor. "It's like goin' home. You don't have to get used to it."

Elmo was intrigued by room service. When first he saw his son
put it into effect, he was amazed. Jerry picked up the phone,
dialed two digits, requested a platter of roast beef, and five minutes later a bus boy wheeled the feast before him.

"You taken ill, son?" Elmo asked. "Seems like you coulda gone
to the dinin' room with ever'body else."

"Don't have to, Papa, when they're willin' to wheel it up to
you. All you have to do is pick up the phone, an' whatever you
want is here in two shakes."

Elmo balked at the notion at first; he never was one for puttin'
on airs. It wasn't until Jerry excused himself momentarily that he
decided to give room service a dry run. Elmo reached for the
phone and listened for a dial tone. The hotel operator answered.
"Co-Coler," whispered Elmo, and promptly returned the receiver
to its cradle. After twenty minutes, he puzzled over the delay in
the arrival of his refreshment and deduced that he had done something wrong. The next time he placed an order, Elmo hollered,
"Hook me up with room service an' send me down a butler."

The family roared, and never a night would pass thereafter that
someone didn't pick up the phone and demand a butler.

One of the worst mistakes Cecil made early on in his employment was taking a camera on the road. In the wrong hands, it
could provide nothing but trouble. One evening in particular, two
girls followed the boys back to the hotel, and worked up enough
nerve to knock on Jerry's door for an autograph. Cecil invited the
girls inside, where they spotted the camera and asked for a picture
with Jerry. Having no space to set up a shot, Jerry hopped in bed
with a girl under each arm while Cecil clicked away with his
Polaroid.

Cecil gave two photos to the girls and put the rest in his shav-
ing kit, forgetting all about them until after he returned home.
Linda Gail found them as she helped him unpack and, taking half
a look at the smut, ran to her mother. Jerry did plenty of fast
talking before he found himself in another scandal, but with
Cecil's help convinced Myra that he would never be so stupid as

to pose with another playmate. It was fortunate, too, that news of an illegitimate child born to one of the fans and rumored to be Jerry's did not get back to Myra. On a subsequent trip, Cecil heard that a paternity suit was in the works. The action was never filed, Cecil discovered, due to the death of the unwed mother during a domestic dispute.

Mamie made several trips with her son to learn firsthand what sort of shenanigans Cecil and Jay had roped her impressionable boy into joining. She had the boys in the band sized up for a bunch of hell-raisers who were responsible for wearing away her son's self-discipline, forcing him to stay up late and drink whiskey. Jerry was anxious to preserve her belief that he was a good boy whose only fault was that he loved his mother too much.

The boys gathered in Jerry's room late one night for a few beers, a case to be exact, and as the evening spun its dizzy way, the floor was littered so that three steps could not be stumbled without kicking a dozen cans. A knock came at the door, and Cecil, always the joker, pranced to answer it in his underwear, thinking it might be another group of girls wanting an autograph. What he found was the mother of his employer standing in the doorway with hands on hips, glaring at the gathering.

"Mamma!" Jerry exclaimed while shoving cans under the sheets, "what are you doin' here?"

"Whose beer cans are these?" Mamie demanded.

Jerry, at a complete loss for an explanation, answered, "Jay's, they're all Jay's."

Mrs. Lewis did not have to say another word. Her eyes, at times such as these, did all the talking. Jay, whom Mamie held single-handedly responsible for all the ills in the world, was riveted in place by sharp-eyed daggers.

In the middle of January 1961, Myra hunted for a new home large enough to accommodate Jerry's extended family, comprised of his parents, Linda Gail, Frankie Jean and her family, his son by a former marriage, his fan club president, his road manager and two or three members of his band. Unable to afford his employees more than starvation wages when he could pay them at all, the least Jerry could do was share his food and keep a roof over their heads. On East Shore Drive in the south Memphis suburb of Coro

Lake, Myra found a home twice the size of their first residence with a swimming pool.

As time drew near for the closing of the sale, Jerry departed on an extended tour of Canada. On the seventeenth, he wrote Myra from Toronto: "Sure hope we get our house, tell everybody I said hello—your husband, the Great Jerry Lee Lewis," which she interpreted to mean "handle all details." Her goal of creating a pad befitting a star was met by offsetting the furnishings against white shag carpets and lavender drapes. In the living room, Jerry's music room and presence chamber, was his favorite recliner, where he was served all meals, and a white grand piano. The latest thing in interior decorating, and which no home was complete without, was a waterfall situated in the foyer.

Jerry came home to his castle and was duly impressed by the statement that wall-to-wall white made—sort of like walking on clouds. The choice was far from practical in a home where a two-year-old was given free rein and family and friends constantly filed in and out, but Myra was able to enforce a rule requiring the removal of shoes before entering, which many a headstrong Lewis was dying to break. The only other modification Myra contemplated was a revolving door to maintain a regular flow of traffic.

Although 1961 was when Elvis Presley's "It's Now or Never" became the vocal single of the year among his five Grammy nominations, he stepped down from the stage and would not perform again publicly, with the exception of movies, until 1969. His retirement officially marked the end of the Golden Age of Rock 'n' Roll. In a year which gave prominence to soundtracks from the movie classics *Exodus, Camelot* and *Sound of Music,* the male vocalists whose turn it was to bask in the limelight were Del Shannon, Bobby Lewis and Roy Orbison. Again, the time for the return of Jerry Lee seemed ripe.

It was February, and Jud Phillips finally persuaded the union to reinstate Jerry on the promise to pay fines, fees and defaults at the rate of one hundred dollars a week. Jud was back on a full-time basis promoting his greatest discovery and conferring with Ray Brown of National Artists on bookings, hoping to mount a comeback overseas to overcome the boycott at home. Jerry's price was two hundred fifty dollars a night, the lowest level in four years.

Nevertheless, the Grades, Sirs Leslie and Lew, coldly refused to discuss Jerry's return to England, and Jud turned to Central America, where the climate and reception were warmer, booking three months in Mexico City and neighboring provinces.

On the ninth, Jerry became the first artist to record at the new Sun studio in Nashville, and Jud made sure the press turned out to witness the "first step on the long comeback trail." The session consisted of four remarkable recordings: "What'd I Say," "Livin' Lovin' Wreck," "Cold, Cold Heart" and "I Forgot to Remember to Forget," destined to produce the only modicum of success he was to enjoy for as long as he remained on the Sun label. These were Jerry's most skillful vocals and proof of his mastery of diverse styles. With the Presley hit, he proved he was as good as Elvis at his own game; the remake of Hank Williams's classic was the epitome of honky-tonk piano; "Livin' Lovin' Wreck," coupled with "What'd I Say" for the single, echoed Jerry's best rockabilly vocals; his rendition of the Ray Charles hit was instrumentally faithful to the original except where he "improved" upon it with frills, trills and glissandi.

The single was scheduled for release on the twenty-fourth at the same time Jerry was to embark for Mexico. These plans were set aside so that he could play more important dates closer to home —Li'l Abner's Rebel Room in Memphis, Birmingham, Meridian and St. Louis's Keil Auditorium—to stoke the grass-roots followers on the single.

Billboard, cautious in speculating on Jerry's revival, heralded "What'd I Say," remarking: "It's been a long, dry spell for Lewis, but this outstanding rendition of the Ray Charles song, once a hit for Charles himself, can bring him back, with the proper push. Lewis's pumping piano is tops and the vocal matches it."

The market was similarly cautious breaking in the single finding an initial response in the R & B ranks; surprisingly, since the Anita Kerr Singers backing Jerry were no Raelets. The country crowd, the only folks to turn out to see Jerry in small but steady droves over the past two years, picked up on the song in spite of the sound having little to offer the true country-music lover. As with "Whole Lot of Shakin'," Jerry translated rhythm and blues for white folks whose purchases were reflected in the pop charts, and "What'd I Say" became the first Lewis record to appear in all three ranks since "Break Up" in 1958. The song remained alive throughout the spring, finding its strongest reaction in April, rated Number 26 in R & B, Number 27 in the country listing and Number 30 in the pop top forty.

The all-important decision as to what song should be released to continue the upward trend was made arbitrarily, like so many other key decisions determining Jerry's career. Sam Phillips would sooner consult a deck of cards than chart action for predicting trends. Ignoring the stirring in the R & B market, Sam sought to exploit the teenagers and country listeners with the mismatched "Cold, Cold Heart" and Otis Blackwell's "It Won't Happen With Me," a "poppy teen-slanted rocker" with a comical approach which missed the mark completely. Otis, publishing the title under the Ray Evans pseudonym, had written the lyrics for Jerry, a plea-cum-popularity-contest:

> *You say you could fall in love with Elvis*
> *And you say you like to hear Jackie Wilson sing,*
> *Wait a minute, wait a minute, pretty baby,*
> *I just wanna tell you one little thing:*

> *Well, your love for Elvis Presley, it wouldn't last very, very long*
> *You'd get sick and tired of seein' him wigglin' past your door.*
> *It's true, Jackie Wilson, oh, he can talk that talk*
> *You'd get sick and tired of seein' him walk that walk,*
> *It wouldn't happen with me.*

Teens ignored Jerry's plea when it was released at the end of June, yet his smooth and gentle version of "Cold, Cold Heart" went straight to the Number 22 slot in the country charts, where it remained for more than five weeks without the first promotional aid. True ol' Hank to come through when all else fails.

Jerry's summer tour covered Michigan and carried him from Fall River, Massachusetts, and Providence, Rhode Island, down the Eastern Seaboard through Florida, where he did two shows a day in different towns for a chain of radio stations. His price was up to four hundred dollars, except when he agreed on fifty dollars less to fill in between dates. Heading home, he stopped in Georgia to play the Fayetteville Drive-In where he costarred with a science-fiction thriller, *The Fly*. From there it was straight to the top: the Moultrie Junior High Gym and the Adel Grade School Auditorium.

There was hardly sufficient time, patience and energy for the trip by car across the width of the nation for Alan Freed's concert at the Hollywood Bowl. Freed, working as a KDAY deejay in Los Angeles, had signed on to emcee a tour for a group of investors. Jerry headlined the show, which included The Shirelles, the most prominent of the black girl groups that became fashionable in the early sixties. Following the Bowl date, the band drove back across America to Montgomery, Alabama, then to where they had begun two weeks before at the Gator Bowl in Jacksonville for another radio-sponsored event paying Jerry's largest guarantee of the year, six hundred dollars.

The right vehicle to carry Jerry back to New York arrived in August. Those Labor Day extravaganzas at the Brooklyn Paramount in years gone by were revived by deejay Murray "the K" Kaufman in a ten-day festival starring Jackie Wilson, and Jerry was selected as the top draw for the white crowd. Jackie had by this time been in the business ten years, beginning with Billy Ward's Dominoes on the old Federal label in 1951. He was an Elvis Presley for black women, dreamy-eyed and pompadour-hair-done, when his solo career began on the Brunswick label. "All My Love," in August 1960, was his sixth hit following the monumental "Lonely Teardrops" in 1958. Jackie's career was rudely interrupted shortly thereafter when a man shot him twice during a show. The Labor Day marathon was to be Jackie's triumphant return to the stage. Jerry Lee Lewis did not see it that way; it was to be his comeback before many of the same people who had set box-office records during the Christmas of 1957.

Altogether, fourteen acts paraded across the Paramount stage four or five times daily. Jackie and Jerry followed Etta James, Clarence "Frogman" Henry, Elvis soundalike Ral Donner, and Brian Hyland, whose string of a dozen hits commenced hardly eighteen months before with "Itsy Bitsy Teenie Weenie Yellow Polka-Dot Bikini." The do-wop groups were represented by The Belmonts, The Chantells, The Cleftones and The Regents, who performed their top-ten hit, "Barbara Ann." Tony Orlando was kicking off his career, and backstage at the Paramount Kay Martin introduced him to her old pal and his future wife, Elaine Berman.

The ten-day exhibition quickly evolved into a war between

Jackie Wilson and Jerry Lee Lewis, and club owners in the Northeast felt the reverberations. Wilson was hot, but Lewis, in the Number 2 spot, made him hotter as the Great Ball of Fire brought black patrons to their feet with numbers that out-Rayed Ray Charles. Club owners now conspired to bring this heated rivalry into their showrooms, having learned from wrestling and boxing promoters that the best way to make a sellout crowd crazy is to let blacks fight rednecks and check the guns and knives at the door. So when the Paramount closed its door behind fifty shows of musical history, booking agents were clamoring to host what had become known as the Battle of the Century: Jackie Wilson vs. Jerry Lee Lewis.

Henry Winn, a black promoter, stacked six other black acts against Jerry in a thirty-day swing through northern Negro night-clubs commencing on Jerry's twenty-sixth birthday. No dates were booked below the Mason-Dixon, since it was nearly impossible for a black man to find hotel accommodations, and while the minstrels trooped about in converted buses, Jerry, Cecil, J. W. and drummer Gene Chrisman drove a new turquoise Cadillac. The first date was the Rocklyn Palace, where owners sold every seat in the house, added more, sold those and charged folks to line the walls and stand over by the cigarette machine.

Jerry's set consisted of three or four songs, usually "Down the Line," "What'd I Say," "Great Balls of Fire" and "Whole Lot of Shakin'." Encores were a necessity, and he battled 'em to a stand-still with "High School Confidential," "Breathless," "Johnny B. Goode" or "Hound Dog." A change was brought about to Jerry's association with the black roots of rock: There was more rhythm to his blues and more soul in his rock 'n' roll.

The show moved on to Newark, Chicago and the bastion of black entertainment, the Apollo Theatre in Harlem, and by that time every club owner east of the Mississippi was calling Ray Brown offering their firstborn for just one date. Jerry was willing and Jackie was able, and the two singers continued throughout October in black venues of the East and Midwest. Along the way, Jerry added "Peanut Butter" and Chris Kenner's "I Like It Like That" to an R & B repertoire which grew to include "Save the Last Dance for Me," Berry Gordy's "Money," and Little Richard's "Long Tall Sally" and "Good Golly Miss Molly."

Performed live, the new additions were brilliantly interpreted, keeping their composers' intentions in mind but once they were recorded in the Phillips studio in Nashville, the addition of horns and reeds swamped the sound, and chirping background vocals of white girls and boys transformed the material into something which the record-buying public rejected. Consequently, "Save the Last Dance for Me" and "Money," released in September and November respectively, managed to sell sparingly wherever the tour took Jerry but were never popular enough in any large area to merit a position on the national charts.

Continuing this same trend in January 1962, Jerry recorded "Ramblin' Rose," replete with three honkin' saxes led by Boots Randolph and the insipid background vocals. The flip side reworked Junior Parker's "Feelin' Good" as "I've Been Twistin'," a countrified version of the dance craze. Ignoring the predilections of the grass-roots followers who had bought his every hit, and failing to satisfy pop-oriented teens, it was wrongly supposed that the Jackie Wilson package tour would establish Jerry as a musical soulmate, thus pleasing no one. As Jud had said of him in the beginning, Jerry Lee Lewis was an action artist that had to be seen to be appreciated; recordings lost something in the translation.

Sam Phillips finally got around to compiling a second album, deceptively entitled "Jerry Lee's Greatest" in that some of the tracks had never been released and were nothing more than filler. "Hello Josephine," "Hillbilly Music," "Frankie and Johnny" and the Jim Reeves hit "Home" were combined with "Great Balls of Fire," "Break Up," "What'd I Say," "Cold, Cold Heart," and "Money," the single that failed as a drawing card for the collection. More than three years had elapsed since the release of Jerry's first album, and in comparison, he pointed out to Jud, Elvis had released fourteen albums in the same period in spite of serving two years in the army. Every other artist he had ever shared a bill with had more LPs than he, yet, he quickly added, who was as versatile or as talented?

"Who has been more maligned and despised?" was Jud's reply.

Christmas that year was not a festive occasion. Jerry was not home until the twenty-fourth, and Myra, on the verge of a nervous breakdown for the past five months, was talking of returning to school to be rid of fan clubs, rock 'n' roll and road shows.

J. W. Brown signed with Todd Records to begin a career of his own, too.

There was bad blood elsewhere in the extended family, involving Linda Gail and Cecil Harrelson. Cecil, twenty-six and recently divorced, had no interest in the flirtations of his best friend's fourteen-year-old sister. The more he balked, the more intent Linda became on capturing his attention. Without result, she resorted to the unconventional, first by lying to her mother that Cecil was her lover and that Mamie should make him marry her, then by becoming engaged to Bobby Goza to make Cecil jealous. Still no response, so Linda married Bobby to really teach Cecil a lesson. She was married three months before leaving Bobby for another man, whom she later married. Bobby killed himself.

And on Christmas morn, two-year-old Stevie was perhaps the only member of the family enjoying the bounty of having been given two of everything in the world. Under a mountain of giftwrap, Mom found her lone present from her husband, a small bottle of inexpensive perfume, a drugstore variety which looked better in the bottle than it smelled on the body. For years, it sat unopened on her dresser, treasured for having been the only personal item Jerry ever gave her. He never understood how the casual mention of discarding the unused trifle could bring tears to Myra's eyes.

Jerry and his tribe of trusted advisors took a long look at the ledger at the end of 1961. All efforts to return him to his former status had gone awry another year. Clearly, the key to a comeback was a pardon for his sins by way of a reclamation of England.

Following the aborted tour, no one could reasonably expect Jerry's recovery from the Child Bride Scandal, and it was not until the British release of "What'd I Say" in April 1961 and its eighth-place showing in the charts that the return of Jerry Lee could be seriously considered. With the first mention of that possibility, Fleet Street broke out in a rash of Scandal revivals, and complications set in when Ray Brown set about negotiating a tour. Jerry was denied an entry permit by the Home Office. The ban angered Decca, his British label, prompting a spokesman to question "What sort of vindictive bureaucracy is at work? If Jerry is being barred because he married a thirteen-year-old girl, then half the Eastern potentates now visiting Britain should be refused entrance. He should be judged purely as an entertainer ... and a man with two records in the best-sellers' list is obviously a top-rate performer people want to see."

And the people's voice was heard by every newspaper in the land, proclaiming Jerry's abundant talent and protesting against the injustice of the Home Office. The letters did not discriminate in their attacks—they blamed everyone remotely connected with Jerry: Sun, for not releasing more of his records and for failing to promote them when they were marketed; the promoters, for failing to invite him back to England; the press, for invading his privacy; and those fans who had been swayed by the pasting and no longer supported him. There was no doubt that there had been a falling-off of interest in Jerry because of unfavorable publicity, but based upon the vast majority of correspondence to England's newspapers, this attitude had been adopted by the people who controlled entertainment, and not by the fans.

"Somebody once wrote that Jerry Lee could have been living with a chimpanzee and still not have it affect his STAGE appearances. I'm with them," wrote one supporter. "The phony, whipped-up sensationalism that surrounded him last time did nobody any good, a lot of people considerable harm, and enraged a lot more who wanted to see the erratic Mr. Lewis perform. It's not too late for him here ... just as long as he doesn't bring TWO wives with him this time. But the best bet is to lay off big press receptions and just get down to the job in hand, i.e., belting it at the piano."

Purely on the strength of such stirring public sentiment, Jerry Lee Lewis was booked into England for three weeks commencing on April 26, 1962. It was the chance of a lifetime in a lifetime of chances.

⑨ *In Loving Memories*

ARILLA LEWIS, MATRIARCH OF THE CLAN, was approaching her ninetieth birthday. Her husband, Leroy, had been gone twenty-five years, and she ceased to travel about visiting her children, grandchildren, great-grandchildren and great-great-grandchildren when she sensed it would not be too much longer before she and Lee were reunited. Arilla died January 23, 1962, a grim start of a black year.

The Lewis clan, due to the longevity of its members and their fruitfulness, had swollen in rank to a large number. Births were celebrated far more often than deaths were mourned, and seldom did an empty place at the table remain vacant. For instance, Frankie Jean, mother of two-year-old Wayne, Jr., and infant daughter Jerry Christina, found herself in the family way again in spite of rarely being at peace with her husband long enough to cooperate. It was no secret that Wayne was a runaround, and fights were loud and frequent. On the night Frankie caught him sneakin' out, she chased him down in a car. Not satisfied with nipping tail feathers, she reached for the gun she always kept handy and sent a slug past Wayne's ear which shattered the windshield of Mamie's Oldsmobile. Had Frankie been a sure shot, her third baby, Michael Lee, would never have known his father.

Jerry was happy to be a thousand miles away, playing one-night stands from Canada to California with Fabian, Bobby Vee and Faron Young. Myra, seventeen and a freshman in business college, had been married four years, a mother for three of them. She was lonely but never alone, living in luxury not as her husband's partner but as a helpmate in the pursuit of his career. She loved a man incapable of loving her in the way she deserved, a man who had her when he wanted her and cast her aside when content, who spent himself entertaining others and drank in order to cope with a three-hundred-date schedule which took him everywhere but the top of the charts. Together, they shared a defiant will to survive; she the stronger of the two in her depthless loyalty and moral sense.

No bond between husband and wife is stronger than the child that unites them, and without Steve Allen Lewis, Myra and Jerry would have found it infinitely easier to have gone their separate ways. Stevie was their big blon' baby, their one mutual happiness.

At age three, Stevie exhibited a natural aptitude for the piano, scary in the way he chorded entire songs and sang better than he could speak. It was as if music had been knit together in the unformed substance of the womb and bred in the bone. His father more or less expected any son of his to excel at the keyboard; his mother saw a potential to excel beyond his father. As they were to discover, Stevie's mission in life was altogether different from making music, and therein lay an iliad of woes.

In Memphis, Easter morning was radiant. For Myra, it was the holiday for dressing pretty and hunting eggs. This year was to be different, for Myra chose this to be the day when she would take Stevie to church for the first time—a fitting initiation, since Easter is what Christianity is all about. She dressed her little boy in orange and olive, cherishing his complete innocence, his blue eyes filled with the light of love, a package bursting with a curious excitement and the anticipation of many marvelous discoveries—like baskets filled with jelly beans and marshmallow bunnies. Like getting out of his Easter outfit and dipping his toes in the pool. It was a blessed day.

In the evening, Myra was busy preparing dinner for Elmo and Uncle George Herron. She was concocting a large pot of her special spaghetti, and guessed over a grocery list while Stevie minded his business and everybody else's, running in and out with a grubby handful of jelly beans. He was suddenly guided into the backyard and stood at the edge of the swimming pool, staring into water made murky by recent rains. He turned on the garden hose and arced a waterfall into the deep end, then backed away and searched for a stick to fish the filemot frith for treasures.

Daring himself to reach farther than he could achieve, Stevie slipped into the pool, his small size making a barely audible splash. The hand of death pushed him down, hitting his head and forcing the last trails of airy spirit from his mouth. He dropped lifelessly to the bottom of the dark pool. The splashing stopped. The ripples spread to the far sides of the cement basin and dispersed. The water was stilled again as quickly as the interruption had disturbed it. In a single, unblinking moment, Stevie was snatched from the earth and ushered before God, purified and spiritually reborn, as in the baptismal font.

Myra walked through the house wondering where her son was hiding. She went into the den where Elmo talked with George. They had not seen him. The threesome hurried outside and began calling Stevie's name with increasing pitch and volume. Myra ran to the backyard, searching, and was distracted by the water running from the hose into the pool. She shivered on the brink of the watery grave and screamed.

Jimmy Haning, a neighbor who heard the call, dived into the pool, making one pass in the shallow end before finding Stevie five feet deep. Other neighbors came pouring out of their homes, having heard the mother's screams a block away.

"Here, I have him," Jimmy called, and handed Stevie to Myra. The baby's face had turned blue, his clotted hair stuck together in locks.

She carried the limp doll a few steps and placed him in the grass while others tried mouth-to-mouth resuscitation. Myra froze, her fists covering her mouth as she wished life into her baby's body. A doctor broke through the crowd and asked that Myra be taken inside as he prepared to open the chest with a pocket knife for heart massage. From the patio, Myra watched the doctor's silhouette illuminated by flashlights against draped bedsheets as he operated for twenty minutes.

"He breathed!" someone called to Myra.

"Thank God!" she sobbed. "He's gonna be all right."

The doctor came into the house and sat beside Myra as firemen loaded Stevie into an ambulance. "There was nothing I could do," he said.

Myra did not understand the meaning of the doctor's pronouncement. She went into the bedroom and called the hotel in Minneapolis where Jerry was staying. Cecil answered.

"Stevie fell in the pool. They've taken him to the hospital. Tell Jerry," she said, and hung up.

Jerry called the hospital. He was told his son was dead. Although he said nothing and showed no emotion, Cecil could tell by the look on his face that it was tragic news. He took the receiver from Jerry and made reservations on the first flight to Memphis. At the airport, it was announced that harsh weather conditions had canceled their flight. Cecil bought a checkerboard from the gift shop and played Jerry match after match until all hope of departing before dawn had vanished. They found a nearby hotel where they napped until sunrise, and took the first flight out when the fog lifted.

In Memphis, Stevie was being prepared for shipment to the Comer Funeral Home in Ferriday. Before Myra was told of his death, Elmo asked the family physician to prescribe a strong sedative for her, then cleared the house of guns, knives, forks, bits of string and anything with which she might do herself harm. When the body was sent to Ferriday, they followed, Cecil driving one car and Jud Phillips another.

Arriving at the farm in Clayton, Jud found Mamie lying on her bed and looked in to check on her.

"Miz Lewis, I am sorry . . ."

"We all are, Mister Phillips."

"If I can get you anything—"

"I'm all right. I jus' don't know who to blame," Mamie whispered, in a tone more in anger than in sorrow.

"How's that again, ma'am?"

"I say I don't know who to blame, whose fault it is."

"Miz Lewis, I don't b'lieve it's a matter of fault. I don't think anybody's to blame," said Jud. "A thing like this is an accident."

"I jus' don't know," she repeated. "I suppose you'll be wantin' a drink about now, wouldn't you, Mister Phillips?"

"Well, yes, ma'am, but I know you don't allow it."

"Elmo!" Mamie hollered. "Reach me my purse an' get some money. Go out an' get Mister Phillips whatever he drinks."

Elmo drove into town for two fifths of bourbon, one of which he hid under the front seat of the car, the other he gave to Jud to be kept out of sight till his glass needed refilling. Elmo repaired to the car for his bracer. After the third disappearance, Mamie confronted him.

"Where you sneakin' off to ever' ten minutes, ol' man? Is that booze I smell on your breath? Are you hittin' the bottle, too?"

Jud walked away from the fight. He roamed the house till he found a pillar of salt standing over the bathroom sink staring into the medicine cabinet mirror. His muscles were pulled into knots. He had been crying. His face was still red.

"I don't believe it," said Jerry. "God, I don't believe it."

In the evening, attendants from the funeral home delivered Stevie to the farmhouse. The coffin was set before the large picture window in the living room which opened onto the front yard. The top of the wooden box was removed to reveal the corpse, his complexion pale except for the purple bump on his forehead. Jerry stood over his son's casket and motioned for Jud to come near.

"Ain't it odd how this happened on Easter Sunday," said Jerry softly. "Jesus died for the sins of all mankind so that we might be saved, so that we'd learn the error of our ways, repent and follow Him. Stevie died on Easter Sunday. Stevie died for my sins so that I might be saved."

"Don't that seem a mite cruel, for God to take a baby 'cause his daddy done wrong?" Jud offered.

"Nossir, not if you've studied the Bible like I done—'Shall I give my firstborn for my transgressions, the fruit of my body for the sin of my soul?' it says."

"You ain't gotta be a saint, though. An' you're not a bad man."

"You gotta be good. You gotta be so good, you gotta be pure. I don't expect you to unnerstand, your brother didn't. We argued about it all afternoon one day. He tol' me rock 'n' roll had the power to save souls. How can the devil's music save souls? The devil ain't never saved a soul. An' I have the devil in me. If I didn't, hell, I'd be a Christian."

"Well, I b'lieve—"

"It ain't what you *believe*, it's what's written in the Bible," Jerry recalled. "You're a sinner unless you be saved and borned again an' be made as a li'l child an' walk before God an' be holy, an' I mean you gotta be so pure that no sin shall enter there, for it says 'no sin.' It don't say 'just a little bit,' it says 'no sin shall enter there,'" he said, tapping out each syllable on the casket. "Unless a man is born again, he cannot see the kingdom of heaven. Whoever puts his faith in the Son has eternal life, but whoever rejects the Son will not see that life, for God's wrath remains on him. You gotta be good, so good . . . An' I can't. I can't do it. An' I know I can't. I'm weak. I'm a sinner an' I'm headed for hell. God is jus' tryin' to get me to do what I promised to do."

"And that is—"

"Preach," Jerry concluded.

The two men shared a long silence during which Jud watched Jerry battle with his conscience. "Mr. Phillips, what do you think I should do?"

"Well," Jud began cautiously, "you know, after the funeral there ain't a whole lot else to do 'cept sit around an' cry, an' that ain't never done much good. You can't bring him back. No amount of preachin' can bring him back."

Jerry nodded, his eyes fixed on Stevie's face.

"I think it would be good for you and Myra to get away from here as soon as possible. No use hangin' around. I'd get away, give myself a chance to . . . you think about it, Jerry. If you still wanna go to England, I'm with you, we'll go. Seems a shame that after waitin' four years, you should have to postpone somethin' this important. Think about it. Let me know tomorrow."

Jud returned to his motel, leaving Jerry in the company of his parents, who had remained in place at the kitchen table for hours. Had they raised their eyes to meet Jerry's, they would have seen the inner turmoil as he considered his ways: He had sown much and brought in little. He ate, but was not filled. Clothed, without warmth. Wages earned for a bag of holes. He looked for much, and lo, it came to little.

"Why?" saith the Lord of Hosts. "Because of My house that lieth in waste while ye run every man for his own house. I do make thee desolate because of thy sins. Thou shalt eat, but not be satisfied; and thy sickness shall be in thine inward parts; and thou shalt conceive, but not bring forth; and whomsoever thou bringest forth will I give up to the sword. Thou shalt sow, but shall not reap.

"When thou vowest a vow unto God, defer not to pay it, for He hath no pleasure in fools; pay that which thou vowest. Better is it that thou shouldest not vow, than that thou shouldest vow and not pay, wherefore should God be angry at thy voice, and destroy the work of thy hands. . . . They that strive with the Lord shall be broken to pieces; against them will I thunder in heaven."

Jerry heard the words of God but did them not. The path was clear before him, the course laid down once before. To England! Home of lost causes. To England! Grave of reputations. England! Where the streets are paved with gold! "They have struck me, and I felt it not. They have beaten me, and I knew it not. When shall I awake? I will seek it yet again."

"It's your fault!" Jerry turned on his father suddenly. "You let him drown. You weren't watchin' him. You were drunk, weren't you? Jus' like right now."

Elmo opened his mouth to protest. Jerry lunged from the table as Mamie took up the accusation.

Lying in the darkened bedroom, Myra was ranting hysterically to no one. She felt a tremendous physical pain, not unlike the throes of childbirth; her inward part a yawning gulf, her throat an open sepulcher. No sedative a doctor could prescribe could stay this torment. "I don't want to live," she cried. "Take me instead. Just bring him back . . . please."

Jerry held her, stroking her hair and shushing her as if she were a sobbing infant. Her breaths came staccato. When she could cry no more, the corners of her mouth relaxed and she felt the sting of parched lips coming together. Falling asleep, she dropped lifelessly to the bottom of a dark pool.

Myra wasn't sure how long she had slept, but awoke in a dim light, feeling mind and body at peace. She stared at the same crack in the ceiling she focused on when Jerry focused on her, and was reminded she lay in the bed in which Stevie was conceived and nursed. She sat bolt upright, and for an instant tried to sort nightmare from reality, hoping they were not one and the same. Jerry cracked one eye to catch a fleeting glimpse of his wife rushing to the living room as if she were answering the call of her baby. There, in silent sorrow, slept her Little Boy Blue, her sailor set endlessly adrift in a wooden ship on a listless lake. Those eyes which should not have been able to summon another tear began to brim and she buckled at the knee. Jerry reached down and picked her up and carried her back to bed.

When next they emerged from the bedroom, Myra was clad in

one of her black outfits, deathly pale against the dark fabric, her face half-concealed and filled with anguish. Jerry was at her side, dressed in a suit which had not seen light of day since he preached. With the silent contemplation of a statue, Myra stepped in to take her last sight and farewell, weeping as J. W. and Cecil fitted the top of the box to the bottom, trapping inside a glimmer of the morning sunlight.

The service passed before Myra like a bad dream shrouded in shadows. Jerry spoke for her, thanking those who came to the church. The procession moved down the dirt road running alongside the farmhouse to where the Lewis family staked their burial ground, where young Jerry played and where his son would play forevermore. Jerry, always next to his child bride, was a tower of strength and reserve, gripping her arm to lend support. When the burial was done, they walked home, Jerry watching the ground and thinking of the past, then looking to the sky and the future, mentally arranging the announcement he made when everyone had assembled.

"I'm goin' to England day after tomorrow," he said. "Myra, too. I talked with Mr. Phillips about it an' I think it's the best thing to do."

Mamie was stunned. "How could he suggest such a thing?" she demanded, as if Jud were not in the room.

"Miz Lewis, it's the best thing to do till this tension aroun' here eases up some. Neither Jerry or Myra need this kind of thing," said Jud.

Mamie harped against the sin and shame of walking away from a fresh grave to sing rock 'n' roll for heathens. It was a sacrilege, she moaned, it was disrespectful of the dead.

Jerry heard her words but did them not. The show must go on. He returned to Memphis on the twenty-fifth, giving him one day to prepare for the month-long business venture. Myra would not be going as yet—she was in no condition mentally or physically for an overseas flight and overextended fans. Her family did not want her to remain home alone, but she flatly refused to go elsewhere and denied those who offered to stay with her. She wandered about the place looking for things that had belonged to Stevie. The day of the funeral, the Hanings had cleaned the house of anything and everything that had been connected with the child. His clothes were gone. His toys were gathered from the floors of closets and from under the couch. Telltale signs a three-year-old leaves during the course of a normal day were scrubbed away. Not so much as the scuff of a small heel remained, save a shelved baby book with few entries and a miniature portrait which hung on the wall like a hatchment.

In her closet, Myra found the only personal item overlooked by the purge—a white, orange and olive checked shirt, green shorts and suspenders and a green bow tie—the suit Stevie had worn to church Easter morning. Fearing it, too, would be taken, she hid it, except for times when she hugged the garments close to her while she cried.

The headline "Jerry Lee Lewis Refuses to Cancel British Trip" caused a new and different sensation in London. Critics asked how he could possibly perform five days after burying his son. What manner of man is capable of such cold, cold heart—a real trouper or a real heel?

"I'm heartbroken, but determined not to let my fans down," Jerry was quoted. "If I can make them happy, it will help to relieve my suffering."

"I never expected him to carry on with the tour after such a tragedy," promoter Don Arden said. "He is to be congratulated for going through with it."

Some reporters did not agree. Hack writers of the vulgar herd who had denied Jerry a fair hearing four years before were crawling out of the gutter with pencils sharpened like stilettos. The tale gathered like a snowball, recounting the Child Bride Scandal and hinting at a greater outrage, Jerry bloodlessly sloughing off his sorrow for the lust of applause—such was the black art of publicity.

On April 27, Jerry received a welcome at London Airport reminiscent of the same scene four years earlier. Harrowed by the harrier hounds of Fleet Street, he was besieged with questions, the first of which was "Where's Myra?"

Jerry, dressed in black suit and tie, answered in a low tone. As he spoke, there was absolute silence except for the click of cameras and the pop of flashbulbs. "Myra's in a pretty nervous state because of Stevie. But she may join me later. It depends on how she feels."

"Don't you think it's rather heartless to return to a tour so soon after your son's death?"

Jerry searched the sea of faces for the commentator. "Nobody was closer to Stevie than I was. But I felt I had to keep on going, keep working. I reckon Stevie's in a lot better place than I am now."

Many who had similar questions forgot them.

"But it's been only six days, Mr. Lewis," another protested.

"The Lord giveth, the Lord taketh away. Blessed be the name of the Lord," said Jerry, and parted the sea of scribes to exit into the English morning.

At his hotel, Jerry was swamped with demands for a more complete explanation of his actions, to which he released a prepared statement:

> The tragedy that overtook me with the death of my young son should have prevented me from coming. How can I undertake this tour after such a terrible thing? The answer is that this tour was very important to me, it meant a lot to me. But then so did my baby. But God saw fit to stoop down and pluck away my boy and there was nothing I could do about it after that. If I hadn't held myself together, I wouldn't be here now. I'd be in the looney bin. I just had to catch hold of myself and say, "Jerry, there is nothing you can do now but continue as you planned. Go to England. People are waiting to see you there." This is what I did. I welcome the chance which the invitation for me to return to Britain presents. I have always felt I should return to rectify any misconceptions people have of me as an entertainer and a person.

The Associated Press wired dispatches from London with news of Jerry's reception in the town he was virtually drummed out of four years previously, and Myra watched the papers to see if her husband had been tarred and feathered upon his return. At last, she found a dozen lines under an inconspicuous heading hinting a "Better Reception Than First Tour Seen by Lewis." Jud was working overtime to do everything in his power for favorable press short of writing the articles himself. He was prepared to buy Jerry's comeback, if necessary.

Jerry's take for thirty-two shows was somewhere in the neighborhood of fifty thousand dollars—approximately twenty-eight hundred dollars a night—from which 10 percent was lopped off the top by the William Morris Agency for their part in booking the tour. Fifteen thousand dollars was earmarked "promotional expenses" by Jud, who set new standards in porterage, causing bellhops to blink at the size of their tips. There were perks for every courtesy, including opening the door, and soon every hotel employee lined up for Jud's coming and going. Then, too, there was Cecil's difficulty in understanding the currency; he tipped cabbies twenty pounds thinking it was the equivalent of a few bucks. Under the circumstances, there was little chance for profit. There were no guarantees or advances, and Jud put all expenses on the credit cards Sam had foolishly lent him, trusting they would be used only in emergencies.

Jud's costliest tactic was his favorite—the open bar. British journalists, many of whom were free-lancers out to find a tale to tell a paper, were unaccustomed to such kindness, and Jud's suite became the most popular pub in town. All interviews were scheduled one hour later than reporters had been told, allowing Jud sufficient time to "put 'em in the right frame of mind," as he liked to refer to getting drunk. By the time Jerry made his entrance, he was roundly greeted by just so many drinking buddies with pads and pencils.

As the first bull session began, one writer, obviously intent on provoking an argument for the sake of colorful copy, approached Jud. "My name is Cassandra, and I'd like to ask you a few questions about the way you and your brother conduct your business."

"Not right now, son, this is Jerry's party," said Jud.

"You'd have to be rather trashy people from a trashy background to record such trash," Cassandra continued.

"Look, fella. I don't know what your problem is, but if you wanna talk about me an' Sam an' Sun, why don't you meet me downstairs in ten minutes and let the others here get on with more important matters," Jud said.

"Right," said Cassandra, and walked out of the suite.

Jud excused himself from the party, went into the bedroom for his coat and stepped into the hallway on his way to the lounge. Cassandra, hiding in a doorway, bopped Jud on the head with the wooden handle of his umbrella. Jud was stunned, and felt for a rapidly rising lump before giving chase. Cassandra, with brolly at the ready for another swipe, decided to run instead and made straightaway for the lobby and into an adjacent shoe shop. Jud pursued, red-faced and furious, blowing into the store scattering shoes in all directions and crashing neatly arranged displays to the floor.

The chase at its closest point allowed Jud the satisfaction of punching Cassandra a few times on the back of the head before the younger man, lighter and fleeter of foot, took the advantage and ran far away, never to be seen again. Jud dragged back to the hotel, where the owner of the shoe shop awaited with claims of mounting damages, lost revenues and ruined reputations.

"What's the tab, chief?" Jud asked impatiently.

"Three hundred pounds," the owner estimated, acting on a tip from the bellhop.

"My ass," said Jud. "We knocked over a few tables and chairs."

"Antiques, sir, every one," said the gentleman.

"Oh, all right, I ain't got time for this crap," Jud said, and borrowed against Sam's credit card. "It was an emergency," he told Sam, who wondered at the tremendous bill from a shoe shop.

The hospitality suite turned out to be a bad idea. Talk turned to everything but rock 'n' roll, and at the end of the party Cecil and Jerry got around to flag-waving and challenged those present that "y'all would've lost the war without us." It wasn't long before television wanted in on the act growing in reputation for causing more than one kind of ruckus, and Jerry was brought into the studio to perform, prompting one reviewer to call it "the television event of the year, the like of which we shall never see or hear again."

On Sunday, April 29, one week after the drowning death of his son, Jerry Lee Lewis ascended once again to win the crown of rock 'n' roll. In the northern industrial town of Newcastle, the Killer performed two shows before near-capacity crowds who greeted him with standing ovations and welcome back banners. "He seemed unusually subdued to Britons," the press reported, "until his final number—'Whole Lot of Shakin' Going On.' Then he let loose, rushing from one end of the stage to the other with his hair flying and jumping on top of the piano." At the second show, Jerry performed fifteen minutes of encores, at the end of which the crowd mobbed the stage chanting "We want Jerry" for ten full minutes.

"I have never had a reception like it," Jerry said. "Not even when I was really hot in the States. I was worried before I went on. I knew that this was one of the most important nights in my career. After that incident four years ago, I was determined to make a comeback in Britain. I knew I could do it, but would the fans accept me? I was just as prepared to be booed off the stage as I was to receive a quiet reception. There they were with big banners, the fans, saying 'Welcome Back, Jerry Lee Lewis'—it was one of the great moments in my life."

Reports of Jerry's reception revitalized Myra's decision to make the trip. He called to tell her of his excitement and that he wanted her there to share it. Still, she wasn't sure she could make it. She had neglected the looking glass, her body wasted in sorrow and confinement. She had no money with which to buy a wardrobe, having indulgently given all of the cash Jerry left her to the church.

In the day of her trouble, Myra sought the Lord. She refused to be comforted. She was troubled and could not speak. Her Bible was her constant companion. But rather than finding fortitude from heaven, she was convinced that Stevie's death was a punishment for her sins. She adopted the severe self-discipline of an ascetic; her life emptied of joys and satisfactions. She left her hair long and straight, gathering it in a bun to further reflect the statement made by her black, fashionless clothing. She looked like living death.

Myra's best friend and neighbor, Maxine Malone, sympathized with her till there seemed to be no end to mourning. "Myra, your husband is an entertainer. He's around a lot of people. They're gonna take one look at you an' say, 'Is that Jerry Lee Lewis's wife?'" Maxine reached for Myra's Bible and opened it. "Won't you tell me what you did, or show me where it says you've done somethin' you should be punished for?"

Myra turned the pages to a well-worn passage, the story of Jezebel the temptress. "Once when Jerry was away, I put on some lipstick. He always tol' me not to, 'cause it was a sin, but I thought it looked good. God took my baby because I put on makeup. Jezebel, that's me," Myra confessed.

With Lois's help, Maxine persuaded Myra to come alive, first by cleaning house and brightening her surroundings, and then by doing the same for Myra herself. They propelled her in and out of shops and coaxed her in and out of flattering outfits, forsaking negative black for the purity of white when she refused to wear colors. Maxine and Lois then pushed Myra into a beauty parlor for a cut and style, and at the end of the project were well satisfied with the results. Myra was railroaded onto an airplane bound for London. Without her cheerleaders, her grief returned as a runner. She was again absorbed in her Bible, and prayed the plane would crash and put her out of her misery.

Landing in London in one piece, she gathered a borrowed mink cape around her and, shielding herself with the Testament, deplaned to find no one to meet her. Jerry had gone to the wrong terminal. When she paged him, he rushed over, disguised in a trench coat and dark glasses, leading a string of reporters and the curious. He noticed how pretty she looked, then spied the book in her hands.

"What's with the Bible?" he asked.

"I got a lot of comfort from this after the accident," she said, as reporters eavesdropped. "In the past few weeks, my favorite passage has been 'Blessed are they that mourn, for they shall be comforted.'"

Before newsmen could further intrude, Jerry spirited his wife to a waiting car. By nightfall, she and her brief statement were all there was to an entire page of the *Daily Mirror:* "Faith: Clutching a Bible, the very young wife of Jerry Lee Lewis flies to join her husband after the tragedy." At the hotel, Myra spoke with reporters, many of whom were as anxious to discuss the events of the past four years as they were to delve into the past week.

"Well, you're back after four years—which adds up to a lifetime for one as young as you," a reporter began.

"That's true," Myra agreed. "I left school when I was twelve. If I had stayed on, I would have graduated this year. A mighty lot has happened to me. I'm eighteen in July, but I guess I feel very, very old."

"Regrets?"

"I sure haven't. I love Jerry, Jerry loves me—that's the real story of my life."

"Are you a religious man, Jerry?" the reporter asked, noticing the Bible.

"Guess I am. I try to live by the Good Book. My mamma an' daddy are very religious. Before I became a singer, I did a lot of preachin'. If I wasn't a singer, I'd be a preacher."

At mention of Stevie, Myra began to weep. "We loved that little boy," she said, then reached for her Bible. "I read the Bible a lot. I think I've found the answer there."

"We're surprised you decided to come under the circumstances," the reporter remarked.

"When Jerry asked me to join him in Britain after Stevie had gone, I didn't know what to think. But my Mamma an' Daddy always told me to do what I thought was right. And I knew my place was beside my man."

Myra excused herself and went into the bedroom while Jerry saw the writer to the door. "That little gal has got more courage and wisdom than anybody I've ever met. When we lost Stevie, it was Myra who was the brave one. There's nothin' I wouldn't do for my wife."

Closing the door, Jerry followed Myra into the bedroom where she sat with her Bible. They were alone for the first time in many days. "What are you doin' with that Bible?" he demanded. "It's beginnin' to bug me. You ain't gonna carry it around all the time, are ya?"

"I might," Myra replied.

"What are you gonna do, preach? If you ask me, it's a little late for all that hypocritical stuff," he said, building up to the accusation that had been fomenting inside him. "That Bible can't cure what ails you, girl. It can't remove your guilt. It can't take away the sins you committed, the ones Stevie's payin' for. It's your fault he's dead—you didn't watch him like you were s'posed to, did you? Answer me!"

Myra began to cry, then wail, in answer to Jerry's indictment. He ran out of the room, frustrated and disgusted with himself. In a few moments, Jud came in and sat down beside her, offering sympathetic understanding and a glimpse of what troubled her husband.

"Listen to me, now, Myra. Don't worry about what Jerry said, forget it. He's just upset. He's got no one else to blame, no one to yell at. It's a terrible thing when life is destroyed, that's why he screams at you. It's not your fault Stevie's gone, and he knows that. I don't b'lieve you could ever do anything that bad. But Jerry thinks he has, and in the last few days he's talked of little else beside his own sins an' goin' back to preachin'. He blames hisself for Stevie's death 'cause he knows there's no goin' back, 'specially after this reception."

Myra understood without answering. She spent the rest of the night as well as the remainder of her stay confined to her hotel room. Except for moving about from town to town, she did not venture out. When Jerry ran out of devices to bring her into the open, he asked Gene Vincent and his wife to help by offering to squire Myra about the countryside. She declined and remained cloistered in consultation with her Bible, searching for strength to withstand her husband's guilt-ridden accusations, hoping God would siphon her soul from its friable shell and deliver it from this living hell. She could bear no more sorrow.

Crowds in every concert locus looked for Myra at Jerry's performances. They chanted her name in the same way they sung for his encores. "You've gotta come to some of these shows," Jerry pleaded with his wife. "People wanna see you. They can't figger out why you ain't there."

Myra was admired for overcoming the trauma of the first scandal and more so for surviving the death of her only child. Gratified by displays of public sentiment, she decided to attend the next show in Mitcham, especially since the masses had become her last source of compassion.

The May 14 date at the Majestic Cinema in Mitcham was typical of the tour: a half-empty house and a wild reception, a puzzling combination. Marked for slaughter, Jerry had brought his hopes to a bad market. Don Arden resorted to filling the bill with as many as fourteen local acts, hoping to drag in enough friends and neighbors to sell a thousand seats. He rarely succeeded and was at a loss for an explanation. Jerry's thirty-minute set was identical to the repertoire honed during the Jackie Wilson tour, only briefer to exclude the Little Richard tunes as Little Richard was a current rival for top honors as England's favorite pianist. Principally, it was his own hits Jerry wanted England to hear him play for the first time—"Whole Lot of Shakin'," "Great Balls of

Fire," "High School Confidential," "Breathless," "Lewis Boogie" and "You Win Again"—as one reviewer put it, "the best rock there is, with a vital dash of country mixed into the middle of it." Why every performance was not sold out could only be attributed to lingering memories of 1958.

Myra watched from the wings, where those seated at extreme angles could spot her from the audience. Calls to her rose during breaks between songs, and Jerry turned to see her looking at him, smiling. It was a scene from long ago, when he picked her out in a crowd and whispered, "I love you" for the first time. He said it again, in the same way.

"Y'all wanna see Myra?" Jerry asked the crowd.

"Yeah!" came the resounding reply, and the chant began, "My-ra! My-ra! My-ra!"

Jerry motioned for her to come out. She shook her head animatedly, not daring to move. He waved again, then ran toward her, grabbed her hand and pulled her onstage. Bathed in the spotlight, she was showered with the crowd's adoration. "We love you," they called, and reached for her hand. These strange, excited, young faces shouted her name, whistling, applauding, cheering. She was awestruck as she stood before them and drank it all in like manna from heaven. Jerry squeezed her hand and led her off again, returning to pummel great balls of fire out of the piano. For one brief moment, Myra was free from everlasting sorrow.

In the four weeks that separated Jerry and Myra from the loss of their son, the reception in England did much to enable Jerry to recover; Myra had survived, but rarely misplaced Stevie in her mind. In his farewell speech to the press, Jerry raved about the tour and promised to return soon for a bigger and better campaign. War with England was ended and a lasting peace achieved. He was the kind of success story the public relished: the small-town boy made good after overcoming two kinds of adversity. Universally condemned, hated both for his private lifestyle and onstage persona, he had not surrendered or fled from the fight. He wanted to be remembered; Myra, forgotten.

In return, the press advanced that Elvis Presley, although continuing to dominate pop charts with his latest, "Good Luck Charm," was cranking out mellow middle-of-the-road ballads and had no real claim to the title king of rock 'n' roll since his discharge from the army and retirement from live appearances. And

with the release of "Return to Sender," it would be seven years
before Presley had another Number 1 hit as only four of his next
thirty-six singles managed to make the top ten. The recently concluded Lewis tour and newest release, "Money," left no doubt as
to who was the British lion of rock 'n' roll. Proclaimed *Disc* in
inch-high headlines, "On Present Form Jerry Lee Lewis Must Be
THE WORLD'S NUMBER ONE ROCK SINGER."

Returning home in June, Jerry went straight to Pittsburgh to
replace Paul Anka at the Holiday House, while Myra went to
Clayton to consult the family's leading theological experts on a
matter she had become obsessed with: the resurrection of her son.
After all, it was not impossible, not if the story of Lazarus or the
miracles of Elisha were to be believed.

To Reverend Sun Swaggart, the man who had put the fear of
God in her when she was thirteen, Myra went to witness his
wonderful work. If miracles were possible, Uncle Sun could perform them. And at the Assembly of God Church in Baton Rouge,
the Swaggarts knew when they saw Myra that they were one step
closer to fulfilling a longstanding goal: the salvation of Jerry Lee
Lewis. Through her, they could reach her absent husband, but she
must be made to surrender first. In her mentally weakened and
emotionally exhausted condition, it was not difficult for Sun to
succeed. He began his sermon by relating the story of Jimmy Lee
and Jerry Lee, cousins closer than brothers, equally talented, who
came upon two roads that diverged: the dirt path, the less traveled
way, serving the Lord for the reward that waits in heaven, or the
street paved with gold, the wide path that many take to make a
fortune on earth. Jimmy walked in the ways of the Lord, plodding
over rough terrain filled with temptations resisted, finding little to
sustain him along the way. He found a good Christian woman to
be his wife, and became the happiest man on earth because he
kept his eye on heaven. Jerry set about the gilded course, hypno-
tizing millions of disciples in the sin that was the devil's music,
succumbing to the temptations of lust and wealth. Along the way,
he married and divorced, married and divorced again, married a
third time to his thirteen-year-old cousin and all the world was
appalled. They were chastised and set upon and had no place to
hide.

"You will remember Easter, a month ago," Sun said. "The day

we celebrate the miracle when Jesus Christ, who died for our
sins, ascended into heaven to be as one with His Father, was also
the day the three-year-old son of Jerry Lee Lewis drowned. How,
you ask, can a loving and merciful God, on the day in which our
faith in Him is at its highest, end a life so young and pure, tortur-
ing the souls of those who loved and cared for him?"

Myra, weeping, begged, "Why?"

"The answer is simple," said Sun. "God plucked the rose from
the vine, took the son from the father, to teach the father a lesson.
'So that the Lord could no longer bear, because of your evil
doings, and because of the abominations which ye have committed, therefore is your land become a desolation, and an astonish-
ment, and a curse, without an inhabitant, as at this day.' It's God's
way of sayin' to Jerry, 'Boy, you've gone too far down the wrong
road, get back 'fore it's too late.' God will take that baby to teach
the daddy to mend his wicked ways, yes, He will. He will end a
life to save one."

And lest Sun fail to drive the point home, he had a reminder for
the rest of his congregation. "It can happen to any of us. We could
all be dead 'fore we reach home tonight. Accept Him when He
calls, you may not get a second chance. Is there anyone here
ready to accept Christ into their life? Anyone wanting to be bap-
tized in obedience to our Lord's command? If so, come forward
and be saved!"

Myra jumped to her feet and ran to Uncle Sun, pleading for
rescue as a woman drowning. Brother Swaggart had won half the
war with the devil. After the service, Myra went home with a
certificate of baptism signed and dated June 10, 1962. She had
taken the first all-important step in bringing her son back to life
among the living. Uncle Sun did not share that same goal—salvation was his game, not raising the dead. Now his most prized
convert was asking for a miracle, and his congregation was waiting with her for it to happen.

At the next meeting, Brother Swaggart preached to a larger
crowd his favorite sermon: The Downfall of Jerry Lee Lewis.
Myra hardly survived the retelling of Stevie's death when Uncle
Sun addressed himself to the subject of resurrection. "Is it possible?" he cried out. "Can it happen?"

Myra froze, watching, waiting. Might Stevie live again?

"Yes," said Sun, and Myra swooned. "Was the disciple Mark

deceiving us when he said, 'Anything is possible if you have faith'? Did not John tell us that Jesus said, 'Anyone believing in Me shall do the same miracles I have done, and even greater ones'? 'The Lord killeth, and maketh alive; He bringeth down to the grave, and bringeth up.' You can ask God for anything in Jesus's name an' He'll do it, chapter fourteen, line twelve, amen, Lord."

Myra was enraptured, dazed by hope and Sun's assurance that God would reward her faith by returning Stevie to her in the flesh. She went home to Memphis, where Stevie recognized his home, for it would be there that he would return as one who had been lost for thirty days. Any day now, Myra was certain her son would come walking into the room as if nothing had happened.

Every evening, she turned out all the lights in the house and prayed aloud for Stevie's resurrection. "'For the Lord hath heard the voice of my weeping. The Lord hath heard my supplication. The Lord receiveth my prayer,'" she repeated endlessly. Late into the morning of the following day, and past the point of fatigue, she went into her closet for her son's Easter outfit, the holy shroud, and cried herself to sleep. Throughout June, the constant vigil continued. Myra saw no one, spoke to no one. She forgot food and family. She concentrated on the sole, singular miracle. Not even the beatified monk pledged to silence could pray with greater earnestness. Still, the child did not come.

He did return, only briefly, and maybe not in the way it had been promised, but Stevie came back to his mother again. He appeared in a dream, that airy silent movie which links the living with other worlds. It was raining. Myra stood at a fence, searching a field covered with high grass and tangled with weeds. In the center of the field, she could see Stevie, barechested, cold and wet, thrashing through the undergrowth, fighting his way toward his mother. Myra reached between the boards in the fence and called to him, but he could not free himself from entanglement and resigned.

Myra woke, the dream developing in her mind. The field of weeds was symbolic of life and all its snares, she thought. Had Stevie lived, would he not have suffered the sins of his father and the long littleness of life that his mother came to know? Wasn't it wrong to wish him back to this mortal coil when certainly he must be in a better place?

It made sense to Myra. The prayer rituals stopped. But the possibility that Stevie might live again did not vanish. Myra continued to attend church, believing there must still be something more she could do. Achieving the next step in the path toward salvation was more difficult, that of receiving the Holy Spirit, and Myra confided in Uncle Sun.

"That may be your problem right there," Sun said of her frustrated efforts. "You got to get that Holy Spirit to do miracles."

"What is the Holy Spirit?" asked Myra.

"Truth," said Uncle Sun.

Jerry spent the first two weeks of July at the Shamrock Club in Keanesburg, a New Jersey resort not far from Atlantic City. It was the first extended booking for his new band, consisting of Ranz McClelland on guitar, Ebb Adair on bass and Morris "Tarp" Tarrant on drums. As an added feature, Jerry employed Charlie Chalmers to play saxophone. When the boys were not onstage, they were usually to be found on the carnival midway, Cecil and Jerry playing the Wheel of Fortune till each had won a dozen stuffed animals.

Jerry insisted Myra spend her eighteenth birthday with him in New Jersey, but she declined to attend his shows so as not to upset her karma. No one courting the Holy Ghost could expect to be visited in a dive. Although Myra was hardly social, Kay Martin and other fan-club members threw a surprise party for her at the motel. It was the first time such an event was held in her honor. Jerry continued to play the Northeast, returning to Atlantic City in August. Myra turned down his offer to tag along. There was another, more important, trip to make. She had her own show to do.

The brothers and sisters meeting thrice weekly at the Barton Heights Church of God were planning a pilgrimage to Chattanooga for the Pentecostal Convention. Not only would Myra attend with tens of thousands of other believers, she was going as a featured guest. Tales of her rebirth in the church had spread far and wide along the evangelical trail blazed by the Swaggarts. Myra was a celebrated sister in her circle.

The convention took place in a great field usually reserved for traveling circuses and carnivals. A massive tent, not unlike the Big Top, was raised to house the ten thousand come to rejoice in the Holy Spirit. A large platform was erected to seat the honored guests, including Myra. Mrs. Jerry Lee Lewis was to stand before the multitude and testify. The child bride of the famous singer had come to attest to the glory of God.

"Yes, I've had new Cadillacs," she said, and men's eyes widened. "Yes, I've had big homes and swimmin' pools," she said, and women dreamed of mansions. "And my husband is known all over the world. But you don't know what an unhappy time it's been—the times I was alone, the times we suffered. I lost my baby . . . I was lost and now am found." Then Sister Myra led the gathering in the singing of her favorite hymn, "One by One."

When she finished her testimony, Myra wondered at what she had said and how she had found the courage to say it. She drew a complete blank. From the reception she received afterward, Myra thought she might have given the audience the secret of life.

"You're the mother of an angel," women said to her, "sent by God to do His bidding. You are an inspiration to us all."

"You're a woman of great strength," men said, "the kind of wife every man would be proud to have."

Myra had never been estimated in such superlatives. She was amazed at the effect she had worked over so many people. Her husband must be blind to the sainted qualities seen in her by thousands of others. Who was wrong and who was right?

Although it was not apparent in his performances, nor indicated by his habiliment, the death of his son worked great changes in Jerry, and the religious metamorphosis of Myra stirred a similar reaction in him. He was again a dual personality, the raging performer and the recalcitrant preacher. On August 17, Myra, Lois, Rusty, Linda Gail and the Malones drove to Jerry's appearance at the Chestnut Club in Kansas City. J. W., back at the bass, suggested everyone come up for a good time. But good times were not what they used to be. Myra had pledged never to set foot in a nightclub where liquor was served and Jerry refused to drink. Furthermore, drinking was not permitted in their presence. And Jerry, who wore plain dark suits onstage, scolded the girls for wearing short pants and exposing flesh, saying it was sinful regardless of their having to make the long trip in a crowded automobile sans air conditioning in 100° temperature. There was no cussin', no fightin' and no chasin' after women. Jerry was the perfect husband and the model man. His career was shot to hell, but he was a straight arrow.

Myra and company returned to Memphis on Sunday as Jerry and company moved on to Philadelphia for a reunion with Dick Clark. Past friendship and unreturned favors were not what put Lewis and Clark back together again, it was Jud's proposition that much money could be made by Dick buying up several dates while pushing Jerry's next single into the charts. The motive was money, not memories.

The record chosen for the concerted effort was Jerry's remake of Chuck Berry's '58 vintage "Sweet Little Sixteen." Clark signed Jerry for an *American Bandstand* appearance on August 23—his first in more than four years—and booked him for the following weekend's supershow at Steel Pier in Atlantic City. Suddenly, "Sweet Little Sixteen" was heard every day on *Bandstand* and creeped into *Billboard*'s top hundred in the high nineties. The reunion took place as planned with Clark in rare form, putting extra-heavy hype on the audience, which was treated to live versions of the new single and "Whole Lot of Shakin' Going On."

The show at Steel Pier was the rage of the East Coast, promising to be the hottest ticket since Alan Freed's Show of Shows. Joey Dee and Brian Hyland headlined the bill, and on the afternoon of the first performance crowds were jamming onto the Pier. They overflowed the grandstands, spilling onto the midway and backing up along the Boardwalk. All ten shows were sold out and still the kids kept coming to the wooden ark, which began to list and sway under the weight.

Clark, in his role as impressario, dictated a list of songs that Jerry should play. Insulted by this intrusion, Jerry walked onstage following Clark's introduction with panties on his head and sang a set of seldom-heard selections. Clark retired to his office on location, disgusted by the display. He watched the chandelier rock under the shock waves of thousands of dancing, jumping, screaming teens and panicked, breaking into a dead run for the Boardwalk before the entire structure crashed into the sea. The amusement rides were closed down, scaring the crowd into a stampede for the exit during which they trampled officials trying to restore calm. The fans returned for the next show, rising to greet Jerry with an ovation which washed over the Jersey shoreline like a tidal wave. A security force enlisted to strictly limit attendance to following shows counted more than forty thousand heads when all was sung and done.

On the Monday morning following the Steel Pier weekend, Jerry drove to the Atlantic City bus station to meet Myra, who was coming to spend a brief vacation before he took off again. Jerry demanded that she now make every effort to be with him rather than waste away at home alone. So he was in a hurry to see her, and quickly became aggravated with the lone baggage handler who could not find Myra's suitcase. The porter, a speech-impaired, middle-aged man named Giacotello, became flustered when Jerry began complaining.

"I'm thorry, Mithter Lewith," Giacotello spat as he spoke, and Jerry grew angrier as the man stumbled over one bag and another, spraying him with apologies. When Giacotello could stand no more verbal abuse, his upbringing in the streets of New Jersey asserted itself, and in his best Brooklyn Dodger bleacher-bum accent, he stood nose-to-nose with Jerry and dotted his face with an objection. Jerry reared back and spat in Giacotello's face, and the old man danced around the terminal, shouting and pointing at Jerry, drawing the attention of a cop who put the collar on the Killer before he could make a getaway.

"He kept spittin' on me," Jerry shouted at the officer, whose expression belied his many years of being sandwiched in street brawls. Jerry was arrested for assault and battery. Jud paid the fifty-dollar bail and took custody of the criminal. He was instructed to be in court the next Wednesday, and by then would be long gone. Giacotello got his name in the paper and the matter was quickly forgotten by everyone—except Dick Clark.

"I can't put up with this stuff, Jud," said Dick, already miffed at Jerry's onstage shenanigans. Clark stopped playing "Sweet Little Sixteen," the record dropped off the charts, and Dick dropped all future dates with the troublesome Mr. Lewis. Jud came to understand Clark's promotion of Jerry's single had been done solely to promote the show at Steel Pier. When the show was over and the money divvied up, the push behind the record ended, too. All Jerry understood was that not once but twice Dick Clark had taken advantage of him, and he would never forget it.

* * *

In October, at a time when Frankie Jean separated from her husband for the final time, she and her three babies moved to a rented place two blocks from her brother on Coro Lake. Out of necessity, she cultivated a closeness with Myra, whose brief experience as a mother went a long way in helping Frankie with her brood.

On an afternoon when Myra and Frankie went out to do laundry, Elmo watched Wayne, Jr., and Jerry Christina while three-month-old Michael Lee napped in a back bedroom. Frankie returned to find Michael missing. Elmo searched the house frantically and found the baby on the floor between the bed and wall. Myra, with a presence of mind she lacked six months before in a similar situation, administered mouth-to-mouth resuscitation while Frankie became fragmented.

Michael Lee died, apparently the victim of an undetected respiratory ailment, and Mamie blamed Elmo, who had already been made to bear the guilt of Steve's death. For the third time in six months, the clan gathered at the family cemetery to inter a baby —Jimmy Swaggart's sister, Jeanette, had buried her only child, another drowning victim, in August. The monument engraver's puncheon was dulled from extensive use insculpting Lewis headstones.

As the football season of '62 kicked off, Jerry was booked into several college campuses for sock hops. A prime date was at Princeton on November 9, the night before the big game with Harvard, and the gym was packed with three thousand students getting up for the event. The Lester Lannin Orchestra played foxtrots for faculty, and Conway Twitty, a Sun alumnus, sang several of the twenty-seven hit singles he had recorded since 1957. Jerry's jukin' broke the place up. The overflow crowd was forced to stand on tables and chairs and sit on the stage. Those who survived the ordeal departed in total exhaustion, much to the delight of the Harvard team, who rallied to a 20–0 victory over the partied-out Princeton eleven. On Saturday night, following the defeat, Jerry played an encore at the Cloister Inn, an exclusive club for one hundred student members.

Sun Records shipped Jerry's "Good Golly Miss Molly" and "I Can't Trust Me in Your Arms Anymore" shortly before Thanksgiving. "Miss Molly," an Otis Blackwell composition, had been a cornerstone for rival pianist Little Richard. "I Can't Trust Me," another mild country tune, was chosen only because it had been penned by the same man who wrote "How's My Ex Been Treating You," the flip side to Jerry's "Sweet Little Sixteen," which went to the top of many key markets, including Nashville. And like "Sixteen," "Miss Molly" entered the top hundred at Number 99 and submerged. The flip side, the country cut, followed its predecessor to the top of the charts in the same key areas.

At the end of the year, with Jerry's enslavement to Sun drawing to a close, Jerry was approaching other labels. Sam was in the precarious position of either spending money to keep his tarnished prize or letting him leave, taking with him what was left of the label. Confident that Jerry could never repeat the phenomenon of 1957, Sam banked on the belief that no other record company would want him. As with every other guess he made about Jerry's career, Sam was wrong.

For Christmas that year, Mamie gave Elmo what he had always wanted—a divorce. After all, she had her son to cater to her every desire. The lowly Elmo, a man of so little consequence that it hardly mattered what he did, moved to a small apartment in downtown Memphis. Free from blame and worry, he was content to become one of the boys, courtin' the ladies and learning to drink all over again.

It would have been Stevie's fourth Christmas, and Myra had no little one to lavish with gifts when the festive season arrived. She spent much of her time in church praying for some sort of miracle, her husband, still struggling with God, chastised her hypocrisy in the same way he shared his guilt for the death of Stevie. The Lord heard the supplication for the rebirth of their departed son and answered Myra's prayers in His own mysterious way. Within her stirred the beginnings of a second baby.

10 *Return of Rock*

NINETEEN SIXTY-THREE WAS OFF TO A BAD start. Myra felt lonely and depressed and thought the best remedy might be nursing the sick. She applied for a job as a candy striper at the Baptist Hospital in Memphis. Two weeks later, she had a severe attack of abdominal pains, the same clonic contractions she experienced in childbirth, at Stevie's death and all anxious moments in between. Dr. Wilson diagnosed her illness as early symptoms of pregnancy.

The last thing Myra wanted was a baby. Although another child would be the only compensation for the loss of Stevie, she was unprepared to reassume the responsibilities of motherhood so soon after his death, afraid of losing this child, too. Twenty to thirty times a day, Myra was nauseated; the mind was forcing the body to reject the fetus. Dr. Wilson recommended she see a psychiatrist when nothing he prescribed lessened her constant pain.

By February, Myra had become bedridden. Her mother was bringing meals to her three times daily when word came that Lois's father had died. The Browns left immediately for Louisiana, leaving Myra unattended. Jerry, on a tour of Ivy League colleges, was in bed with the Asian flu. Lastly, an ice storm blitzed Memphis, knocking out power and telephone lines and completely cutting off Myra from the outside world. It was not until midnight two days later that Jerry came home to find his wife starving. He found the cupboard bare, retrieved a stale end piece of bread from the garbage and handed it to her. Delirium set in.

When Lois returned with the sad story of her father's funeral,

Myra interrupted her to say, "As sorry as I am about Grampa, I wish I could trade places with him. Jerry still blames me for Stevie's death. His family hates me. They're always sayin' I run around on him an' spend all his money. I'm sick an' I'm miserable an' I don't want this baby."

Jerry would have no more of Dr. Wilson; Myra's depression was the physician's fault. If she needed doctoring, Doc Ratcliffe was the only man for the job. Back to Clayton he took her, back to the farm where she suffered her first pregnancy with a child now buried in the cemetery out back. Doc Ratcliffe studied Myra closely. "Judging from your condition, you won't have this pregnancy to worry with much longer," he warned. "You stand a good chance of miscarriage any day now."

The threat of losing another baby awakened the maternal instinct in Myra, making her want the child desperately, as much as she wanted Stevie's return. And the only way she might keep this baby was to make up for lost time by taking extraordinary care of herself. She went home to Memphis, away from the Lewises and Louisiana, away from psychiatrists and cemeteries. Right up to the last minute, Myra would have this baby alone.

After Mamie divorced Elmo, she moved to a rented house in Memphis to be near her son. The farm in Clayton fell to disuse, so Jerry sold it to buy a house in Ferriday near the church on Louisiana Avenue and kept it seven years, principally for holidays. That the Lewises were living communally on Coro Lake presented a multitude of problems for Myra and Jerry, the first being what to do with Linda Gail.

She had married twice before her sixteenth birthday, rash and determined in the Lewis way. Unable to achieve a response from Cecil Harrelson, the love of her life, Linda decided to teach him another lesson. She met a sailor on leave named Jim Bushlen. The next day, they were engaged. On day three, they married. On day four, Jim remembered leave doesn't last forever and regulations required his eventual return to base. Obviously endowed with a poor memory, Jim forgot to tell Linda where he was stationed, forgot her altogether, and was never heard from again. Show business, more particularly joining her brother's act, was the best way to kill two proverbial birds, fame and family, with one stone: onstage with Jerry and backstage with Cecil. And the pressure was on from Mamma for Jerry to help his sister along with her plans, both personal and professional.

When he could stand the nagging no longer, Jerry dragged Linda Gail into the studio to record his last single to be released while under contract to Sun. He was back at the old studio in Memphis to record "Teenage Letter," and Linda chose the Charlie Rich compositions "Seasons of My Heart," which they sang in duet, and "Sittin' and Thinkin'," which she sang solo. Her third selection was "Nothin' Shakin' but the Leaves on the Trees," at the end of which producer Scotty Moore, who thought he'd heard it all, shook his head as if trying to rid his mind of the music. The cacophany of the duet was godawful. As Jerry attempted to lead, Linda fought him every measure of the way with an ill-timed, out-of-tune caterwaul which made the hair stand up on the back of Scotty's neck. And when going it alone, Linda proved to be un-worthy of the time and expense it took to shape a sophomoric style into something listenable.

Regardless of the record's utter failure, Linda Gail became part of a package deal to be included in all of Jerry's future live perfor-mances. She joined the show in Birmingham, Alabama, and as April moved into May, Linda moved to the same level as Jerry's bandmembers and was paid thirty-five to forty dollars a day. One distinct advantage of her kinship to the star was that she could— and did—forward all bills for clothing, food and other expenses to her brother. And of equal if not greater importance, Linda moved into Cecil's heart and bed, thereby beginning a saga of her own.

Don Seat's last act as manager was to book Jerry for a third tour of Europe during all of May and the first week of June. Economics would once again prevent taking the band. Drummer Tarp Tarrant would be the only musician going with Jerry, and the indispensable Cecil Harrelson would attend as personal manager. The itinerary involved working the London vicinity for one week, flying to Berlin to perform at a prom for children of military personnel, to Hamburg's Star Club, L'Olympia in Paris, and re-turning for a week in Scotland. Jerry was paid eighty-five hundred dollars for the British dates, and an itemized account of his personal profit added up to one hundred dollars after commis-sions, fees and pick-up musicians were paid.

Promoter Don Arden searched for local talent to fill the bill, and coming across an item in the trades he contacted a band who had won a poll of concertgoers at a recent bash at Wembley. Three months before, the group had released their first single, which went to the top of the charts. The band was The Beatles, the song, "Please, Please Me." Brian Epstein told Arden that The Beatles had just completed a tour as opening act for Tommy Roe, a Judd Records discovery, and that the foursome's dues-paying days were over. In Epstein's humble opinion, The Beatles were moving toward stardom faster than Roe. "In fact, The Beatles are touring England with Roy Orbison and Gerry and The Pacemakers while Lewis is here," Epstein said. "The Beatles are top of their own bill."

Arden next approached another fledgling act, The Rolling Stones, who were to The Beatles what Jerry was to Elvis, a wilder, raunchier act. It was no secret that the Stones were fans of Jerry's. Guitarist Brian Jones had for several years used the stage name Elmo Lewis while working in clubs. At any rate, the Stones were also unavailable, and Arden arranged a number of smaller acts to open for Jerry.

The press prepped the populace for Jerry—"The Supreme Rockster," "Mr. Excitement Unlimited," "The Riot-Raiser Superb"—with a fresh story to push his reputation to new heights: While performing in an American club, he took a flying leap onto the bar and ran the whole length of it, still singing and kicking drinks and bottles all over the place. "The wildest man I know," added Gene Vincent.

Five thousand fans jammed the stalls for two shows at the Croydon Theatre in London to see the Wildman. An even greater success was the "Rock Across the Channel" promotion, a day-long excursion from Southend to Boulogne, France, on the ferry "Royal Daffodil" which included performances by Jerry at sea and at the casino in port. The *New Record Mirror* spoke of "Rock Across the Channel" as "one of the best performances by the greatest white rockster still performing . . . sounding even better than the discs which had made him so famous."

During the voyage, a bevy of reporters encircled Jerry to ask a variety of questions, including an appraisal of the Sun situation and whether he would reenlist in four months. "I think I'm gonna sign a contract with RCA for a maximum of six months," he announced. "They'll issue two or three singles and one LP. If they plug 'em hard enough and manage to bring my name back into the charts I'll stick with 'em. Personally, I think they'll be able to do that, but if not, I'll change once again."

Once that bit of news spanned the Atlantic, reporters were asking Sam Phillips for his reaction. He was sorry to report that he and Jerry were unable to come to terms on a new contract, blaming interference from giants in the industry. "The competitive bidding among major labels will ruin the independent record companies," said Sam, avoiding promotion and support of Jerry's product, or the lack of it, and the true nature of their differences.

On the other hand, a Mr. Frank Casone, owner of Memphis's swank Oriental Club and Jerry's new manager, was talking about Las Vegas, a starring role in a film of the Hank Williams story, dropping names like producer Joseph Pasternak and avoiding names like RCA. No one bothered to call the man actually negotiating Jerry's contract, Cecil Harrelson, or the company which was running to the front of the bidding war, Mercury Records. While the Killer pitched a little woo to the *Fraüleins*, Cecil was pitching PR to Mercury's owner, Irvin Green.

In London, Jerry and Cecil ducked out of a party and hailed a hack back to the hotel. The driver, excited by his celebrity passenger, attempted to impress Jerry with a stretch of first-rate speeding, and the boys took the first opportunity to hop out at a traffic light before they were killed. A Jaguar pulled alongside the curb, and the driver, a muscular man with a curly pompadour, offered to give them a lift to the hotel.

"I don't ride with strangers," Jerry declined.

"I'm really a fan of yours," the driver persisted. "I've got every record you ever made."

"Thanks, anyway," Jerry refused.

The driver hailed another cab for Jerry and Cecil. At the hotel, they discovered the Jaguar had followed and the driver wanted to introduce himself. "I was a builder up until the time you began your career," the fan said. "I quit and started singing in pubs in Wales. I changed my name from Tom Woodward to Tommy Scott, and I've just started a band called The Senators. I haven't won any auditions, but it won't be long. I try to sing just like you."

"Well, lots of luck to you, Tom," said Jerry.

"Could I trouble you for an autograph?" Tom asked, and was obliged.

Two years later, following Jerry's recording of "Green, Green Grass Of Home," Tom Woodward, a member in good standing of the Jerry Lee Lewis International Fan Club, recorded the same song, thereby surpassing his idol and becoming idol to millions as Tom Jones.

Jerry descended the gangplank of the plane into the arms of his wife, mother and manager, all wearing dark sunglasses, the token of hunted celebrities. A photo of the reunion in the newspaper looked more like graduation day at the Academy for the Blind. There was a catered reception that evening at the Oriental Club, hosted by Mamie Lewis and Frank Casone.

It was no secret that the way to Jerry Lee Lewis was through his mother, and long before Casone breathed the first word of his intent to manage Jerry's affairs, he courted Mamie to gain access to her son. Casone had been a partner in Las Vegas's New Frontier Hotel before coming to Memphis to open the Oriental, a private club for card holders shelling out one hundred dollars for exclusivism. Casone boasted his influence in Vegas could work Jerry into the hottest clubs on the Strip at dollar figures unseen in several years. In exchange for Vegas on a silver platter, Jerry had to agree to make the Oriental Club his home base. A twenty-four-foot-high neon sign depicting Jerry at the keyboard was erected, and Casone called every beat writer in the country to spread the news. "I'm gonna shoot Elvis off the hill," he said, and coming from a man who once dodged a murder rap, some thought the claim to be more than braggadocio.

When Casone guaranteed Jerry a stint at the Thunderbird Lounge in Vegas for two weeks in August at ten grand per week, Jerry signed his life away, or at least the next five years of it. Casone, in Jerry's estimation, was the epitome of the big-time nightclub hotshot, and his Italian heritage coupled with rumors of an unsavory past spelled clout to the Killer. At the culmination of his courtship, Casone made Sam Phillips look like a piker, and in the end promised to be a terrible foe.

* * *

Mamie visited her son frequently while he was home in June. In the middle of the month, she had a most important mission for him. "Y'know, there's somethin' been botherin' me a long time," she said. "Your brother Elmo is still buried out on Snake Ridge. Ever'body since then been buried in Clayton."

"He's down there with Grandaddy Lee an' the rest of the Lewises, Mamma," said Jerry.

"I don't want him down there with the rest of the Lewises," Mamie grumbled. "I want my boy with my mamma an' daddy, next to Stevie an' near where I'll be an' you'll be, too. I want Elmo moved to Clayton. Now."

"Mamma, I don't even know where he's buried," Jerry whined.

"I do, an' all the more reason why he should be moved, so's he won't be forgotten completely."

"Yeah, but it's been twenty-five years. They ain't nothin' left of a eight-year-old boy after that long."

"Get what there is an' bring him home," Mamie demanded.

Jerry called Cecil into the room. "Listen, I want you to drive Mamma down to Snake Ridge an' get my brother."

Cecil looked at them and waited for the punchline. "What brother?"

"Elmo, Junior," said Jerry.

"Oh, is he ready to come visit for a spell?" Cecil kidded in return.

"I'm serious, Cecil. Mamma's gonna show you where he's buried. She wants him moved to Clayton to be with the rest of us."

"You're serious." Cecil squinted at Jerry.

"It shouldn't be too difficult. Here's some money. Get somebody to help you."

Cecil, Mamie and Linda Gail drove Jud's 1960 Cadillac to Louisiana for the exhumation. Mamie led them to Snake Ridge, a long forgotten tract of land far from civilization where pioneer members of the Lewis clan encamped more than one hundred years before. They walked along the unkept remains of simple graves and found the linden tree shading the unmarked grave of Elmo, Jr.

Cecil came back the next day with help, a seventy-year-old black man with callused hands and a back bent from years of hard labor. The pair worked in half-hour shifts till the tops of their heads dipped below ground surface. After scraping past six-foot depth, Cecil began to cuss, thinking Mamie had brought him to the wrong place. He pressed down another foot and found bits of rotted wood.

The two men carefully excavated the remains from the soil. Little of the casket remained, a handful of splinters and six handles of brass or pot metal. Elmo, Jr., was basically intact. All of his clothing had disintegrated except buttons and belt buckle. The skull, still matted with short bristles of hair, frail and white without its overcoat of skin, was cracked where the truck struck him in 1938. One arm rested on an empty formaldehyde bottle. When Cecil had ladled the last of the find into the new casket, he hastily filled in the hole and returned to Clayton, where Elmo, Jr., was placed next to his maternal grandparents and nephew.

It was all part of the job as personal manager to Jerry Lee Lewis, a job that paid ten dollars a day, room and board, and all the laughs and tears a man could handle.

From its first day to its last, the month of August 1963 was the busiest on record for the stars, major and minor, of the Lewis circus. There was a birth, a marriage, a new contract, new recordings and the various awards, accolades, spats and congratulations to go along with them—all in all, a typical time in the life and times of Myra and Jerry Lee Lewis.

August 1. Jerry arrives in Las Vegas to begin two weeks at the Thunderbird Lounge for nineteen thousand dollars. With him are aide-de-camp Cecil Harrelson and erstwhile protégée Linda Gail Lewis, who informs the aide-de-camp she is well into the fourth month of pregnancy with his child and recommends he make some provision for their immediate future.

August 2. A sellout crowd greets Jerry opening night at the Thunderbird. The Ink Spots, Liberace and The Kingston Trio, appearing at three rival casinos, wonder where everybody went. Having no plans for the remainder of the evening, Mr. Harrelson, twenty-seven, and Ms. Lewis Goza Bushlen, sixteen, marry in an all-night wedding chapel on the Strip. The happy couple, penniless, homeless and on the way to becoming parents, are invited by the bride's brother to move in with him and his family.

August 3. A twenty-four-hour hotline is installed between the Lewis home and Dr. Wilson's home to provide emergency consultation in case of a delivery premature to September 5. Mamie calls to inform Myra that she can expect a visit from in-laws in two weeks.

August 4. Jerry Lee Lewis is acclaimed "astounding" and "the surprise hit of the Strip" by Vegas columnist Ralph Pearl, thereby insuring a continued sellout of each performance.

August 5. Cecil Harrelson enters into final stage of contractual negotiations with Irvin Green, owner of Mercury Records. Producer Shelby Singleton acts as Cecil's counsel.

August 6. Jerry is quoted in the press with reference to his contract with Sun expiring at end of the month: "I am open to bids. I am also interested in getting my records back on the most-played lists around the country. My records have sold without any promotion by Sun."

August 7. To which Sam Phillips replies in print: "I am not happy with the situation. I took Lewis when he was a twenty-one-year-old inexperienced youth from Ferriday, Louisiana, and produced four million-selling records on him before his career took a nose dive."

August 10. Design issues album "Rockin' With Jerry Lee Lewis," a compilation of four Sun cuts on one side backed with the duo of Frank Motley and Curley Bridges on side two.

August 11. Liberty releases "Great Balls of Fire" on anthology LP "Original Hits Number 9."

August 13. As the Thunderbird date draws to a close, competing clubs are bidding for Jerry's return. Cecil arranges to meet Mercury execs during the first weekend in September for contract signing.

August 15. The Lewis troupe heads home, where Mamie awaits the newlyweds. In concert with Linda Gail, Mamie fosters rumors that Myra has been a whore for anyone who would have her in the past year and that her child will have dark hair to prove it, intent upon dissolving Jerry's marriage and disenfranchising the baby in the same way Jane Mitcham and Ronnie were disposed of.

August 17. Frank Casone advises his client that he is to begin a week-long engagement at the Vapors Club in Hot Springs, Arkansas, allowing a seven-day leeway before the predicted date of birth of Phoebe Allen/Mark Allen Lewis, names chosen by the mother.

August 19. Linda Gail reminds Myra not to dispose of her maternity wardrobe after the birth of her child saying a "friend" could sure use it.

August 24. Jerry leaves for Hot Springs. His last words to Myra: "If you have the baby, it better be a boy. It ain't manly to have girls."

August 25. Jerry begins the first of seven nights at the Vapors Club. Sam Phillips communicates last-minute final offer before Sun sets September 6.

August 27. Mamie and Linda Gail depart for Ferriday, having moved Myra close to a nervous breakdown with accusations of adultery and the illegitimacy of the baby. Myra, one week from her due date, is home alone.

August 28. Calm before the storm.

On August 29, Lois and J. W. Brown, afraid of Myra being left unattended, sent ten-year-old son Rusty to spend the night with his sister. Rusty, hampered by crutches necessitated by a malady of the legs, slept on a pallet beside Myra's bed to be near any emergency.

Toward midnight, Myra felt a trickle of water and employed the hotline to Dr. Wilson. Wilson said it sounded like kidney trouble, but given the closeness to Myra's due date, perhaps she should come to his office for a look-see. Myra, unable to rouse Rusty, beat him with a crutch. Startled into believing an emergency had arisen, Rusty hopped about the house in hysteria.

Next, Myra phoned her mother. At the mention of water, Lois went into seizures and, unable to drive, ordered Myra to pick her up on the way to Dr. Wilson's. Leaking freely, Myra made it to the Brown's, unloaded Rusty and acquired Lois, now speaking in tongues.

At Dr. Wilson's office, Myra's water broke and she was told to proceed directly to the hospital. Deciding to attend to Lois first, Myra phoned Maxine Malone and found the number out of order. Myra and Lois drove to the Malones, where Maxine, also unable to drive, hopped in the front seat next to Myra and restrained Lois.

Meanwhile, at the hospital, Dr. Wilson was wondering what had happened to his patient when two fair-to-middlin' midwives and a mother-to-be with towel stuffed up her gown limped in.

Tranquilizers are administered to Lois and Maxine as Myra was whisked to a room.

After being served her favorite aperitif, glucose, Myra made several attempts to reach Jerry in Hot Springs. "Now we're gonna give you a little something to help you relax," were the last words she heard before dropping lifelessly to the bottom of a dark pool.

At five A.M., a nurse wakened Myra, saying, "Wake up, Miz Lewis, you have a little girl."

"Don't kid me," said Myra, feeling her distended stomach. "I'm here to *have* the baby. I haven't had it yet."

Enter Phoebe Allen Lewis, a blond spittin' image of her ol' man except for her mother's blue, blue eyes.

"Phoebe?" the nurse questioned.

"Rhymes with Stevie," Mrs. Lewis explained.

Lois called Mamie at six A.M. with the glad news. "Miz Lewis, Myra had a little girl!"

"What color hair does she have?" Mamie pursued, and was not happy with Lois's reply.

Lois called the new father in Hot Springs. "Jerry, Myra had a little girl!"

"Well, I'll be doggone," he said.

"Seven pounds. A blue-eyed blonde."

"Well, I'll be dadgummed."

On August 31, Mamie and Linda Gail returned to Memphis. Mamie declined to visit her granddaughter in the hospital, complaining that elevators gave her claustrophobia, and dispatched Linda Gail for a description of the infant. That night, Mamie called Jerry in Hot Springs to tell him Uncle Lee Calhoun was in the hospital for what might be his last time, but wasn't. "He's seein' devils," she related. The next day, Jerry, who had yet to drive 175 miles to greet his newborn, drove twice as far to see his uncle at Mamie's insistence.

On September 2, Myra went home with Phoebe. She was awaited by her parents, arranging a white bassinet laced with pink ribbon, and Mamie and Linda Gail. Myra wondered what could have kept her husband.

After the Browns departed on errands, Myra turned around to find Linda and Mamie walking out the door with suitcases in hand, having argued briefly about a topic unknown to her. The pair tore out of the driveway in Mamie's car, returning in sixty seconds so that Linda Gail could take the keys out of the ignition to Myra's car. Myra, alone at home with a three-day-old baby, had no means of transportation.

On the fifth, Myra, without having heard so much as a hello from her husband in a week, was surprised to see him pull up in the driveway. In no hurry to see his wife and daughter, Jerry began leisurely rooting through the trunk for his clothes, until Myra ran outside and dragged him in to the house, chattering about their beautiful baby.

Jerry approached the crib with caution, expressionless. Standing with feet together and hands clasped behind his back, he bent at the waist to peer inside. "Yeah, she's a fine li'l baby, ain't she?" he said, and walked out of the room.

For two weeks, the Killer would have absolutely nothing to do with his daughter. She could scream her head off and Jerry wouldn't budge out of his easy chair. Myra began to think Mamie had convinced him Phoebe was not his, but as Jerry explained to Cecil, "I always said I didn't want a daughter an' I still don't. A man needs sons to carry on his name. Girls—you can't do nothin' with 'em. They only grow up an' leave you for another man."

It was during the third week, perhaps when those cobalt eyes first adored her daddy, that his cold, cold heart melted. He picked her up and held her for the first time, and seemingly never put her down again. Father and daughter sat together, ate together, and shortly thereafter slept in the same bed. Jerry rarely called her by her given name, preferring to refer to her as "My Heart."

In the second week of September, trade journals proclaimed the signing of Jerry Lee Lewis to Mercury Records, a five-year pact for fifty thousand dollars, half to be paid upon signing, half at the end of three years. In his first session, Jerry recorded a dozen songs, which were released on various albums over the next four years under Mercury's Smash banner. Considering his past performance, Smash decided to market him as Sam Phillips had, attempting to please fans of country, pop and rhythm and blues. From the wealth of material, Smash selected Jerry's remake of Ray Charles's "Hit the Road Jack" and the countrified "Pen and

Paper" to be his first single. At the same time, plans for an album of remakes of his greatest hits on Sun was projected for Christmas. The task of coproducing the "Old Master" was assigned to Jerry Kennedy, a session guitarist for Elvis, and Shelby Singleton, producer of Mercury artists Johnny Preston, Bruce Channel and the Big Bopper.

"I don't like that nickname, Old Master," Jerry complained. "I ain't old."

"Jerry, that's what some people call God," said Cecil.

"Oh, then it's okay," said Jerry.

Not even God could save "Hit the Road Jack" from its fate as a pop flop, submerged below the top hundred songs of October 1963. "Pen and Paper" crept into the country top forty in February of the next year. Once Singleton and Kennedy had given Jerry's best music a facelift Nashville-style, his hits bore little resemblance to the originals. Gone were the echo vocals and simple instrumentation, and in their place were big-city refinements which glossed over the spontaneiety so vital to Jerry's sound. There were horns and strings and a female chorus likened to The Chipmunks who approached each track in the same way with the same "uh-huh" to Jerry's every statement. The life was gone, the innocence missing, and the overall effect was like drinking watered-down whiskey. As much as Singleton and Kennedy tried to add, the more they took away, till "The Golden Hits of Jerry Lee Lewis" had none of their original appeal. The fact that the album sold at all was due to the opportunity fans had to buy twelve of Jerry's best songs in one package.

In mid-October, Jerry opened at the world's largest nightclub, the Chez Paris in Chicago. It was the date onlookers dubbed the turning point in his stage career, what the *Times* announced as "Jerry Lee Lewis On Way Back Up After Career Nose Dive." Friends and family witnessed a change in the man; he was shopping for new cars and told Myra to find the finest interior decorator to remake their home from top to bottom; he was drinking again. As Jerry said in the *Times* interview, "You've got to keep swingin' an' keep smilin' through life," and for the time being, he was all smiles.

Everyone remembers where they were on November 22, 1963, when President Kennedy was assassinated in Dallas, Texas.

Schools sent children home, businesses closed, and everywhere could be heard the sound of cries and news bulletins. On that same day, Parlophone released an album entitled "With The Beatles," released in America as "Meet The Beatles," containing the song which changed the popular-music culture of the civilized world, "I Want To Hold Your Hand." Released November 29, the song created Beatlemania among the young, and parental animosity not seen since "Whole Lot of Shakin' Going On" made Jerry Lee Lewis the Rebel Angel of 1957.

Four Englishmen, ranging in age from twenty to twenty-three, succeeded in creating a new fad, making all that came before dated and obsolete. They wore matching collarless worsted suits the color of London smoke and narrow ties over white shirts, straightlegged trousers topping pointy-toed, high-heeled boots, and a new hairstyle for the sixties, a natural, greaseless mop growing over the ears, eyes and down the neck. They played the same music as their forefathers—American rhythm and blues, southern rock 'n' roll and Motown. The novelty was their British accents and clean, fresh harmonies in sound. It was asked of John Lennon what was his ambition for The Beatles. "To be bigger than Elvis," said he, and finding Presley's "Bossa Nova Baby" and "Kissin' Cousins" falling away to make room for "I Want To Hold Your Hand" and "That Boy," there was evidence that Lennon had achieved his goal for the moment. The question was then asked, as it had been so many times before of other fads, will Beatlemania last?

"No," came the answer from Jerry Lee Lewis. "These Beatles lack just one thing. Talent. I hate to say this, but I ain't afraid to say it. They're a great bunch of boys, but they're just doin' what Elvis started back in fifty-six. And they ain't never gonna be half what Elvis an' Jerry Lee Lewis were 'round those times. I don't care even if they're making carloads of money. I can name you a thousand rock 'n' roll singers with no talent who've made themselves a million dollars. They've gone down well in the States because there've been no big rock 'n' roll groups in America for five years. All this hollerin' an' screamin' ain't nothin' new. And it ain't nothin' to what it was when Elvis an' me started.

"I was makin' ten thousand dollars a day then. Jerry Lee Lewis was the Number One rock 'n' roll singer in 1958. And that's the truth. Then I got married, and the bad publicity cost me a billion dollars. They sure slammed me hard. I guess people were jus' lookin' for some excuse to kick the music.

"So I still say The Beatles are limited. If I'm still goin' in ten years time, I'll be the oldest teenager in the business. And I ain't reckonin' on retirin' yet. If I do ever give this life up, I reckon I'll go back to preachin'. I might be an ol' farmer. Don't you be sayin' I'm gonna do that, though," Jerry told the reporter. "The way I feel now, I'll jus' go on rockin' an' rollin'."

Industry reports in early 1964 revealed "Pen and Paper" topped out at Number 36 in *Billboard's* country chart, and the "Golden Hits" album had risen slowly but surely toward the top twenty. It had been three years since *Billboard* had recognized a Jerry Lee Lewis production, and Smash was confident that the February release, "I'm On Fire," would be his next million-selling single. Other reports indicated Beatlemania might be nothing more than collective momentary insanity. Reviews originating in Paris showed a Beatle concert at L'Olympia, scene of Jerry's triumphs, to be disastrous. Parisians preferred Trini Lopez to "Yeah! Yeah! Yeah!"

"I'm On Fire" was thought to be so explosive that Smash canceled plans to record all other songs in consideration and rushed it to the plant for immediate release. It took six weeks to show up in the charts at Number 99, advanced one notch and died. On a purely aesthetic level, those who knew Jerry and his music felt it was one of the finest rock recordings ever produced. The fan club touted it as the hottest number since "Great Balls of Fire." Regardless of its artistic merit, "I'm On Fire" was put out by a flood of Beatle releases. The Fab Four not only held all top seven positions in *Billboard's* pop singles chart, they owned five other positions in the hot hundred.

It became a matter of survival for Jerry, a battle he had fought his whole life long, and his recourse lay in the wit and wisdom of the counterattack. If England was invading the colonies, the Killer would spearhead an assault of Europe, where attitudes were still provincial. A three-week blitzkrieg was set for March 17— twelve dates in England and campaigns in France and Germany.

Jerry's take amounted to $11,500. Again he was barred from bringing his own band. Don Arden, making every effort to accommodate Jerry, offered passage for two by boat and all expenses. So quickly were Jerry and Cecil forced to prepare for an opted flight that there was little time for good-byes. Cecil left over Linda Gail's protest that she was made to stay home with Myra and raise babies. She had given birth to "Little Cecil" hardly a month before, and four o'clock feedings weren't half the fun of rolling in from a show at four A.M. It was time to send Cecil back to school for another lesson: If he wasn't there to satisfy her, the order could be filled elsewhere. "You're gonna hear some rumors about me when you get home," she warned him. "None of 'em are gonna be true."

When Cecil was in England, Linda Gail conducted an open and notorious affair. She even decided to voluntarily admit her indiscretion to her husband when he came home, and their separation went into immediate effect as she moved out of the bedroom she shared with Cecil to the room across the hall, legalities to follow whenever he could get around to them. The schism in the Harrelson half of the household had not the slightest effect on the Lewises. It seemed a joke to Jerry, especially when he stirred in his sleep and heard Cecil or Linda sneaking into each other's bedrooms.

On the other hand, Myra had no complaints with her mate. They had recently been featured in the *Press-Scimitar's* home section showing off the work of a New York hairdresser-cum-environmental-architect who had transformed the Lewis's typical tract home into a showplace complete with a piano-shaped swimming pool. Walls were knocked out to create a gigantic living room, and one side of the dining area was glassed to overlook the pool and patio. A bay window was added to the living room, where Jerry's baby grand piano was elevated on a stagelike pedestal. Windows and walls were completely covered by lilac drapes, the floor by wall-to-wall lavender carpeting. Conventional lighting fixtures were replaced by purple-tint chandeliers. The decorator went wild with lounges: custom-designed free-form chairs in bluish purple, high-backed settees in shimmering white and a massive couch resplendent in brilliant tangerine. Behind the couch, what else but mirrored panels antiqued in black and gold veins. The pad was completed only after a brick and stone fountain was entrenched between the living room and dining room. Towering green plants turned the nook into a garden alcove lit by emerald-green spotlights. The overall effect was described by the staff writer as "California-style Arabian Nights."

When Jerry received the bill he went into shock. The damage came to thirty-five thousand dollars—all of Jerry's Mercury money and more—and he estimated he could have built and furnished a new home for the same sum. "I thought you said this guy was a friend of yours," Jerry said to Frank Casone.

"He is," Casone replied.

The front page of the *New Musical Express* for March 20, 1964, headlined The Beatles' latest hit, "Can't Buy Me Love." Throughout the journal were ads hawking Beatle boots and collarless jackets. The inside cover posed the question "Elvis Finished?" and in a review of the Big E's latest flick, *Viva Las Vegas*, in which he sang a soppy version of "Santa Lucia," the *NME* critic referred to Presley as "one of the once-greats on the pop scene."

There had been a changing of the guard, and if Presley was being regarded in the past tense, Jerry wondered how the British press would assess his tour. On page 17 of the same *NME* issue, lost among bits on The Mary Kay Trio and ads announcing dates for The Kinks, Freddie and The Dreamers, and The Rolling Stones, appeared the meek greeting, "Welcome to Jerry Lee Lewis Again." The question in everyone's mind: Will Jerry live up to expectations or will he follow the downhill slide of Elvis Presley?

The answer came from Birmingham in the following week's *Express*, "Jerry Lee: Sensation."

"If ever a man earned his pay, Jerry did," said the reviewer. "He packed more excitement, energy and sheer electrical impact into his eleven numbers than you could find in a shop full of LPs. Not even the wild scenes that Little Richard created on his tour matched those by Jerry Lee at Birmingham."

"Artists come and go like passing clouds," began another commentary. "Others change their styles to keep abreast of the times, while still more develop an entirely new approach as they achieve professional maturity. But despite all the undulations on the pop music scene, one factor remains constant throughout the years—a dynamic bundle of energy known as Jerry Lee Lewis."

And although Jerry was referred to here and there as an "old timer," a television executive overseeing the production of Jerry's broadcast compared him to Sinatra and Judy Garland. "He knows everything there is to know about audience reactions and emotions. In his own field, Jerry Lee Lewis is just as great."

His fourth English tour of duty was completed amidst sellout crowds and universal acclaim from the press. His crowning victory was having won the land that gave birth to The Beatles at a time when Beatlemania was at its peak. Jerry's European label was compelled to capture his German date on tape for the album "Live at the Star Club, Hamburg."

Returning from abroad in April, Jerry proceeded directly to Nashville to work on his next single, to be released in June. Trouble waited for him in Memphis, where Frank Casone and Ray Brown were involved in a power struggle. Casone, trying to cultivate his client into a Vegas act, was battling Brown, who was booking the Killer on the same circuit he had traveled over the past six years. One wanted a few prestigious dates, the other bread-and-butter money. Ignoring Casone, Jerry continued to accept bookings from Brown. Casone waved his contract in Jerry's face, showing the clause naming him sole manager, agent, representative and adviser, and demanded 25 percent of the receipts as also provided in the contract.

Jerry refused Casone his percentage of shows he did not book, and left for Port Washington, Wisconsin, on a tour of the Midwest for Ray Brown in mid-May. Meanwhile, Casone filed suit against Jerry, Myra, Ray Brown and the bank, seeking to attach all property and enjoin Brown from paying Jerry until an accounting had been made.

In the two weeks between instigation of the suit and the hearing on May 25, many hidden aspects of Jerry's manager came to light. The biggest shock was discovery of Casone's connection with Sam Phillips and the secret pact between the two which would have steered Jerry back to Sun Records. The scheme backfired, as did the one between Casone and the interior decorators attempting to bilk Jerry out of thirty-five grand, half of which was to have been slushed to Casone. Jerry refused to pay the major portion of the decorators' bill, and they, too, filed suit. "Come get your pool," Jerry told them. "You ain't gettin' another dime outta me."

In hearing Casone's complaint, the court interpreted his management contract to mean he was not Jerry's sole *booking* agent, and the absence of that one word was fatal to Frank's case. Jerry was vindicated and Casone was denied proceeds from bookings arranged by Brown.

Let bygones be bygones, said Casone, and invited Jerry and Cecil to his home to discuss future involvements in a friendlier atmosphere. A fight between Cecil and Casone started within two minutes, and it was then that the gangster in Casone asserted itself. Threats of bodily harm came fast and furious.

"Mess with me an' I tell the cops what really happened to the Oriental Club, how you torched it for the insurance. Mess with me, Frankie, an' see who gets burned next." Cecil stormed out of the house with Jerry running behind him, laughing as he usually did when Cecil got cranked up.

"Y'know, Cece, I think you should handle all my bizness from now on," Jerry said. "We unnerstand each other, you 'n' me. We don't need no contracts between us. You look after me an' I'll look after you."

"It's a deal, Killer," said Cecil, shaking hands on it.

"Say, Cece, who was it started that Killer bizness, anyway?"

"I b'lieve it was you."

"No, I b'lieve it was you started that," said Jerry, eyeing his friend. It was one of Jerry's toying tests designed to catch a confidant off-guard. He was always baiting little traps and thawing out snow jobs. Cecil was one of the few men who earned Jerry's respect, and no matter how great a star he might have been or might become again, the last thing he needed was a friend to lie to him or build false hopes. He was safe with Cecil. As best friends, coworkers and brothers-in-law, Jerry and Cecil set out, two country boys with a high school education and a half between them, to master the maverick show business.

The next step, "She Was My Baby" and "The Hole He Said He'd Dig for Me," was another pop/country sandwich, half of which the public swallowed. There was no attraction for anglophiles, but the flip side, likened to a Hank Williams composition, found spotty support from country stations. For all the pushing Smash was doing to make Jerry king of rock 'n' roll again, the public cried out to deaf ears for country songs.

"I tell you what I see happenin'," Jerry Kennedy told Jerry Lee. "The country stations are playin' your music, but as long as you continue to record rock, you'll never gain their total support. Quit rockin' an' go country, and they'll make you top ten again."

"Never," said Jerry, refusing to hang up his rock 'n' roll shoes for instant country stardom.

At the Municipal Auditorium in Birmingham, Alabama, Smash recorded Jerry's concert for "The Greatest Live Show On Earth" album. In the opinions of those whose opinions mattered most, this was Jerry's brightest moment on vinyl. It was his music the way it should be played and recorded, without interference from producers and the inhibitions of the studio. "We're recordin' a live album so you may hear songs you may have never heard me do before and songs I may never do again," said Jerry, and treated listeners to hits by other singers sounding like they were written just for him—Little Richard's "Jenny, Jenny" and "Long Tall Sally," Chuck Berry's "Memphis" and "No Particular Place to Go," Ray Charles's "I Got a Woman," and Buck (Never let 'em forget you're country) Owens's "Together Again." There were no horns or strings, no backing vocals except for the screams of thousands.

"High Heel Sneakers" was chosen as the single from the album, and Jerry Kennedy and Shelby Singleton knew if this wasn't a hit, they'd *all* go back to farming. September was chosen for the release date. It seemed like the perfect plan was about to unfold when, as if the gods had intervened, The Beatles descended like a plague of locusts. Their first American tour wiped out twenty-four cities and broke every entertainment record that had ever been established. The Kansas City show at Charlie Finley's ballpark alone netted $150,000. Hotels hosting the band sold used sheets and pillow cases for one thousand dollars and one-inch squares of same for a dollar. Maids in these same hotels went bald pulling the hair out of their heads when they found fans willing to part with fortunes for a lone Beatle lock.

The Beatles went home taking America's wealth with them. Smash proceeded with their plans, and the album took off in the right direction toward the top forty but failed to draw the attention it deserved. For one week in November, "High Heel Sneakers" ranked Number 91 in the pop charts. As The Beatles thrilled ten, twenty, thirty, forty, fifty thousand and more, Jerry played to twenty-five hundred at DePaul University, a couple thousand at the Tupelo Fair, and performed for a benefit in Memphis to raise funds for the family of Dean Manuel, who died in the same plane crash that killed Jim Reeves in July. Keep swingin', keep smilin'.

*   *   *

In November, one week before returning to England, Jerry was front-page news in the local paper. Complete with photos of him at home with Myra and Phoebe was an interview entitled "A Lot to Overcome Says Star as Career Takes Upward Turn," still describing his course in its comeback stage.

"It may seem like England is taking the lead in pop music now," Jerry said, "but that's not really true. It's just that the U.S. temporarily left the field wide open, and groups like The Beatles, who copied the American style, took advantage of an opportunity. Now that they've caught on, American deejays are dusting off our early records. We rockers are back on top again."

His position on The Beatles was softened for British reporters, who told Jerry that he had a great effect on John, Paul, George and Ringo in their formative stages. He returned the compliment, saying The Beatles had "done more than anybody to get my sort of music back in the charts." He claimed an affinity for their fight to overcome the disillusionments of trying to get on in show business in the same way he fought for his sort of music, but went no further.

"Kids don't look at me the same way they look at Elvis and The Beatles," Jerry explained. "At first they looked at Elvis as a sex symbol. Then they looked at The Beatles because of their hair. But they look at me because I have talent. I can't say they don't have talent. They have a different sound. But with me, the teenagers get pure talent, no gimmicks like sex or long hair. Each time I give the best I can."

"Then who's fighting who?" the writer asked.

"I ain't fightin' nobody. I came over here to release my records and my fans won't buy them unless they're pure Jerry Lee Lewis." A far cry from his last British interview, wherein he blasted The Beatles as talentless bums and confessed his fondest desire was to get a part in a biblical film.

For this tour of England, Jerry insisted on bringing his own band, consisting of drummer Tarp Tarrant, bassist Herman Hawkins, and guitarists Butch Hutchinson and Larry Nichols. Each man was paid five hundred dollars for four weeks' work, including one Dick West, acting gopher now that Cecil had been promoted. They opened on November 17, one week after The Beatles had completed the same rounds, and therefore it was no surprise to promoters when only two hundred fans showed up for Jerry's first show in Bristol and the second show was only half-filled.

Three days later, Jerry got a peek at the current rage, The Rolling Stones, who opened for him on the television program *Ready Steady Go!* and who were more impressed with Jerry than he was with "Time Is On My Side." The Animals opened for him later in the tour, and he was damned if he could figure out what all the screaming was about when they moaned and groaned "The House of the Rising Sun" or how it got to be Number 1. Returning to England for the second time that year, the fourth in little more than two years, had been a mistake. The timing wasn't right, the focus had shifted, and none but fanclub lifers showed up to lend support. Jerry returned home planning not to wander too far again for a long while.

A new rock 'n' roll television show aired on ABC in the fall of 1964. Improving on the *American Bandstand* format of playing records for the studio audience to dance to, *Shindig* offered live performances by top acts. *Shindig* was produced by Jack Good, an Englishman who had written in glowing terms about Jerry since his beginning. Jerry's agreement to appear on Jack's show on December 30 began a long association responsible for keeping Jerry before the public in the coming lean years. On the same night that Willie Nelson made his national television debut on *Shindig* singing "Don't Let Go," Jerry sang "Jenny, Jenny," "Mean Woman Blues" and closed the show with "Whole Lot of Shakin' Going On."

Shindig was a success, and judging from the letters mailed to the network, Jerry had a great deal to do with it. Jerry was asked to make the first of four return visits to Shindig in the next year. So on New Year's Eve, a time when one reflects over the past year and makes plans for the next, Jerry had something to be thankful for: A productive year that, had it not been for the British invasion, Chuck Berry's comeback and the new sounds coming out of California, would have made him a star all over again.

"The Greatest Live Show On Earth" reportedly sold one hundred thousand copies, thrice that many by Jerry's count, and reached the top forty in *Cashbox* and *Music World* in January 1965. Jerry was booked into Kentucky, Ohio, Texas and Indiana during the first six months of the year at $500–$750 a night, with three *Shindig* dates spliced at two-month intervals, the first occurring on February 17. That same show debuted three new acts: Sonny and Cher, Glen Campbell, and England's latest group, The Moody Blues. Perhaps the confrontation with these fresh faces caused Jerry some slight discomfort, for he repaired to his dressing room to peroxide his darkening hair bright yellow.

As a favor to Jerry, Jack Good permitted Linda Gail to sing on *Shindig,* which ultimately led to her being added to *Shindig*'s touring show and a recording contract with ABC-Paramount. More important, Jerry introduced "Baby, Hold Me Close" from his forthcoming album. The song was written by Jerry with Bob Tubert, vice president of Monument Records, armchair critic and lyricist hobbyist. It was a rockin' rhythm-and-blues number with horns and a funky piano break, another dance instruction in the style of "Whole Lot of Shakin'."

With the release of "The Return of Rock" album later that month, Jerry embarked on an uncharted course stretching over the next three years and spanning five albums and seven singles, none of which had any greater chance of discovery than a message in a bottle. That is not to say he was in a rut or that these sixty songs were unmerchantable. On the contrary, Jerry Lee Lewis was packaged five different ways, and it is this lack of direction, not his versatility, that caused listeners to scratch their heads in wonder at what Mercury was trying to sell.

"The Return of Rock" collected an even number of rhythm-and-blues and country songs with three rockers written by Chuck Berry but coming too late to take advantage of Berry's brief resurgence upon his release from prison. The best of Berry's singles struggled to reach Number 95 that year, his finest material having been covered by everybody in the business. The British youth were following R & B rockers of a new generation led by Eric Clapton, Jeff Beck, Peter Townshend and their godfather, John Mayall. Instead of leading the parade, Jerry and Chuck Berry were falling behind the new wave. The timing so vital in creating new trends had fallen off. Chuck and Jerry had lost the art of what the English were mastering: innovation.

Sam Phillips released Jerry's "Carry Me Back to Old Virginia" and "I Know What It Means" on the heels of "The Return of Rock" in mid-March. It was an experiment that failed in its attempt to cash in on Mercury's promotion, and was not attempted again for six years. In June, Jerry divided a tour of northeastern campuses to tape *Shindig* on the fifteenth, the purpose of which was to promote another single, "Rockin' Pneumonia and the Boogie Woogie Flu." For lack of a better gimmick, Jerry recorded the song using a harpsichord, not exactly a main ingredient of authentic rock 'n' roll. Nevertheless, it was Jack Good's "Pick of the Week," even if it was nobody else's.

Jerry's coperformers on *Shindig* included The Righteous Brothers and soulmate Jackie Wilson, with whom he sang "Whole Lot of Shakin'" as a finale. The British singing duo Chad and Jeremy were also on the show, and Jerry paid more attention to the length of their hair than the sound of their music.

"What do you think people'd say if I cut my hair real short?" Jerry phoned to ask his wife.

"Why would you want to do that?" Myra asked.

"These British groups are makin' long hair a farce, an' I'm gettin' tired of it."

"People'll think you've lost your mind, Jerry," she said, but was not surprised to find her short-shaved husband singing on *Shindig* two weeks later.

With a new image came a new album, "Country Songs for City Folks," arriving in the fall of 1965, a renovation of style and format. Producers Singleton and Kennedy opined that rock music was going places Jerry could not follow, that the rock 'n' roll days were over, leaving the country market wide open. They attempted to make the transition smoothly, portraying Jerry as a contemporary artist by depicting him on the cover in a dark suit against a cosmopolitan high-rise building, the title intended to invite sophisticated listeners inside, where they were met by a dozen country cousins—all new material, with the exception of "Crazy Arms" overhauled in an upbeat. The album covered hits of the day such as "Wolverton Mountain," "North to Alaska," Johnny Cash's "Ring of Fire" and Roger Miller's "King of the Road," and Jerry's remake of "Green, Green Grass of Home" was excerpted for a single. Unfortunately, it was released while Porter Wagoner's hit version was still charting, and Jerry's copy, sounding nothing like him vocally and deleting the piano for harmonica and acoustic guitar, was no improvement on the original. If Jerry's album sold only one copy, it was to Tom Jones, who covered

"Green, Green Grass of Home" and made a passel of green, green money.

As the cornerstone for Jerry's cataclysmic change in direction taking place three years later, "Country Songs for City Folks" was reissued as "All Country," with a new cover depicting him in worksuit, dungarees and boots, standing in the middle of a dirt road shaded by the green, green grass of home, and sold infinitely better. However, Jerry was reluctant to release the original album in 1965, and made Shelby Singleton promise not to proclaim he had gone completely country in advertising. It was this lack of conviction, this fear of alienating rock 'n' rollers, that kept country radio from taking the product seriously, thereby further delaying Jerry's country crossover. That "Country Songs for City Folks" did not sell well proved Jerry's point that he could not forsake rock for all the cash in Nashville.

On the night Jerry played to five hundred at the Blue Angel Club in Fort Wayne, Indiana, The Beatles played Shea Stadium to fifty-five thousand. The next week was Jerry's thirtieth birthday, the magic number traditionally separating generations of music makers. Candles on the cake silently standing at illumined attention said more than the loudest criticisms. Jerry was not a kid anymore. He watched his final performance on *Shindig,* comparing himself to The Yardbirds, The Pretty Things and Billy Preston, noticing the widening gulf between himself and the younger set.

For his birthday, Myra gave Jerry a Lincoln limousine replete with tape recorder, stereo, bar and refrigerator. It was similar to the model used by the President of the United States, and set Myra back seventeen thousand dollars. Although it was the snazziest means of travel, the cost of the limo's upkeep was impractical, and the long, low-riding luxury item, nicknamed the "lemonsine," sat out of commission before Jerry was another year older. Myra made up for her well-intended mistake by giving him something more practical, a white convertible Cadillac. The limo, if good for nothing else, provided Cecil with the inspiration to write a song, "Lincoln Limousine," which Jerry took credit for creating.

Theorists of what makes a popular song would not by the end of 1966 be able to formulate a working theorem for success upon hearing the widely diverse styles that made it to the top of the charts that year. Sgt. Barry Sadler, a lone soldier without instrument or backup band, had a colossal hit with "Ballad of the Green Berets." The Association scored mightily with "Cherish," and The Righteous Brothers repeated earlier successes with "Soul and Inspiration." The Four Tops had the top R & B hit with "Reach Out, I'll Be There," and an anonymous group of studio musicians calling themselves ? and The Mysterians sold a million copies of "96 Tears." Herb Alpert, a nice Jewish boy who kept up with his trumpet lessons, placed three albums in the top ten within the twelve-month span.

Nineteen sixty-six was the year The Beatles remembered "Yesterday," and released their tenth album, "Revolver," regarded as the peak of their career. The Beatles quit the road by August and became a studio band, concentrating on cultivating innovations which would serve as a touchstone for a generation growing up during the experimental phase of the drug culture. It was an offhand remark made by John Lennon in the *London Evening Standard* that, when taken out of context, provoked burnings of Beatle books and records. "The Beatles are bigger than Jesus Christ," said John, not satisfied with merely topping Elvis. Blasphemy, cried many of the same people who had been offended by the redoubtable Mr. Lewis, thus giving rise to a Beatle boycott.

It was a poor year for Elvis and a good one for his able replacement. Of Big E's seven entries, three failed to make the charts and "Love Letters" showed only as high as Number 19. Tom Jones, the Lewis protégé, had a Number 1 hit with "Green, Green Grass of Home" and captured the collective heart of womankind. The frustrations of Jerry's misguided recording career, now into its tenth year, showed no signs of the kind of success he had once bargained for with God. To make it to the top again was all he asked in return for his promise to return to a good Christian life; the top, a place he had been once briefly, which he had forgotten the way to, and which he could not recognize upon his return.

Nineteen sixty-six was a lost year in the memories of Myra and Jerry Lee Lewis. Two hundred and fourteen dates and a five-week tour of Europe obliterated the calendar. What free days there were in Jerry's schedule were lost in transit, visits to the studio and a few quiet moments at home.

Ebbtide Club, Reviere, Mass., Jan. 9–15; Clayton Club, Selmer, Tn., Jan. 12; Brock's Club, Lexington, Ky., Jan. 13;

Essex House, Indianapolis, In., Jan. 14; The Platters, Cadillac, Mi., Jan. 15; Holiday Ballroom, Chicago, Il., Jan. 16 . . .

The single "Sticks and Stones," a Ray Charles hit suggested to Jerry by a fan, backed with "What a Heck of a Mess," was released in January. The flip side was a clever attempt on Jerry's part to write a country tune. The album following this release was "Memphis Beat," the newest description of Jerry's particular brand of ballad. According to liner notes, Memphis Beat was part traditional jazz, part rock, a hint of "old riverboat shuffle," the joy and blues of gospel, and the soul of spirituals. This collection, more than any other, showed the error in attempting to include something for everyone.

"Memphis Beat" contained a filler cut, "Whenever You're Ready," written by Cecil Harrelson and sounding something like what he must have said to Linda Gail on the night she proposed: "Whenever you're ready/ Just let me know/ I'll pack my clothes/ And away we'll go." Only recently had Cecil spent idle moments jotting down lyrics on spare pieces of paper and the backs of contracts, the idea being that by recording their own material, he and Jerry could divide the publishing fees paid to Jerry Lee Lewis Music, Inc. Cecil was part owner, although he never saw a penny of his 20 percent. Acknowledging the good idea, Jerry and Cecil sat down together to write "Lincoln Limousine," undoubtedly the song receiving the strongest criticism since "Old Black Joe."

Intended to be a folk-rock eulogy for John Kennedy, its quick pace caused *Record Mirror* to complain, "The most controversial of the Kennedy tributes is 'Lincoln Limousine' by Jerry Lee Lewis, who sings apparently lightheartedly about the shooting in Dallas. He might just be sincere, but it doesn't sound in good taste."

In October, the release of "By Request, More of the Greatest Live Show On Earth" album was timed to correspond with Jerry's tour of Europe. Some placed sales of the first live album on the sunny side of half a million units, the best-selling of his Smash albums to date. So it seemed like a good idea to try it again, this time choosing Panther Hall in Fort Worth, Texas, where Jerry could still spy the color to the boys' necks—ain't no har growin' down thar—and it was the feel, not so much the sound, which made this taping better than the first.

It was a different atmosphere altogether when Jerry took the same show to classy suburban nightclubs in Bradford, Newcastle, South Shields, Middlesborough and Stockton, England. The press flocked to see him as always. In the event that there was no new scandal, there was always history to kick around with the quotable Killer. Tom Jones was present at both shows in Bradford to make Jerry's introduction from the stage. Proclaiming Jerry the "best entertainer in the world today," Tom stepped aside to watch Jerry prove it. His immaculate dinner jacket was ripped away and the Killer roared out from underneath the finery. At the end of each performance, he left the stage in the midst of rioting, looting and rampant vandalism wreaked by rabid supper clubbers.

Backstage, Jerry was interviewed by Poppin' Johnny and Gaspin' Gus, editors of *Sun Sound Club Magazine*, who got off to a bad start by asking, "A lot of folks say that you got your style from Mickey Gilley. Is that true?"

"Man, who's been sayin' that?" Jerry roared. "I taught that guy all he knows. He got it all from me."

"What do you think of Mickey?"

"I just don't like copycats. I'd rather have the real thing."

"As a beginner, then, who were your biggest influences?" Gus recovered.

"Well, now, I just don't figure that I had any influence, apart from my fans, that is. I'd say my fans were my biggest influence."

"Compare the music you perform today with the good ol' days at Sun."

"The difference between rock music today and the rock music of yesterday is much the same as it is with religion today and back in the times of Jesus Christ," Jerry illustrated. "The religion is not the same as it was in biblical times and never can be again. It's the same way with rock 'n' roll. It isn't the same as it was in the beginning. Another example is the way they make cars. Man, when I got my first Buick, I thought it was the greatest car ever. I've had better cars since, but I'll never forget that Buick."

After completing the two-week tour of supper clubs, Jerry traveled to Germany, Switzerland and France, where his music was undergoing a revival of phenomenal proportions. The top hundred poll in France for October and November revealed that Jerry led all others with fourteen songs, including "Long Tall Sally" at Number 7, "High Heel Sneakers" at Number 10, and "Money" at

Number 14. His closest competition came from The Rolling Stones, who owned Number 1, "Satisfaction," among their twelve entries. The Beatles followed with eight, three of which were in the top ten. Elvis also had eight, although "Do the Clam" at Number 26 was his best showing.

Jerry returned to England for one week and a closing night in London on November 14. Toward the end of his final performance, as he played the last strains of "Great Balls of Fire," a riot turned the hall into a free-for-all. When the action moved too close to the Killer, he employed the microphone for the only other thing it could be used for beside screaming for help, a trick shot, a boomerang action which bounced off an attacker's face and returned to Jerry for a repeat. When the device was employed later at the Roseland Ballroom in Atlanta, Georgia, the impact caused an overzealous fan to go into epileptic seizures and die, an unfortunate freak incident for which Jerry was held blameless.

. . . Stardust, Bloomington, In., Dec. 12–15; Jet Set, Indianapolis, In., Dec. 16; Eagles Lodge, Connersville, In., Dec. 17; Diamond Club, Dayton, Oh., Dec. 18; Hungry Eye, Indianapolis, In., Dec. 19–20; Stardust, Chicago, Il., Dec. 21.

11 *She Even Woke Me Up to Say Good-bye*

AFTER TWO YEARS OF BATTLING ABC TELEVI-
sion executives over programming philosophies, *Shindig* producer
Jack Good threw a stack of records through his office window,
kicked down the door and stomped it to pieces, then fled to a
mountain hideaway where he decided to finish a pet project, a
rock 'n' roll version of Shakespeare's *Othello*. He planned to have
his script ready in June 1966, rehearsals to begin in Philadelphia
by September. The show would move to Broadway and two other
cities, then to Hollywood to turn the play into a motion picture.
For the role of the noble Moor, Good had former professional
football player Roosevelt Grier in mind. Iago, the villainous co-
lead, was perfect for Good's favorite rock 'n' roller, Jerry Lee
Lewis.

Jerry did not cotton to the idea at first. His main objection was
moving North, and being absent from music two or three years
would be equally unnatural. Acting itself was too confining, totally foreign to the spontaneous style he had perfected. He had
already turned down a recurring special-guest star role in television's highest-rated program. *Bonanza* wanted him two or three
times a season to play the part of a saloon pianist and Jerry declined, saying he was interested only in a bona fide starring role.
Now Jack Good was offering him a role on his own terms and
Jerry was forced to face his real fear: ridicule.

"Actually, you'll speak very few lines," Good explained.
"Most of your bit will be sung at the piano. I'll send the script,
and if you decide it's not for you, I'm sure Bobby Darin will take
it."

Jerry received the seventy-page script entitled *Catch My Soul*, bound in imitation black leather with his name embossed on the cover in gold letters. Leafing through the work, he spotted Iago on practically every page, relieved to find most lines one or two sentences long. A note accompanying the script listed a change in opening location to Detroit, at the bottom of which Good included a handwritten note explaining that the principal comic element of the play was Jerry's southern interpretation of Shakespearean speeches. It was not a production for serious students, nor an attraction for the average theatergoer. Instead, Good hoped his work would be viewed in the spirit of fun, and its greatest gain might be interesting youthful rock 'n' roll fans in something loftier than comic books, but it was not to be expected.

Jerry began studying his lines while touring in his Lincoln limousine. He recorded cues on tape, leaving pauses for him to speak his part. Just when he began to make progress with Iago, Good called to say Detroit was out and his brainchild miscarried. Not to worry, said Good, leave me but a little to myself.

In January 1967, Jerry's organization was disrupted by a shake-up at Mercury, desertion in the ranks and cancellations of shows. Charlie Fach replaced Shelby Singleton as his producer, and Shelby was only too happy to dump the dilemma of what to do with Jerry so that he could start his own label. Guitarist Charlie Freeman, having offended Jerry by admitting to atheism, quit the band after Jerry refused to bail him out of jail on a drug charge; drugs were okay, but a Memphis Beat had to love Jesus if he wanted to keep his job. Then the announced tour of England in April was sacked when promoters declined to meet Ray Brown's price. Perhaps another shift in European moods was the real reason for the change in plans, as British kids were heading in a new direction toward psychedelia. Their critics panned washed up Little Richard, looking like this year's Zulu, and accused the back-sliding Chuck Berry of being a "bullet-headed Yank with dollar signs for eyes." It wasn't safe to be in the export business at present.

Forced to remain at home, Jerry played Boston's Where It's At club on January 6. Tarp Tarrant was behind the drums, Danny Daniels at the organ, and Jackie Harrell replaced Charlie Freeman on guitar. The new bass player was J. W. Brown. Back into the fray whenever Jerry needed him, Jay forgot hard feelings when there was a job to be done. After thirty days without pay, he returned home on his own airline ticket and waited for Jerry to call again.

The Summer of Love was beginning in San Francisco's Haight-Ashbury district, where the newest counterculture was hatched. The hippies, long-haired and brightly attired anti-Vietnamese War activists and Magical Mystery tourists, were dropping acid and out of society. They were polar opposites of young blacks on the East Coast rioting for basic human rights. Jerry Lee Lewis was earning a living somewhere between the conflicts. He played jerkwater towns where "draft evaders" were people hoping to avoid catching cold and "taking a trip" still meant piling the kids into the camper for a weekend away—towns like Lebanon, Kentucky, Connersville, Indiana, and Jonesboro, Arkansas, where folks went to church, saluted the flag and hoped the horrors of the headlines would not threaten their peace and quiet. For the blue-collar worker in Blytheville and the nine-to-fivers in Fort Worth, Jerry sang "It's a Hang Up, Baby" and "Turn On Your Love Light," the only singles he had to offer that year to folks who finally bought that copy of the "Golden Hits" album they'd been meaning to buy and never found the answer to the puzzlement, "What is a Moby Grape?"

At home, Myra had nothing to occupy her time but a precocious child who had become too much to handle. Phoebe, in the Lewis way, rejected every attempt at discipline, and as if she weren't enough of a problem, Jerry was forever expressing his desire to have another son to carry on his name. But another baby did not seem to happen, and Myra and Jerry eyed each other with suspicion, wondering whether the other was still biologically capable of parentage. Those attacks of nerves which gripped Myra's stomach like a fist returned with debilitating regularity. She was losing control.

Phoebe had apparently read all the child-rearing books, for she seemed determined to break all the rules. She could walk before she was a year old at a time when most infants are learning to crawl. By age four, she exhibited the same marvelous musical ability her father had passed on to her brother. Unlike her brother, though, Phoebe was a troublesome child. Whereas Stevie had spent hours on end playing contentedly by himself, Phoebe was always creating a nuisance, a lion within a lamb. Dissatisfaction was the first feeling she learned to express; anger, the first emotion she displayed.

As a last resort, Myra searched Memphis for a nursery school which met her strict standards and found one on the opposite side of town. But Myra's emotional dependence on the child made it nearly impossible to leave her every morning at eight not to return till five. Myra did not know what to do with herself. Maxine Malone, Tarp's wife, Judy, and people she met at church completed her circle of friends. When, for the sake of friendship, she ceased to spend the livelong day with her companions, she had nothing to do but tidy an already spotless house. She went bowling every Tuesday. She played bridge every Wednesday. To occupy the rest of the week, she developed an interest in ceramics which led to the purchase of a kiln to set up a workshop in the garage. When she had mastered the craft, she began to teach classes five days a week. Winning three first-place ribbons at the Memphis Ceramics Association Show was the only accomplishment in her life.

Leaving Phoebe all day in the care of strangers created feelings of guilt in Myra. One morning she drove her daughter to school, but only after persuading Phoebe to untie the car doors from the inside, and walked her to the front door of the nursery where she had the sudden impulse to scoop her up and head for home. She returned to the car alone and sat behind the wheel wondering where to go. She had no shopping to do, no friends to visit or classes to teach, so she sat there till noon. She walked across the street to a drugstore for lunch and returned to the car, where she waited till five. Thus began Myra's practice of spending the entire day sitting nine hours in her station wagon parked across the street from Phoebe's nursery school. She took to bringing a blanket to spread out in the bay of the automobile, a picnic and several magazines to while away the hours. Why? It was too far to go back home.

Myra kept a boarding house occupied by itinerant labor, freeloading inlaws and the six dependents of Jerry Lee Lewis. She had mastered the art of cooking for two or twenty-two, and learned to live through periods of prolonged solitude spelled only by occasional three-day weekends when her home turned into a hotel. Myra counted the number of nights she had spent alone with her husband since their marriage: the same three she recalled ten years ago. The house was filled with tension. There were no new hits. Nothing was happening. The same old clubs for the same money Jerry made in the beginning, a contract in its fourth year yielding no royalties and not likely to be renewed. It was all making Jerry drink to forget these things.

Myra never knew who would walk in the door in the guise of Jerry Lee Lewis. She hoped it would be the blond, smiling kid, the skinny shaker on his way to the top. The man she usually met was the Killer, the lean, mean honky-tonk pianist wired from weeks on the long road, depleted by pills as the road became endless, still on his way back up the ladder. He took pills to pep him up for another performance, pills to calm him down to sleep, the abstention from which made him nothing but irritable when at home. He usually arrived unannounced in the middle of the night, wanting a hot meal and hot sex.

"I can't sleep at night anymore," Myra complained. "I lie awake all night and nap for a few hours at dawn."

"Take somethin'," Jerry recommended. "Look in my bag."

"No, I'm afraid. Know what makes me sleep? Rain. I remember when I was a child we had a tool shed in the backyard. The rain against its tin roof wasn't like regular rain, it was different. And it always made me sleepy. We don't get enough rain these days."

Before returning to the road, Jerry hired workmen for a home-improvement project. They sawed holes in the ceiling of the master bedroom where speakers were installed. A recording engineer hooked up a sound system in the attic. Dark curtains were hung, and a self-winding tape came from the studio. There was a switch on the wall by the bed which turned on the system; sixty minutes of rain falling on a tin roof. With curtains drawn and tape activated, the bedroom was Bible-black and shelter from the storm.

Myra's rest was disturbed by the sound of a diesel truck approaching. Odd that a semi should pass through their subdivision far from shipping lanes. She heard it again the next night and the next. The engineer had recorded the sound of a passing truck while taping the rain. Actually, it wasn't rain, only the sound of a garden hose sprayed against sheet metal. Now that's real love, Myra thought, when a husband makes somebody hold a hose against hammered tin to simulate the sound of rain for the benefit of his wife's sleep. It gave her something to think about while listening for the truck. She couldn't go to sleep till that truck had passed.

In June, Mercury took Jerry down the wrong road and branded him "Soul Man" like big black letters on a dead-end sign. "Soul My Way," parenting his only pair of singles for 1967, had three songs which could qualify for the soul stigma, otherwise it was more of the same old mistakes. "It's a Hang Up, Baby" substituted a clavichord for piano, and "Turn On Your Love Light" dispensed with keyboards altogether for a rhythm revue brass section, and when the piano is missing from a Jerry Lee Lewis number, it's *really* missing. Jerry's cover versions failed to match or better those of his competitors—"Dream Baby" became a big hit for Glen Campbell, Mickey Newbury's "Just Dropped In" was a smash for Kenny Rogers, and "Hey Baby" did not equal the original by Bruce Channel. Cecil Harrelson contributed "Shotgun Man," which attracted a Rolling Stones' offer to record it for a piece of the publishing that was refused.

"He Took It Like a Man," written by Jerry Lee Lewis, was a song *nobody* would touch. A tribute to those who personified grace under pressure, Jerry erred in making biblical characters the subjects of his lighthearted lyric. To wit, the beheading of John the Baptist was described: "When the axe fell down Johnny didn't even frown/ He laid there/ He took it like a man." Yet another black mark extending the blacklist of his music, this time for sacreligiousness.

At a time when Bobbie Gentry and Bobby Goldsboro were the hottest tickets in country sound and Lulu and The Association had the top pop hits, there was no interest in soul Jerry's way among longtime fans and nothing to attract the new. While on a swing through California, Jerry played the Palomino Club in North Hollywood, which rated a review by Robert Hilburn in *The Los Angeles Times*. Hilburn observed the audience was made up of the "25–30 age group which ten years ago was buying the records that were reshaping popular music." In other reviews, such as the August report in the *Fort Worth Star-Telegram*, the title "grand old man of rock" was bestowed on the thirty-two-year-old singer.

"I've seen 'em come and go, but I'm the onliest one who has

his songs played consistently on country stations, rock stations and Negro stations," Jerry resumed.

"Has switching your style to country increased your popularity?" the writer asked.

"Man, I've been doin' country music from the word go. What was I doin' ten years ago? 'You Win Again' is what I was singin'. You think that ain't country? Oh, sure, they called it rock 'n' roll. Now I do it again and they say I'm going country. I'm doin' the same kind of music I always did. I'm doin' Jerry Lee Lewis."

Doing what he had always done was not earning the kind of money he once made. At the end of the year, he had grossed $114,175.86 and it had cost $89,190.79 to earn it. From the $30,000 overage, more than $5,000 was given to the church and dependents outright, the rest was gobbled up in maintaining the clan. So when Jack Good called at Christmas to say rehearsals for the on-again-off-again production of *Catch My Soul* were definitely on for January, Jerry decided it wise to spend the first five months of 1968 acting for $900 a week. There would be far less expense in remaining stationary, less fatigue, and fewer numbers to support.

The opening had been moved a third time to Los Angeles on March 2 and the lead had been awarded three times before William Marshall, who had played Othello in other companies, took it for keeps. Following a six-week run and two-week hiatus, the show would open on Broadway, a promise of more money and a movie to follow. It was to be the first time in his life that Jerry would be absent from the club circuit for a prolonged period and he wasn't sure he could adapt. It was the perfect time for a change in direction; with the youth market following Jimi Hendrix and Cream, Jerry's future, if there was one, was not in the rock field. The total commitment to country music was inevitable, but he was not receptive to the idea.

It was producer Eddie Kilroy and songwriter Jerry Chestnut who asked Jerry Lee to listen to a song written in the way they thought his country transition would sound best and to which he would least object. Chestnut had written "Another Place, Another Time," a handsome melody about a lonely man at bar-closing time, not hillbilly but unmistakably country. The song was nothing special in Jerry's opinion, nevertheless he consented to try it out in the studio. All at once, and in what looked like the end of days with Mercury, the label had what they were looking for as the one low lament forever changed Jerry's fortunes. Because Jerry Kennedy was contractually Jerry Lee's lone producer, Eddie Kilroy was chased away, not to be seen in the producer's chair at a Lewis session for twelve years. In the meantime, he went to the newly formed Playboy Records with a green Mickey Gilley and beat Mercury at their own game with a Lewis soundalike.

With a feeling of malcontented optimism, Jerry left Nashville to pursue a stage career, having recorded a dozen country songs —fiddle, steel guitar and all—which failed to excite him. For the next three months, he lost himself in the antiquity of Shakespeare and seldom thought of the songs which were going to completely change the rest of his life.

Rehearsals for *Catch My Soul* began January 8, giving Jerry scarcely one week to relocate. He found a furnished apartment a half-block off Sunset Boulevard on Olive Street and returned to Memphis to fetch his family. Myra packed as much as she could squeeze into her new Eldorado, which Cecil drove when everyone departed on the fifth. Their Hollywood home consisted of one bedroom, one bath, a living room-dining room and an out-of-date kitchen equipped with half a stove, single-basined sink and ice box. No matter how nicely decorated, the place looked limited except for the fenced terrace in back. Cecil lived across the commons. Mae Boren Axton, housemother of Heartbreak Hotel and publicist for Linda Gail Lewis, lived not too far away on Sunset.

For Myra, the next three months promised to be everything she had ever wanted out of life—a quiet little place with no one to share it but her husband and baby. There were no road trips or entourage, and having Jerry eat his supper at the dining room table every night at the same time was a sheer delight. He spent his ninety-minute lunch break at home, too. He worked from ten in the morning till ten at night. She had two pans of hot water waiting for his aching feet when he came in. "My job is to see that Jerry get to work on time, which is of most importance in Hollywood," Myra wrote the Malones. "I can't remember when he was this happy. Me, either."

So contented were they that Jerry suggested they consider making Los Angeles their permanent home, and he told Myra to drive around the different neighborhoods to see what she could find.

She idled through exclusive sections of Beverly Hills, mostly for the enjoyment of spotting movie stars' homes rather than finding a home for herself. She had heard of too many cases where moving to Hollywood had made careers fly high while marriages fell apart, and she wasn't for that. She read the movie magazines. She knew what went on at Hollywood parties.

With Jerry on the West Coast, it wasn't long before a whine came up out of the East from two who had been forsaken, Mamie and Linda Gail. "We jus' have to come," Mamie phoned to say, "find us a place near y'all." And Jerry did as he was told and found his mamma a nice apartment two blocks off Hollywood Boulevard where she could stand on the front steps and see the rear of Grauman's Chinese Theatre. Myra's idyll was ended as in-fighting with in-laws resumed. Normalcy, however brief, left an empty feeling at having lost what she had waited ten years for and would never find again.

From Jerry's salary came rents and expenses in maintaining three apartments and feeding six people. The Memphis Beats following him out to LA to back him in the play were not making near as much, forcing them to crowd a motel room to save on multiple rents. Ken Lovelace, separated from his wife to replace Jackie Harrell on guitar, attracted Linda Gail, who was hoping for a fourth husband before her twenty-first birthday. Their affair received little notice until Ken moved in with Linda and Mamie. They were soon married, or said they were, in a clandestine spot in Anaheim. Jerry and Myra chose not to become involved in discussions about Linda's affairs or the complications in Ken's marital status, but it wasn't long before Cecil quit to escape from the maddening circus.

Catch My Soul took its title from a line wherein Othello professes his love for his wife, saying, "Perdition catch my soul, but I do love thee!" It was one of the Bard's better efforts for creating phrases that have found their way into common speech; *Othello* also contains the original references to jealousy as "the green-eyed monster" and sexual intercourse as "making the beast with two backs." Oft quoted is Iago's speech on the relative worth of money compared to the value of a good reputation: "Good name in man and woman . . . /Is the immediate jewel of their souls. /Who steals my purse steals trash . . . /But he that filches from me my good name/Robs me of that which not enriches him/And makes me poor indeed"—particularly poignant when delivered by Jerry Lee Lewis.

Of course, by the time Good reworked the masterpiece, and when spoken by Jerry, the lines bore little resemblance to their former selves. "Jerry's accent seems to take the starch out of Elizabethan structure without disturbing the meaning and force of his speeches," Good told a critic. "The coupling of Jerry Lee Lewis and William Shakespeare seems not to corrupt either. Iago becomes as much Lewis as Lewis becomes Iago, because Jerry is one of those persons who exists like fixed points on a compass by which everything else must be judged. Thirty-two years of southern individuality is not about to be bent out of shape by three hundred sixty-four years of dramatic tradition."

Iago was a cunning schemer with sentiments not unlike the actor's. Vexed at the union of a black man and white woman, he destroys them by moving Othello to insanity with unfounded rumors of his wife's infidelity. Othello smothers her moments before learning the truth from Mrs. Iago. Othello wounds Iago. Iago kills his wife. Othello kills himself, Iago is banished, Cassio becomes governor, stagehands clean up the mess and everybody goes home. "Whatever may be the theme of *Othello*, *Catch My Soul*'s theme is a very obvious one: the clash of contemporary white and black cultures, a clash that tends to be symbolized in young minds in terms of popular music. Othello speaks in a style reminiscent of Martin Luther King and sings music in the general idiom of Motown Records, Detroit. Iago sounds a bit like George Wallace and sings songs of the Sun Records, Memphis variety. The whole piece is presented with comic-strip clarity as a medieval morality play," Good explained.

Quite an ambitious undertaking. A rare feat in theater, to sum the essence of the strident sixties within the framework of a seventy-minute Elizabethan play. However, Good played to the wrong crowd. His production was part of a subscription-supported season patronized by the cuff-link crowd, whereas it had been designed to attract "young people who read Shakespeare and dig The Righteous Brothers." On March 5, the curtain went up before an opening-night crowd decked out in tuxedoes and gowns, patrons of the arts every one, dukes and duchesses of society. They were confronted by Jerry Lee Lewis sporting a devilish goatee and blackened coiffure, singing vandalized verse from a green gilt grand piano pulpit belching red smoke. Every major publication was represented by critics, who attacked everything from the decor of the theater's men's room to the shine on the actors' shoes.

Variety: "Jerry Lee Lewis, quondam rock-roll sensation in acting debut, makes of Iago an often chilling contemporary schemer, despite a sing-song recital of lines. While the many show elements are top notch to weak, the combination is erratic."

Los Angeles Times: "When Lewis tells a wiggling chorine: 'Shake it and break it and wrap it up and take it,' it fits the play better than 'O, mistress, villany hath made mocks with love.'"

Associated Press: "Nowhere was the cultural gap more blatant than in the performance of pop singer Jerry Lee Lewis as Iago. He is secure in his blues-shouting of the songs, but his rendition of the *Othello* soliloquys in his native Louisiana tone is something else."

Open City: "What the large audience witnessed was a lavish, overly-loud hodgepodge of bad music, grotesque scenery, cluttered choreography, unimaginative and distracting lighting and acting poor to the point of irritation—especially on the part of Jerry Lee Lewis."

Los Angeles Free Press: "What *Catch My Soul* needs is a Ray Charles or a Little Richard or an Otis Redding to play Othello to Jerry Lee Lewis's Iago—an Othello with soul, a soul to catch. Without an Othello who knows from inside his guts what it's like to be black in a white man's world, *Catch My Soul* takes ten steps backward for every step it takes forward in terms of concept."

Rolling Stone praised the play as "the first serious offensive by rock upon the sham that is the American 'musical' theater," and *Cash Box* recommended West Coasters catch the show, but there was other news in the same issues of the music magazines of far greater importance to Jerry. The release of his new single, "Another Place, Another Time," was his first breakthrough in ten years. Country deejays were convinced that the new Jerry was the old Jerry, the one who came out of Louisiana singing Hank Williams and Jimmie Rodgers before he got all shook up, and Mercury guaranteed there would be no backsliding to boogie. The question was put to Jerry: Whither wilt thou goest, Broadway or Nashville?

On April 13, the curtain dropped for the last time on *Catch My Soul*. In the last week it grossed more than eighty-seven thousand dollars, the largest take of the run. "Another Place, Another Time" had already sold one hundred thousand copies and ranked Number 3 in the country top ten. The big question was answered for Jerry when the Schubert Theatre withdrew its support and Jack Good's hopes of finding a Broadway home were ended. Ray Brown wasted no time in planning a tour for Jerry commencing on the day following his return to Memphis.

In her heart, Myra knew a hit record meant the end of domestic tranquillity. Together, she and Jerry had toughed it out over the long, lonesome road, bonded by pain and adversity, joined only by love and the hardships they had endured hand in hand. Death, doom and disaster were elements they came to know and learned to live with, disappointment they could handle. Success was quite different. Victory, hard fought and bitterly won, was the beginning of the end. There were going to be changes now that the struggle was over. Forgotten were his promises to retreat to a pastoral life; Jerry would walk the streets paved with gold alone.

"What's Made Milwaukee Famous (Has Made a Loser Out of Me)" was Number 2 on the country charts in June 1968, in spite of the cornball lyrics transforming the Killer into the lonesome loser persona so popular with fans of that ilk and Jerry's difficulty with creating a new image. One promotion pictured him glumly reflecting over a can of beer at the end of a bar, another depicted him in a purple velvet Nehru jacket picking flowers in an open field. Mercury obviously had no idea how to promote a fifties shaker reborn in the psychedelic sixties as a country singer.

"I've been country all my life," Jerry remarked, "only thing is I'm a little bit more serious about it now. I'm not a rock 'n' roll singer. Even if rock 'n' roll is revived, I would stay country."

And on the strength of that bold promise, country radio kept its part of the bargain by making Jerry a hit all over again.

"She Still Comes Around (To Love What's Left of Me)" was another Number 2 chart entry at the end of September. And at the end of 1968, in the very last week, "To Make Love Sweeter for You" became Jerry's first Number 1 hit since "Great Balls of Fire." The only element depleting the force of his comeback was the release of a duet album with his sister, and even then they managed to inch into the top ten with "Don't Let Me Cross Over" in May 1969. "One Has My Name, the Other Has My Heart," sans Linda Gail, climbed to Number 3, yet later in the year their duet on "Roll Over Beethoven" plummeted to Number 71, a warning from country radio to shed dead weight and refrain from further temptations of backsliding to rock 'n' roll.

Good fortune breeds parasites, and Jerry's prosperity brought Sam Phillips out of the woodwork to take advantage of him again as the Mercury contract came to an end. With Kemmons Wilson, founder of the Holiday Inn hotel chain, Sam started a new label simply dubbed Holiday Inn Records and tried to win Jerry over by equalling Mercury's offer. Jerry had the satisfaction of turning him away, but Sam devised other means by which to exploit the artist who once made Sun shine. Oddly, it was Cecil who motivated Sam toward the wise decision to regenerate his label.

"I'll give you ten thousand dollars for all rights to Jerry's Sun tapes," Sam offered Cecil. "There's about a hundred and sixty songs, most of 'em ten years old by now."

"Think that's a fair price?" Cecil asked.

"It's more than fair."

"Well, I'll give you a hundred an' fifty thousand if you'll sell 'em back to us," Cecil said, secretly knowing Mercury's intention to buy the Lewis archives for two hundred thousand dollars.

Sam gasped. "For that much, I'll throw in the publishin' rights."

"Sold," said Cecil. "How you want your money?"

"Lemme ask my accountant an' I'll get back to you. But we got a deal, now, a verbal contract. You've bought them tapes," said Sam, then began to think about the proposition. He called Shelby Singleton, now head of his own label, and asked his opinion on why a bag of old chestnuts should fetch such a high price.

"It's obvious," said Shelby, "Jerry's a hit again, an' you got some of his best stuff in the can unopened. It's worth a fortune."

When next Sam spoke to Cecil, it was to inform him the deal was off. He gave no reason, but soon everyone learned that Shelby Singleton had purchased the entire Sun library for $250,000, leaving 25 percent in the hands of Sam Phillips and reorganizing as Sun International. One of their first releases was "Invitation to Your Party," recorded by Jerry Lee Lewis in July 1963. In July 1969, the song went to Number 6 on the charts, leaving Jerry to wonder at its fate had it been released and properly promoted six years before. Sun International pulled the same stunt in making Jerry's 1963 vintages "One Minute Past Eternity," "I Can't Seem To Say Goodbye" and "Waiting for a Train" Numbers 2, 7 and 11 respectively, equalling or bettering the new songs released by Mercury. Everyone made money on Jerry's music except Jerry. But every time Cecil engaged attorneys to recover a fortune in unpaid royalties or challenge ownership of the masters, Jerry would override him, saying, "I got two companies puttin' out hits on me. Don't sue."

Nineteen sixty-nine began with three weeks of sellouts in Lake Tahoe. In March, Jerry was special guest on Tom Jones's television show in London, then played to standing room only in New York. He took part in The Monkees' television special in March. In June, he was tied with Buck Owens for *Billboard*'s Country Music Artist of the Year in record sales, prompting invitations to appear on *Hee Haw, The Glen Campbell Show,* Dick Cavett, Ed Sullivan, and in concert at Carnegie Hall. In December, Jerry headlined the Toronto Rock 'n' Roll Festival, a two-day outdoor event notable for the debut of John Lennon's Plastic Ono Band and memorable appearances by Bo Diddley, Chuck Berry, Gene Vincent, Little Richard, Alice Cooper, The Doors and Screamin' Lord Sutch.

The album "She Even Woke Me Up to Say Goodbye" spawned two Number 2 hits, the title cut by Mickey Newbury and "Once More With Feeling" by newcomer Kris Kristofferson. It was undoubtedly Jerry's finest album, a return to improvisation sorely lacking on previous efforts, bringing the Killer persona of stage fame into the recording studio for the first time. He refashioned Merle Haggard's "Workin' Man Blues," Faron Young's "Wine

Me Up" and Ivory Joe Hunter's "Since I Met You Baby," employing his deepest chest voice and perfect piano breaks, what Jerry called "hangin' it in." Lest anyone forget, "Whole Lot of Shakin'" was worked into his version of Chuck Berry's "Brown-Eyed Handsome Man." It was a great album. It was a remarkable year. Why, then, was Jerry unhappy? What was the source of his discontent? His past, the one thing he could not change.

The real disasters in Jerry's life did not occur until after he got what he wanted. Waiting ten years to be rightfully restored made him mad, knowing he possessed the talent which would have earned him a hundred hits had the ban on his music not been imposed. The same promoters and disc jockeys participating in the boycott now gathered around him like old pals. Jerry seemingly never met an enemy. Thus, he could find no one to blame for his mistreatment or bear his anger and frustration. Myra, his only companion through the lean years, was also a constant reminder of his struggle; he did not blame her for his failure, rather accused her of mismanaging his success.

Success was far more difficult than failure for Jerry to handle —opposition provided a challenge which required every resource he could muster to win the fight, but stardom asked nothing more of him than to enjoy his belated just desserts. The luxuries of luminance were showered upon him, and he gathered them in with open arms. Alas, with every pill, each sip from the bottle and stranger's kiss, the guilt which drives Pentecostals insane or to the altar welled up within him. And what of his promise, his part of the deal struck with his God of bargains? He was obliged to surrender worldly gain for unfinished work for the Lord, an obligation he refrained from meeting again and again, for which he would be punished again and again. Myra was a constant reminder of his covenant. She became the scapegoat for his frustrations and the lamb for his sacrifice. Jerry broke his promise, choosing rock 'n' roll over religion and Mammon over Myra. The Lord withdrew His spirit from Jerry, but saved Myra from a terrible fate.

The Big Hurt began with a thousand smaller ones, telephone calls perverting Jerry's guilt into Myra's fault. He had been away from home three days, enjoying life in the fast lane, when he awoke at four A.M. and was confronted with the embodiment of deadly sin in the shape of a whore lying beside him. His guilt came as a runner. He called home, shouting accusations of adultery at himself, using Myra as his alter ego.

"You motherfuckin' whore, who the hell do you think you are?"

"Is that you, Jerry?" she said, half-asleep.

"Who's it s'posed to be, you slut? You expectin' a call from somebody else?"

"Jerry, are you all right?"

"Whaddya mean am I all right? Of course I'm all right. I never been better."

"Why are you callin' in the middle of the night?"

"Who the hell are you to tell me not to call in the middle of the night? I'll call you anytime I want, an' you better be there. Alone."

"I've never been unfaithful to you, Jerry. You know that."

"Whoa, now, you weren't no virgin when I married you, y'know."

Myra paused. "I'm a good wife. I keep a nice home . . ."

"You ain't the one bustin' your ass out on the road," he interrupted, "stuck in the backseat of some damn car—"

"Somebody has to raise Phoebe," she reasoned.

"My mother can do that. You should be here with me," he said, watching his lover leave the room.

"You're lucky to have a good home to come home to," she added.

"Well, then, jus' call me Mr. Lucky."

The next day, when the demons had fled, Jerry called Myra to apologize. "I'm sorry, baby, I don't have nobody else to beat on. It won't happen again," he promised, and it wouldn't happen again until the next night, when at three or four in the morning, Mr. Hyde hollered accusations at his wife only to retract them the following day. It happened the same way nearly every night that Jerry was on the road, and he was gone twenty-five days out of every month. As unnerving as it was, Myra was not about to leave Jerry for a little thing like nightly abusive phone calls. She was made of stronger stuff. So was he.

At Jerry's insistence, Myra sometimes joined him on the road. He punished her by staying out all night with the boys, leaving her alone in a motel room till he was good and ready for bed, then arrived drunk and expecting her to treat him like one of his party girls. In the morning, he started bitchin' before his feet hit the floor. He was the same at home, but because Myra forbade his drinking in the house, her ceramic workshop was converted into a playroom laughingly referred to as the "den of iniquity" where he could howl at the moon to his heart's content. "If you don't like what I do," he threatened, "you can walk on down the road an' take your clothes with you. Jus' leave Phoebe with me."

Back came Myra's nervous attacks, tying her stomach in knots and causing her face to erupt in shinglelike patches. Her doctor prescribed powerful tranquilizers when injections of cortisone failed. Medicinal dependence plunged her into long spells of depression when she wanted to do nothing but sleep. She lost interest in life. She was wretchedly unhappy. When all else failed, Myra returned to church. Fleeing from the hellhole late one night, she stumbled into her church and knelt at the altar, praying and crying incessantly. She would not be comforted. She returned home only to have her husband taunt her. "You're a real Christian, ain'tcha? Yeah. God punished you, didn't He, girl? Took your son away from you."

Myra broke. She ran out of the house into the backyard screaming. She fell to the ground, pleading for the earth to open up and swallow her. She did not want to live.

It's not the first year of marriage that's hard, it's the last one, and like most of their thirteen years, Myra and Jerry spent 1970 apart. He called to check up on her morning, noon and night, cussing and accusing her of the sins of every whore in hell. While driving through Texas in June, Jerry stopped at a roadside pay station to call Myra for her daily allotment of grief and she hung up on him till he ran out of dimes. "She knows I can't get to her," he declared. "But I'm gonna buy me a damn plane so the next time she hangs up on me I'll fly home an' beat hell outta her," and the next day dropped twenty-five thousand dollars on a dilapidated DC-3 to that end.

Jerry gradually worsened. One July morning, Myra woke to find her husband and her father still drinking in the den of iniquity from the night before. A fight started, and Myra called the police. Jerry knocked her to the floor and threatened to kill her if she ever made a stupid mistake like that again.

Jerry came home one hot August night lookin' for love at the wrong place, wrong time.

"No," Myra croaked in her sleep.

"You don't tell me no," said Jerry.

"I just did," she yawned.

"To hell with you," said Jerry, and locked himself in the bathroom with his medicine jar.

Now was the perfect chance to leave him. Myra pulled on a housecoat and got in her car, not knowing where she was headed. Jerry tried to stop her, threw rocks when he couldn't get her door open. He pursued, passed her on a deserted stretch and ran her off the road. He forced her to return home, where she was made to pay dearly for her transgressions.

"If you ever leave me again," he kissed her, "I'll throw acid in your face."

He tightened his grip. "If you ever leave me, I'll throw you in the river," he said, kissing her again.

"Leave me," he kissed her hard, "an' I'll kill ya."

At wit's end, Myra came down to one final course of action: If she could not escape, she would kill her husband before he killed her. No, she couldn't commit murder. Hurt him maybe, or cripple him. Illness was the best idea. Confinement to bed would cause him to rely on her and give her the chance to nurse him. Illness would cause her to take pity on him and turn her hatred to love again. So she set out to the pharmacist for a potion to make him sick as a dog. She didn't know what to look for, avoiding bottles with skull and crossbones to search among the diuretics and emetics, hoping to find some mild poison causing him to nearly defecate to death. She sorted through sneezewort, soapberry, snakeroot and wintergreen till she found oil of eucalyptus, a derivative from the myrtle shrub used since times ancient to open the sinuses. At supper that night, Myra slipped a vial into Jerry's milk, not sure what was going to happen. She watched him take a sip, then blanch.

"This milk has soured," he complained, and poured it out, thereby sparing Myra from life imprisonment or, at the very least, Jerry's stomach ache.

The idea of divorce ran hot and cold with Myra until August, when "the other woman" called. Myra hesitated to believe the report, but if it was true, she would have a way out of this unhappy marriage without taking a guilty conscience with her. She could tolerate drinkin', dopin' and the phone calls, could even cope with physical abuse, but adultery was the unforgivable last straw. She was furious, yet the Bible had taught her to forgive seventy times seventy offenses a day, and she sat Jerry down in an effort to get him to open up to her. Communication was difficult, as it had always been.

"I want you to know I'm aware of what you're doin'," she said, placing her hands in his. "The only thing I can say is please stop."

"Baby, I know I been workin' too hard an' stayin' away too long. I'm gonna cool it. Don't worry."

Jerry did not pick up on Myra's message, and she could not bring herself to mention adultery, fearing his short fuse. She did not know what else to do. She had to have proof before taking legal action. After all the mistreatment she had suffered, she was going to make certain of his sins, then shove them down his throat. She wanted evidence. She wanted photos. She wanted revenge.

Myra called the first listing in the telephone directory under detectives and retained Accredited Security Systems, made up of a married couple named Ken and Marianne and their flunky, Pete Malito. It was the kind of bumbling operation which gave private eyes a black eye. The Three Stooges Meet the Killer. They agreed to take the case for twenty-five dollars an hour plus expenses, and spent August and September tailing Jerry from town to town, bugging his hotel rooms, setting up misfiring photographic surveillance in closets and peeking through keyholes. They either missed every chance to catch their quarry or botched the snare, but because they were employed by a wealthy pigeon, they were in no rush for results. Myra shelled out thirty-thousand dollars to learn she was married to an absolute angel.

"Send us to Australia with him in October," the Keystone Cops pleaded. "That's where we'll really nail him."

"No," said Myra. "I'm puttin' a stop to this right now. You're off the case." Drowning in a sea of insanity, Myra killed a bottle of Valium and called her secret agents before lapsing into a coma. Ken, Marianne and Pete rushed over to pour coffee down her and keep her up. Pete never let go. At the end of a marriage to a pregnant wife with two children, Pete let Myra know that she could call on him for anything and reminded her often.

Jerry called to say he would not be home for another day or two, then surprised her at three A.M. of the same day by showing up and complaining there was no supper simmering on the stove. He fixed himself a bologna sandwich and glass of milk, throwing food all over the place, then entered their bedroom and thumped Myra three times on the noggin to demand why she didn't arise to serve her master. Startled from her sleep, she lifted her arms to ward off his blow and struck him. He grabbed her fists and beat her face black and blue. "Look, Phoebe," Jerry said to their seven-year-old, "your mamma's gone crazy. She's hittin' herself in the face."

Myra could not go out of the house for a week. Her eyes were swollen and her face was bruised. Her husband needed help, and she took it upon herself to save him from himself. She began by going into his bag for his pills, the blue and yellow diet ones that wired him for action, and flushed them down the toilet. When his stash was discovered missing, he flew into a rage, bashing out the patio sliding glass doors and bashing Myra to the floor. She grabbed their daughter and hid in the bedroom behind locked doors until Jerry took off for a nightclub.

The phone rang at three that morning, and demons cursed her in shrill voices. Myra pulled a pearlhandled pistol from the night-stand and put it to her head and told Jerry what she was about to do. The demons went silent. Then, very softly, he said, "Put the phone close so I can hear it go off."

Something inside Myra snapped. She looked at the phone as if it were a person, then at the gun, and ever so easily put it back in the drawer and slowly closed it. She beat the telephone into a thousand pieces, screaming "No! No! No!" No sonofabitch was ever going to make Myra kill herself. She knew then she was getting out and taking her daughter with her.

The phone rang in the kitchen; perhaps it was Jerry frantically trying to save her from suicide. Picking up the receiver to relish his reaction, she heard another voice. It was a fan of Jerry's, a car salesman from Oklahoma City named Jackie Mansell.

"I shot my wife in the face accidental when she tried to stop me from killing myself," Jackie said. "I thought she was cheatin' on me and was gonna leave me for another man. I think she's gettin' a divorce."

"That's funny, I am, too," Myra admitted for the first time.

"Really?" Jackie perked. "I been in love with you for years, Myra. I'm sendin' a plane after you tomorrow."

"Jackie," she said, "I've never had those kind of feelin's for you—"

"I'm comin' to Memphis tomorrow, Myra. Get ready," he said, and hung up.

Myra spent the next three days in a motel while Jackie camped out on her doorstep waiting for her to come home. At the end of the third day, he gave up and went back to Oklahoma City, where he sealed himself in his garage, left the motor running and gassed himself to death.

It was October, and Jerry left for Australia on the twenty-fifth for three weeks. Myra was at home spending most of her time in church, praying for strength and guidance without a sign from heaven. A friend approached her with the tale of a remarkable woman in Waycross, Georgia. "Sister Little," the friend said, "is an angel of the Lord. She will tell you which way to turn."

Myra called upon Sister Little, identifying herself only as Sister Lewis. "I'm calling to ask your advice about my marriage. What can you tell me?"

"I can't tell you anything," said Sister Little, "but if God has something to say to you, He will reveal it through me. I'll pray about it. You must pray, too, sister."

Six days passed without word from Sister Little. It was the last day of the month, Halloween, and Sister Frances had come to comfort Myra's woes. "Let's call Sister Little," she said, and Myra placed the call as Frances listened in.

When Myra identified herself, Sister Little began to weep and wail and speak in tongues and prophesy. "Behold, my daughter, I have seen your tears and heard your cries. Demons of death and dementia are all around you, a dark cloud surrounds your home —alcohol, adultery, suicide and drugs. God has opened the door for you to leave. You have stayed, and argued with the Lord. Get out. Get out now. I see murder, a murder and a suicide. Get out. God has shown you the way. He has opened the door. Why won't you go?"

Myra was in hysterics. Frances was crying, too. The doorbell was ringing, ringing, ringing; demons come for tricks or treats.

The next dawn, a Sunday, Myra was in church, where she was

uplifted in a new and higher spirit. The night of ignorance in which she had made all of life's important decisions was lifted away. God made a crooked path straight, and she could no longer resist God's will. No longer was her highest mission in life to be the wife of Jerry Lee Lewis. To her credit, and to her detriment, she had continued to stand beside him even while he rose up against her, and there was too much anger and frustration in him to change. She considered herself lucky to have known him, and faced the grim possibility that she would never find true love, for every man thereafter would have a legend to live up to and surpass. One feast, one house, one mutual happiness was all she ever desired, and the one wish she was never granted. She could not have loved him more, only longer.

On Monday, Myra made straightaway to an attorney's office and spent the entire day relating her unhappy tale, finding it impossible to put into words her experiences of the past dozen years. "Our troubles began as soon as we were married, when Jerry spent three days in Los Angeles with a girl named Lynn," Myra began, and satisfied her counselor's curiosity with a litany of misdeeds upon which a petition for divorce could be based; silly, in the way a description of the torment caused by Jerry accusing her of Stevie's death ran alongside the tale of how he once hit her with a plate of spaghetti.

Myra spent the next day apartment hunting and found a place on Candace Drive in Whitehaven where she stored a set of dishes, pots, pans and blankets and moved her clothes and the washer and dryer. Everything else needed to begin life anew was new. By Friday, Myra had strengthened her fragile grip on life and was prepared to move herself and her daughter to their new home on Sunday. She wanted to serve him personally, for it would be too cruel to have an officer do it. She took the precaution of bringing a plainclothes warrant officer with her to the airport and hired Pete the detective for protection in case of violence.

The plane taxied to a stop at the terminal gate. It was three A.M., and the passengers were fatigued from the long flight. The Lewis party had been partying for the past forty hours, raising so much hell on the flight from Australia that the plane stopped in Fiji to put them off. They were still wound up like an eight-day clock when they touched home. Jerry emerged, surprised to find Myra come to greet him so late and in inclement weather.

"I was thinkin' you'd better be here. I knew the other wives would be waitin', so it's a good thing you came, too," he said, cocking his sunglasses over his head and putting his arm around her.

She betrayed him with a kiss. "Jerry, this man has something for you."

The warrant officer pulled back his jacket to reveal his badge. "Mister Lewis, you wanna step over here so I can talk to you?"

"No. You can say whatever you got to say right here."

"You are hereby officially served in the matter of Myra Gale Brown Lewis versus Jerry Lee Lewis in an action for divorce . . ."

"What is this, baby?" Jerry questioned.

"You heard him, Jerry. That's what it is."

"Get outta my way," Jerry said, shoving the officer aside. The officer went for his gun, and Jerry moved past him, saying, "I said get outta my way!"

They walked to the car, still arm in arm, the tears beginning to cloud Jerry's vision and roll down his face. "Myra, I don't jus' love you, I worship your guts. You're my whole life."

"Get in, Jerry. I'll take you home."

Pete pulled up behind them in another of the Lewises' Lincolns, and Jerry asked, "Who's he?"

"A detective. I've had you followed."

Jerry sank in his seat, covering his eyes with his hand. "Myra, you can't leave now. Our life together is gonna be so beautiful. Things are just now gettin' good again. I know I done you wrong. I know I hurt you, but, baby, you never said anything. You never gimme a warnin'. I didn't know it was this bad. I can't b'lieve you'd do me this way."

Myra did not speak. She took Jerry inside, where the entourage had assembled to learn what had happened. They congregated in the den of iniquity while Myra fixed her last supper for her husband.

"Can you b'lieve this li'l girl is tryin' to divorce me?" Jerry asked, trying to crack her defenses with a smile. "Idn't that the most ridiculous thing you ever heard?"

He reached for her hand as she walked by and felt her small, cold fingers. "Let's go to bed, baby," he said, as two sleepless days and nights closed in on him.

She followed him into the bedroom, where he fell back on the mattress, still dressed. He was totally exhausted, mentally, physically and emotionally. Myra sat next to him, holding his hand.

"Don't leave me," he murmured as tears leaked from the corner of his eyes onto the pillow. He skimmed below the surface of sleep, waking whenever she stirred to repeat, "Don't leave."

He fell fast asleep, and she withdrew from his clutch. She walked through the dark palace without pain or remorse, no sudden impulse to change her mind, no well of emotion for fond memories. She stepped out into the November night, cold and wet, the sheeted rain providing a perfect good-bye. And as she left the driveway for the last time, she saw him standing at the front door, arms reaching out, crying, "Please, don't leave."

Epilogue

CRAWLING FROM THE WRECKAGE OF THEIR home, Jerry tried everything in his power to win Myra back, including surrendering his life to Christ. He made a full confession: He admitted their misfortunes were God's punishment for his sins, not hers. He admitted the spiteful interference of his family, promising it would cease. He pledged never to look at another woman, drink another drop or pop another pill. He'd even give up rock 'n' roll, for God's sake, if she'd only come back.

Myra did not believe him. Jerry was willing to put it in writing, a signed contract, giving her every penny of his royalties for the rest of his life, what amounted to millions of dollars, for her love and affection. It wasn't worth it, she said.

On December 11, 1970, Walter Cronkite announced on the national evening news that Jerry Lee Lewis had given up rock for gospel, cancelling all shows and vowing never to set foot in a nightclub again.

"I've made a stand for God," said Jerry. "I'm just letting people know openly that I went back to the church and I got myself saved, and the Lord forgave me my sins and wiped 'em away." And in support of his longstanding heavenly debt, Jerry recorded his "best album," a gospel collection entitled "In Loving Memories," for Christmas.

"It won't last," Myra said of Jerry's salvation. "He's just doing this to get me back."

Church members appealed to her in Jerry's behalf. Her preacher appeared on her doorstep with the penitent to offer testimony of the miraculous conversion. "He's changed," said the preacher. "Look at him. He's fasted five days!"

"I'm a Christian," said Jerry. "If you're a Christian, you'll forgive me," but the Lord hardened her heart.

He wept openly, continually. "Hasn't she punished me enough?" he begged of Lois and J. W. Brown, and they, too, were so moved by his humility that they sponsored the reconciliation.

Myra, to her own amazement, was resolute in resisting her husband, the love of her life, the father of her children. She visited a psychiatrist to ask his advice. "After all I've been through, I think I might be crazy," she said. "If I ain't crazy, I must be nuts for remaining sane." The doctor could not untangle that knot.

Ten days after his sanctification, Jerry came to see Phoebe, at two A.M., trying to kick Myra's unanswered door down. "I've got a gun," he said, and bashed out a window to crawl inside as Myra phoned police.

The police asked for Jerry's autograph and went away. Myra, defenseless, had burglar bars installed, and called Pete Malito to protect her from evil. Pete avowed it would become a full-time job.

Mamie Lewis had been treated in Houston, Texas, for aches and pains in August 1970. She had cancer of the everything—heart, lungs, and esophagus, and she was spared the details, according to her children's wishes. She was given six months to live, and those six months would be made as comfortable as possible.

"I mustn't be too sick," Mamie said to her family. "Y'all always seem so happy around me." And the strain of putting up a pleasant front destroyed her daughter's nerves. Jerry only visited twice in the end of days, unable to withstand the pain of watching the light of his life flicker and fade. His parting tribute was the purchase of a new Cadillac which was parked and left unused outside Mamie's bedroom window for her to admire.

Cecil Harrelson was the only person to nurse Mamie. For the last three months of her life, he attended her around the clock, making excuses for absent kin and comforting her fears with assurances that she was weathering a bout with hepatitis.

On Easter Sunday, when Jerry could no longer withstand

haunting memories of Stevie and the pending death of his mother, he broke faith with God, reneging on his spiritual commitment to go on a bender. Late into the following day, Cecil found him at the Vapors nightclub in the company of demons, and gave Jerry the news that his mother had lapsed into a coma. She died April 21, 1971.

If ever Jerry suffered a deeper hurt than this, no one knows it; he could not speak it. His soul was bound up with his mother's soul, his heart with her heart; all the good was gone.

Three weeks after losing his mother, Jerry lost the only other woman in his life as the final decree of divorce ending his marriage to Myra was entered; it was the final blow.

"Remember, Myra," he said, "you're no 'Lizabeth Taylor. You're too dumb an' ugly for no man to ever want you." Insults and preying upon her weakness proved no more successful in chasing her back to him than salvation and repentance.

Myra married her bodyguard on September 3, just to prove Jerry wrong; somebody would take her. She tried to call it off two days before, but Pete, so close to a fortune, threatened a nervous breakdown, and she relented.

Pete worked for an insurance company for two hundred dollars a week. He applied for a job with the Memphis Police and was stonewalled by Jaren Pate, a sheriff's secretary with clout at the courthouse and girlfriend of Jerry Lee Lewis. Pete was fairly run out of town, getting on with a car-rental agency which moved him and his family to Atlanta.

Pete knocked down $158 a week. Myra received one thousand dollars a month from her settlement and with it purchased a house, cars and anything else they needed. Jealousy of Jerry drove Pete crazy. No trace of Myra's former life could be found in their home, not even a piano. Pete suggested that he and Myra could never have a real family unless all assets were lumped in a communal pot for each to share and share alike. Refusing to compromise Phoebe's secured future, she advised Pete to dig for gold elsewhere. She was alone again. She was twenty-nine.

Jerry married Jaren thirty days after Myra remarried. "She's drivin' me crazy," was the way he explained Jaren's proposal, and he went through the charade more out of spite than love; that, and because Jaren was pregnant. They did not last two weeks. Di-

vorce proceedings dragged on over the next ten years; Myra had
halved Jerry's fortune, and it would not be halved again.

From the time Jerry Lee Lewis, Jr., was thirteen, he expressed
a desire to join his daddy's act. In August 1970, he replaced his
mentor, drummer Tarp Tarrant, while Tarp was in the hospital.
Upon Tarp's return to action, Junior became deputy drummer,
tambourine shaker, backup vocalist and Dad's warm-up act.

Junior heard the song of fools and learned the words by heart.
Not only did he learn how to rock but how to live like a rocker.
His father, his shining example, was powerless to preach abstention while showing the reckless way. Jerry's attempts at repri-
manding his son turned into fist fights, and matters only became
worse.

Before he was nineteen, Junior was in and out of mental hospi-
tals and drug addiction wards five times, spending anywhere from
two weeks to seven or eight months at a stretch drying out. He
had inherited the tolerance and constitution of his ancestry, and
rebounded for more in the Lewis way. At the hospital in Mande-
ville, Jerry foisted the blame for Junior's ruin on Jane, Tarp and
the other bastards in his band, and demanded the boy's release
into the custody of his ailing grandmother.

At Mamie's funeral, Junior was in distress. Thanking the
preacher for his kindness, Junior invited him to come back again
real soon. And the preacher returned in his black suit, Bible
opened to the last rites, for the burial of Junior on November 13,
1973. He had gone to a garage to tow a repaired car with his jeep
and on the way home the hitch came loose, causing the car in tow
to sway, hit a bridge abutment and flip over, breaking Junior's
neck.

The Lord hid His face. Jerry bore His rage, His fierce wrath
and the terrors which put his friends far from him and his family
into darkness. Let no male child issue forth; every victory vanity,
downed and strangled every joy.

In the ten years following his divorce from Myra and the loss of
his loved ones, Jerry was always at the center of some sort of
conflict. Everything he touched became lost, broken or bruised.
He killed off all of his followers in drinking bouts, but they continued to follow. Band members were drugged into oblivion, used

up and discarded like squeezed dry tubes of toothpaste; they made no sound; no one opposed his views. He came down on women, tearing them to pieces, yet they continued to come into his company. He amused himself by embarrassing his fans, but still they are there. He tempted death in ways no illusionist can master: breathing fire from the hash-filled bowl, swallowing drugs till his belly burst, blindly speeding down dark country roads, a torque of twisting arms and legs on the brink of destruction or conversion; always some sort of conflict for which there is no solution.

The seventies read like a police blotter: suits for assault, arrests for disorderly conduct, incarceration for driving under the influence of drugs and alcohol, wrecking a Rolls, crashing a Corvette, suits for divorce, hundreds more for cancelled shows and defaulted payments on cars, homes and airplanes. He rented office space and shot through the walls into adjoining businesses. He shot his bass player, at neighbors, and was accused of comin' after Elvis. A contract was taken out on Myra's life. So many liens were placed against his recording contract that royalties were exhausted. The Internal Revenue turned his life into a nightmare, raiding his home for stuff to sell at public auction and showing up at box offices all over the country to confiscate receipts. He was hospitalized for a broken nose, influenza, ulcers, gall bladder, respiratory failure, drug abuse, exhaustion and a ruptured stomach, a boomerang-shaped scar evidencing a onetime less than 5 percent chance of survival. Jaren and Linda Gail pressed for his committal to a mental institution. He ripped the tubes from his nose and the needle from his arm and walked out of the hospital unassisted, threatening to kill whoever signed commitment papers. He went home to install an iron door to his bedroom, hid guns in every corner, and went into his game room to sail his records edgewise into the walls where they remained embedded, a monument to gleeful rage.

The press had a field day all the while; count on the Killer for colorful copy. Jerry, who had learned that headlines don't always mean glory, never trusted the truth with any reporter; they lied. No matter what he said, or how it was intended, his words were twisted around and thrown back in his face. If the press wanted lies, they would print *his* lies. If they were dumb enough to believe he set fire to pianos, he might as well tell 'em what they wanted to hear. Jerry himself lost track of the truth, falsifying facts and calling the results a higher truth. Interviews turned into indignation, and the press lost sight of the setbacks and tragic losses which robbed him of a livelihood and the joys in life.

"Fame," said Jud Phillips, "creates images around its victims and heroes. Fame is the sum of misunderstandings that gather around a fool."

In September 1976, following an all-night bout with the bottles, Jerry and his bass player, Butch Owens, sat in the den of Jaren's home in Collierville, Tennessee, listening to dubs from a forthcoming album. They weren't the greatest songs Butch had ever heard, and Jerry asked Jaren to bring him his .357 magnum to change his mind. Toying with the revolver, Jerry fired, an obstructing bottle causing the bullet to fragment but imbedding Butch with a spray of glass. Butch was made to lie down on the front lawn so as not to bleed on Jaren's white carpet; his wife was forbidden to use Jaren's phone and ran next door. At one time or another, the media reported that Jerry and Butch were playing Russian roulette, Butch had insulted Jerry's music, Butch had been giving dope to Myra's brother, Rusty, who worked as Jerry's drummer from 1975–77, Butch had kept dope purchased for Jerry, and that Jerry was taking target practice at the bottle. The real reason lies somewhere in a combination of all theories. Butch sued for compensatory and punitive damages in the original amount of four hundred thousand dollars, which was whittled away to less than half that amount on appeals, and of which no part was paid by the Killer.

Whether Jerry meant to shoot Elvis Presley on the night of November 23, 1976, the media did not seem to care. It was late at night and Jerry Lee Lewis turned up at the gates of Graceland under some ungodly influence, a gun surfaced, and the press took it from there. Jerry maintained that he had come to Presley's rescue, that the bloated Caesar was wallowing in the throes of drug-induced death and he called Jerry repeatedly for help—help which Jerry refused him till it was too late. Elvis was dead within a year, and while the press was concerned only with whether he and Jerry had been friend or foe, Jerry knew in his heart that it was another life he would have to account for to the Lord.

Elmo Lewis died July 21, 1979, at age seventy-one. He spent the last ten years of his life raisin' hell, like his daddy before him.

He and his son alternately shared a bottle and swapped barbs, and one of their more heated exchanges nearly ended the relationship altogether when Elmo took a shot at Jerry, hitting a bystander instead.

Elmo boasted his own arrest record down at the police station, and once dodged another drunk driving charge by ditching his car, moving over into the passenger's seat and convincing highway patrolmen that a crazy man had been driving and ran off into the woods. As in the thirties, Elmo continued to dabble in moonshine and was charged with possessing untaxed whiskey. "I can understand DUI and resistin' arrest," he said, "but what's this bit about untaxed whiskey?"

"Untaxed—bootleg, moonshine," the officer defined.

"Now, you gonna have to prove in court I didn't pay the tax on that goddam whiskey," Elmo defended.

At a time when Jerry thought nothing of giving his mother two, three thousand in cash, he wouldn't spare his father twenty bucks to buy a new pair of shoes, for he knew Elmo would either throw the money away or give the shoes to someone less fortunate. Like his daddy, Jerry was generous to a fault in caring for his family and friends, and what he did not give away, people freely took from him. Long before the end of his life, Elmo had nothing, and when cancer began to waste him away, he moved into the caretaker's house on his son's estate in Mississippi. A few months before his death, Elmo made one last request of Myra.

"I once recorded a hit song," he said. "It was back in sixty-one or thereabouts. Jerry took me down to the studio to record 'Mexicali Rose,' and ever'body tol' me it was a hit—Jud, Cecil, you remember, Myra, you heard it. It was a hit. But Jerry wouldn't let Sam release it. Mamie never wanted me to have nothin', an' Jerry had to do like Mamie said. The only thing I ever wanted was to hear my song on the radio," and he began to cry.

Myra attempted to purchase and release "Mexicali Rose" by Elmo Lewis so that his last and only wish might be fulfilled. No one at Sun knew where it was after eighteen years, or where to look, doubting it had ever existed at all. When attendants came to ferry him to the hospital for the last time, Elmo paused to take sight and farewell of an old, toothless friend with whom he had shared the caretaker's cubicle—a weathered Starck upright.

* * *

The audience sat stonily composed as the man directed a spot-light to illuminate the Bible on the piano's music rack. He was drunk, or worse, and stopped singing hymns to preach the gospel. The message was confused: Beware great balls of fire.

"Hey, Jerry, play somethin'," someone called.

"Hey, why don't you lemme do my show," he replied.

"Well, do it. Sing."

"How 'bout 'Up Against the Wall, Redneck Motherfucker'?"

"How'd you like me to whip yer ass for you one time?"

"Brother," Jerry advised, "I hope you brought a gun bigger'n mine."

"How big *is* your gun, Jerry?" joked the foe.

"Send your wife backstage an' I'll let her touch it."

From out of the wings stepped another preacher. "Show's over, folks. Jerry, come with me."

"Jimmy Lee Swaggart, what the hell are you doin' here, son? Hey, what're you doin'?"

"I'm takin' you home, Jerry," said Jimmy, and carried his cousin from Ohio to Baton Rouge in his private plane for a week of nourishing food and sobering thought.

"We came close to making a breakthrough," Jimmy said later. "I don't know if it will be tomorrow, or five minutes before he dies, but I'm firmly convinced Jerry's gonna make it. He's been runnin' from God all his life and he knows he can't run forever."

And in February 1982, as he presided over the funeral of Arthur Gilley, Mickey's dad, Jimmy Lee Swaggart, recently returned from a crusade of China, made another attempt at redeeming one of his own. "Whosoever among you believes you wouldn't go to heaven with Uncle Arthur if you died today, come forward."

Only one man came to the altar, the prodigal son.

Jimmy Lee asked, "Will you accept Christ as your savior?"

He still waits on an answer from Jerry Lee Lewis.

Index

PRISCILLA,
ELVIS
AND ME

The sizzling, sensational love story that starts where Priscilla Presley's bestselling autobiography left off!

PRISCILLA, ELVIS AND ME

MICHAEL EDWARDS

Michael Edwards' passionate romance with Priscilla Presley burned hot and fast. From the early, heady days of sexual passion and romantic bliss, to the terrible fights sparked by Lisa Marie's blossoming womanhood, *Priscilla, Elvis and Me* is a love story that is wrenching in its honesty and unflinching in its telling—an intimate look at a "perfect" love in a frozen moment of time... in the shadow of a legend.

With 16 pages of intimate photos!

Famous Lives
from St. Martin's Press

LIBERACE: THE TRUE STORY
Bob Thomas
_____ 91352-4 $3.95 U.S. _____ 91354-0 $4.95 Can.

THE FITZGERALDS AND THE KENNEDYS
Doris Kearns Goodwin
_____ 90933-0 $5.95 U.S. _____ 90934-9 $6.95 Can.

CAROLINE AND STEPHANIE
Susan Crimp and Patricia Burstein
_____ 91116-5 $3.50 U.S. _____ 91117-3 $4.50 Can.

PATRICK SWAYZE
Mitchell Krugel
_____ 91449-0 $3.50 U.S. _____ 91450-4 $4.50 Can.

YOUR CHEATIN' HEART:
A BIOGRAPHY OF HANK WILLIAMS
Chet Flippo
_____ 91400-8 $3.95 U.S. _____ 91401-6 $4.95 Can.

WHO'S SORRY NOW?
Connie Francis
_____ 90386-3 $3.95 U.S. _____ 90383-9 $4.95 Can.

Publishers Book and Audio Mailing Service
P.O. Box 120159, Staten Island, NY 10312-0004

Please send me the book(s) I have checked above. I am enclosing
$ _____ (please add $1.25 for the first book, and $.25 for each
additional book to cover postage and handling. Send check or
money order only—no CODs.)

Name _____

Address _____

City _____ State/Zip _____

Please allow six weeks for delivery. Prices subject to change
without notice.

Capítulo Uno

Adam Chase tenía derecho a conocer a su hija. Mia no podía negárselo, pero el corazón le sangraba todavía como si tuviera doce cuchillos clavados. Renegaba de su conciencia por haberla llevado esa mañana a Moonlight Beach. Los dedos se le hundían en la arena de la orilla mientras caminaba con las chanclas en la mano. Hacía más frío del que se había esperado y la niebla que llegaba del mar cubría la playa con un manto sombrío. ¿Era un presagio? ¿Había tomado una decisión equivocada? La inocente carita de Rose se le presentó en la cabeza. La llamaba «mi melocotón» porque era el bebé con las mejillas más sonrosadas que había visto en su vida. También tenía los labios muy rosas y cuando sonrió por primera vez, ella se derritió.

Rose era lo único que le había quedado de su hermana Anna.

Miró hacia el mar y vio, como había esperado, la figura de un hombre que nadaba más allá de las olas que rompían en la orilla. Si podía fiarse de lo poco que había indagado, tenía que ser él. Adam Chase, arquitecto de fama mundial, vivía en la playa, era solitario por definición y también era un nadador empedernido.

La brisa le levantó el pelo y se le puso la carne de gallina. La misión que la había llevado allí era descomunal. Tendría que ser de granito para no estar asustada en ese momento.

No sabía qué iba a decirle. Había ensayado mil posibilidades, pero ninguna había sido la verdad.

Volvió a mirar hacia el mar y vio que estaba saliendo. Algo le atenazó la garganta. Había llegado el momento. Calculó los pasos que tenía que dar para interceptarlo en la arena. Sintió otro escalofrío. Él se levantó en las aguas poco profundas. Tenía las espaldas anchas como las de un vikingo y a ella se le aceleró el corazón. Se acercó con unas zancadas largas y ágiles. Ella se fijó en su pecho musculoso, en su elegancia y fuerza. Las pocas fotos que había encontrado no le hacían justicia. Era hermoso como un dios. Sacudió la cabeza y sus mechones veteados por el sol soltaron unas gotas de agua que le cayeron por los hombros.

–¡Ay!

Algo se le clavó en la planta del pie y notó un dolor muy intenso. Se lo agarró y se dejó caer en la arena. La sangre brotó al instante, se quitó la arena con la mano y se quedó boquiabierta. Tenía un corte de una botella de cerveza rota. Si no hubiese estado mirándolo como una boba...

–¿Te has hecho daño?

La voz profunda le retumbó en la cabeza, levantó la mirada y vio el gesto de preocupación de Adam Chase.

–Sí –asintió con la cabeza–, me he cortado.

–Malditos niños –Adam miró la botella rota